Farming
&
Wildlife

A practical handbook for the
management, restoration and creation
of wildlife habitats on farmland

John Andrews and Michael Rebane

Published by The Royal Society for the Protection
of Birds, The Lodge, Sandy, Bedfordshire SG19
2DL.

ISBN No: 0 903138 67 0

Typesetting by Bedford Typesetters Ltd, Bedford
Artwork by Dan Powell
Design by Philip Cottier
Figures by Rob and Rhoda Burns
Printed by KPC Group, Ashford, Kent.

RSPB Ref: 375/94

Cover Photographs:
Cattle grazing *(R Hosking, FLPA)*
Swaledale sheep *(David Woodfall)*
Gulls following plough *(J Hawkins, FLPA)*

Authors:

John Andrews joined the RSPB staff in 1970 and was Head of Conservation Planning 1972–85. He was the RSPB's Chief Advisory Officer from 1985 until 1991 and is now a consultant specialising in habitat restoration and management. His address is Andrews Ward Associates, 17 West Perry, Huntingdon, Cambs PE18 0BX.

Michael Rebane was the RSPB's Terrestrial Adviser from 1990–94 with responsibility for the provision of management advice on upland, woodland, lowland heathland and agricultural ecosystems. Prior to joining the RSPB he was Reserves Manager with the Scottish Wildlife Trust for nine years. He now works from Crete as a tour leader and wildlife and travel writer.

Authors' Note

In writing this book we have both drawn on an accumulation of information derived over many years, in the course of our day-to-day work, from dozens of professional and amateur research workers, site managers and advisers in many organisations throughout the UK and overseas. Without that firm foundation of knowledge, it would not have been possible to contemplate undertaking this project and we wish to record our sincere thanks to all those people on whose work we have been privileged to build.

The RSPB and the authors wish to express their grateful thanks to the following organisations and individuals who contributed actively to the production of the handbook.

Contributors

For some chapters, detailed information on particular aspects of management, including otherwise unpublished material, was prepared by contributors from outside the RSPB or by RSPB research staff. A number of individuals also gave up time to talk at length to the authors about aspects of their management work or current research. All the farm case studies were provided by FWAG advisers, farmers or crofters. All these contributions listed by chapter and for subject are given below.

Nicholas Aebischer	Game Conservancy	Chapter 2 (Partridge)
Paul Bright	Mammal Society	7
James Cadbury	RSPB	5
John Casely	Long Ashton Research Station	2
Andy Chadwick	Forestry Authority	7 (Deer)
Sarah Corbet	University of Cambridge	2 (Bumblebees)
Keith Corbett	Herpetological Conservation Trust	4 (Reptiles)
Peter Corkill	English Nature	3
Adrian Darby and staff of the Kemerton Estate		2
Jack Donovan		2,3
Tim Dixon	English Nature	3
Paul Edgar	NE Hampshire Heathlands Project	4
Andy Evans	RSPB	2 (Stubble & birds Cirl Bunting)
Rob Fuller	British Trust for Ornithology	
Andrew Hoodless	Game Conservancy	7 (Woodcock)
Tony Hutson	Bat Conservation Trust	7
Richard Jefferson	English Nature	3
David Kendall	Long Ashton Research Station	2
Albert Knott	English Nature	3
Stuart Lane	English Nature	
Bob Lord	English Nature	3
Jonathan Marshall	Long Ashton Research Station	2
Maurice Massey	English Nature	3
Simon Nobes	English Nature	4

Pete Robertson	Game Conservancy	7 (Pheasants)
Dave Sheppard	English Nature	4 (Invertebrates)
Mike Shrubb		2,3
Nick Sotherton	Game Conservancy	2 (Partridge, Rare weeds, Beetle Banks, Conservation headlands)
Paul Toynton	English Nature	3
Tony Warne	Joint Nature Conservation Committee (JNCC)	7
Bernard Wilson	Long Ashton Research Station	2
Jeremy Wilson	British Trust for Ornithology	2 (Mixed farming, Organic farming, and Use of crops by birds)
Doug Woods	Somerset Trust for Nature Conservation	7
Malcolm Wright	English Nature	4

Case Studies

William Baker	Farmer	Chapter 2
Edward Baxter	Farmer	2
Jamie Boyle	RSPB	6
Mervyn Browne	Farmer	5
Joy Greenall	Oxfordshire FWAG	2
Christine Hall	Perthshire FWAG	5
Christopher Hawkins	Farmer	7
Juliet Hawkins	Suffolk FWAG	7
Stuart Jackson	Leicestershire FWAG	8
David Jenkins	Coed Cymru	7
Richard Knight	FWAG	All
Alison Lea	Suffolk FWAG	2
Mr & Mrs E H Lewis	Farmers	7
Dr & Mrs Morgan	Landowners	3
Angus MacDonald	Crofter	6
Richard MacMullen	Norfolk FWAG	4,7
Joe Nourish	Farmer	8
John Rampton	Farmer	4
Matthew Rampton	Norfolk FWAG	4
Dave Robinson	Trustees of Chatsworth Settlement	10
Alison Rothwell	RSPB	6
Jeff Simpkin	Lancashire FWAG	9
Chris Smith	Buckinghamshire FWAG	9
Sara Smith	Derbyshire FWAG	10
Stan Terry	Farmer	9
Trustees of the Chatsworth Settlement		10
Brian Tustian	Farmer	2
Graham Ward	Farmer	9
Roger Wardle	Farmer/Lincolnshire FWAG	3
Roger Wardle	Trustees of Chatsworth Settlement	10
Sarah Warrener	Fife & Kinross FWAG	2
Andy Webb	Norfolk Naturalists' Trust	4
David West	Oxfordshire FWAG	1
Mrs Kelaart	Farmer	1

Reviewers

Each chapter was sent out in draft for critical review. All those who thus contributed to the final form of each chapter and thereby to the overall approach of the handbook are listed below. A number of organisations also looked over the final draft.

Stewart Angus	Scottish Natural Heritage (SNH)	Chapter 6
Helen Armstrong	SNH	5
Martin Auld	RSPB	4
Lloyd Austin	RSPB	2,3,5,6
Ian Bainbridge	RSPB	7
Colin Bodrell	MAFF	All
David Braithwaite	Bishop Burton College of Agriculture	4
Bob Brown	RSPB	2
Roy Brown	University of Plymouth	4
Martin Buckland	ADAS	7
Roger Buisson	RSPB	9

J P Byrne	ADAS	5
James Cadbury	RSPB	5,6
George Campbell	Scottish Crofters Union	6
Elaine Carlisle	DANI	2
Jim Carmichael	Northern Ireland Agricultural Producers' Union	All
Eric Carter		2
Andrew Clark	NFU	All
Nigel Critchley	ADAS	2,3,4
Allison Crofts	Royal Society for Nature Conservation (RSNC)	3
George Cussons	Rothamsted Experimental Station	2
John Day	RSPB	5
Isobel Drury	RSNC	9
Catherine Duigan	Countryside Council for Wales (CCW)	5,9
Janet Egdell	RSPB	6
John Elcock	Scottish Agricultural College (SAC)	2
Andy Evans	RSPB	4
Ceri Evans	RSPB	4
Malcolm Florey	National Association of Principal Agricultural Education Officers	All
Sam Franklin	RSPB	2
Tony Gent	English Nature	4
Graham Gill	Forestry Authority	7
Charles Gimingham	University of Aberdeen	4
Harry Gracey	DANI	All
John Graham	Shuttleworth College of Agriculture	2
Rhys Green	RSPB	6
Joy Greenall	Oxfordshire FWAG	3
Peter Grieg-Smith	MAFF	2
Christine Hall	Perth & Angus FWAG	5
Rachel Hamilton	Otley College	4
Maurice Hankey	Scottish Landowners' Federation	All
Judith Harris	MAFF	All
Jenny Heaney	SAC	2,6
Andrew Heaton	Severn Trent NRA	9
Terence Henry	Greenmount College of Agriculture	2,3,7,8
Peter Hobson	Otley College	4
David Howell	SNH	9
Andrew Humphries	Newton Rigg College	5
Jonathan Humphrey	CCW	8
Neil Hutton	Shuttleworth College of Agriculture	2,7,8
Digger Jackson	RSPB	6
Christine James	Hertfordshire FWAG	7
Richard Jefferson	English Nature	3
David Jenkins	Coed Cymru	7
Pam Johnson	SAC	2
Paul José	RSPB	9
Chris Judson	SOAFD	All
Roger Key	English Nature	7
Keith Kirby	English Nature	7,8
Richard Knight	FWAG	All
Alison Lea	Suffolk FWAG	2
Phil Lyth	N Yorkshire FWAG	5,9
Jayne Manley	English Nature	5
Will Manley	Royal Agricultural College	3,4,7
Chris Marrable	Conservators of Ashdown Forest	4
Rob Marrs	University of Liverpool	4
Nick Marshall	RSPB	7
Eric Meek	RSPB	5
Clive Mellon	RSPB	2,3,5,7,8,9
Ian Melrose	National Farmers' Union (Scotland)	All
Nick Michael	English Nature	4
Hilary Miller	CCW	8
Ian McCall	RSPB	9
Davy McCracken	JNCC	3,5,6
Jane MacKintosh	SNH	3
Richard MacMullen	Norfolk FWAG	9

Judith Mobbs	Otley College	4
Andrew Moorhouse	Wiltshire FWAG	8
Nicola Muggeridge	Conservators of Ashdown Forest	4
David Newborn	Game Conservancy	5
John Nicholls	Conservators of Ashdown Forest	4
Phil Nicolle	British Association for Shooting and Conservation (BASC)	7
Hugh Oliver-Bellasis	Farmer	2
Kevin Owen	Farmers' Union of Wales	All
Debbie Pain	RSPB	5,8
Mary Painter	RSPB	4
Steve Parr	CCW	8
John Phillips	Heather Trust (formerly Joseph Nickerson Reconciliation Project)	5
Bruce Philp	West of Scotland Agric. Coll.	3,4,5,8,9
Tony Prater	RSPB	2
June Randell	Dumfries & Galloway FWAG	3,8
Mark Redman	British Organic Farmers	2
Richard Robinson	SNH	6
Carol Russell	Central Scotland FWAG	7
Alastair Rutherford	Countryside Commission	2
Paul Sayers	ADAS	All
Jane Sears	RSPB	9
Jim Simpson	Ulster Farmers' Union	All
Nick Sotherton	Game Conservancy	2,8
Andy Stewart	Greenmount College of Agriculture	
Tim Stowe	RSPB	6
Nigel Symes	RSPB	4
Paul Tabbush	Forestry Authority	7
Gareth Thomas	RSPB	All
Rachel Thomas	English Nature	7
Paul Toynton	English Nature	3
Roger Turner	RSPB	7
Colin Tubbs		4
Una Urquhart	RSPB	5
John Waldon	RSPB	2
Nigel Webb	Institute of Terrestrial Ecology	4
Geoff Welch	RSPB	3
Derek Wells		3
Steven Westwood	Countryside Commission	8
Gwyn Williams	RSPB	All
Iolo Williams	RSPB	5
Jeremy Wilson	British Trust for Ornithology	2
Mandy Wilson	SNH	5
Michael Wolstenholme	Farmer	7
Alan Woods	Country Landowners' Association	All
Robin Wynde	RSPB	4
Martyn Wrathall	SAC	3

Steering Group
An RSPB staff group advised on all aspects of the production of the book. The following were members of the group for part or all of the duration of the project.
Melinda Appleby, Mark Boyd, Mike Brown, Lennox Campbell, Jim Dixon, David Elcome, Graham Elliott, Chris Gomersall, Debra Royal, Jane Sears, Sylvia Sullivan.

Project Support
Much material for tables, figures and features was compiled and drafted by Sarah Niemann and Nick Milton. Sarah Niemann also co-ordinated the compilation of the case studies.

Acknowledgment
Production of the book has been sponsored by The National Grid Company plc, the owner and operator of the electricity transmission system in England and Wales. Additional financial support was provided by the Ministry of Agriculture Fisheries and Food. We are grateful to both organisations.

Contents

Foreword

No one these days underestimates the influence of agriculture on our
countryside and wildlife, and its contribution to overall biodiversity. While
nature reserves and other protected areas are clearly important for
conservation, many species depend upon the wider countryside, most of
which is farmed.

In the post-war years the intensification of farming in the drive to increase
food production led to the loss of many of the habitats and the wildlife which
they supported. Our responsibility in the '90s is to avoid losses and (where
possible) to restore some of the key habitats. That requires the commitment of
the Government and its countryside agencies, the non-governmental
organisations (NGOs) of which the RSPB is pre-eminent and, most importantly
of all, of farmers and landowners.

The Government and its agencies are providing a strong lead with policies and
measures which encourage land management practices that are more
sympathetic to the needs of wildlife. So too are the NGOs, and I particularly
welcome the publication of this handbook by the RSPB. It will help provide
the link between the policies and financial incentives and the practical delivery
by farmers of the land management which will benefit our wildlife.

The handbook is a very thorough piece of work and I wholeheartedly
commend it to the farmers and other land managers, their professional
advisers and those involved in agricultural training throughout the United
Kingdom.

Gillian Shephard.

Minister of Agriculture,
Fisheries and Food

Endorsements from other organisations

Farmland is the essential element which makes up most of the wider countryside. It supports much of our native wildlife, common species in the main but also those which are uncommon and threatened.

Many wildlife habitats on farms are now fragmented remnants of originally larger areas and their full interest is often unrealised. This book is a valuable asset which will help advisers and farmers get the best for wildlife from their land.

The case studies give a practical indication of the potential on offer. The challenge is to recognise and realise that potential, and farm in a way to best fit the needs of wildlife, the farm and the farmer. FWAG's national, county-based advisory service will ensure that the recommendations outlined in this handbook can be tailored to meet the specific requirements of each farm. FWAG welcomes the publication as an important element of support for all concerned with managing the countryside.

Farming and Wildlife Advisory Group

As we approach the 21st century the people of Britain, and our political leaders, are increasingly focussing their attention on farming practice, wildlife and the countryside. Farmers and others who have responsibility for the countryside have an important role to sustain and further develop this heritage.

This handbook provides a very good practical approach for the long-term benefit of wildlife and farmland. It recognises the value of much of our existing landscape and farming practice and it will go a long way to ensure a managed countryside of continuing diversity and interest.

Present and future farmers and others involved in countryside management decisions, have an excellent handbook and a wide range of species should have an optimistic future.

It provides a guide to the major habitats, species and the effects of management. A most helpful reference is that of methodology, to which both farmers and students will be able to relate.
We would commend its use in agricultural colleges as a valuable text for all students.

National Association of Principal Agricultural Education Officers

The RSPB has a well-deserved reputation for providing scientifically-based advice on land management for the benefit of wildlife. In many cases that advice has been put into practice on RSPB reserves and refined in the light of experience thereby gained.

The *Farming and Wildlife Handbook* presents up-to-date advice on how best to manage each of the major farmed landscapes in the UK for wildlife. It should become an invaluable reference source for agricultural colleges, farm advisers and farmers.

It is widely recognised that the abandonment of traditional farming systems poses a major threat to biodiversity. Government schemes will play a central role in tackling this challenge. This Handbook should help. We therefore commend it to all those involved in seeking to protect, maintain and enhance our national wildlife heritage.

Country Landowners Association
Scottish Landowners' Federation

The UK farming unions welcome the publication of the RSPB's *Farming and Wildlife Handbook.* At a time of rapid change for farmers and the countryside, farming practice is being asked to provide an ever more diverse range of 'goods'. One of the most important is countryside care. CAP reform is opening up new opportunities and challenges for both farmers and conservationists – for instance set-aside can be managed positively for an appreciable wildlife gain. It is for the agricultural community and conservation groups to work together to ensure the maximum gain for wildlife can be integrated within modern, practical and profitable farming.

By compiling a wide range of data on habitat management and relating it to farming systems, the RSPB has produced a valuable reference for wildlife conservation. On the basis of information contained in the Handbook we hope farmers will receive a high standard of professional advice suited to their farming needs. However, the interpretation of this information will be crucial as environmental considerations will vary from site to site. Farmers should only progress with conservation efforts after a careful consideration of the options open to them and with professional assistance if required. We hope that the Handbook will become a valuable reference for farmers and their advisers and help them to produce the conservation goods of the future.

Farmers' Union of Wales
National Farmers' Union
National Farmers' Union (Scotland)
Northern Ireland Agricultural Producers'
Union
Scottish Crofters Union
Ulster Farmers' Union

1. Making Wildlife Management Decisions

1. The use of the handbook

This handbook provides practical advice on methods of management of wildlife habitats on farms. It is presented so that it can be used easily by farmers, farm advisers and agricultural colleges.

The book is divided into ten chapters. This chapter explains how to use the book, how to evaluate the importance of different wildlife habitats and decide on priorities for their management, and how to prepare farm wildlife plans. The nine following chapters cover the major wildlife habitats found on farms – arable land, grassland, heathland, upland and rough grazings, machair, farm woods, hedges, wetlands, walls and buildings.

Each chapter contains five sections.
- Section 1 describes the habitat, the key requirements of its wildlife and the effects of farm management on it. This background information is important in assessing the quality of habitats on the farm and in understanding the reasons for different types of management.
- Section 2 explains how to make decisions on appropriate conservation management. It lists the information that should be collected before decisions are taken, summarises the main choices

and indicates what help may be available.
- Section 3 provides the basic prescriptions to enable farmers to manage, enhance or create the habitat on their farms.
- Section 4 lists books and other reference material which will give further information for readers who are interested in knowing more about the natural history of the habitat or who need additional guidance on unfamiliar management methods.
- Section 5 contains a case study of work which has been carried out on a typical farm.

All the most important points are summarised. Photographs, figures and tables provide supporting information. Each chapter also contains features which describe the needs of selected species that are either closely associated with farms or are of great conservation significance; some are both.

At the end of the book, appendices list organisations that may be able to provide further advice, codes of practice, and legal considerations that relate to farming and the environment.

2. Surveying the wildlife interest on farms

- Survey is important to assess the wildlife value and potential of the farm.
- Check with conservation bodies for existing information.
- Map habitats and assess their condition using the guidelines given in the habitat chapters.
- Add information on rare species, if known.

2.1 Farming systems
Different types of farm hold different types of wildlife. Mixed farms will generally hold more species than specialised livestock or arable farms, for three main reasons. First, arable and pasture support different plants and invertebrates and provide different feeding and breeding opportunities for birds and mammals: where both types of land are present on a farm, there will be the potential for greater wildlife diversity. Second, some species have complex

requirements and need two or more different field types to be available on the farm. Lapwings, for instance, nest on spring tillage but prefer to take their chicks to feed on pasture. Third, where several different crops are grown, there is better continuity of food supply and suitable habitat structures than on a farm with only one crop. For example, skylarks nest in crops less than 30 cm tall and if the farm holds winter cereals, spring cereals, roots and grass leys, the birds can make a series of nesting attempts and so rear more young than in a farm with only one crop type.

In practice, the amount of wildlife on the farm is very dependent on the type of management. If arable crops and grass are managed intensively, even on a mixed farm few wild plants will survive, invertebrate variety and abundance will be reduced and there will be few opportunities for feeding or successful breeding by birds and mammals.

Organic farming excludes as far as possible the use of artificial fertilisers and pesticides, relying on crop rotations, animal and green manures, legumes and mechanical cultivation techniques to maintain soil fertility and control pests. This approach may have a range of benefits for wildlife because it can mean a return to mixed enterprises and, perhaps, a restricted ability to control wild plants and invertebrates in the crops. However, it does not always follow that organic farming is better for all wildlife. As with conventional farming, much depends on the intensity and sensitivity with which management is undertaken.

To that extent, all types of farming system can make a contribution to the conservation of wildlife and a main aim of this book is to enable farmers and their advisers to make informed decisions related to their existing operations, rather than advocating any change in overall farming practice.

2.2 The need for survey

Wildlife varies greatly from farm to farm. Underlying factors such as soil type, climate and location mean that the list of species that are likely to be found in Antrim, for example, is very different from that of Fife or Sussex. Some habitats are only found in

one part of the UK – thus, machair is almost confined to the Western Isles, most lowland heathland is found in counties south of the Thames and so on. Neighbouring farms with similar soils and weather may have very different sets of wildlife because of past management decisions and current practice. All this means that every farm needs to be assessed on its merits.

In practice the approach is usually to note what habitats are present, assess their suitability for wildlife and, if possible, record the presence of any rare species. This section explains the process step by step, and the relevant chapters set out what should be recorded for the different habitat types. However, before starting, it is useful to understand the general principles on which all assessment is based and thus the type of farm survey which will be required.

The broad aims of conservation are to maintain the present numbers and distributions of all wildlife throughout the UK and, where possible, achieve some recovery of those species and habitats which have diminished most in recent years. The 'bottom line' is to prevent species from becoming extinct, though it is accepted that the numbers of some pests need to be controlled. The species regarded as most important are therefore those which are rare nationally or are rapidly declining in numbers; either situation may mean that extinction is a real risk. Rare farmland species include the corncrake and the marsh fritillary butterfly. The grey partridge is one species that is declining seriously. Sometimes a species that is generally widespread and thriving may be rare or declining locally and so merit careful management in that particular area.

In addition, some species which are quite common here in suitable habitat are regarded as important because the UK holds a large part of the European or world population and so has an international responsibility for their protection. Bluebells and breeding curlews fall into this category.

In practice, assessment of a farm's wildlife would never be able to take account of the status of all the species that are present for two reasons. One is the simple practical impossibility of finding out what occurs – a small unimproved meadow may contain hundreds of invertebrate species for instance, plus dozens of different plants. The second reason is that the abundance and distribution of many of these species will be unknown anyway. Species for which good information is available include most flowering plants, some insects (especially butterflies and dragonflies), amphibians, reptiles, birds and mammals. This leaves hundreds of other plants such as mosses and fungi, plus most invertebrate groups, for which information is incomplete.

Because of this, when faced with the need to survey and assess an area and decide on management, the usual approach is to consider mainly the habitat as a whole and to note the presence of important species, if known. The better the condition of the habitat and the bigger it is, the more likely that declining or rare species will survive in it, whether or not anyone knows they are there.

Often, conservation management is considered for only one part of the farm, such as a wood or a pond. The danger with this approach is that a habitat of greater importance may be overlooked. It is better to assess all of the farm first and then decide which parts to manage for wildlife. However, in either case, a survey should be carried out before deciding on management. If grant aid is to be sought for management or habitat creation, contact should be made with the relevant grant-awarding body to discuss the degree of information needed.

The survey involves three stages – checking with the conservation bodies for information they may hold on habitats and species on the farm, mapping and assessing the present condition of the habitats on the farm and noting past and present management. These stages are described in more detail below and Section 3 of this Chapter explains how the results of the survey should be evaluated.

2.3 Recording information
Whatever the source of information, it is easiest and clearest to record the location, context and extent of important habitats or species on an up-to-date map of the farm.

Maps are normally required to support applications for grants to manage or create wildlife habitats. The larger the scale the better; normally 1:10,000 is suitable but where more detail is required then a scale of 1:2,500 may be necessary. Much of the information collected can be summarised onto the map. An example of a completed farm survey map is given at Figure 1.1, page 14.

The habitats to be noted are:
Arable land
Improved grassland
Semi-improved or unimproved grassland
Lowland heath
Hill and rough grazings
Woodland
Hedges, farm trees and scrub
Watercourses including ditches
Ponds and other waterbodies
Other wetlands such as marsh or areas which regularly flood
Walls and farm buildings
Other habitats such as machair, saltmarsh, gravel pits

2.4 Sources of information on sites
In much of the lowlands and some upland areas of the UK, all the habitats have been mapped by 'Phase 1 surveys' which record broad habitat types using a standard colour code and key. They often also include information on the condition of the site and on uncommon species. This means that, before ground survey is undertaken, it is worth checking with the official conservation agencies, the Wildlife Trust and FWAG for relevant information that may have already been collected. Check that the information is up-to-date and that conditions have not changed on the farm since it was collected.

The best sites nationally are designated by the official conservation agencies in Britain as Sites of Special Scientific Interest (SSSIs) or, in Northern Ireland, as Areas of Special Scientific Interest (ASSIs). The official agencies are responsible for identifying these sites and informing farmers and all other owners and occupiers of their interest. A list of operations that might be harmful to these areas is sent to the farmer, who must consult the agency before carrying out any of these operations. Advice on management is available.

Only a very few areas are officially designated and there are thousands of additional wildlife areas on farms that are highly important. Often their existence is known to local authorities and wildlife trusts and information on their value is usually passed on to the farmer. Advice on management and financial incentives may be available.

2.5 Habitat survey

As well as simply mapping the habitats, either by taking information from an existing 'Phase 1 survey' or by walking the farm and recording their extent, it is essential to record information on the condition of each habitat. The range of information required will vary from habitat to habitat and is set out in full in Section 2 of each chapter. There is no reason why the farmer should not do his own habitat survey as the main features of importance are not difficult to identify and map. The guidance given in each chapter is intended for use by people without special wildlife survey skills. It should usually be possible to carry out the habitat survey at any time of year but if, for instance, it is essential to identify trees, the work may have to be timed for when they are in leaf.

On large estates, the use of up-to-date aerial photographs may be a valuable aid in finding and mapping small areas of habitat. Older photographs and old maps are useful to find out about past management, which is important in assessing the likely value of some habitats. The information to be collected enables the habitat to be assessed in terms of:

- **Habitat rarity.** If there is little of the habitat surviving in the UK, then probably most of the species that depend on it will be declining or rare. Rare habitats on farmland today include flower-rich permanent pasture and hay meadows.
- **Vegetation structure and composition.** If the habitat has a varied structure and contains the typical range of plants, it is probable that it will support a wide variety of other wildlife. Most land which is being actively farmed holds only the crop plants. It has a very simple vegetation structure and composition and supports only a restricted range of persistent pests or other species which can tolerate the conditions. The overall variety and abundance of wildlife is low and most species are common because the habitat is abundant.

- **Site size.** In general, larger sites are more diverse in structure and composition than small ones, so they hold more species. Also, the larger the site is, the less the likelihood that any harmful event, such as accidental fire on a heath or spray-drift into a wetland, will affect the whole area.

2.6 Species survey

Normally species surveys are not practicable or necessary for decisions on managing farm habitats. The recommended habitat management methods will maintain conditions suitable for both common and rare species. Often, when rare species are found to be present, their requirements are unknown anyway so that the best that can be done is to continue to maintain the conditions in which they have survived so far and hope that this is sufficient. However, if information is available, the locations of scarce species should be mapped so that the sites in which they occur continue to be managed to maintain the present conditions and are not inadvertently destroyed.

In a few situations, there are good reasons for looking for particular rare species. For example, stone-curlews may breed in sugar-beet fields on the sandy soils of parts of East Anglia and, as they are rare and at risk from field operations, it is important to know if they are present. Where such special cases apply, they are mentioned in Section 2 of the relevant habitat chapter.

For a minority of rare species there is good information on habitat needs so that it is possible to manage areas to increase the extent of suitable conditions or even attract species which are absent. For instance, some rare birds and plants could be treated in this way. Survey for these species and the production of detailed management schemes requires specialist assistance.

The collection of information on species is tied to the seasons. Most work is done in spring and summer but some areas, such as sites which flood in winter, may need survey at other times of year.

If lists of species are available as a result of previous surveys by the conservation bodies, they will usually indicate whether any uncommon species are present.

3. Making wildlife management decisions

- Different wildife habitats have different conservation importance.
- The condition of the habitat affects its value for wildlife.
- Management priority should be given to uncommon habitats.
- Take into account the needs of rare species.
- Habitats in poor condition should be restored.
- Where there are only common or damaged habitats on a farm, management is still well worthwhile.
- Habitat creation is valuable but a lower priority than maintaining existing habitats.
- The introduction of species is inadvisable except in special circumstances.

3.1 Conservation priorities

Wildlife conservation on a farm involves making choices. There will be limits to what can be done, imposed by cost, practicality and personal interest. Some species or habitats will be more important than others. It is rarely the case that the most worthwhile wildlife management is also the cheapest and easiest thing to do!

The first stage is to evaluate the results of the survey and decide which are the most important parts of the farm and of each habitat. Some habitats are themselves rare and are likely to hold nationally rare species. Normally, these should have first priority for conservation management. Others are locally uncommon. A few are widespread and support only common species. Based on the rarity of habitats nationally and the typical range of species which an area in good condition might hold, the relative importance of farm habitats, including cropped land, is likely to be as follows:

Habitats likely to be nationally important
Unimproved permanent grass including pasture, hay meadows and wet grassland.
Lowland heath.

Moorland with extensive heather, bilberry or other similar shrubby growth.
Machair.
Woodlands which have been on the same site for centuries and contain native trees.
Extensive (>1 ha) marshes and reedbeds.

Habitats likely to be of county/regional importance
Semi-improved grassland with some surviving wild flowers.
Plantation woodlands of native tree species.
Large (>1 ha) waterbodies.
Small (<1 ha) marshes and reedbeds.
Land that remains surface damp until midsummer.
Land that floods in winter for at least 2 weeks.
Unpolluted rivers, streams and ditches.

Habitats likely to be of local importance
Ponds and other small (<1 ha) waterbodies.
Scrub.
Big hedges with trees.
Old trees in fields.
Spring cereals and some spring-sown rootcrops and field vegetables.
Conservation headlands.

Habitats likely to be of limited value for wildlife
Winter cereals and most other intensively managed crops.
Improved grass.
Tightly-trimmed or stunted hedges.
Plantations of non-native trees.
Polluted wetlands including ponds and ditches.

The value of a habitat is affected by its condition. The most important elements of habitats are described in Section 1 of each chapter and, by comparing the results of survey with the descriptions, it is possible to decide on the quality of the habitat. Thus, if most of the elements are present and fit the description of good condition, then the habitat is of high quality. It may well hold uncommon species. The main aim should be to maintain it unchanged so that it continues to support all the wildlife.

If only one or a few of the elements are present and in good condition, the habitat as a whole is likely to have fewer species but the best areas may still hold important ones. Aim to continue to manage such areas correctly and, if there are enough resources available, attempt to improve the rest of the habitat.

If all parts of the habitat are in poor shape, it is unlikely that important species have survived. However, depending on the type of habitat and on the proximity of a thriving population, at least the more mobile species such as birds and some insects may be able to recolonise if suitable management is commenced.

Overall, give top priority to maintaining important habitats which are in good condition. If resources permit, deal next with restoring the condition of important habitats which have deteriorated and, after that, with any common habitat examples.

If information on species is available, it is possible to check whether any of them are locally or nationally rare or declining by contacting FWAG, who will also be able to give guidance on appropriate management. If necessary they will contact the official conservation agency which holds lists of all nationally rare species, commonly known as 'Red Data' lists. Flowering plants, birds and many invertebrate groups have been covered and Red Data lists for other groups are being prepared. Existing lists are periodically updated, taking into account any increases or decreases in populations.

Some wildlife species have legal protection. Again, information is available from the official agencies.

The vast majority of areas of wildlife habitat on farms are not especially important in themselves but still have a vital role to play in maintaining the abundance and distribution of many wildlife species. Often such areas can be improved for wildlife without great cost or inconvenience. County FWAGs are the main agencies involved in giving advice on their management.

It cannot be emphasised too strongly that a farm that only contains common habitats like hedges and field margins will still make a valuable contribution to the fabric of the countryside by managing them in ways

sympathetic to the needs of wildlife. More people get enjoyment from brimstone butterflies, hawthorn blossom, buttercups and skylarks than from rarities.

3.2 Habitat creation

In addition to the management of existing features, farmers are now being offered financial help to restore or create certain wildlife habitats, for example through the Environmentally Sensitive Areas scheme, Countryside Stewardship and Tir Cymen and a range of new measures .

To ensure that these schemes are successful and worthwhile, it is important to create or restore habitats which are most appropriate to the soil type and locality and, indeed, the farm. Forethought should be given to how long-term management will be carried out. Advice is normally given as an integral part of the scheme and is also available locally from most official conservation advisers and FWAGs. Where guidance is not provided within the scheme itself, the best course would be to re-create the wildlife habitats previously occurring on the farm and the soil types, with priority given to any uncommon habitat such as heathland.

Basic guidance on methods of creating habitats is given in the relevant chapters. As techniques and experience are developing rapidly, further advice should be sought before starting work.

Habitat restoration is not a substitute for protecting the original habitat and should always be seen as a lower priority than managing any important habitats that exist on the farm. This is because it may be possible to restore the main elements of the vegetation, such as tree cover or heather, but in most cases much of the other wildlife will not recolonise. For instance, new farm woods contain few if any of the uncommon plants to be found in ancient woodlands; wildflower plantings, though attractive to common butterflies and bumblebees, lack many of the rare insects that live in old permanent pasture. However, habitat restoration or creation is worthwhile on farms where most or all of the original habitats have been lost.

Ponds and other wetland areas usually become of value to a wide range of wildlife in less than five years and sometimes in their first season whereas, at the other extreme, it may take a new woodland at least 50 years to reach a condition where some less common species of plants and insects might begin to colonise.

The best chances of success come where a small surviving area of habitat can be extended, allowing its surviving wildlife to colonise the new area gradually.

Always use native species and, if possible, use seeds or plants that come from stock which grows naturally in the locality. Some plants and seed mixes come from the Continent and have growth forms different from the native varieties. Consult the leaflet *Growing Wild Flowers From Seed* (see page 11) for further information about approved seed stockists.

3.3 Introductions

The introduction of plants, including trees and shrubs is fundamental to the creation of most habitats but the introduction of invertebrates or vertebrates needs to be approached with considerable caution. Unless conditions are exactly right, they will probably die out within a generation or two. Many species will colonise in time once conditions become suitable. The only grounds for deliberate introduction are where the species is sedentary, and the sites where it occurs are remote from the new habitat so that natural colonisation is unlikely. A number of criteria should be satisfied before any introduction takes place. These include:

- Release only into geographical areas where the species previously occurred.
- The requirements of the species should be known and met.
- Enough individuals must be released to allow for natural losses.
- The removal of individuals from the donor site should not jeopardise the species' survival there.
- All legal requirements should be met. Some species cannot be captured or translocated without a licence from the official conservation agency.
- The success of the operation should be monitored.

3.4 Financial incentives and schemes

There is an increasing range of financial incentives for managing farm land to take into account the needs of wildlife. Many schemes overlap and some are restricted to specific areas. Schemes are operated by government agencies including the Agriculture Departments, Forest Authority and the official wildlife conservation bodies. Local authorities and National Parks also provide grants. Lists of those available quickly go out of date. To be of most help a leaflet has been produced containing this information. To obtain a free copy of the most recent version please send an A5 stamped addressed envelope to the RSPB at The Lodge, Sandy, Bedfordshire SG19 2DL.

3.5 Planning wildlife management on farms

Straightforward decisions on one feature or habitat on a farm, such as changing the frequency of hedge trimming or introducing conservation headlands, do not need a detailed plan. However, to take account of all the opportunities that may exist to look after wildlife, much the best approach is to prepare a farm wildlife plan. This can cover not only the management of habitats but also, if wished, it can be used to help assess the pros and cons of changes in the detail of crop management and in the handling of wastes and possible pollutants, thus integrating wildlife conservation into all aspects of farm practice. Such a plan can also include information on landscape, historic and archaeological features of interest.

There are several different ways of preparing farm wildlife plans, which are sometimes also called farm conservation plans. They all set out a sequence for making decisions and deciding on appropriate action. Like any other farm project, wildlife management is most likely to give worthwhile results if it is planned in advance. The following checklist summarises the points to consider.

3.6 Farm wildlife management checklist

1. Decide how much of the farm to consider.
- Only one habitat or part of the farm.
- All the farm, perhaps plus operations which may affect wildlife. For this, you will need to produce a farm wildlife plan. Follow the format given in Table 1.1

2. Decide who will prepare the plan.
- Farmer alone — follow guidance in this chapter and the relevant habitat chapters.
- Farmer appoints adviser. Contact FWAG or other advisers (see Appendix I). Adviser must liaise with farmer over decisions on management.
- If the plan will cover any land designated as SSSI/ASSI, the official conservation agency must be consulted at this stage.

3. Will the work be eligible for grant aid or other incentives?
- Check with the relevant agencies or ask FWAG.
- Ensure that your survey conforms to any rules in order to obtain grants.

4. Check for information on the farm's habitats and species.
- Contact FWAG and the Wildlife Trust for existing up-to-date information such as 'Phase 1 Surveys' which map all habitats across many areas of the UK and may have covered the farm. Mark this on a large scale map.

5. If current information is not available, carry out a habitat survey.
- Mark on a large scale map all the habitats and features that you are considering managing (for a list see the farm wildlife plan format in Table 1.1).

6. Add information on uncommon species.
- Also record on the map the location of any uncommon species noted during surveys of the habitats.

7. Assess habitat quality.
- Follow the guidance given in Section 2 of the relevant habitat chapters. Map the features described. No special skill is required for this.
- Refer to Section 1 of each chapter for background information on the aspects of habitats that are most important for wildlife.
- Using that information, decide which habitats or areas within habitats are of good quality,

which are moderate and which are in poor condition.

8. Consider the need for species surveys.
- If the habitat quality is high, there are likely to be rare species present. It is rarely necessary to confirm this by survey but, if it is wished to do so, consult FWAG or the Wildlife Trust about methods and employ an experienced specialist.
- In some cases, it is important to survey for particular species. Where this is so, guidance is given in Section 2 of the relevant habitat chapters.

9. Decide on ideal priorities for management.
- Refer to the list on page 6 for a ranking of farm habitat importance, or take advice from FWAG.
- Ideally, give priority to the habitats that are least common locally and nationally, and to areas which are in good condition as these are most likely to hold important wildlife.
- Consider what might be achieved in both long and short term by maintenance and enhancement of existing habitats and by the creation of habitats.
- If rare species are present, ensure that management will take them into account.
- Do not ignore common habitats. They are the backbone of the countryside and hold the species that give pleasure to most people.
- Consider restoration and creation of habitats.

10. Weigh up the practicalities.
- Refer to Section 3 of the relevant habitat chapter to find out what management is required.
- Has the farm the skills, manpower and equipment to do the work?
- What are the practical implications for the running of the farm?
- What are the financial implications including management costs, loss of income due to reduced production, income from grants, incentive payments, sales?
- Are there legislative constraints?

11. Finalise the plan.
- Prepare a map with all the management decisions marked.
- Supplement this if desired by a short written work programme and budget, listing the objectives and the management required, including a note of work priority, timing, labour and cost.

Table 1.1: Format for farm wildlife plans

PART 1 BACKGROUND
List the following information.
1. The Farm
Farm location.
Farm size, tenure and available labour.
Farm type plus other relevant information, eg shooting interests.
Farm buildings, their use and location.
Livestock. List the livestock types and numbers.
Crops. Map and list the crops grown and any rotations.
Soil type. Note the type(s) across the whole farm.
Set-aside. Note option chosen and management.
Site designations and conservation schemes. Map and give details of land notified as being of
    wildlife or other importance, eg SSSI, ESA.

2. Farming Operations
Fertiliser use, rate of application, timing, type of applicator. Any observed effects on habitats, eg
    run-off into ditches.
Measures to alter soil pH.
Pesticides used, the target species, rate and timing, type of applicator. Any observed effects
    on wildlife.
Livestock management. Note timing and intensity of grazing, seasonal practice, use of
    supplementary feeding and mineral blocks. Any effect on wildlife, eg overgrazing.
Farm wastes produced, the treatment and method of disposal. Effects on wildlife.
Environmental and wildlife management. List any conservation measures undertaken (see
    Agriculture Departments' codes of good agricultural practice on air, water and soil). Note
    practices specifically undertaken to benefit wildlife.

3. Wildlife Habitats
Map location and extent of:
    Arable land.
    Improved grassland.
    Semi-improved or unimproved grassland.
    Lowland heath.
    Hill and rough grazings.
    Woodland.
    Hedges, farm trees and scrub.
    Watercourses including ditches.
    Ponds and other waterbodies.
    Other wetlands such as marsh or areas that regularly flood.
    Walls and farm buildings.
    Other habitats such as machair, saltmarsh, gravel pits.

Record the locations of uncommon species if necessary.

4. Wildlife Management Options
    Assess habitats and record:
        Existing interest and potential of each habitat.
        Management being undertaken on existing habitats.
        Creation of habitats.
        Management for individual species.
        Indicate the conservation importance of different actions.
        State the wildlife management aims of the farmer.

5. Opportunities and Constraints imposed by the farming system
Financial implications. Management costs, loss of income due to reduced production, grants
    and incentive payments, income from product sales.
Management requirements. The work required to maintain/enhance the wildlife interest and
    the manpower/equipment implications.
Legislation. Will this affect the management prescriptions?
Integration with other farm activities.

Table 1.1: Format for farm wildlife plans (cont'd)

PART 2 THE PLAN

6. Work Programme and Budget

Each decision on habitat management or changes in farm operations is recorded, with:

Priority – degree of importance of each task.

Labour – the number of man days or hours required.

Cost – capital, revenue and income if any.

Timing – when the work should be carried out (season and year).

7. Annotated Map

Show the farm boundary, field numbers, wildlife habitats and important features, and a brief description of the management proposals. All maps should show north, be dated, use a scale, show a key to wildlife habitats.

8. Summary

If wished, a short summary of decisions may be prepared.

9. Further Help and Advice.

Append any technical fact-sheets or advisory leaflets.

4. References and further reading

Batten, L A, Bibby C J, Clement P, Elliott, G D and Porter, R F 1990. *Red Data Birds in Britain.* T and A D Poyser.

Bibby, C J, Burgess, N D and Hill, D A 1992. *Bird Census Techniques.* Academic Press.

Bratton, J H (ed) 1991. *British Red Data Books: 3 Invertebrates other than insects.* Joint Nature Conservation Committee.

Buckley, G P 1989. *Biological habitat reconstruction.* Belhaven Press.

Farming and Wildlife Trust and Schering Agriculture 1988. *Farm Conservation Guide.* Green Science.

Fry, R and Lonsdale, D 1991. *Habitat Conservation for Insects.* Amateur Entomological Society.

Fuller, R J 1982. *Bird Habitats in Britain.* T and A D Poyser.

Farming and Wildlife Advisory Group 1992. *Handbook for Environmentally Responsible Farming.* FWAG.

Kirby, P 1992. *Habitat Management for Invertebrates.* pp. 11–18. RSPB.

Lack, P 1992. *Birds and lowland farms.* HMSO.

Nature Conservancy Council 1990. *Handbook for Phase 1 Habitat Survey.* NCC.

Nature Conservancy Council and Botanical Society of the British Isles 1987. *Growing wild flowers from seed.* (Leaflet. Now available from English Nature.)

O'Connor, R J and Shrubb, M 1986. *Farming and Birds.* Cambridge University Press.

Perring, F H and Farrell, L 1983 (2nd edition). *British Red Data Book I, vascular plants.* Royal Society for Nature Conservation.

Rodwell, J R (ed) 1991. *British Plant Communities* Vols 1–3 (to be completed in 5 volumes). Cambridge University Press.

Shirt, D B (ed) 1987. *British Red Data Books: 2 Insects.* Nature Conservancy Council.

Stubbs, D 1988. *Towards an introductions policy.* Wildlife Link.

Tait, J, Lane, A and Carr, S 1988. *Practical Conservation: Site Assessment and Management Planning.* Hodder and Stoughton.

Wright, F J 1990. *Environmental Handbook for Agricultural Trainers.* Agricultural Training Board.

Case Study: Farm Wildlife Plan

Farm details

Farm:	Hall Farm, Moreton, Oxfordshire.
Tenure:	owned by Hall Farm Ltd, managed by the farm manager, Tony Morrison.
Size:	187 ha covered by this farm plan (total farm area 526 ha).
Altitude:	48–69 m.
Soil:	three distinct soil types: Thames river alluvium; Cretaceous and Jurassic sandstone, siltstone and clay; river terrace gravel.
Crops:	173 ha under arable and 14 ha permanent pasture. Intensive 2 wheats - barley - oilseed rape (-pulses) arable rotation. There is a small area of permanent grassland used for horse paddocks and livery with some fields cut for hay.
Wildlife features:	despite the large fields and open landscape Hall Farm has a wide variety of wildlife habitats including watercourses, long established grassland, individual trees, hedgerows and ponds.

Hall Farm has been owned by the Hedges family since 1932 and in 1982 the estate was divided. The landscape at Hall Farm consists of large, open arable fields with prominent boundary features, comprised of wide drains and streams with mature shrubs and riverside trees or old roadside hedges. The farm also contains a scheduled ancient monument which is believed to have been excavated for a small fortification but was never completed. An extensive network of sown grass rides follow the perimeter of the larger arable fields following a horse riding trail. Horse riding and livery is a significant diversification enterprise in the farm.

Farmer's aims
Primary aim
- To enhance and improve existing wildlife and landscape features within the context of the farming system.

Secondary aims
- To produce a practical work plan including possibilities for the creation of new wildlife habitats and landscape features which will improve this farm's attractiveness for wildlife and amenity.
- To identify sources of finance to fund conservation management.

Background
Farm conservation plan produced in April 1993 by FWAG, in draft for discussion with the farmer, as a basis for planned wildlife improvement. Plan can be updated and reviewed according to farm policy, seasonality and availability of labour.

Methods
The existing wildlife features have all been mapped (see Figure 1.1). Their wildlife interest and potential have also been described in the farm conservation plan. Proposals for management and new wildlife features have also been prepared, extracts of which accompany Figure 1.1.

As with any intensive arable farm a number of the farming operations have potentially damaging operations for wildlife. The major operations are outlined in the plan and modifications suggested to lessen their impact. A suggested work plan for the next 7 years has been prepared along with outline details of the relevant grant schemes.

▶▶▶

Achievements

Primary aim
● Farm conservation plan prescriptions produced in draft to guide management, enhancement and creation of wildlife features in the farm now being discussed.

Secondary aims
● Work plan produced.

● Relevant grants identified to fund work.

Future management
Confirmation of proposals contained in the farm conservation plan. Detailed specifications for individual sites, and grant applications will be prepared by FWAG as required.

The Hall Farm area was suggested as a compact unit for the initial plan and it is intended to expand the report to cover the remaining farm area in due course.

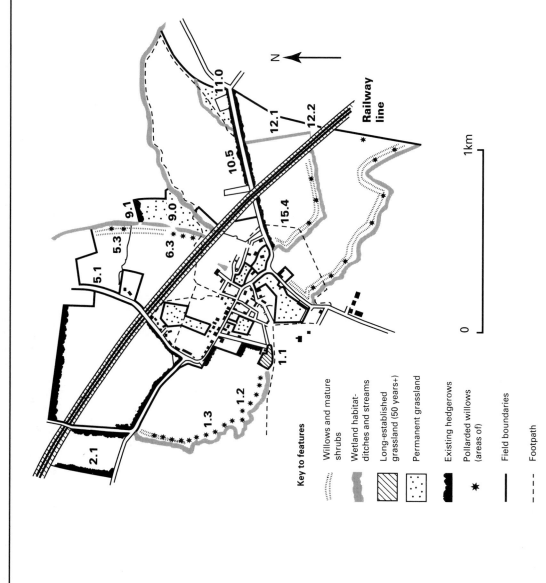

Key to features

▨	Willows and mature shrubs
▨	Wetland habitat- ditches and streams
▨	Long-established grassland (50 years+)
▨	Permanent grassland
◼	Existing hedgerows
✳	Pollarded willows (areas of)
——	Field boundaries
- - -	Footpath

0 ⊢——————⊣ 1km

Figure 1.1 Farm Wildlife Plan – Hall Farm, South Moreton, Oxfordshire.
Note: The above plan and accompanying management prescriptions were produced by FWAG. This is an extract and does not contain the full set of prescriptions but highlights the range of potential management work planned for wildlife on the farm. Figures on the plan refer to sites listed in Table 1.2.

Table 1.2: Extracts from farm wildlife plan
Hall Farm, South Moreton, produced by FWAG

SITE	DESCRIPTION	MANAGEMENT PRESCRIPTION
1.1 Ancient mound	Irregular mound probably dug in 1220, which seems to have been intended for a small fortification.	Scheduled site, continue to manage by light grazing. Prevent any further development of scrub. Do not plant trees or shrubs on or near mound. Leave soil undisturbed.
1.2 Riverside boundary	Parish boundary, important wildlife and landscape feature consisting primarily of old pollarded willows.	Pollard willows every ten years when dredging is carried out. Leave some piles of dead wood. Plant occasional bankside shrubs, eg, guelder rose.
1.3 Meander plantings	Areas inside deep meanders planted with mixed broadleaves.	Maintain suitable weed control for first five years. Beat up failed trees with alder, new willow stems and low shrubs such as guelder rose, grey willow and dog rose. Remove unsuitable trees such as beech and conifers.
2.1 Young hedge	Dense predominately hawthorn hedge, 2.5 m tall. Significant wildlife corridor.	Lay hedge in two consecutive seasons (years 1 and 2). Leave established hedgerow trees. After laying leave hedge untrimmed for a few years allowing new shoots to grow.
5.1 Grass verge	Steep grass verge unsuitable for hedge or tree planting.	Ensure wide grass margin and bank are maintained (2 m +). Allow grass to develop into tall tussocky sward for beneficial insects and small mammals.
5.3 Tall trees and shrub boundary	Important wildlife corridor and landscape feature.	Plant replacement black poplars and pollard mature willows. Manage shrubs by careful siding up with hedge trimmer when necessary (every three years).
6.3 Pond	Steep sided, small field pond, low existing wildlife value.	Excavate banks to create more convoluted shape and gradual sloping banks. Create marshy area and plant shrubs and occasional trees, move fence out (Year 1).
9.0 Grass meadow	Long-term grass sward established around 12 years ago. Well used footpath along southern boundary.	Re-seed part of the field with a native grass mixture and selection of wild flowers (Year 1). Leave wide margin for wildlife and footpath. Manage as a hay meadow with a late cut. Possibly harvest wild flower seeds.
9.1 Hedgerow	Mature hawthorn and blackthorn hedge.	Trim on a three-year staggered rotation allowing bushes to fruit.
10.5 Hedgerow	Old hedge containing six species; hawthorn, blackthorn, spindle, field maple, ash and willow. Gappy in places.	If possible trim on a three-year staggered rotation. Long term, coppice and gap up.
11.0 Pumping station field	Old grass ley, some finer fescue grasses present.	As this field is used for hay consider increasing the species interest by no further nitrogen or chemical applications and cutting slightly later. Leave a 1–2 m unmown strip around the field for insects and small mammals.
12.1 Drain bank	No margin present, important wildlife corridor.	Establish 2 m permanent grass margin to prevent fertiliser and chemical drift entering drain. Mow every 2–3 years.
12.2 Corner planting	Field corner with some established trees.	Plant up a small mixed copse. Ash, wild crab apple, field maple, alder, hawthorn, hazel, dogwood (Year 2).
15.4 Future pond	Wide margin with potential for small pond feature.	When cleaning drain excavate wide meander feature to increase still water habitat for wildfowl.

2. Arable Land

1. Factors influencing wildlife

1.1 The context of arable farming

- Technological developments in arable farming have brought about greatly increased productivity with consequent loss of wildlife.
- Current developments are increasing the potential to retain at least some wildlife alongside efficient arable farming.
- Set-aside and other schemes now present opportunities for habitat re-creation.

Most people are well aware of the remarkable advances in arable productivity achieved in the last 50 years. Mechanisation freed additional land for tillage by removing the need to grow grass to feed horses, which had for centuries provided the motive power for cultivation and carting, and enabled vastly increased work rates in everything from ploughing through drainage to grain drying. Plant breeding, artificial fertilisers and pesticides have also contributed to greatly increased productivity. The economic context of agriculture, latterly within the Common Agricultural Policy, gave farmers the confidence to invest and to specialise. Specialisation has permitted the development of exceptional standards of husbandry and the most efficient use of capital.

This chapter does not assume that, in order to benefit wildlife, a farmer will alter his decisions about which crops to grow or about the main methods of management. The conservation of the many species that depend on arable farming has to be through ways which do not impose unacceptable cost or complication. There is a growing body of knowledge to show how at least some wildlife can be retained within the context of an efficient farm and this process is helped by advances in the understanding of the role of natural organisms such as money spiders and ground beetles in insect pest control, and in the development of specific pesticides and

accurate application systems for farm chemicals. New policies for agriculture, to reduce production or to benefit the environment, open up the prospect of restoring more of the wildlife of arable farms. Because many hundreds of wildlife species are dependent on arable, and some are now extremely rare, these measures are important in addition to conservation on other farm habitats. However, as land is taken out of production, there is also the prospect of re-creating rare and important habitats such as lowland heaths or seasonally-flooded hay meadows. These are discussed in the relevant chapters.

1.2 Wild plant variety and abundance

- Nearly 300 kinds of wild plants grow on tilled land.
- Many are annuals adapted to exploiting bare ground and with long-lived seeds.
- Some of the arable weeds are now amongst the rarest plants in the UK.
- Wild plants are important as food and cover for other wildlife.
- Most of the insect species that occur on arable are harmless to the crop and some are beneficial.
- Plant seeds and invertebrates are sources of food for game and other birds.

Nearly 300 species of wild plants have been found growing on tilled land in the UK. Some, such as wild oats, barren brome and cleavers, are serious competitors with the crop and must be controlled but most occur in small numbers or are low-growing plants which may have no significant effect on yields. Many of these wild plants are sources of seed which is eaten by birds and small mammals.

Tillage provides ideal conditions for a number of plants that have evolved to exploit bare ground. In nature, bare ground is a fairly uncommon and short-lived habitat produced by events such as spates, landslips, fire or trampling by large herbivores. Plants adapted to exploit it are annuals, which germinate rapidly, grow fast and produce copious seed, often in a matter of weeks. To do this, they need freedom from competition and, once other larger or longer-lived plants appear, the first colonists are overshaded, deprived of moisture and nutrients, and quickly die out. However, their seed may be widely dispersed by wind or water currents; some of these plants have seeds equipped with hooks and get carried off in the pelts of mammals and the plumage of birds. Most importantly, many of them have seeds that are long-lived and can persist in the soil for many years, awaiting the chance event which once again produces bare ground in which they can germinate and renew their seedbank.

Many of these annual weeds were serious crop pests. Now, most of them are amongst our rarest plants. For example, the corn buttercup has disappeared from about 95% of its former range. Shepherd's needle, corn marigold and pheasant's eye have also greatly declined. Not surprisingly, corncockle, with seeds that are poisonous and hard to separate from wheat, is probably now extinct as a wild plant in the UK (Feature 2.1: Arable weeds).

Wild plants are important as sources of food and cover for much other farmland wildlife, especially insects. For instance, field pansy provides a nectar source for butterflies while poppy and fumitories are eaten by many other insects. Many crop pollinators such as bumblebees (Feature 2.2: Bumblebees and field margins) depend on wild plants for nectar and pollen at the time when the crop is not in bloom. Over a thousand different insect species spend part of their life cycles in cereal fields and at least 150 kinds of spider have been found in them.

The vast majority of these invertebrates do no harm and many are beneficial (Feature 2.3: Beneficial insects). They include crop pollinators and predators of crop aphids all of which are of positive benefit to the

farmer. There are approximately 350 species of non-specialist aphid predators found in cereal crops, perhaps the most important of which are hoverflies and ladybirds.

Most of these invertebrates are also potential food for gamebird chicks, particularly partridges, as well as birds such as lapwings and skylarks, and mammals such as field mice or shrews.

1.3 Crop type and structure

- Different species make use of different crops.
- Those which feed on the crop may be significant pests but some can be tolerated as their effect is slight.
- Crop height and density affects its use by wildlife.
- Few birds make use of tall, dense cereal crops.

It is difficult to know to what extent different crops might potentially be used by wild plants and insects because efficient management to produce clean crops and high yields tends to remove most of this wildlife. Typically, the species that survive in particular crops are ones with an ability to become pests because the conditions suit them, such as grasses like barren brome in cereals and some broadleaved weeds in broadleaved crops where herbicides cannot be used on them. Similarly, some mammals and birds feed directly on the crop and may therefore become pests. For instance, cabbages and rape can be subject to severe damage by pigeons.

Many creatures feed on particular crops or use them as cover for quite short periods during the growth cycle, for instance, skylarks feed on some sugar-beet seedlings but do not eat the foliage of mature plants. Similarly, greenfinches may take ripe oilseed rape seed but ignore the plant for the rest of the year. As a result, their effect on the crop may be insignificant in most years.

Birds nesting in other habitats may make use of standing crops for feeding. For instance, yellowhammers, whitethroats, robins, blackbirds, dunnocks, greenfinches and tree sparrows frequently fly from hedges or woodland into the edges of crops, especially later in the season when the crop may hold large numbers of invertebrates.

Few mammals live entirely in cereal fields – hares and field mice make much use of woodland for example, but several species, including rabbits and roe deer, feed on the foliage of a wide range of crops.

Crop height and density affect the temperature and humidity within the crop and at the soil surface because of the shading effect and influence on windspeed. Thus they can determine the overall survival of wild plants and invertebrates. In turn, the abundance or scarcity of these natural food resources affects other wildlife such as small mammals and birds.

For birds, the value of a crop as a foraging place or potential nest site depends not only on the available plant and invertebrate food supply but also on its structure and stage of growth. They determine the ease with which birds can move through it and also affect their vulnerability to predators. For example, grey partridge (Feature 2.4: Grey partridge) broods avoid areas where the overhead canopy of the cereal crop is very sparse as there is insufficient concealment from birds of prey, but the chicks find it difficult to move through dense vegetation, such as close-growing cereal stems or matted grass, so that their feeding rate falls and survival may be affected.

In general, crops become less attractive to birds as they grow taller and denser, although tramlines allow access to ground level in an otherwise impenetrable crop and are much used by some species.

During the breeding season several birds choose to nest in arable fields, perhaps the most familiar being the skylark, which for successive nesting attempts may move between crop types according to their structural suitability. A key factor is crop height, which must be less than 30 cm. A typical series of choices might be: in April, winter cereals; in May, spring cereals, and in June, root crops. Birds make little use of tall crops for nesting but in a few areas marsh and Montagu's harriers breed in autumn-

sown cereals. Quail may also be heard calling from within cereal fields particularly in the drier southern part of the UK.

1.4 Timing of cultivation and sowing

- Timing of cultivation and sowing affects wildlife.
- Some plants need autumn cultivation and others germinate after spring cultivation.
- Spring tillage is an important nesting habitat for some birds.
- Autumn-sown crops become too tall and dense by spring for birds to nest.
- Winter stubbles are an important feeding habitat for birds.

The timing of sowing is an important factor for much wildlife on arable land. It impinges on the germination times of plants which depend on bare ground and so are largely or wholly confined to tillage. Many rare arable weeds germinate in the autumn, some in both autumn and spring and some only in spring (Feature 2.1: Arable weeds). The widespread switch to autumn sowing is probably a cause of the decline of species such as corn marigold, weasel's snout and night-flowering catchfly that germinate in spring.

The timing of cultivation also affects the present generation of problem weeds. Wild oats germinate in the spring and, because of the shift to autumn sowing in much of the UK, have become less of a problem compared with barren brome and black grass, which are mostly autumn germinators.

Spring tillage is important for feeding and for nesting by several bird species. It makes soil invertebrates available at a time of year when they are otherwise difficult to locate and creates the nesting conditions required by lapwing, stone-curlew (Feature 2.5: Stone-curlew) and oystercatcher. These birds will only nest where they have good all-round visibility so that they can respond in good time to approaching predators. In addition, they pick their food, which includes earthworms and beetles, from the surface of open ground so that they need extensive unobstructed areas over which to forage.

Autumn-sown crops become too tall and dense by spring for the birds to nest. Where these birds have declined it is partly because of the shift to autumn sowing dates, though an important additional factor may be the disappearance of mixed enterprises, because the birds tended to move their chicks to nearby pastures which were better feeding areas with more insects than the arable land.

Where stubble is left through the winter, spilt grain, weed seeds and insects are utilised by a range of species including partridges, pheasants, flocks of finches and buntings, jackdaws and rooks. By the spring much of the available food will have been eaten and ploughing then renews the supply of accessible invertebrates and, to a lesser extent, seeds at a time of year when some farmland birds have difficulty in finding sufficient food.

Today, it is generally only in more northern areas of the UK that spring sowing still leads to stubbles remaining through the winter. With the widespread shift to autumn sowing, many formerly common seed-eating birds such as corn bunting, tree sparrow and linnet have undergone serious declines and the cirl bunting (Feature 2.6: Cirl bunting) was reduced to fewer than 150 pairs in part because of the loss of this important winter habitat.

Pink-footed geese and greylag geese also use stubbles, feeding mainly on spilt grain and winter growth and switching to grazing cereal crops, pasture or field vegetables when this is exhausted.

1.5 Pesticides

- Pesticides are an essential part of arable farming.
- Herbicides have made many formerly widespread plants rare and greatly reduced food resources for invertebrates, birds and mammals.
- Insecticides may also have significant effects on many non-pest insect species.
- Pesticide drift can affect adjacent habitats.
- Seed treatments and molluscicides can also affect wildlife.

Pesticides are an essential part of the operation of almost all farms and have been a key factor in the increase of yields through the control of crop pests, diseases and competitors. For example, until the 1940s, much weed control was achieved by cultivation and the use of rotations, but, as these are not wholly effective, small numbers of weeds survived and produced seed, so ensuring their perpetuation. Since the introduction of herbicides, the potential to wholly eradicate many broadleaved plants has increased. Formerly widespread plants including rough poppy, shepherd's needle and corn buttercup are now very rare.

The practice of spraying the 'green bridge' to reduce the risk of carrying over crop disease and to help in weed control also removes plants that pose no problem to the crop but are both habitat for insects and a food resource for small birds and mammals.

An important cause of repeat infestation by barren brome and some other pernicious weeds is the practice of spraying out the plant community of the hedge bottom. This removes the perennial plant cover which resists colonisation by such annual weeds.

Many species of invertebrates are affected by the use of non-specific insecticides and, indirectly, by the use of herbicides, which destroy their food resources.

The great decline in the grey partridge on farms and its extinction from some parts of the UK is due to poor levels of chick survival primarily resulting from food shortage. Partridge chicks feed mainly on beetles (leaf beetles, small diurnal ground beetles and weevils), moth and sawfly larvae and many kinds of plant bugs (Feature 2.4). The abundance of these insects has been greatly reduced by insecticides, by some fungicides which also have insecticidal properties and by herbicides which remove the wild plants on which many of these insects depend.

Pesticides may cause significant harm to non-target plants or invertebrates even at less than the recommended application rate – impairing growth and competitive ability, reducing feeding rates and mobility, increasing vulnerability to predators and so on. This means that aerial drift of even small amounts of a formulation may have effects outside the cropped area, affecting the field margin and habitats such as ponds. The amount of drift depends on a combination of factors, including wind-speed, temperature, humidity and the type of sprayer used. Generally, the greater the wind-speed, the higher the boom above the crop and the finer the spray, the greater will be the risk of drifting.

Seed treatment is a valuable method of delivering pesticides to target pests and diseases without spreading them through the environment. However, this may introduce special risks for seed-eating wildlife, including some finches and buntings. Seed that is carefully buried as it is sown presents much less hazard than if some is left exposed on the surface. Many of the features of treated seeds apply also to granules and molluscicide pellets, which are eaten by the same range of wildlife species. If the pesticide is formulated with a nutritious cereal base, pellets may be eaten as food in the same way as seed, with consequent harmful effects.

1.6 Fertiliser use

- Artificial fertilisers have harmful effects on most wild plants.
- Wild plants that can exploit high nutrient levels are potential crop pests.
- Manure releases nutrients more slowly and is better for wild plants.
- Manure increases soil organic content, soil invertebrate abundance and the food resources of some birds.
- Slurry application is not beneficial to wildlife.

Fertilisers have significant effects on wildlife. Most plants have evolved to make efficient use of very small amounts of nutrients because concentrations are rather rare in natural habitats. As a result they have little ability to respond to high levels. Modern crops have been developed to respond to appropriate artificial nutrient applications with greatly accelerated growth and yields. The effect is that they can out-compete most wild plants by

depriving them of light and moisture. Some of the latter disappear entirely and others survive only poorly, producing less seed than when growing in less fertile soil. There are a few weeds which evolved to exploit high nutrient levels, growing rapidly and producing copious seed. Some of these remain amongst the handful of plants that are potentially serious crop competitors.

Manure has far less effect because it contains lower concentrations and releases them slowly. Its organic nature also has important effects on the abundance of soil fauna such as earthworms and tends to produce land which is good for feeding by birds, including lapwings and golden plovers, rooks, gulls and thrushes. Green manures may have a similar effect. However, as with so many interactions between arable farming and wildlife, the story is complicated because frequency of cultivation also has an effect on earthworms, the numbers and variety of species being reduced by the physical effects of tillage.

Slurry can be toxic to soil invertebrates such as earthworms. It lacks much of the organic component present in manure, and nutrients are rapidly available to plants. Its use is not beneficial to wildlife.

2. Options and assessment: planning management

2.1 Wildlife assessment of arable land

- Note the existing interest and the farming activities it depends on.
- Greatest interest is likely to be in spring-sown crops, at field margins and adjacent to other habitats.
- Ground-nesting birds may be present in spring and summer.
- In winter, a different set of wildlife may be present.
- Consider the possible beneficial and harmful effects of changes in current practices.
- Identify fields where set-aside could bring most wildlife benefits.
- Ideally, produce a farm wildlife plan to help decide on the optimum ways of maintaining wildlife in arable fields.

The assessment of wildlife on arable fields needs to consider four questions – what wildlife is present, what crops and areas of the farm does it depend on, what impact would changes in crops or their management cause, and what potential is there for increasing the wildlife interest without unacceptable effects on farming operations, crops and overall costs? It will be found helpful to do this following the farm wildlife plan format set out on page 10 as this presents a systematic approach to weighing up the opportunities and constraints imposed by the working of the farm.

The general principles of wildlife assessment are also described in Chapter 1. Table 2.1 covers the wildlife assessment of arable land specifically.

As section 1 of this chapter makes clear, most efficiently managed arable fields hold very little wildlife, especially where crops have been sown in the preceding autumn and are well grown by April. As a general rule, there is likely to be more wildlife in spring-sown crops and on those parts of the field where, for whatever reason, growth is poor in spring. Also, with the exception of some ground-nesting birds, most surviving wildlife interest is likely to be close to the edge of the field. This is because wild plants are most likely to survive here, where they suffer less competition from the crop, and because such plants are likely to attract insects and birds. As these areas are usually in the 'front line' where weed invasion is fought most intensively, assessment needs to consider whether management for wildlife and weed control can be integrated effectively, for instance by maintaining cultivated strips or permanent plant cover.

The presence of wildlife at the field's edge also reflects the fact that most invertebrates, birds and mammals that use the cropped area also need the habitat and shelter provided by hedges, ditches or adjoining uncropped land such as woodland. Assessment should pay particular attention to parts of the crop which adjoin such areas and it is here that greatest benefits are likely to come from special management measures such as 'conservation headlands'. Other chapters explain how to assess these habitats and what wildlife value they have.

Normally, the farmer will know if birds such as lapwing, oystercatcher or stone-curlew nest on the farm. FWAGs and the other conservation bodies will provide detailed advice on management for birds, rare arable weeds or other species where requested.

Assessment needs to take account of the changing wildlife interest of the field right through the year. A field that holds little in spring and summer may be important for roosting or feeding by golden plover in winter, for example.

Finally, consideration should be given to identifying fields where particular wildlife benefits can be achieved through rotational or long-term set-aside.

Table 2.1: Wildlife assessment of arable land

INFORMATION REQUIRED	METHOD	REASON FOR INFORMATION
1. Conservation status and interest	Contact FWAG initially.	Very little arable land in the UK has been scheduled as SSSI. However some information on rare species or semi-natural features such as hedges or ditches may be kept.
2. Past management	Check farm/estate records. Check historical information. Examine past/present aerial photographs.	Worth undertaking when considering habitat re-creation on the farm possibly through set-aside. Also the best chance of arable weeds is in fields most recently switched from spring to autumn sowing.
3. Current management	Map crop types and note rotations and times of sowing.	Different crops have different wildlife values. Rotations may be an alternative to agrochemical inputs so reducing effects on wildlife. Spring-sown cereals are of higher wildlife value than winter-sown. Size of fields and juxtaposition of crops to other habitats also affects wildlife interest. May suggest changes of crop distribution around the farm. Also guides survey for uncommon species.
	Note fertiliser use, including type and methods, amount, timing of application.	Review of practice to assess impact on wildlife, eg preventing fertiliser application into ditches and streams and field margins.
	Note pesticide use, including type and methods, amounts, timing of application. Note effect on target/non-target species.	Review of practice to assess impact on wildlife, eg protecting hedge bottoms, creation of conservation headlands. May suggest modifications to current use.
	Record post-harvest management.	May be important for a different group of species.
	Record management of rotational set-aside land, such as herbicide use, timing of mowings and cultivations, use of natural regenerations/sown cover crop.	To consider present wildlife usage and potential to modify to benefit uncommon species. To consider effect of management on wildlife.
4. Presence of non-injurious and uncommon arable weeds	Note presence of non-injurious and uncommon arable weeds.	Of wildlife conservation value. Consider allowing to set seed to maintain in seedbank.
5. Other wildlife features	Map uncultivated field corners, farm tracks, field margins, 'conservation headlands', 'beetle banks', hedges, dry-stone walls, ditches, ponds, isolated trees. (For other habitats see relevant chapters.)	May be the only areas of wildlife interest on the farm and have specific conservation and management requirements.
6. Rare and sensitive species	Record exact location of rare species. Note presence of ground-nesting birds. Note vegetation structure in vicinity. Seek specialist guidance.	Arable land can support a number of rare breeding birds such as stone-curlew and Montagu's harrier. A number of rare arable weeds may also be present. The location of these is important as they can easily be inadvertently destroyed.
7. Boundaries	Locate and assess fences, hedges.	To identify potential for field margin management.

RSPB: Farming and Wildlife

2.2 Management needs and opportunities

- Integration of significant wildlife benefits with efficient arable cropping is difficult.
- Review agrochemical uses and maximise use of target-specific pesticides.
- Consider giving special treatment to field margins.
- Where ground-nesting birds occur, take measures to avoid destruction of eggs or chicks.
- Look at the opportunities provided by set-aside to restore wildlife.

There are no easy ways of increasing wildlife on arable land. To a large degree this is because the declines of species are the result not of single factors but of several in combination. For instance, to restore ideal conditions for breeding birds such as lapwing would require spring sowing on fields that had been manured and were adjacent to unimproved pasture. To restore rare arable weeds needs not only reduction in, or cessation of, herbicide use but also correct timing of cultivation and sowing – autumn for some species, spring for others. Restoration of the big flocks of finches and buntings that once used winter stubbles means not only a change in sowing date but also toleration of broadleaved weeds through the winter period. Perfect conditions for grey partridge would be sparser crop density – involving lower sowing rates and less nitrogen, plus toleration of arable weeds to provide ample food for the chicks, and good nesting cover available in broad margins of permanent grass and herbs.

Even so, there are several courses of action which will bring worthwhile results for wildlife.

First, the more target-specific pesticide applications become, the better. Many plants and invertebrates in crops do no harm and some are beneficial to crop pollination or pest control. A review of agrochemical use on the farm, including fertilisers, may indicate ways in which wildlife gains can be achieved. Bear in mind the overall effects of change. For instance, replacement of herbicides by cultivations may be disadvantageous to some ground-nesting birds without increasing the numbers of wild plants in the crop. In this case, use of herbicides which kill only the problem weeds would be a better approach.

Second, there are benefits to both pest control and wildlife from giving special treatment to field margins. There are a range of options to suit different situations such as strips of perennial vegetation a minimum of 1 m wide and 'conservation headlands' where applications of broad leaved herbicides and insecticides are limited but conventional management of the rest of the crop is not affected.

Third, where there are ground-nesting birds, particular care should be taken to avoid damage to eggs or chicks during spraying or cultivations. It can be surprisingly difficult to spot them once the adult moves away from the nest or the motionless, crouching young; some patient searching may be needed. Once located, they may be moved to one side and carefully replaced in the same spot once the tractor has passed.

Fourth, rotational or long-term set-aside could be managed in ways which would create suitable conditions for species that once thrived on arable.

Long-term set-aside and some other schemes may also be used to restore other habitat types, and methods are given in the relevant chapters. However, it is not necessarily a good trade-off to lose uncommon species that depend on arable and replace them with a different set of wildlife requiring a different habitat. FWAGs and the other conservation bodies can give advice on the relative merits of different courses of action. An increasing range of financial incentives are available for wildlife management on farms. Take advice on the opportunities which may exist (see page 8).

3. Management of arable land

3.1 Use of pesticides and fertilisers

- Follow all legal requirements and the advice in the Code of Practice.
- Use pesticides only when pest threshold levels are reached.
- Use target-specific formulations wherever possible.
- Use insecticides early and late in the day to minimise effects on bees and other non-target insects.
- Take great care to avoid spray-drift.
- Consider alternative means of pest control and their implications.
- Clear-up spillages of treated grain.
- Ensure fertiliser applications do not affect field margins and other habitats.

In the UK controls to ensure the safe use of pesticides are covered by the Food and Environment Protection Act 1985. This Act is operated through the Control of Pesticides Regulations 1986, which determine the manner in which products may be applied and the responsibilities that users must accept. A code of practice to give guidance on these matters is published by the agriculture departments and the Health and Safety Commission (see Appendix II: Legal considerations).

Always follow exactly the permitted conditions of use specified on the label, with care to observe any restrictions such as time of day, crop growth stage and weather conditions. Failure to comply may increase the hazard to wildlife and even minor carelessness or accidents can have serious consequences.

It is recognised good husbandry and financial sense to use pesticides only when pest numbers justify action; this approach also benefits wildlife. As well as monitoring levels of weed and pest infestation to spray at the most cost-effective time, reconsider the pros and cons of cultivation to control weeds, selection of resistant crop varieties, adoption of a suitable rotation pattern, and management of field margins to encourage beneficial

insects and prevent spread of weeds into crops.

The incidental killing of non-target predatory insects such as rove beetles and hoverflies may increase the likelihood of recurring pest problems and the need to re-spray. Pest numbers recover much more rapidly than their predators. Thus, when spraying becomes necessary, selective pesticides should be used to minimise or avoid harm to non-target wildlife. Advice on formulations with least effect on wildlife is available from FWAGs.

If possible, spray in the early morning or evening when most flying insects are not within the crop. During those times when bees are at risk notify your spray liaison officer 48 hours prior to spraying. Spraying should ideally be carried out in a steady force 2 light breeze blowing away from susceptible land. In general, larger droplet sizes drift least. On warm still days, very small droplets may be produced and these may drift out of the target field. Similarly, stronger winds are also likely to result in spray-drift. Never spray in winds of force 4 or above. Drift can also result from 'bounce' at the end of the boom so shorter booms set low are preferable. Important habitats vulnerable to spray-drift include ponds, woodland edges, hedges, unimproved grassland and field margins. If possible, avoid spraying the outermost 10 m all round the field so as to minimise the risk of drift onto hedges or other areas important for wildlife.

As the field margin is the zone most used by the wildlife of arable fields, it is very beneficial to give it special treatment at all times.

When drilling treated grain, particular care is needed where the drill turns at the edge of a field and any spillage should be buried or removed.

Fertiliser and animal manure should not be applied to grass strips alongside field boundaries or to buffer zones around ponds, old grassland or other areas of wildlife value. With spinner applicators it is difficult to keep applications out of sensitive areas including field margins so particular care is needed – fit a deflector if necessary.

In England, Nitrate Sensitive Areas have been designated by MAFF in an attempt to reduce levels of nitrate leaching. Further information can be obtained from them.

3.2 Field margins

- Uncropped field margins can be managed in ways which are valuable to wildlife, and aid pest and weed control.
- Perennial grasses and herbs growing at the field margin will not invade the crop but will suppress problem weeds such as cleavers and barren brome.
- Tussock-forming perennial grasses are also the overwintering habitat of beetles and spiders which prey on crop pests.
- Establish a strip of perennial grasses and other plants at least 1 m wide at the field margin by assisting natural colonisation or by seeding.
- In large fields, create additional grass strips ('beetle banks') for predatory insects.
- Always keep all pesticides and fertilisers out of the established margin or beetle bank.
- If necessary, manage margins and banks by mowing.
- Where there is a heavy weed burden, use a 'sterile strip' about 1 m wide between the crop and the margin or bank to assist weed control.

A strip of uncropped land at the hedge bottom or along the fenceline can have great value for wildlife especially where it adjoins a well-structured hedge, pond or other habitat (Figure 2.1: Field margins and conservation headlands). It provides breeding cover for gamebirds and the overwintering habitat for invertebrates that prey on crop pests such as aphids, but it has been seen as a reservoir of harmful weeds and has often been deliberately sprayed out in consequence. Correct management should result in reduced crop pest and weed problems plus significant benefits for wildlife.

Less than a quarter of all the plant species that grow in field margins are able to colonise beyond 2.5 m into the crop because their seeds do not spread any further. Most of them, and those which can get well into the field, are killed anyway by crop competition or cultivation. Of those which can persist in the crop, only a very few are able to become pernicious weeds necessitating control. Reinfestation of the crop can be greatly reduced by correct management of the field margin.

These weeds become a serious problem for two reasons. First, they are annuals and therefore produce copious seed and can respond rapidly when cultivation or the use of broad-spectrum herbicides creates bare ground and frees them from competition by other plants. Second, unlike most other annual and perennial wild plants, they have the ability to respond to high inputs of nitrogen (Figure 2.2 Effects of nitrogen fertiliser on field margins). However, being annuals they are at a disadvantage in competition against perennial plants because their seeds can only germinate and grow in the occasional gap in the cover so where there is a well-established community of tussock-forming grasses and broad-leaved herbs, the main problem weeds such as cleavers and barren brome are absent or only present in small numbers.

This means that they can be brought under control by re-establishing a marginal strip at least 1 m wide, composed of perennial, tussock-forming grasses such as cocksfoot, false oat grass and Yorkshire fog. These resist colonisation by the pernicious annual weeds and also compete with couch, so preventing or slowing its spread.

Perennial tussocky grass is also the overwintering habitat of rove beetles, ground beetles and spiders which prey on aphids and other crop pests. Dense grass cover with plenty of grass litter, providing stable temperature conditions throughout the winter, can hold up to 1,500 of these predators per square metre (Feature 2.3). In spring, they disperse into the adjoining fields and begin to consume insect pests, thus limiting the build-up in their numbers and possibly delaying or

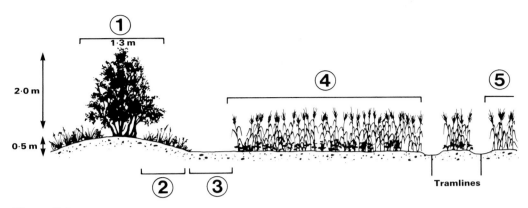

Figure 2.1
Field margins and conservation headlands — management guidelines

1. *Hedge.* Trim hedges every other year and keep to a maximum height of 2 m. Do not allow hedge to overgrow adjacent grassy strip, which is the vital area for nesting partridges.

2. *Grassy bank/nesting strip.* The area used for nest sites by gamebirds and for overwintering beneficial insects. At least 1 m wide and preferably sited on a bank. Should be composed of perennial grasses and other non-weedy herbaceous species. Avoid spray and fertiliser drift into this area. Allow build-up of dead grass material essential for successful nesting, but top the vegetation every 2–3 years to avoid scrub encroachment.

3. *Boundary or sterile strip.* Purpose is to prevent invasion of crop by cleavers and barren brome where they have become abundant. Should be at least 1 m wide. Maintain by rotovation in February/early March. Do not spray out grassy bank. Drill crop farther out into the field to leave area of bare cultivated ground for the sterile strip. Avoid spray-drift by shielding nozzle down to ground level. Not essential for conservation purposes — purely intended for weed management.

4. *Conservation headlands.* The area between the crop edge and the first tramline (usually 6 m wide according to boom width). This is an area of crop treated with selective pesticides to control grass weeds, cleavers and diseases while allowing most broadleaved weeds and beneficial insects to survive. Ploughing of headlands is recommended especially on heavy soil or where grass weeds are a problem. Avoid turning furrow onto grassy strip as this can create ideal conditions for annual weeds. Choose headlands next to good nesting cover. Avoid headlands infested with difficult weeds (especially barren brome and cleavers).

5. *Sprayed crop.* Treat as normal. Avoid drift into headland. Use only safer aphicides.

(Source: Boatman, N 1990. Field Boundary Vegetation. *The Game Conservancy Review of 1989. No 21,* pp 58–61. Game Conservancy.)

preventing serious infestation, especially in the early part of the season before the pests start to breed. This means that pesticide use may be reduced, with consequent savings. In addition, the less use that is made of insecticides, the more harmless insects will survive and provide food for other wildlife such as gamebirds and skylarks.

Where permanent plant cover no longer exists, consider restoring it on a strip around the field at least 1 m wide. If it is wider, as well as having greater wildlife potential, it can then double as an access track. In addition, where rabbits are a problem, a wider margin will help to reduce crop damage and facilitate control.

If the field margin is heavily shaded, it may be difficult to get perennial vegetation to grow so the first step will be to cut back, lay or coppice overgrown hedges, especially

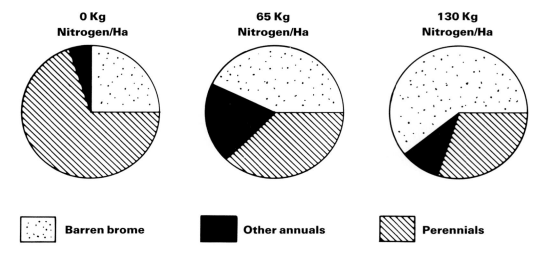

Figure 2.2

Effects of nitrogen fertilisers on field boundary vegetation. The relative proportions of different components of field boundary vegetation (measured as dry weight) in plots treated with three different levels of nitrogen fertiliser. Increase in fertiliser application caused a significant increase in amount of barren brome together with a reduction in the perennial component of the boundary vegetation.

(Source: Theaker, A and Rew, L 1992. Fertilisers and the Field Boundary. *The Game Conservancy Review of 1991*, pp 52–54. The Game Conservancy.)

those which run east-west and have permanent shade on the north side. The overall long-term benefit to a wide spectrum of wildlife will greatly outweigh the short-term loss. However, because some wildlife depends on big hedges, the best approach would be to spread the management over several years so that some stretches will have regrown before others are cut, and to keep any which are not causing a shading problem (see page 254).

Once conditions for plant recovery are suitable, there are two main courses of action – managing natural regeneration or planting seed. In either case, as with any crop, correct seedbed preparation is important. Germination and growth depend on a good tilth but it is important to cultivate the margin shallowly to minimise damage to the hedge roots. Establish a clear plough line at the edge of the area to be planted so that in subsequent management of the adjoining land bare soil is not turned onto the vegetated margin, creating a seedbed for the problem weeds.

If natural regeneration is the chosen method, when it appears check its

composition and, if necessary, spray the field margin using the most selective weedkiller to control any serious infestation by the main problem weeds but allow all other plants to survive. Time spraying to hit the weeds while they are small plants and vulnerable to low dosages so that incidental effects on other plants are minimised. Note that adequate control may not result from use of the normal tractor-mounted boom as the tip will be difficult to control and may snag on the hedge. A better method would be to fit a single lance sprayer or, if the job is small, to use a knapsack sprayer.

Perennial grasses and other plants will gradually colonise and progressively restrict the ability of the annual weeds to germinate and grow. As this happens, spraying can be reduced and, finally, stopped.

If seeding is the preferred method, follow normal weed-control practice prior to sowing the grasses. The best time to sow is early autumn or even August on heavy soil. Later sowing runs the risk of seedlings suffering frost damage. The alternative is to sow in spring. Drill or hand sow with perennial grass appropriate to the soil type, such as cocksfoot at $3g/m^2$ or Yorkshire fog at $4g/m^2$ or, better, a 50:50 mix of the two at the recommended rates.

Other native perennial grasses such as fescues, bents and meadow grasses could also be incorporated in small amounts (up to 20% of the total composition) and this would increase the incidental value of the margin for grass-feeding butterflies such as the meadow brown and marbled white and for grasshoppers. Incorporating perennial wildflowers will have even greater general benefit to wildlife as it will provide a range of food resources for songbirds, small mammals, bumblebees and many other insects but will increase cost and require greater care while they are becoming established (Feature 2.2). Information on the establishment of wildflower grasslands is given on page 76.

Once establishment or restoration of the field margin begins, great care must be taken to avoid spray-drift or accidental fertiliser application. Broadcast-type (spinner) fertiliser applicators are particularly bad in this respect but can be fitted with deflectors.

When the grasses reach a height of 10 cm, cut them down to 5 cm to encourage tillering and speed up the closing of the sward. Once fully established, a perennial grass margin may not need cutting at all unless the hedge is spreading into it by suckers or seedlings. If it is solely composed of grasses, the build-up of litter will be useful as cover for overwintering insects. However, if broadleaved plants have been sown, it is best to take a cut every autumn or winter so as to prevent the grasses becoming too dominant and swamping the other plants. Care must be taken not to destroy the tussocks used by hibernating insects or to scalp the surface and create bare ground which weeds can colonise.

If it is found that harmful weeds still colonise the crop from the narrow bare edge between the new margin and the crop, the solution is to establish a sterile strip about 1 m wide on the cropped area that can be managed by cultivation or spraying with the nozzle shielded to ground level or,

better, by using selective weedkiller. Time the application for November or December if possible; at this time the cleaver and brome plants, being annuals, are small and actively growing so that they are killed by dose-rates which will not cause significant harm to well-established perennial grasses should drift onto the margin occur. Do not establish a sterile strip where there are uncommon arable weeds growing (Feature 2.1).

With very large fields where the centre is 200 m or more from the edges, consider also creating grass baulks or 'beetle banks' within the field to support predators of insect pests and provide habitat for other wildlife including gamebirds. This will reduce the time it takes for predatory insects to disperse through the crop in spring from their overwintering sites in the grass tussocks. During normal autumn cultivation, create a ridge down the centre of the field about 0.4 m high and 1.5 to 2 m wide. Leave a gap of about 25 m at each end to allow easy movement by machinery so that the field can still be worked as one unit. The ridge will occupy about 0.1 ha of a 20-ha field and can easily be ploughed out if it ceases to be required at some future date. The strip should be sown with the tussock-forming grasses cocksfoot and Yorkshire fog as described above.

If desired, top the flower-heads of the grass before seed-set but take care not to damage the structure of the grass tussocks. Topping may also be needed to control scrub invasion though in principle this could be managed to produce a hedge, with consequent benefits to a wide variety of wildlife. As with the margin, a sterile strip may be needed to facilitate weed control.

It will take two or three years for margins and 'beetle banks' to develop into suitable habitat for overwintering insects and spiders, when they may come to hold densities of over $1,500/m^2$. It is then essential that insecticidal sprays are only used on the crop when pest numbers reach threshold levels (or spraying is a contractual requirement). Select sprays that have minimal effect on beneficial species.

3.3 Conservation headlands

> - To benefit grey partridge and other wildlife, create 'conservation headlands' in the outermost 6 m of the field.
> - Do not attempt to create conservation headlands on land with serious weed infestation.
> - Do not spray with insecticides or broadleaved herbicides.
> - Only use pesticides to control cleavers, grass weeds and crop disease.
> - If nitrogen inputs are also reduced, rare arable weeds may benefit.

Wildlife management may be extended from the field margin into the crop by creating 'conservation headlands' (Figure 2.1). On the outer 6 m of the field, insecticidal pesticides and broadleaved herbicides are not used at all, but selective compounds are applied when required to control cleavers, grass weeds and crop disease. If broadleaved weed abundance becomes so great as to interfere with combining, a pre-harvest application of glyphosate can be made (but not on malting barley). However, if 'headlands' are maintained on fields that do not have a serious weed problem and ideally adjoin margins with an established perennial plant cover (plus if necessary a rotovated strip), it may be possible to withhold almost all pesticide applications. The majority of the field may be fully sprayed with the usual complement of pesticides (but wherever possible using formulations that are target-specific) and care should be taken to avoid spray-drift.

The original objective of conservation headlands was to improve the breeding success of grey partridge, but other wildlife also benefits. The great increase in broadleaved weed density and variety may result in up to a threefold increase in those insects on which partridge chicks depend (Feature 2.4). In consequence, both partridge and pheasant brood size is likely to increase. Butterflies make greater use of conservation headlands because the weeds provide them with nectar sources and some are caterpillar food plants. Pesticide drift into hedges is reduced and this can be important for the very wide variety of insects that live in hedges.

Provided that nitrogen inputs are also reduced, the technique can be combined with management for rare arable weeds. The areas required for them may be quite small.

Overall yield loss in conservation headlands is likely to be 5-10% and this amounts to 0.3-0.6% of the yield of an average field. The presence of weeds in the crop at harvest can slightly increase grain moisture content and drying times. Weed seed amounts may necessitate extra cleaning, though they are unlikely to exceed approved levels for feed crops if mixed with the grain from the whole field. Where game shooting is important, the grain from headlands may be used to feed the birds through the winter.

It is important to realise that partridge hatching success may be nullified by bad weather at hatching time in June or by predation by foxes or corvids, and not to give up the technique as a consequence of a bad season, especially in view of the other benefits provided for wildlife.

3.4 Rotational set-aside

- Set-aside is designed to reduce surpluses but it can be possible to manage it to benefit wildlife.
- Give particular attention to land adjoining good wildlife habitats such as big hedges.
- In most situations, the best approach is to allow natural regeneration which should not be cut, ploughed or herbicided in March to July.
- If weed control is essential, undertake it outside this period if possible. Whatever method is used is likely to harm wildlife.
- If cover must be mown, work from the centre outwards to avoid killing birds and mammals.
- If herbicides are used, select the most target-specific formulation or confine treatment to seriously affected areas only.
- For most wintering birds, retain stubbles.
- Do not apply slurry to set-aside land managed for wildlife.
- For rare arable weeds, cultivate after harvest or in early spring.
- For breeding lapwing and some other species, aim to create bare ground by early March.

While rotational set-aside is a scheme designed to reduce crop surpluses, the land may be managed to benefit wildlife in a number of different ways. Regulations govern the scheme and may change from year to year but must be complied with; exemptions may need to be sought from the appropriate agriculture department where the result will be good for wildlife.

Best overall results for most wild plants, insects and spiders, mammals and birds would come from allowing the land to regenerate naturally and not carrying out cultivation, cutting or herbicide application between mid-March and mid-July, so avoiding destruction of flowers and allowing invertebrates and birds to use the habitat for feeding and breeding.

Any form of weed control is likely to reduce the value of the land to wildlife and the choice of method is important. In most cases, the least overall impact will come from target-specific herbicides confined to areas where infestation is serious or, where practicable, by spot-treatment. In addition, it may be necessary to top thistles or other injurious weeds if they appear in the field and threaten to seed into adjoining grassland but bear in mind their value as nectar sources and the ease with which they can be eradicated from tillage.

Management for wildlife will be particularly beneficial where it is on land which adjoins other habitats such as big hedges, ponds, woodland or scrub. This is because many species have complex requirements and use several different habitats in the course of a season or even during a day. Because warmth is very important to butterflies, bees and many other insects, sheltered, south-facing fields are likely to be particularly favoured.

For overwintering birds and for seed production by some rare arable weeds, allow the stubbles to stand after harvesting. Spilt grain or other crop seeds, weed seeds and soil invertebrates will provide food for finches, buntings, thrushes, gamebirds and geese amongst others (Feature 2.6). Some of the insects, such as sawflies, that are food for game and other birds in the breeding season, overwinter in the soil and are also likely to be much more abundant where the ground is not cultivated immediately after harvest.

Adult sawflies begin to appear in early May and the larvae feed on cereals and grass in June and July, so providing food for partridge and other birds. The ideal situation would be where natural regeneration provides such feeding habitat for insects and birds into late summer. Where there is a good growth, this will also provide nesting cover for gamebirds and skylarks and it should not be cut or cultivated before mid-July to avoid destruction of nests and brood-rearing cover. If action is essential to control weeds, use selective herbicides or leave some continuous strips untouched, especially those adjacent to grass margins, big hedges or woodland.

Many species of small mammals will forage in volunteer cereals or a cover of annual weeds. Populations fluctuate greatly from year to year so it does not follow that, even if conditions are ideal, the result will be a bonanza for barn owls but, in general, these birds are likely to benefit from maintaining naturally regenerated plant cover for as long as possible through the year.

Where a dense natural cover does not develop and plant growth is sparse and short, the open conditions may attract breeding lapwing and, in some parts of the UK only, stone-curlew or oystercatcher (Feature 2.5). Such conditions can of course be created before the beginning of March (when the first lapwings may be settling to breed in the south), either by cultivating to produce a suitable surface or by ploughing before mid-winter so that frosts will do the job. Do not cultivate in the period mid-March to mid-July to avoid any risk of destroying eggs or young.

Where it is known that rare arable weeds are present or were present in the past, cultivation should be timed to encourage their germination – October for autumn-germinating plants and March or April for spring germinators. If the past history of wild plant occurrence is known, the correct timing can be related to particular plants. So that it can set seed, the resultant growth must not be cut, cultivated or treated with a broad-spectrum herbicide in the summer months. This makes it essential to select areas, such as those adjoining well-established permanent cover in the field

margin, which will not suffer from problem weeds. Otherwise, use selective herbicides which will not harm broadleaved plants.

Set-aside provides an ideal opportunity to restore permanent plant cover on the field margins without any risk of pesticide or fertiliser input in the first year and with easy access for management. Once this has been done, problems of weed invasion into arable crops in subsequent years should be reduced and there will also be gains in wildlife variety.

Where geese are a pest on winter cereals or spring grass, it may be possible to hold them on the set-aside areas provided that an efficient scaring programme is applied to the vulnerable fields. Ground to hold wintering geese may be fertilised and sown with grass but this will remove its value to other birds. Permission from the appropriate agriculture department is currently needed for the use of fertiliser.

If a cover crop is established, care should be taken with spring or summer cutting, which poses particular dangers to leverets and roe deer fawns concealed in the tall growth. If cutting is necessary, work from the centre of the field outwards so driving animals towards the hedges. The attachment of scaring devices such as tractor-mounted flushing bars is a technique that has been used with some success, especially if a forage-harvester is used.

4. References and further reading

Andrews, J 1992. Some Practical Problems in Set-aside Management for Wildlife. *British Wildlife* Vol 3 No 6 329-336.

Deane, R 1989. *Expanded Field Margins*. Nature Conservancy Council.

Firbank, L G, Carter, N, Darbyshire, J F and Potts, G R (eds) 1990. *The Ecology of Temperate Cereal Fields*. Blackwell Scientific Publications.

Farming and Wildlife Advisory Group 1992. *Arable Farming and Set-aside*. FWAG.

Farming and Wildlife Advisory Group 1992. *Farming and Field Margins*. FWAG.

Farming and Wildlife Advisory Group 1992. *Farming and Pesticides*. FWAG.

Game Conservancy Annual Reviews. Containing a range of papers on the requirements of wildlife, both plants and animals, found on farmland. Game Conservancy Trust.

Game Conservancy 1992. *Management of Rotational Set-aside for Game*. Game Conservancy Trust.

Lack, P 1992. *Birds and Lowland Farms*. HMSO.

Marshall, E J P 1988. *The Ecology and Management of Field Margins Floras in England*. Outlook on Agriculture, Vol 17, No 4.

O'Connor, R J and Shrubb, M 1986. *Farming and Birds*. Cambridge University Press.

Way, J M and Greig-Smith (eds) 1987. *Field Margins*. BCPC Monograph No 35. British Crop Protection Council.

Feature 2.1: Arable Weeds

1. **Pheasant's eye**
   On soils over chalk or limestone. It now occurs, however, no farther north than Berkshire, and is known at only 13 sites in the country. Strong association with rotations including grass leys, possibly indicating more extensive farming regimes. Found to grow best and to produce most seed in late-sown winter wheat.

2. **Corn gromwell**
   Both on chalky clay and on heavier clay soils. Corn gromwell produces most seed in October-sown winter wheat. It is fairly resistant to some of the most commonly used broadleaved weed herbicides, and competes well with cereal crops in the presence of high levels of nitrogen. Despite this, corn gromwell has become increasingly rare in recent years because of earlier sowing of winter cereals.

3. **Corn marigold**
   On sandy, acidic soils and areas with high rainfall. Associated with a history of spring barley or root crops, and in experiments, corn marigold was most successful when sown in spring crops. The increased use of winter-sown cereals have probably contributed to the decline of this species. Locally common in some parts of the country.

4. **Lesser snapdragon**
   Also associated with sandy, acidic soils but more restricted to the south-west of Britain. Found mainly in fields in which either spring barley or root crops were normally grown and, in experiments, produced seed only in late-sown spring crops. Very uncompetitive in cereal crops, and it may be that the increased acreage of winter-sown cereals coupled with higher rates of nitrogen application have contributed to its decline. It is also susceptible to herbicides. Lesser snapdragon seed may be quite persistent in the soil, which may help its continued survival.

5. **Rough poppy**
   Rough poppy is still widely distributed on chalky soils in the south-east of England, but has gone from most of its formerly recorded localities in the rest of the country. A poor competitor with cereal crops at high nitrogen levels, and very few plants or seed are produced except in spring or late winter-sown crops. It is also susceptible to most of the commonly used herbicides. The continued survival of this species, like the corn poppy, is probably due to the long persistence of its seed in the soil.

6. **Corn buttercup**
   This species has undergone the most severe decline of any of Britain's plants in recent years. Good populations were found in only five localities, mainly on calcareous clay soils in the south-west Midlands. Found to grow and produce seed only in winter crops sown in October and November. It performs poorly in competition with crops when high levels of nitrogen are applied and is also susceptible to most of the herbicides in common use. Seed production very low, even under optimum conditions, and seed longevity in the soil is believed to be poor. Corn buttercup has therefore been very susceptible to changes in farming practices.

7. **Shepherd's needle**
   Shepherd's needle was once a considerable problem weed even preventing the cereal harvest on occasions, but is now found in very few localities on heavy, calcareous soils, mostly in Suffolk. Grows best and produces most seed in autumn-sown crops. Shepherd's needle competes well with cereal crops, even when high levels of nitrogen are applied, but is very susceptible to most commonly used herbicides. Low potential for seed production, and the seed is thought to have little persistence in the soil.

8. **Night-flowering catchfly**
   Still widespread on light, sandy or
   calcareous soils, especially in the east of
   the country as far north as Yorkshire. It
   is mainly spring-germinating and occurs
   largely in spring barley and root crops.
   Competes poorly with cereals when high
   levels of nitrogen were applied. As this
   species flowers late in the summer,
   plants can persist and produce seed in
   cereal stubbles only in the few places
   where they remain for long enough.

Night-flowering catchfly was found to be
susceptible to most of the commonly
used herbicides. The seed is believed to
be long-lived, and seed production can
be high, and this probably accounts for
its continued survival.

Information adapted from Wilson, P, 1991.
*Factors affecting the distribution of rare arable
weeds.* Game Conservancy Review of 1990.
Game Conservancy.

Uncommon arable weeds, and their main soil type and main region of distribution within Britain. From Wilson, P J, 1990. The ecology and conservation of rare arable weed species and communities. Unpublished PhD thesis, University of Southampton.

COMMON NAME	SOIL TYPE	DISTRIBUTION
Extremely rare (found in fewer than 20 10-km squares)		
Pheasant's eye	Chalk/brash	S E England
Blue pimpernel	Chalk/brash	S E England
Loose-flowered silky bent	Sand	E Anglia
Broad-leaved cudweed	Chalk/sand	S England
Western fumitory	Sand/loam	Cornwall
Corn buttercup	Clay	S W Midlands
Shepherd's needle	Clay	E Anglia
Spreading hedge parsley	Clay/loam	S England
Broad-fruited corn salad	Clay/chalk	S England
Rare (found in between 20 and 50 10-km squares)		
Lesser quaking grass	Sand/gravel	S W Britain
Rye-brome	Clay	S England
Fig-leaved goosefoot	Clay/peat	S England
Broad-leaved spurge	Chalk/clay	S England
Dense-flowered fumitory	Chalk	S E England
Small-flowered fumitory	Chalk	S E England
Vaillant's fumitory	Chalk	S E England
Long-stalked cranesbill	Chalk	S E England
Mouse-tail	Clay	S Midlands
Rough-headed poppy	Chalk	S E England
Corn parsley	Chalk/clay	S England
Small-flowered buttercup	Clay	S W England
Small-flowered catchfly	Sand/gravel	S W England
Slender tare	Clay/brash	S England
Uncommon (found in between 50 and 150 10-km squares)		
Corn marigold	Sand/gravel	All Britain
Narrow-leaved hemp-nettle	Chalk	S E England
Corn gromwell	Chalk/clay	S England
Weasel's snout	Sand/loam	S W Britain
Long-headed prickly poppy	Sand/chalk	S E England
Night-flowering catchfly	All soils	E Anglia
Green field speedwell	Sand/loam	S W England
Decreasing		
Bugloss	Sand	All Britain
Treacle mustard	Sand	E England
Catmint	Chalk	S E England
Stinking mayweed	All soils	S England
Dwarf spurge	All soils	S England
Babington's poppy	Clay	E England
Small-flowered cranesbill	Sand	S England
Stone parsley	Clay	E England
Thale-cress	Sand/clay	S England
Sharp-leaved fluellen	All soils	S Britain
Field woundwort	Sand/gravel	S W Britain
Thyme-leaved sandwort	All soils	All Britain
Round-leaved fluellen	Chalk/clay	S E England
Knotted hedge parsley	Chalk/clay	S England
Small toadflax	Chalk	S E England
Henbit	Chalk	S England
Grey speedwell	Chalk	S E England
Cut-leaved dead-nettle	Clay/sand	E Anglia
Flixweed	Sand	E Anglia
Venus' looking glass	Clay/chalk	S E England
Wall rocket	Chalk	S E England
Common storksbill	Sand	All Britain
Dwarf mallow	Sand	S England

Feature 2.2: Bumblebees and Field Margins

Bumblebees prefer the perennial flowers of established vegetation. Annual weeds of disturbed or cultivated ground rarely attract them. Large patches of flowers are much more valuable to bumblebees than odd scattered plants.

Vegetation of high wildlife value, such as water meadows or ancient grassland, contains a wide range of flowers used by bumblebees. Field margins can also support some valuable plants.

Bumblebees have an annual life cycle. A colony is founded by a single overwintering queen. She emerges in spring to find a suitable nest site, building a small chamber into which the first eggs are laid. These develop into infertile workers. By summer the colony has grown and later eggs develop into fertile males and young queens. Mating occurs in late summer, after which the males die. The young queens then overwinter and start new colonies the next year.

Bumblebees use a variety of nest sites. Some favour grass tussocks and several establish colonies below ground in the disused nests of mice or voles. Brown bumblebees make their nests of moss at the ground surface and are vulnerable to trampling by livestock and cultivation.

Bumblebees require perennial plants which flower from March until September. This provides a continuous supply of pollen and nectar. Pollen and nectar are used to feed the brood in the nest, nectar to provide energy for flight. In spring young queens are dependent on early flowers such as willow and white dead-nettle. During the summer bumblebees forage from a wide variety of wild flowers. Proboscis length varies between species and influences which flowers are visited. The two-banded white tail has a short proboscis and visits open and short-tubed flowers such as bramble, heather and knapweeds. The three-banded whitetail has a much longer proboscis and feeds on tubular flowers such as foxglove, woundwort, red clover, thistles and honeysuckle.

Bumblebees play an important role as pollinators of both wild flowers and crops. Those species with long probosces, particularly brown and three-banded whitetail bumblebees, are important pollinators of field beans and red clover. Those bumblebees with medium-length probosces are useful pollinators of crops with short flowers, such as white clover, lucerne, bird's-foot-trefoil and borage.

Management

Feeding Pollen and nectar from a wide variety of flowers growing in sunlit situations. Protect field margins, ditch sides, hedge bottoms, woodland edges and permanent pasture from herbicides. Retain bramble patches. Establish wildflower mixtures containing labiates, legumes and knapweed, eg on field margins, set-aside or the rides of new farm woods. Field crops are not in flower early enough to enable newly-emerged queens to start their colonies, so retain or plant willow and other early nectar and pollen producers.

Nesting Keep sunlit areas such as field margins and south-facing woodland edges to grow tussocky grass cover. Do not plough. Minimise vehicle traffic over these areas. Avoid herbicide drift. If necessary, top in winter to prevent scrub encroachment. If summer cutting is essential, eg on set-aside, set the cutter at least 15 cm above the ground to avoid surface nests.

Insecticides Minimise mortality by care to avoid spray-drift into feeding and nesting areas. Turn off the outer sprayer when working field edges or, better still, maintain unsprayed headlands. Do not spray crops on which bees are feeding. Bumblebees start feeding earlier in the day than honeybees and go on later in the afternoon.

Field margin plants with flowers attractive to bumblebees			
	FLOWERING PERIOD		
PLANTS	SPRING	EARLY SUMMER	LATE SUMMER
Sallow	o		
Wild cherry	o		
Dandelion	o		
White deadnettle*	o	o	o
Common vetch*		o	
Bush vetch*		o	
Tufted vetch*		o	
Hogweed		o	
Wild roses		o	
Hedge woundwort*		o	
Honeysuckle*		o	
Red campion*		o	o
Foxglove*		o	o
Bramble		o	o
Common figwort*			o
Common mallow			o
Great willowherb			o
Rosebay willowherb			o
Greater knapweed			o
Lesser knapweed			o
Black horehound*			o
Spear thistle*			o
Teasel*			o
Lesser burdock			o

Flowers attractive to bumblebees with long probosces.

Source: Corbet, S and Fussell, M. 1991. *Farming and Bumblebees* FWAG (unpublished leaflet).

Feature 2.3: Beneficial Insects

While the value of bees as crop pollinators and ladybirds as predators of greenfly is well known to farmers, the value of the natural predators of other pests is less well known.

Aphids are serious pests of cereal crops in the UK. If their natural predators such as ground beetles, rove beetles, spiders and hoverflies can be encouraged on agricultural land, then it may be possible to reduce the reliance on aphicides.

Hedgerows and field margins can provide good overwintering habitat for these predators. In addition, if these habitats are rich in flowers, they in turn supply a source of nectar and pollen for those adult hoverflies that occur in cereal fields in the spring and summer. The larvae of more than 20 species of hoverfly feed on aphids.

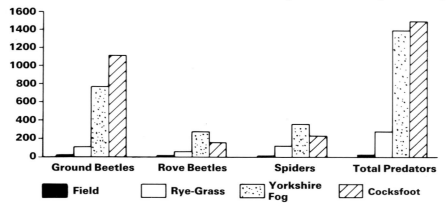

Aphid predator densities within a cereal field and on a grass ridge built across it, winter 1988/89. (Adapted from: Thomas, M 1990. Diversification of the Arable Ecosystem to Control Natural Enemies of Cereal Aphids. *The Game Conservancy Review of 1989***, No 21, pp 68–69. Game Conservancy). This figure shows that in certain grasslands aphid predator densities exceeded 1,500 beetles per sq m and cocksfoot and Yorkshire fog were preferred for overwintering.**

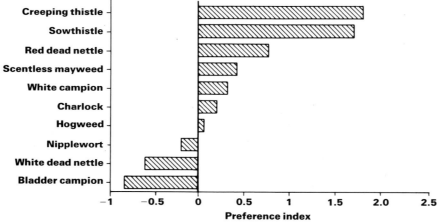

The species of commonly occurring arable weeds which are preferred by an economically important species of hoverfly, Hampshire, June 1989. Preference is shown by values greater than zero; avoidance by values less than zero. (Adapted from: Cowgill, S 1990. The Ecology of Hoverflies on Arable Land. *The Game Conservancy Review* **of 1989, No 21, pp 70–71. Game Conservancy.)**

Feature 2.4: Grey Partridge

Over the last 40 years, numbers of grey partridges in the UK have declined by over 90%.

Partridges usually nest at the edge of a field, at the base of a hedge, on a bank or in long grass from the end of April to early June. The ideal field size for partridges is about 10 ha. Nesting banks need to be a minimum of 1 m wide and at least 0.5 m high. Long dead grass from the previous year should be left to provide nesting cover. The ideal hedge height is less than 2 m, without taller trees or branches that could act as look-out posts for predators. Hedges should be cut every second or third year in January or February.

The hen lays up to 16 eggs, the largest clutch of any species of bird. The chicks hatch in mid to late June and spend most of that time in cereals or in other long grasses feeding mainly on insects such as sawfly larvae, leaf beetles, weevils, plant bugs, plant hoppers and ground beetles many of which feed in turn on broadleaved weeds inside the crop.

Young chicks (up to about three weeks of age) are almost entirely insectivorous.

The use of insecticides in brood-rearing areas such as cereal fields reduces the numbers of chick food insects. The use of herbicides and the reduction of broad-leaved weeds further decrease numbers of insects.

Selective spraying of the outer margin of cereal crops ('conservation headlands') or set-aside land managed to produce good-quality brood-rearing habitats are beneficial and can increase chick survival rates.

By late summer the birds form coveys feeding on weed seeds and gleaning grain among the stubbles. In winter and spring most partridges feed by grazing on growing cereals, weeds or pastures, especially those with clover and grass leys.

Natural regeneration under stubbles is one of the options for management of rotational set-aside and can prove valuable for winter feeding.

(Source: Prepared from information supplied by Aebischer, N J and Sotherton, N W, of the Game Conservancy.)

Feature 2.5: Stone-curlew

Stone-curlews are large (length *c*. 41 cm), plover-like birds which live on light, stony soils, where their streaked, sandy brown plumage keeps them well camouflaged. They have short bills, long, yellow legs and striking lemon-yellow, owl-like eyes. In flight, the bold black and white wing pattern is noticeable. Stone-curlews are difficult to find by day, but their wild, shrieking cries carry far at night.

Stone-curlews have declined by at least 85% since 1940, to around 160 pairs. These are largely restricted to the Breckland region of East Anglia and to parts of the West Country. There are also a few birds scattered throughout the chalk hills of East Anglia and the East Suffolk Sandlings.

Stone-curlew

Reasons for the decline
Formerly, stone-curlews nested on the short turf of tightly grazed chalk downland or grass-heathland. Today, much of this type of land has been turned into arable farmland or commercial forestry. Much of what remains has deteriorated to rank grass, bracken or scrub because of reduced grazing by livestock and rabbits. More than half of British stone-curlews now nest on farmland in spring-sown crops, but the shift to winter cereals and away from mixed farming has made many areas unsuitable.

Essentials for stone-curlew survival on arable farmland

Bare or sparsely vegetated ground for nesting
Stone-curlews make a scrape on bare or sparsely vegetated ground and nest from early April to August. Spring cereals and most pea and bean crops grow too rapidly to remain suitable for the birds after mid-May. Carrots, sugar and fodder beet, kale, maize and onions can offer favourable habitats for nesting because they cover the ground slowly in the spring and early summer. Stone-curlews will often return each year to the same field where suitable crops are grown in successive years.

Safety from farming operations
Nests and chicks in crops are at risk from rolling, tractor hoeing, irrigation (which can waterlog them) and other farming operations. Stone-curlew chicks do not run away when threatened, but instinctively freeze on the ground. Their superb camouflage makes them extremely difficult to see.

Suitable feeding places
Stone-curlews feed mainly at night in short vegetation or bare ground on earthworms, beetles and woodlice. They prefer tightly grazed pasture, but also feed in outdoor pig fields. Early in the season, the birds can feed in spring-sown arable fields, especially where the application of farmyard manure or a previous ley has increased the number of soil animals. Very often, it is the loss of livestock from a farm that has resulted in a rapid decline in stone-curlews.

Conservation on arable land
Stone-curlew nests can be very difficult to locate, even when adult birds are known to be using a field. If you think you have stone-curlews on your land, please contact the RSPB, whose trained staff may be able to help you protect birds and nests without disrupting normal farming operations.

Look out for stone-curlews

When working with a tractor, you may see stone-curlews sneaking away from a nest or chicks, and it is worth checking the area for them. If you find a nest, it can be marked with sticks in the crop row 15 m on either side so that the tractor driver can avoid it. The markers can easily be removed when work on the field is finished. There are usually two chicks, which leave the nest immediately after hatching but they may remain within the field.

Roll spring cereals early

If rolling can be carried out in March, or at the latest before 10 April, then few stone-curlew nests will be at risk, although spring cereals are a poor nesting habitat because of their rapid growth.

Take care when tractor-hoeing sugar-beet. Efficient weed control is essential, but tractor-hoeing can destroy stone-curlew nests and kill chicks. If tractor-hoeing is unavoidable, mark the position of the nest, and avoid it. It is also much safer to hoe before the eggs hatch because chicks stray from the nest and are difficult to find.

Delay hand-hoeing sugar-beet

If you know of a nest, delay hand-hoeing until the chicks have hatched and left the nest because the sitting bird may desert the eggs if kept away for too long. The eggs take 25 days to hatch, but the chicks are active almost immediately.

Farmyard manure

Use farmyard manure on fields with spring-sown crops. This should increase the number of earthworms, beetles and other soil invertebrates on which stone-curlews feed. Sheep grazing of beet tops can also be beneficial because the sheep manure fields, which increases the number of invertebrates.

Consider alternative uses of arable land

Opportunities are available for re-creation of lowland heath and chalk downland, or for the management of rotational set-aside.

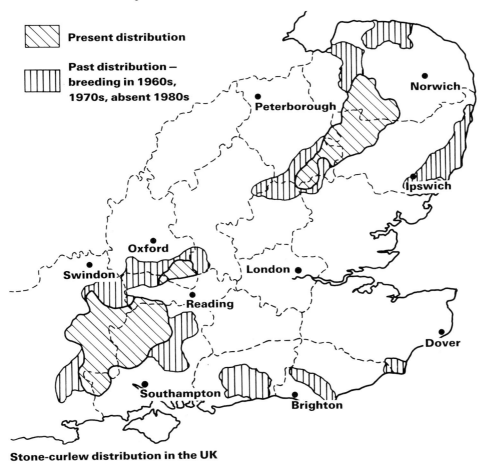

Present distribution

Past distribution —
breeding in 1960s,
1970s, absent 1980s

Stone-curlew distribution in the UK

Feature 2.6: Cirl Bunting

Cirl buntings have declined greatly in Britain over the past 50 years and there are now only 300 pairs, almost all restricted to south Devon.

They prefer to nest in thorny scrub and thick hedgerows. Favoured sites are gorse bushes, bramble and blackthorn although they will nest in almost any hedgerow shrub providing it is bushy enough. In the breeding season they have a home range which usually extends over several fields.

Chicks of cirl buntings are fed a varied diet of invertebrates, including caterpillars, moths, beetles, aphids, ticks and mites. By far the most important component of the diet is grasshoppers. Studies in south Devon have shown that they can comprise 75% of the diet in August. In heavy rain when insects are difficult to find, they switch to feeding their young on seeds, especially cereals.

Cirl buntings are dependent almost entirely upon weed-rich stubble fields for their winter food supplies. Research in Devon has shown that over 90% of foraging was made on stubbles, even though this covered a very small percentage of the total land area. Cirl buntings feed not only upon spilt grain but also on the small seeds of annual weeds. The more broadleaved weeds in a stubble, the more likely cirl buntings will feed in the field. They also like to feed near hedgerows, rarely venturing more than 30 m from the field margin (see bottom left).

These stubbles have become increasingly rare with shift to winter cereals and the use of herbicides. Other changes have also reduced the availability of food in winter. Cirl buntings used to be known as 'village buntings' because they regularly came to barns, stockyards and threshing yards.

As they rarely move more than 1 km from their wintering site (see bottom right), if the wintering population can be maintained, they are likely to breed in the following year.

Management
- Avoid hedge cutting between March and September, and carry out a 2-3-year rotation.
- Retain some patches of scrub in addition to bushy hedges.
- Retain unimproved and semi-improved grassland as a mosaic with arable land and hedgerows to provide invertebrate food in summer for chicks.
- Retain stubble, preferably unsprayed and close to hedgerows through the winter. This can be provided through 'conservation headlands' and rotational set-aside.

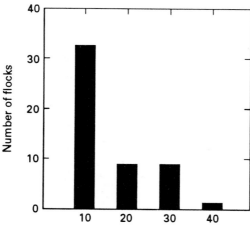

Distance from hedge (m) cirl buntings venture when feeding in winter

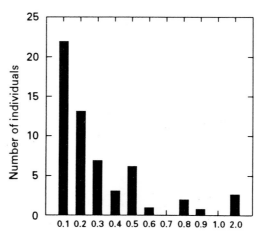

Distance between wintering site, where ringed and breeding territory (km)

Case study: Grass Margins

Alison Lea

Over 80% of the fields now have permanent grass margins 2–4 m wide.

Farm details

Farm:	Bower House Farm, Kersey, Ipswich, Suffolk
Tenure:	Mr Baker, owner-occupier
Size:	300 ha
Altitude:	40-75 m
Soil:	clay/loam soils
Crops:	133 ha winter wheat, 26 ha winter barley, 7 ha spring barley, 26 ha oilseed rape, 43 ha spring oilseed rape for industrial use (set-aside), 17 ha beans, 18 ha peas, 4 ha permanent pasture.
Other wildlife features:	ancient broadleaved woodland, modern mixed woodland, new broadleaved plantation (Farm Woodland Scheme), ponds, good network of indigenous species mixed hedgerows, wildflower meadow, scrub, many ancient pollarded trees.

Mr Baker has owned the farm for three years and runs it as a limited company; previous management was not sympathetic to conservation. The surrounding countryside is open and rolling with occasional woods, some of high conservation value, and mostly arable farms. Mr Baker has replanted two semi-natural ancient broadleaved woodlands (each *c* 2 ha) which were storm damaged; 9 ha of new woods have been planted on former arable land; several ponds desilted, opened up and enlarged; and new hedges planted. Permanent grassland has been laid down. Existing hedgerows are now managed sympathetically for wildlife. A FWAG farm wildlife plan has been implemented.

Farmer's aims
Primary aim
- To provide the best possible conditions for native wildlife and through this to benefit intensive arable farming.

Secondary aims
- To provide the best conditions for hedges and associated wildlife.
- Provide access for pedestrians and machinery all round farm.

▶▶▶

- Provide wildlife corridors to link various habitats.
- Provide conditions to support high populations of agriculturally beneficial invertebrates.

Background

Resources: No grants available for improving/managing widened grass margins. Some labour needed to set up and manage margins, most effort required in first year. Land take is the main cost but loss of yield has been negligible and margins fit in with farming practice. Also machinery needed for maintenance.

Constraints: None

Source of advice: Suffolk FWAG; farm plan forms the basis for the conservation work on the farm but there is a continuing input of advice.

Methods

In 1990 margins averaging 0.5 m wide were created. By 1993 80% of field margins had been expanded, all by seeding, to a minimum of 2 m, allowing thickening of hedges and maintenance using small tractor with mower, and to 4 m wide on all woodland margins and other places of high conservation value, eg around ponds. Seed mixtures were of two basic types: tussock producing (50% cocksfoot), and fine grass (based on fescues/crested dogstail). Sowing rate 16 kg/acre (40kg/ha). Extent of margins in 1993 2 m – 16.8 km; 4 m – 6.1 km giving a total of 4.7 ha. Problems encountered were spray-drift in year 1 onto small areas and earth bared by heavy machinery, moles, horses (trespass) and drainage machinery.

Establishment: Margins mown 4-6 times to 75 cm in 1st year; no herbicides applied. Edge of grass established with *careful* cut of plough. End of 2nd year: careful tillage to avoid creep into margin when ploughing. 3rd year; mowing regime fully established, no weed control necessary, other than by mowing.

Cutting regimes
1. Pedestrian routes – cut at 75 mm or higher 2–4 times annually (next to crop)
2. Margins for invertebrates, birds, small mammals - cut only when necessary to avoid scrubbing over or seeding too many weeds, eg thistles. Top July-March.

Achievements

Primary aim
- No scientific monitoring done to see if wildlife populations have increased but general feeling is that they have. No adverse effects on arable operations.

Secondary aims
- Hedges have widened naturally - better bases." Access, both private and public (footpaths) vastly improved. Access for combine better - not taken into consideration at start.

Future management
- extend margin network to cover whole farm.
- reduce pesticides and fertiliser getting on to margins (pneumatic spreader is to replace spinner).
- monitor crop pest levels and only apply the minimum amount of insecticides necessary.
- attempt to monitor populations of predatory invertebrates.
- creation of beetle banks across larger fields.

Case study: Conservation Headlands and 'Beetle Banks'

Sarah Warrener

4.8 km of 'beetle banks' are planned to extend the network of conservation headlands

Farm details

Farm:	West Gilston Mains, Fife, Scotland
Tenure:	Mr Baxter, owner-occupier
Size:	486 ha
Altitude:	76-213 m
Soil:	Till derived from Carboniferous sandstones and shales
Crops:	winter wheat (99.6 ha); oilseed rape (86.7 ha); spring barley (64.0 ha); winter barley (10.9 ha); vining peas (16.2 ha); set-aside (47.8 ha); permanent pasture (68.0 ha).
Stock:	500 ewes
Other wildlife features:	Mixed woodlands and ponds

The farm has been owned by the family since the mid-19th century. It is well wooded in a landscape with very few trees. The woods (which were laid out for shooting) are a mixture of broadleaves and conifers of varying ages. 12 ha have been planted recently under the Farm Woodland Scheme with a high proportion of native species. There are several excellent ponds with high conservation interest on the farm.

Farmer's aims

Primary aim
- To enhance the sporting potential by providing good feeding for gamebird chicks.

Secondary aim
- To increase the diversity of plants and animals on the farm.

Background

Resources: Initiated in 1991 with no financial support on all cereal headlands. Anticipated yield loss and increased harvesting costs considered acceptable.

▶▶▶

Constraints: None
Source of advice: Game Conservancy

Methods
No residual herbicide was applied to the outer 4 m (a boom section) of the winter cereals; no contact herbicides used on the spring barley. The farm has no black grass, sterile brome or wild oats to contend with, though there was some difficulty encountered at harvest with cleaver infestations. In subsequent years some problem headlands were sprayed out, but on balance most gave no difficulty. Good crop establishment has kept competition with wild plants to a minimum. The establishment of conservation headlands under set-aside was considered, but rejected because of the rotational obligations.

Achievements
Primary aim
- No grey partridge counts took place before autumn 1992 when the programme was well underway. Formal predator control was initiated in mid-1992 and results for the 1993 season will be monitored. There is now about 20 km of suitable nesting habitat for partridges.

Secondary aim
- No formal census of butterflies or wild plants was carried out but no cereal aphicides have been required in the summer months since the introduction of conservation headlands which would suggest an increased beetle population. Raptor numbers have increased markedly.

Future Management
Beetle banks (grass ridges in the middle of fields) are being introduced as the rotation permits; 4.8 km are planned and will be in place within a year. The same grass mix (cocksfoot, perennial rye-grass, timothy, rough stalk meadow grass and wild clover) will be sown around all the fields in a 2-m strip to improve the quality of nesting habitat on the farm. This will complement the network of conservation headlands.

Case study: Cereal Production on an Organic Farm

Farm details

Farm:	Oatleys Farm, Turweston, North Bucks
Tenure:	Mr and Mrs Tustian, owner-occupiers
Size:	154 ha
Altitude:	122–137 m
Soil:	Very mixed (limestone, loam, clay)
Crops:	24.3 ha permanent pasture, 24.3 ha winter wheat, 12.2 ha spring wheat or oats, 12.2 ha red clover one-year ley, 64.4 ha five-year leys. 14.2 ha spinneys, 2.8 ha roads and buildings.
Stock:	55 Hereford x suckler cows, progeny to 18 - 24 months, 230 Suffolk x ewes, 70 Suffolk x ewe lambs, 20 free range sows, 200 laying hens, table poultry.
Other wildlife features:	2 established spinneys: one probably 100 years old, the other probably ancient woodland. All hedges laid. Magnificent display of cowslips. One of only two known colonies of giant bellflowers in Buckinghamshire.

The family have been on the farm for 59 years and it is farmed as a husband and wife partnership. Most sizeable trees were cut down for an airfield which was built to the north side of the farm during the war, making the farm very exposed. The family have always enjoyed shooting as a hobby and started planting spinneys in 1963, primarily to encourage pheasants. Since then some 8 ha of trees, two ponds and 1,000 m new hedges have been established. The farm has twice won first prize in the Buckinghamshire FWAG competition for encouraging wildlife in conjunction with sound farming practices.

Farmer's aims
Primary aim
- To encourage a greater diversity and abundance of species of wildlife.

Secondary aim
- To create an attractive farm environment and reduce exposure to weather.

Background
Resources: No extra labour has been employed, the family have planted and maintained the new spinneys. From 1963-1971 no advice or financial support was available; in 1974 the Countryside Commission provided planting grants. In 1990, 1991 and 1992 6.8 ha of broadleaved woodland has been established under the Farm Woodland Scheme.
Constraints: None.
Source of advice: From 1971 the Game Conservancy gave advice, in 1974 the Countryside Commission; more recently FWAG has helped enormously.

Methods
Management carried out: A 3-m grass strip is left round arable fields to control the spread of problem weeds. This is also beneficial in encouraging natural predators. The field rotation is vitally important to the system of farming and to bird populations.

The seven-year rotation involves years 1–5 under grass ley with high clover content. Year six winter wheat, stubble ploughed February. Year seven spring wheat, undersown with five-year grass ley.

This means that a quarter of the farm is stubble during the winter and as there are always some weeds in the organic system many birds, chiefly seed feeders, winter on the farm, often in huge flocks. Farming organically means fodder conservation takes place much later than in current systems, often when birds have fledged.

Achievements
Primary aim
- A balance has been achieved and no synthetic fertilisers, pesticides or fungicides are used. Kestrel, sparrowhawk, tawny and little owls are common; hobby, barn, long-eared and short-eared owls are seen occasionally.

Secondary aim
- The farm is far less exposed, more interesting and visually more attractive than in 1963.

Future management
Mr and Mrs Tustian are soon to retire, and hope the farm will continue in organic management.

Robert Book, Environmental Picture Library

Juliet Bailey

2.1 The production of high-yield, weed-free crops requires skilled management throughout the year to prevent serious losses as a result of weeds and invertebrate pests. Attempts to improve the wildlife value of cropped land must take these into account and, ideally, help to foster wildlife species which themselves combat pests such as crop aphids.

2.2 Over 300 plant species have been found on arable land. Some, such as corn marigold, were once widespread but most of them are now rare in crops, mainly because of the use of herbicides. As they have declined, so too have the insects and birds which depend on them. Today, most arable land supports little wildlife.

RSPB

Michael Rehane

2.3 & 2.4 Spring tillage attracts nesting birds such as lapwing and, as here, stone-curlew in sugar-beet. The widespread shift to autumn sowing has resulted in a decline in both species. Care should be taken with farming operations where ground-nesting birds are known to use a field.

C H Gomersall, RSPB

D Sewell, RSPB

2.5 Winter stubbles offer good feeding conditions for finches and buntings especially where there are also seeding weeds. Birds such as cirl bunting have declined owing to a combination of the shift to autumn sowing and fewer weeds in the crops.

2.6 Skylarks only nest in crops that are less than 30 cm tall. On mixed farms the birds may raise successive broods as different crops grow to the required height during the course of spring and summer. Few birds make use of tall or dense crops for breeding.

Hawk-eye Photo Library

V Miles, Environmental Picture Library

2.7 Most agrochemicals affect both pests and beneficial or harmless wildlife in the crop. By avoiding or restricting the use of sprays for a boom's width at the outer edge of the crop, it may be possible greatly to improve conditions for game such as partridge and for rare arable plants without significant loss of yield. In all spraying operations, it is essential to prevent drift onto uncropped land such as hedges or ponds.

2.8 The field margin offers good opportunities to integrate wildlife management with good farming practice. Perennial plants provide food and cover for much other wildlife and resist colonisation by arable weeds such as barren brome or wild oats.

Juliet Bailey

Juliet Bailey

2.9 Where the hedge bottom is sprayed out, conditions are ideal for infestation by annual weeds such as cleavers which then spread into the crop. Food and cover for wildlife are largely absent.

2.10 An excellent compromise is to encourage a permanent plant community at the field boundary, and maintain a sterile strip between it and the crop. The plant cover will increase the abundance of insects such as hoverflies and predatory beetles, which spread into the crop and feed on aphids and other pests.

3. Pastures and Meadows

1. Factors influencing wildlife

1.1 Grassland age

- The best grasslands for wildlife are unimproved and have a long management history.
- Their value for wildlife reflects skilled management for livestock and hay production.
- Improved grasslands support a very limited range of wildlife.
- Grassland containing a rich variety of plants is now rare.
- New wildlife grasslands are worth creating but not a substitute for old unimproved fields.

The grasslands which are best for wildlife are the product of skilled farming management. Some may be of great antiquity. As the forest cover was cleared, grasses and other plants which required open, unshaded conditions spread and flourished. The variety of plants which an individual field, hill or valley came to hold was determined by soil type, drainage, location and use. Often the land contained a great variety of different grasses and herbs, which in turn supported an abundant insect fauna, providing food for birds such as corncrake and lapwing.

By 1700, efforts were being made to improve the productivity of grasslands by sowing clover but it is only in the last 60 years or so that plant breeding and the re-seeding of land, together with drainage, mechanisation and the use of herbicides and artificial fertilisers, have brought about a dramatic increase in grassland performance. As a consequence, the characteristic variety of wild plants has been replaced by a small number of highly productive grasses, sometimes grown with white clover. These improved grasslands support a very limited range of wildlife. The pastures and meadows best for wildlife are those which are still unimproved and have the longest history of traditional management.

Throughout history there have been many changes in the extent of grassland.

However, even when livestock production was at a low ebb, every farm needed pasture and hay to feed its oxen or, later, its horses as without them little land could be cultivated. When horses were replaced by machinery, farms no longer required grass keep. At the same time, tillage ousted livestock from large areas of the lowlands of the UK. As a result, there has been a substantial loss of grassland of all types from most lowland regions.

These changes in the nature and extent of grassland have had two important consequences. One is that grassland containing a rich variety of plants is now rare throughout the UK and there have been corresponding declines in the fauna. The other is that, though it is possible to sow grasslands that contain an attractive variety of wild plants and attract some insects such as bees and hoverflies, the grasslands are not recolonised by the rarer plants and insects because they no longer survive in the surrounding area. This is very different from the situation in the past when unimproved grass was widespread; whenever tillage was reverted to grass, for whatever reason, a rich variety of plants and other wildlife could recolonise the land from nearby fields and headlands.

This means that it is most important to retain old unimproved grassland and continue traditional management.

1.2 Plant variety and sward structure

- Grassland structure and composition determine what wildlife will occur.
- Grazing and mowing have different effects. Some plants are restricted to pastures, others to meadows.
- In unimproved grasslands, both grazing and mowing maintain conditions for a rich plant community.
- The greatest variety of plants occurs in fields with a low nutrient level.
- Many invertebrates need particular plant species for breeding and feeding.
- Tall and tussocky grassland can hold large numbers of small mammals which are preyed on by, for example, barn owls.
- A number of birds of conservation importance breed or winter on grasslands.

Both grazing and mowing can create conditions in which a wide variety of plants can grow together – sometimes over 100 species in one field. This is because these activities have two important effects. They prevent the most vigorous plants, which are usually the commoner grasses, becoming too dominant. They also prevent a build-up of dense plant litter, which inhibits the germination and establishment of seedlings and the growth of short species.

Grazing and mowing produce some important differences in the plant composition and the structure of the vegetation. Many pasture plants are low-growing species with basal rosettes, such as the plantains, which escape grazing but are vulnerable to shading and do not thrive in hayfields. Conversely, many meadow plants are tall species, which do not survive intensive grazing or trampling.

However, the availability of nutrients is also an important influence. Grasses and clovers respond to nutrients more vigorously than most other plants, thus outgrowing and replacing them. This means that a field enriched by fertilisers will hold a much smaller variety of plants than one which has not been treated.

Plant diversity is important for the many invertebrates which depend on particular plants. For example, many adult butterflies will feed at a variety of nectar plants but will lay their eggs on one particular species of plant for their larvae to feed on. Thus, the small copper butterfly lays its eggs on sorrels, the marbled white on fescues and the northern brown argus on common rock rose (Table 3.1: Butterflies of grassland). Several species of bumblebees nest in grasslands and feed on the nectar plants; their requirements are described in Feature 2.2.

Topography and plant structure are also important. Some invertebrates require extreme warmth and will only use low-growing plants in open, short-cropped swards on south-facing slopes (Feature 3.2: Grassland structure and butterflies), or bare ground where they can hunt, bask or lay eggs in the warm soil. For some species, grass tussocks provide concealment from predators and protection from extremes of temperature and humidity. They can be particularly important as hibernation sites for beetles.

Both pastures and meadows can contain large populations of small mammals, including shrews which feed on invertebrates and short-tailed voles which diversify the grassland structure by eating grass stems and roots and by creating runs. Populations are largest where cover is dense and grass is dominant in the sward. Tight-grazed fields will hold relatively small numbers. Harvest mice need tall herbage and may use hayfields before mowing. These animals support predators including weasels, stoats, kestrels and barn owls.

A number of declining or rare birds breed in unimproved grasslands. They include lapwing, grey partridge, corncrake, stone-curlew, curlew and, in damp fields, snipe and redshank. Each of these species has particular requirements for nesting and chick-rearing in terms of invertebrate food, wetness of fields and appropriate vegetation structure. For example, lapwings require extensive short swards whereas snipe need taller cover and moist ground (Feature 3.1: Breeding waders and grassland).

Table 3.1 : Butterflies of grassland

SPECIES	LARVAL FOOD PLANT	FLIGHT TIME	DISTRIBUTION
Calcareous grassland			
Adonis blue	Horseshoe vetch	May-Jun, Aug-Sept	S England
Brown argus	Common rock-rose	May-Jun, Jun-Sept	S England, Wales,
Chalkhill blue	Horseshoe vetch	Jul-Sept	S England
Dark green fritillary	Common dog violet and other *Viola* spp.	Jul-Aug	UK
Dingy skipper	Bird's-foot-trefoil	Apr-Jun	UK
Duke of Burgundy fritillary	*Primula* spp. esp. cowslip	May-Jun	England
Grayling	Fine and medium grasses	Jul-Sept	UK
Lulworth skipper	Tor grass	Jul-Aug	SW England
Marbled white	Fescue grasses	Jul-Aug	S England, Wales
Northern brown argus	Common rock-rose	Jul-Aug	N England, Scotland
Silver-spotted skipper	Sheep's fescue	Jul-Aug	S England
Silver-studded blue	Bird's-foot-trefoil, rock-rose, heather, gorse	Jun-Aug	S England, Wales,
Small blue	Kidney vetch	May-Jun	UK
Damp grassland			
Marsh fritillary	Devil's-bit scabious	May-Jun	N Ireland, NW Britain
Damp moors and bogs			
Large heath	Hare's tail cotton-grass, white-beaked sedge, purple moor-grass	Jul-Aug	UK
Scotch argus	Purple moor-grass and blue moor-grass	Jun-Jul	NW England, Scotland
Other grassland habitats			
Chequered skipper	Purple moor-grass	May-Jun	NW Scotland
Common blue	Bird's-foot-trefoil and restharrows	May-Jul, Aug-Sept	UK
Essex skipper	Mainly cocksfoot	Jul-Aug	S England
Gatekeeper	Fine and medium-leaved grasses	Jul-Sept	England, Wales
Green hairstreak	Gorses, rock-rose, and bird's-foot-trefoil	Apr-Jul	UK
Large skipper	Coarse grasses, especially cocksfoot	Jun-Aug	England, Wales S Scotland
Meadow brown	Fescues and meadow grasses	Jun-Jul, Aug-Sept	UK
Orange-tip	Garlic mustard and *Cardamine* spp.	May-Jun	UK
Ringlet	Medium and coarse grasses	Jun-Aug	UK
Small copper	Sorrels	Apr-May, Jul-Aug	UK
Small heath	Fine-leaved grasses such as fescues	May-Sept	UK
Small skipper	Mainly Yorkshire fog	Jun-Aug	England, Wales

Table 3.1 : Butterflies of grassland (cont'd)

SPECIES	LARVAL FOOD PLANT	FLIGHT TIME	DISTRIBUTION
Wall brown	Coarse grasses	May-Jun, Jul-Aug	UK

Adapted from Lane 1992 *Practical Conservation – Grasslands, Heaths and Moors*. Hodder and Stoughton.
Note: while some butterflies may have a UK distribution this does not necessarily mean they are common. Many now have extremely scattered distributions.

Hay meadows are important for birds such as corncrake. Stone-curlews nest on close-cropped chalk downland as well as grass-heaths.

Improved grasslands, whether they are permanent and dominated by a rye-grass sward or a temporary grass and clover ley are of limited wildlife interest, and support very few wild plants. Improved grasslands also support little in the way of fauna with a few notable exceptions, for example grazing geese. Some improved grasslands with a high spring and early summer watertable can also support breeding and wintering wildfowl and waders.

1.3 Pastures and grazing

- The grazing by livestock has created pastures that are rich in wildlife.
- Grazing favours low-growing plants and birds which need open conditions.
- Both overgrazing and undergrazing can lead to the loss of plant diversity and a decline in overall wildlife interest.
- Unimproved pastures are rich in invertebrates, especially if they contain a mosaic of plant structures created by low-intensity grazing.
- Different types of stock have different effects on the vegetation composition and structure of pastures.
- Sheep are more selective feeders than cattle.
- Cattle eat a wider range of coarse herbage than sheep.

- Horses are very selective grazers and can lead to an increase in rank vegetation.
- Trampling by stock, especially cattle, at high densities can destroy the nests of ground-nesting birds.

Unimproved pastures have developed their wildlife interest through livestock management as part of a farming system. Provided that the grazing regime balances stocking rates and densities with the amount of food the pasture can offer, wildlife conservation and livestock production can continue to be integrated.

Grazing favours low-growing plants and consequently those ground-nesting birds that require open conditions for breeding or feeding. It removes plant material gradually and can produce more variety in structure than mowing so it consequently creates conditions suitable for a greater number of invertebrates. Undergrazing will allow rank grasses and unpalatable plants to spread, whereas overgrazing can lead to excessive poaching and weed invasion. Both can lead to a loss of plant diversity and associated wildlife.

Pasture that has a wide variety of plants and a range of plant structures including short swards, tall herbage, scattered grass tussocks and limited areas of bare ground is likely to hold a wide range of invertebrate species. This mosaic is best produced by low-intensity grazing. It is usually easiest to achieve in larger fields where there are likely to be natural variations in slope, surface drainage and aspect which affect plant growth.

A number of invertebrates feed on livestock dung and are, incidentally, very important in causing its breakdown and the recycling of the nutrients it contains.

Cattle, sheep and horses have different plant preferences, feeding and dunging habits. Their plant preferences determine the structure of vegetation and composition of the sward. Sheep tend to be more selective feeders than cattle so that, unless they are stocked at high density, they concentrate on the areas of vegetation they find most palatable and produce a mosaic of short-cropped areas interspersed by ranker growth. This structure may be beneficial for many invertebrates. However, it alters the composition of the sward because it favours the spread of unpalatable plants. Sheep also prefer to eat plant flowers and so reduce or prevent seed production. This may also reduce the abundance of invertebrates that feed on flowers or seeds.

Cattle will eat a wider range of the coarser plants than sheep so that the effect of grazing is more evenly spread. Because they tear at foliage rather than biting it off, they tend to open the sward more than sheep and, being heavier, their trampling is more likely to expose bare soil. On fields where there is a build-up of plant litter, they will break up the mat more rapidly than sheep, so encouraging new growth and germination.

Horses are very selective, overgrazing certain areas and ignoring others, leaving the vegetation to grow coarse and rank. This effect is compounded by the fact that horses regularly use the same dunging areas, so that nutrient enrichment occurs and affects the composition of the vegetation, favouring vigorous, coarse growth. The result may be bad for plant richness but some grasshoppers, for example, often do well with this mix of short and tall herbage.

Where mixtures of stock graze, they tend to create a rather even sward with little structural variety but the spread of

vigorous or less palatable plants is well controlled.

Trampling by cattle, horses and, to a lesser extent, sheep increases the variety in the grassland structure by providing niches for plant germination and microhabitats for invertebrates. However, trampling can also cause the loss of eggs and young of some ground-nesting birds.

On their paths and where animals congregate, bare areas are created. These can be attractive to some invertebrates and a number of uncommon plants that can cope with trampling but cannot tolerate competition from other plants. However, where trampling is severe, poaching can occur and be subject to invasion by plants such as thistles and docks.

Rabbits can maintain swards of wildife value similar to those produced by sheep but, like them, may foster the spread of unpalatable plants. They may also create patches of bare ground susceptible to weed invasion.

1.4 Meadows and mowing

- Hay meadow management creates conditions for a rich variety of taller plants than are found in pastures.
- Hay meadows are less good for invertebrates than pastures. They lack varied vegetation structure and bare ground. Food resources are mostly destroyed when mowing takes place.
- Aftermath grazing increases the variety of plants.
- Meadows shut up from early spring to mid-summer are important for ground-nesting birds which require tall cover.
- Timing of the cut determines whether early-flowering or later-flowering plants thrive.
- Cutting methods and patterns affect wildlife. Cutting in towards the centre can kill nesting birds and mammals.
- Meadows with a high summer watertable and winter flooding are of special importance.
- Intensive silage production is of little wildlife interest.

Mowing favours tall-growing plant species, such as globe flower, snake's head fritillary and great burnet, that are intolerant of intensive grazing or trampling and so do not survive in pasture. Most are perennials so that it does not matter if cutting sometimes occurs before they can set seed, whereas others spread by runners or rhizomes so the precise time of mowing is unimportant. However, the only annuals that persist in hay meadows are those which always set seed before normal cutting dates, such as hay rattle: this is an important plant because it is semi-parasitic on the more vigorous grasses and may reduce their growth, so enabling less vigorous plants to survive.

Cutting dates vary from year to year depending on the weather and quality of the crop. They also vary depending on soil type, location, altitude, aspect and climate. It might once have taken a farm about a month to complete the cutting of all its fields, creating significant differences between the variety of plants found in the early cut fields and those cut four weeks later. Today, modern machinery makes the process much quicker and hay fields containing late-flowering plants are becoming particularly rare. In general, agriculturally unimproved swards retain their optimum condition longer than those which have been improved or re-seeded so that cutting dates are less critical except in relation to the weather.

Mowing is a dramatic event because it removes all of the plant growth in one operation, is less selective than grazing and does not produce the structural variety. These effects are very important for invertebrates and birds.

Hay meadows do not support such a rich diversity of invertebrates as pastures. This is partly because they do not contain as great a variety of vegetation structure and partly because of the abrupt change of conditions when mowing takes place. As a result, meadows are mostly used by mobile species which can move around between sites. However, they do contain a number of rare species, and produce nectar, pollen and other food resources, which can be visited by insects that breed in adjoining habitats.

Meadows that are shut up for hay from early spring to about mid-summer are potentially good for ground-nesting birds, such as redshank and snipe, which require cover. The timing of mowing is an important factor because nests and chicks are destroyed or exposed to predators and the best sites are those where wet ground conditions prevent mowing until after the young have hatched.

Aftermath grazing can increase the variety of plant species which grow in a meadow. If continued to the end of the growing season, it determines the availability and type of nesting cover for birds in the following spring, and thus the species and numbers which will attempt to nest. In northern areas in particular, spring bite is also taken before the field is shut up for hay. At this stage, trampling can cause losses of early nests and eggs as well as reducing cover from predators.

Meadow-nesting birds have suffered with the change from hay to silage (earlier mowing dates) and improvements in mowing equipment (faster mowing speeds). The birds and their eggs and chicks are still present when cutting begins and adult birds and chicks cannot escape the faster cutting machinery. Mammals such as deer fawns may also be killed.

Silage production is of low overall wildlife interest where the grass has been re-seeded, heavily fertilised and two or more crops are taken off each year. A less-intensive silage production system can retain some wildlife value especially where re-seeding has not taken place and where cutting still takes place in late summer.

Land subject to winter flooding was preferentially chosen for hay production because of the beneficial nutrient inputs, and because arable production and spring grazing were precluded. Most of these areas are now protected from regular inundation and may have been underdrained. Where the traditional system exists it should be maintained as it has high importance not only for plants but also for wintering and breeding waterfowl (Chapter 9).

1.5 Other management operations

- Burning can be used to bring neglected grasslands back into condition for grazing.
- Burning can reduce plant and invertebrate diversity.
- Rolling can crush anthills, and birds' nests and chicks.
- Chain harrowing can be used to bring neglected grassland into condition but could lead to invasion by weeds.

Burning can be used as a last resort to start the restoration of a long-neglected grassland. It can remove litter, stimulate growth and open the sward enough for new seedlings to establish. However, this can lead to invasion by bracken, thistles and gorse. Different plants have different resistances to fire so if undertaken regularly it can lead to a loss of plant diversity with those 'fire resistant' species becoming more common. For example, burning can be used to reduce the dominance of problem species such as tor-grass but, if not followed by grazing, tor-grass will come back even more vigorously.

Many invertebrates are sedentary, so burning has the potential to wipe out populations if undertaken on a large scale. Mosses are also particularly vulnerable because they do not have underground root or rhizome systems that escape the fire.

Chain harrowing and rolling are techniques used to cultivate and improve grasslands but have the potential to damage wildlife, and their use on unimproved grassland should be carefully considered. Both operations can destroy anthills, and the nests and young of ground-nesting birds. Additionally, where the pasture or meadow supports early-flowering species, rolling and chain harrowing can reduce or prevent flowering and seeding.

Chain harrowing can have wildlife benefits in breaking up thick vegetation 'mats' on neglected land and so encouraging new growth and germination but if the gaps created are large, thistles, docks and ragwort may invade.

1.6 Nutrients and lime

- Artificial fertilisers encourage rapid growth by agriculturally-productive grasses and clovers. This leads to the loss of wild plant richness.
- Farmyard manure releases nutrients at a slower rate and has much less effect on plant richness.
- Use of slurry results in a reduction of plant diversity, can smother or scorch the sward and cause pollution problems.
- Liming affects the plant composition of grasslands and can destroy plants which are characteristic of acid soils.

Nitrogen produces rapid growth from vigorous agriculturally productive grasses; phosphate similarly favours clovers and other legumes. The great majority of other grassland plants respond much more slowly so that artificial fertiliser application causes a rapid change in the sward composition, with the majority of plant species being outcompeted, over-shaded and suppressed. This leads to the loss of wildflowers and less-competitive grasses. As grasses become dominant, there is a dramatic decline in invertebrate richness also. These changes begin to take place with even the lowest levels of artificial nitrogen application on either pasture or meadows.

Farmyard manure is different from artificial fertilisers in its effects. Its nitrogen content is variable and it releases nutrients more slowly so that the more vigorous species do not become as dominant. The organic component of manure is important to some invertebrates, including earthworms, which are a major food of some mammals and of birds including the lapwing, snipe and thrushes.

Not all grasslands used to receive farmyard manure regularly and some land, such as chalk downland, was never manured at all. Manure was always in limited supply and, after arable, priority was given to hayfields. Traditional practice was that the manure would be applied in autumn and spring, so far as it was available.

Where possible, hayfields were sited on ground subject to winter flooding, which annually helped to replenish nutrients.

Slurry, like artificial fertilisers, produces a sudden release of nutrients and as a consequence causes similar changes in plant composition, leading to a decline in species, diversity. It can cause further damage through scorching and smothering vegetation and can cause pollution problems in run-off.

In the past, lime was applied particularly to those grasslands where soil acidity restricted the growth of grass through limiting the availability of nutrients. Liming is particularly harmful to the wildlife interest if applied to unimproved acid grassland pastures. Today, liming is most likely to be carried out to correct the acidifying effects of the application of artificial nitrogen.

1.7 Soils

- Soil type influences the wildlife of grasslands.
- Calcareous, neutral and acid grasslands support different plant communities. These in turn support different invertebrates and other wildlife.

Soil types have important influences on the wildlife of grasslands. This is partly because some plants and animals require particular soil conditions. For instance, snails are particularly numerous in calcareous grassland because of the abundance of lime with which they construct their shells. It is also because the natural fertility and drainage of some soils restricted the type of grassland management to grazing, while other soils were favoured for hay production.

Calcareous grasslands are uncommon outside England and found, for example, on the chalk downs of Wiltshire and limestone dales of Yorkshire. They were mostly used as pasture for sheep and beef production and some of them were impoverished as an incidental result of moving the stock which grazed them by day onto nearby arable fields at night so as to enrich the tilled land with the animals' dung. The effect of this impoverishment was to reduce the vigour of grasses and increase the opportunities for many herbs which can thrive in nutrient-poor conditions. As a result, such areas became uniquely rich in the variety of different plants they held.

Neutral grasslands were formerly the commonest type in England, being spread across the clay and loam soil of the lowlands. There were also extensive stretches on peat soils in the Fens and elsewhere. Being more fertile than the calcareous grasslands, they could support both dairy and beef cattle. The best neutral grasslands were used for hay production with grazing of the aftermath and sometimes early spring grazing also. Many of the most productive meadows were found in river valleys where annual winter flooding helped to replenish soil nutrients. Water meadows were a highly specialised type of grassland in which relatively warm water rising from springs at the foot of the chalk was run over the land to foster the growth of grass for sheep early in the year. The productivity of the soils and the types of management encouraged many plants which do not occur in either calcareous or acid grasslands and this supported a different range of other wildlife.

In some coastal areas extensive grasslands were created on reclaimed saltmarsh and the marsh itself was also grazed at low tide. These areas often held large numbers of breeding and wintering wildfowl and waders.

Acid grasslands are the most widespread type of pasture. They are still extensive in the north and west of the UK in both upland and lowland farms. Today they are predominantly grazed by sheep. Acid grassland is uncommon in lowland England. It is mostly associated with the free-draining sands of the Midlands, East Anglia and the south, and is particularly associated with heathlands. It supports a quite distinctive range of plants, though it usually holds fewer species. As well as reading this Chapter, reference should be made to Chapter 4 for further information on the management of acid grassland on lowland heaths or Chapter 5 for hill and rough grazings.

2. Options and assessment: planning management

2.1 Wildlife assessment of pastures and meadows

- Assessment of wildlife value is based on management practice, sward structure and composition.
- Where information on scarce and sensitive species is available, it should be included in the assessment.

Experienced grassland farmers will have no difficulty in identifying unimproved fields with their variety of wild grasses and numerous other plants. They will also have a keen appreciation of how to manage stock and hay production to keep the land productive in the long term without inputs of artificial fertilisers. For the purpose of this handbook, it is usually sufficient to know whether a field is unimproved, semi-improved or improved and then to apply the guidelines set out for grazing or mowing, modifying these to take account of particular aspects of their wildlife importance if desired.

However, there are a number of circumstances in which it will be useful to take stock of the wildlife interest (Table 3.2 Wildlife assessment of pastures and meadows). It should always be done if a change of management is being considered, such as a shift from hay to permanent pasture, or where a field which has been neglected is now to be brought back into management. It is also good policy to review wildlife interest periodically to ensure that a gradual decline is not taking place, perhaps due to some aspect of management which could be changed without difficulty.

Assessment will usually be a condition of grant aid and it will also be required as part of the production of a farm wildlife plan.

The general principles of assessment and guidance on sources of information are described in Chapter 1 which should be read in conjunction with this section.

To find out more about the overall wildlife value of a field it is ideally desirable to look at it at several different times of year. For example, use by breeding birds can be assessed in early spring. The plant composition is easier to assess later in the year when grasses and other plants flower. Invertebrates of some species will be active for only a few days or weeks in spring and summer. However, in practice, it is rare to have the luxury of looking at the site over a long period, but a good deal can be judged at any time of year from the soil type, the condition of the sward and information on the management history.

For example, in some fields it will be obvious that the sward contains a great variety of wild flowers and it is reasonable to assume from their presence that there will be considerable invertebrate interest too, depending on the vegetation structure which develops in spring and summer. Pastures are likely to be better for invertebrates than meadows. It is not necessary to attempt to work out in detail how many plants or what species of invertebrates are present in order to make sound decisions on wildlife management. Similarly, where it is known that fields have a high summer watertable, it is likely that waders will attempt to breed and appropriate decisions can be made about timing of mowing and grazing without the need for comprehensive survey.

Obviously, where there is a good chance that rare species are present, it is useful to know so that the risk of inappropriate management is minimised. Guidance and advice are available, especially when the assessment forms part of a grant application for management, restoration and re-creation of grassland (see Appendix I).

Where consideration is being given to the re-creation of grassland for wildlife, thought should be given to soil type, residual nutrient status, context, existing wildlife interest and other factors. These are discussed on page 76.

Table 3.2: Wildlife assessment of pastures and meadows

INFORMATION REQUIRED	METHOD	REASON FOR INFORMATION
1. Conservation status and interest	Contact FWAG initially.	If the pasture or meadow is unimproved, information on its wildlife interest may have already been collected. This will assist in the assessment. Many unimproved grasslands (at least in the lowlands) may have a special designation (such as SSSI or ASSI). Certain conditions may need to be satisfied before any changes in management can take place.
2. Past management	Check farm records. Check historical information. Examine past and present aerial photographs.	The longer a field has been unimproved grassland, the more likely it will be of wildlife interest and contain rare species. If it has never been ploughed or improved, it is likely to have a very high interest. Some leys and recent re-seeds may have some bird interest.
3. Current management	Note grazing practice, including livestock types, stocking rates, timing of grazing and use of supplementary feeding.	Essential in maintaining or increasing wildlife interest of grassland. Use in conjunction with other information collected and adjust where necessary. Supplementary feeding areas can damage unimproved grassland.
	Note mowing practice, including cutting dates, cutting methods and details of aftermath grazing (see above).	Essential in maintaining or increasing wildlife interest in meadows. Use in conjunction with other information collected and adjust where necessary.
	Note other management practices such as chain harrowing, rolling or burning.	Can be harmful to wildlife in some grasslands.
	Note use and application of lime and fertilisers. Specify type and application details particularly rate.	Encourages the growth of the more competitive species of grass and leads to a loss in plant diversity. Can also cause enrichment and pollution of watercourses. May identify opportunities for reduction in rates, changes in type of fertiliser, or application methods.
	Note weed control measures undertaken including target weed species, reason for control, method, timing and success. Give full details of any herbicides used.	Will identify scale of problem. Some weed control measures are harmful to wildlife.
4. Boundaries to grassland	Map location and condition of fences, hedges, drystone walls and dykes.	To identify work to make stockproof especially when grazing management is to be reinstated. To assess the use of hedges and walls in shelter and protection from spray-drift.
	Land-use surrounding grassland.	To identify areas for possible extension of grassland through arable reversion or less intensive management.

▶▶▶

Table 3.2: Wildlife assessment of pastures and meadows (cont'd)

INFORMATION REQUIRED	METHOD	REASON FOR INFORMATION
5. Grassland composition and structure	Note presence and abundance of plants other than agricultural grasses and clovers or common 'weeds'.	If a wide variety of herbs and grasses are present then grassland likely to have wildlife interest. Calcareous and unimproved grassland will hold the greatest number of species. Grass leys, reseeds and grassland with heavy inputs of fertilisers will contain fewest species.
	Map extensive areas of tall coarse grassland, tussocks and areas with deep litter layer.	May suggest undergrazing and need to adjust grazing regime or restoration of management. These features can, however, provide wildlife interest if part of a mosaic.
	Map areas of bare ground, very gappy swards and presence of 'injurious weeds'.	May suggest overgrazing and need to lower grazing levels, take stock off completely or modify supplementary feeding practices.
6. Trees, scrub and bracken	Record location, distribution and abundance.	Depending on size of the area, some can be of wildlife benefit.
		However, may suggest that where management has lapsed, control of invasive scrub or bracken may be needed.
7. Other important grassland features	Note features such as wet ground, pools, anthills, earthbanks, ridge and furrow.	All can be of wildlife importance and need to be taken account of in management; anthills will be destroyed by rolling/harrowing.
8. Rare or sensitive species including breeding birds	Map the location of rare species present/thought to be present.	Unimproved grasslands (especially in lowland UK) are rare and so are some species.
	Note vegetation structure in vicinity.	The presence and needs of these species should be built into future grassland management.
	Seek specialist guidance.	

2.2 Management needs and opportunities

- Where unimproved or semi-improved grassland remains, it should be managed with the needs of wildlife taken into account.
- Ploughing, re-seeding and the use of artificial fertilisers and herbicides are harmful to wildlife and should be avoided.
- Mowing and grazing are vital operations that need to be continued.
- Where the existing wildlife interest is high, continue past practice.
- On wet grasslands, correct hydrological management is also critical.
- Unimproved or semi-improved fields that are overgrazed, undergrazed or abandoned can be restored for wildlife.
- Improved grasslands and some leys can have value for birds and offer considerable scope for enhancement.
- With changing priorities, reversion from arable land to permanent grassland of wildlife value can be feasible.
- Advice and incentives are available for management, restoration and reversion to grassland.

Where unimproved or semi-improved grassland or rough grazing still forms part of a farm, it is important to maintain or enhance the wildlife interest because the habitat is now rare.

Do not plough, level, re-seed or cultivate by direct drilling, slot seeding or oversowing as this will change the composition of the sward and destroy the wildlife interest. Do not apply herbicides. If there is serious infestation by injurious weeds, a combination of control by cutting and grazing should be used. Only if these fail should use of a weed wipe or spot spraying be considered.

Fertiliser reduces the plant diversity of the grassland sward by increasing the competitive vigour of grasses. Avoid all use of artificial fertilisers or slurry on unimproved fields as their application will

destroy the wildlife interest. On semi-improved fields which still retain some wildlife interest, do not increase existing levels of fertiliser application and where possible reduce inputs, perhaps by substituting manure for artificial fertiliser.

Where the wildlife interest is high, it is important to continue existing grazing management or, on meadows, to take a hay crop. Do not alter existing livestock type, stocking rates and timing, or the timing of mowing. Financial incentives may be available.

The management of grassland that floods in winter or is surface-damp in spring and early summer needs to take into account hydrological requirements as well as any cutting or grazing regimes; these are covered on page 305. Wetland areas on farmland are scarce so any further drainage should be avoided. There may be opportunities to enhance the wildlife on wet grassland on the farm and advice should be sought.

Though improved grassland may have little wildlife value when intensively managed, modifications of grazing, mowing and hydrological regimes can create suitable conditions for breeding waders such as snipe, hunting areas for birds of prey like barn owl (Feature 3.3: Farming and the barn owl) and even habitat for corncrakes.

Some unimproved and semi-improved fields are relatively poor for wildlife because they are overgrazed, grazed at the wrong times, or even abandoned. Where unimproved grassland still exists on the farm but is no longer managed as part of the farm enterprise, for wildlife, it is important to restore the former management. Depending on when management was last undertaken, it may now be an urgent priority. The prime objective would be to reduce the dominance of rank grass and the build-up of plant litter, which will cause many plants and invertebrates to die out and to combat invasion by scrub.

Where stock are no longer available, consider using a grazier or, though not ideal, mechanical methods may be substituted for grazing. Where land is overstocked, finance may be available to help adapt the enterprise. There are increasing opportunities to obtain financial payments for suitable management.

Incentives and advice are also available, for example through Environmentally Sensitive Areas and some other schemes, to revert arable land or ley grassland to permanent grassland that can be managed for wildlife conservation (see leaflet *Financial incentives*). The type of grassland to be created will depend on soil type, climate, drainage, whether the field will be grazed or mowed and conservation priorities. Even sites with high residual nutrient levels have potential if they are appropriately managed.

3. Management of pastures and meadows

3.1 Management of pastures

- Where unimproved pastures survive, they should continue to be grazed to maintain their long-term productivity as part of the farm, without increasing inputs.
- Use sward composition, structure and height to guide management.
- Avoid overgrazing, as this creates bare and poached ground, reduces plant and invertebrate interest, and tramples nests of ground-nesting birds.
- Avoid undergrazing as this leads to an increase in growth of vigorous rank grasses and eventually scrub, and a loss of wildlife interest.
- Do not re-seed or use artificial fertilisers or slurry on unimproved or plant-rich pastures.
- To avoid losses of scarce plants and invertebrates, summer grazing should be at low intensity only, especially where the unimproved field is small.
- As a general rule, graze calcareous grassland with about 0.5 cattle or 2.5 sheep per ha/yr, neutral grasslands with 1 cattle or 4 sheep per ha/yr and acid grasslands with 0.4 cattle or 2 sheep per ha/yr.
- Avoid supplementary feeding and the use of ivermectin in unimproved grasslands.

Where a farm still holds unimproved pasture, it is important that it continues to play a full part in the farming enterprise.

Unimproved grasslands developed and maintained their wildlife interest through decisions about livestock production, not flowers, invertebrates or birds. The principles which applied then still apply today. Take what the field has to offer and then move the stock to another pasture, whether this means low-intensity grazing for a long period or a relatively high stocking rate for a short one.

The best guide for conservation grazing management is vegetation composition, structure and sward height. Overgrazing will destroy variation in sward structure, and at its extreme will create bare and poached areas and reduce plant variety, with lasting effects on invertebrates. Undergrazing should also be avoided as this also reduces wildlife interest, leading to an increase in the growth of vigorous rank grasses and scrub. Low-growing herbs are lost, as is plant diversity, and conditions can become unsuitable for many invertebrates and ground-nesting birds. The sward should not be altered by re-seeding or high nutrient inputs.

If stock are no longer kept, consider letting the grazing under an annual licence or other arrangement which specifies livestock type, numbers and timing; it may be useful to give minimum and maximum numbers of grazing days desired. Failing that, apply a mowing regime which removes all cut material.

If the field is in good condition, the ideal is to continue the existing level of grazing. If farm circumstances dictate a change of

Table 3.3: A guide for stocking rates of sheep (S) or cattle (C) for five grassland types (Numbers expressed as animals per ha)

NUMBER OF GRAZING WEEKS PER YEAR	CALCAREOUS GRASSLAND S.	C.	NEUTRAL GRASSLAND S.	C.	ACIDIC GRASSLAND S.	C.	MARSHY GRASSLAND S.	C.	DUNE GRASSLAND S.	C.
2	60	15	100	25	50	12	–	12	20	4
4	30	8	50	12·5	25	6	–	6	10	2
6	20	5	33	8	16	4	–	4	7	1·5
8	15	4	25	6	12	3	–	3	5	1
10	12	3	20	5	10	2·5	–	2·5	4	1
12	10	2·5	17	4	8	2	–	2	3	0·6
14	8·5	2	14	3·5	7	1·5	–	2	3	0·5
16	7·5	2	12·5	3	6	1·5	–	1·5	2·5	0·5
20	6	1·5	10	2·5	5	1	–	1	–	–
24	5	1	8	2	4	1	–	–	–	–
36	3·5	1	5·5	1·5	3	0·5	–	–	–	–
Annual stocking rate (52)	2·5	0·5	4	1	2	0·4	–	–	–	–

Adapted from Nature Conservancy Council (1986) *Potentially Damaging Operations Manual*. NCC and Massey, M 1993 pers. comm.

Notes: 1. These are a guide to stocking rates. For most areas of wildlife interest seasonal grazing is advocated; that explains the absence of year-round levels for marshy and dune grassland.

2. There may be considerable variation across the UK in relation to latitude, altitude, exposure and rainfall, in addition to vegetation composition, height and structure.

livestock type, bear in mind that this may result in some change in the relative abundance of different plants and in the overall structure of the vegetation. The result may not be harmful – it may indeed be beneficial – but it is important to watch for the undesired spread of vigorous and unpalatable plants, such as tor grass on calcareous soils and mat-grass in the uplands. If this occurs, for whatever reason, they should be grazed in early season when they are palatable and stocking rates may need to be increased so that animals will be forced to eat them.

Horses are normally undesirable as the sole stock on pastures. If horses must be grazed on unimproved grass, run other livestock, ideally cattle, so that they graze the areas which the horses leave. Where horses are the only stock available, topping of rank vegetation and weed control may be needed.

On most farms the bulk of the grazing will be improved and any unimproved fields will therefore be used quite selectively. The tendency will be to put animals with high nutritional requirements such as milking cows and ewes just before lambing onto the better keep and to graze the unimproved land with barren ewes, wethers, store cattle and so on. It is important to ensure that this does not lead to unimproved fields being undergrazed.

If possible, do not put stock treated with ivermectin onto unimproved pastures. Ivermectin is excreted largely unaltered in the dung and remains powerfully insecticidal. This reduces the number and variety of insects in dung, thereby slowing down its decomposition. This can lead to a reduction in food resources for insectivorous birds such as curlew and chough (see page 160).

Where ivermectin is used, pour-on or injected formulations are preferable to a bolus because bolus formulations result in ivermectin being excreted in dung over a longer period of time.

Guidelines for stocking rates are given in Table 3.3 but decisions must be taken on a

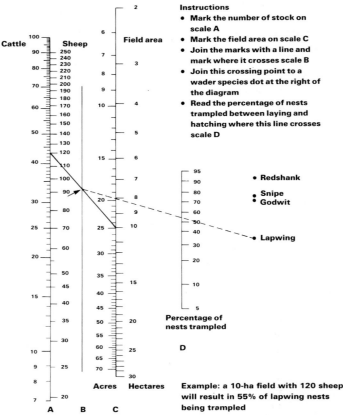

Figure 3.1
The risk of nest trampling for different waders. The number of nests that will be lost can be calculated from the area of the field and the number of stock. The number of stock should be fixed at a level that results in as few nests as possible being trampled. This chart gives the risk of trampling for the whole incubation period, which differs with species.
Adapted from Green, R E 1985. *The management of lowland wet grassland for breeding waders.* RSPB.

field-by-field basis, depending on soil type, vegetation composition and state, growing conditions, past management and existing conservation interest. Rates may need changing from year to year.

Grazing has different effects at different seasons. In early spring when growth is commencing, it helps to reduce the vigour of the more aggressive grass species. Effects on wildlife are minimal. However, by late spring the eggs of ground-nesting birds may be at risk of trampling (Feature 3.1:) and early season flowers may be grazed off so that they cannot set seed. If too many stock are present through the summer, flower production will be greatly reduced, affecting the availability of pollen and nectar for invertebrates and reducing or preventing seed production. Invertebrates are most active at this season and there may

be losses of eggs laid on plants. Ground-nesting birds are at their most vulnerable up to about mid-summer (Figure 3.1: Risk of nest trampling).

From August on, grazing is unlikely to have any seriously detrimental effects and the aim in unimproved pastures should be to remove all the growth of the preceding year by the end of the season. If possible, it is beneficial if some tussocks or rank corners remain at the onset of winter for use as invertebrate hibernation sites.

If the field holds ground-nesting birds, it will be important to leave it in optimum condition for them to settle in the following spring. Different species require different sward heights (Feature 3.1). Autumn grazing is also important in creating a short sward for grazing by geese and other wildfowl.

Stock being fed in winter should not be allowed to stand out during the day on unimproved grassland as their trampling and dunging will severely damage the vegetation.

When unimproved grassland was widespread, it would have been unimportant that many areas were grazed hard through the summer as there were always other fields where grazing was light so that plants could set seed, and insects and birds could breed, in turn recolonising adjoining land when conditions changed. Now that most unimproved pastures are small and isolated, if they are grazed hard in summer there is a danger that species will be lost permanently. For this reason, it is best if summer grazing on unimproved fields is at low intensity only. The critical period is roughly from the start of April to mid-August but precise dates will be earlier in the south than the north, in the lowlands than in the uplands, and will vary from year to year.

If it is practicable in relation to the working of the farm, with small fields it will be best to avoid summer grazing altogether and to concentrate more intensive grazing in early spring and autumn.

On larger pastures, overall wildife richness can be maintained by low-intensity grazing all through the growing season. This is because stock will be able to graze selectively and there will also be enough variation in site conditions for some plants to flower and set seed and for the invertebrate fauna to flourish. If it appears that flower production is poor, it may be due to stock numbers being too high and they should be reduced at this season, with an increase in the autumn to ensure that the field is not undergrazed.

The one exception may be on land with high numbers of breeding birds as even small livestock numbers may cause losses of eggs and chicks through trampling. It will be best on such pasture not to graze in the nesting season.

However, it is very important to remember that in the long term all the wildlife on the site depends on the condition of the plants and not to jeopardise this by aiming for short-term success with any one species. For instance, if hard summer grazing is needed to control the spread of dominant grasses, this should be done even if it means that there will be little flower production for a year or two.

If possible, avoid supplementary feeding on unimproved grasslands. It can result in poaching and localised enrichment due to dunging which can damage the sward, reduce the plant diversity and introduce weeds. If supplementary feeding is unavoidable, site it on ground with least interest, such as a trampled gateway or where animals shelter. The same rule applies to watering sites which tend to concentrate grazing pressure.

3.2 Management of meadows

- Maintain existing mowing regimes on meadows with a high wildlife value.
- Where possible, cut hay late one year in five to allow seeding of meadow plants.
- For ground-nesting birds, ideally do not cut before early July in the south and August in the north.
- If cutting early, adopt a mowing method that enables birds and other wildlife to escape.
- Where aftermath has been grazed, continue to do so.
- Apply manure at traditional rates where this has been done in the past. Do not apply artificials.
- On sites in river valleys, maintain or restore winter flooding regimes and high spring watertables.
- Do not cultivate or re-seed unimproved or plant-rich meadows.

Maintain existing mowing regimes in meadows with a high wildlife value. Plants and other wildlife are influenced by cutting date. Traditionally, fields were cut in the same sequence from year to year. This sequence reflected their fertility, closeness to the farm buildings and other factors. Using horses, the whole process of hay-making may have taken a month or so. As a result, fields cut first contained mostly plants which flower early and those cut last held plants which flower later. If possible, retain the established sequence of cutting in unimproved fields.

There are two problems with deliberately delaying until late summer the cutting of fields traditionally cut last. One is that hay will lose condition. The other is that the hay may not be harvestable at all if wet weather ensues. In some areas, financial incentives may be made available to cover these risks. Otherwise, leave cutting until late one year in five to allow plants to set seed.

Breeding birds may be present in unimproved meadows and in fields improved and cut for silage. The timing of cutting is significant as losses of eggs or chicks are likely before early July in southern England and Wales, mid-month in northern England and Northern Ireland and the start of August in Scotland.

The pattern of mowing is also important. Mowing entire fields in a spiral from the outer edge inwards drives mammals and birds, including chicks, towards a central 'island' as they do not want to break cover. As a result, they may be killed by the mower during the final few cuts. If this method is still used, it is worth leaving the last stand of hay overnight so that birds and mammals can make their escape and then cutting it at very slow speed the next day.

It is also possible to mow in one of a number of alternative methods, which give mammals and birds an increased chance of escape into nearby fields, ditches or hedgerows. Though these take a little longer they are worthwhile because of the rarity of many ground-nesting bird species. One technique is to mow first across both ends of the field to make turning areas and then to mow across the field in strips from end to end so that birds can escape on the other side of the field (see page 181). The slower the mower travels, the greater the animals' chance to avoid being killed.

Where aftermath grazing and early spring grazing have been practised, they should be continued if possible as cessation may result in the loss of some plant species. Past practice should not be changed. For instance, introduction of spring grazing may eliminate plants like hay rattle which grow early in the season. Take account of the guidelines in the section on grazing, page 68.

Hay meadows on land that did not regularly flood in winter were usually fertilised with manure. It is most important not to use artificials or slurry on unimproved meadows and not to increase the amounts of manure used as any of them will lead to loss of plant richness. If manure is not available, from the wildlife point of view it is best to use nothing. See the guidelines on page 74.

Meadows that still flood in winter are particularly rare and important for wildlife. They contain plants such as meadow-rue that do not grow in dry meadows or in pasture. They may also hold breeding waders such as snipe, which feed in the moist ground. Maintain the whole hydrological regime as far as possible (see page 305). As well as flooding, it is very desirable to maintain a high watertable until the time for haycutting approaches and the level is dropped to allow machinery onto the field. Where flooding has ceased and penning levels have been dropped, restoration may be possible. In some areas, financial incentives will be available to help with costs.

3.3 Weed control

- Control injurious weeds and prevent their spread through skilled grazing management. Avoid practices such as overgrazing that create large expanses of bare ground or gappy swards. Do not site supplementary feed areas on unimproved grassland.
- Topping or cutting are preferred control methods on plant-rich fields.
- If herbicide use is unavoidable, use a weed wipe or spot spray target weeds only. Never blanket spray.
- Tolerate small numbers of weeds as all have wildlife value.
- Herbicides should be used in accordance with the Control of Pesticides Regulations 1986.

Weeds can mean different things to different people but this section refers mainly to those listed in the Weeds Act 1959. These are creeping thistle, spear thistle, broad-leaved dock, curled dock and ragwort.

The spread of thistles, docks and ragworts normally occurs on bare ground or gappy swards which arise through overgrazing or poaching. Poaching can occur when stock numbers, particularly cattle and horses, are high and congregate in wet areas and around feeding sites. Weed seeds can be brought in with supplementary feed and through nutrient enrichment in traditional dunging areas, which produces conditions suitable for dock establishment. Nutrient enrichment also favours nettles. Rushes can sometimes become a serious problem on wet sites, and bracken can become a problem on acid soils and hill pastures (its control is covered on pages 116 and 153).

Serious weed infestation affects both grazing and hay production and can also reduce plant diversity and other wildlife interest. However, all these plants are a natural component of grasslands and in small numbers add to its wildlife value. Thistles and ragwort are valuable nectar sources for many bees, butterflies and other insects, while some invertebrates feed on their foliage or seeds. Nettles are food plants for peacock butterflies and some other species. Thistle and dock seeds are important for some finches. Rushes are used as nest cover by curlews and the seeds are eaten by birds.

The prevention of weed infestation is preferable to being faced with the situation of losing hay or grazing, and having to undertake some form of control. Aim to maintain the sward in good condition through manipulation of stock, stocking densities and adjustments to periods of grazing based on the quality and amount of food available and what grazing pressures it can withstand. To minimise the effects of poaching around feeding and watering sites, locate them permanently in 'sacrificial' areas such as gateways where poaching is almost unavoidable anyway. Fence off other poached areas to allow them to recover or reduce stocking levels. If possible, do not site supplementary feed areas on unimproved grassland as weed seeds can be introduced and germinate successfully in the poached areas around the feeding sites.

On unimproved fields avoid all use of herbicides if possible. Instead, use a combination of cutting and grazing. Docks are most likely to become a problem on fields grazed by cattle or horses. Prevent seed production by cutting before the plants flower and if possible replace cattle by sheep for a period as they will graze regrowth. Thistle cutting must be done before they have developed flower heads which will otherwise spread seed even after they are cut. Spear thistles are biennial and can be eradicted by cutting but creeping thistle spreads by underground rhizomes so repeat cutting will be needed.

Ragwort is particularly problematic as it is toxic to stock, particularly young animals, cattle and horses. Adult cattle and horses will not eat it while growing but may do so when it has been cut in the field or in hay. Cut to prevent seed production and remove from the field. Sheep will eat ragwort and have been used to graze young plants or regrowth but this is particularly inadvisable with young animals or where there is a substantial infestation.

A combination of topping, twice if necessary, and grazing with cattle works well with rushes.

Care should be taken where ground-nesting birds are present. The ideal would be to walk the field and mark nests with canes but this is not likely to find all the nests or to be practicable. Drive as slowly as possible whilst cutting to give birds the chance to move out of the way.

When herbicides are necessary, use the most selective available, apply as directly as possible, preferably through a weed wipe or by spot-spraying. Also use in accordance with the Control of Pesticides Regulations and follow the code of practice. On unimproved grasslands use herbicides only as a last resort. Some fields will hold rare thistles such as meadow thistle and these should not be killed.

3.4 Fertilisers, manure and lime

- Do not apply artificial fertilisers or slurry to unimproved grasslands.
- If grassland has been semi-improved but some wildlife interest survives, restoration will require stopping application of all nutrients for a period.
- Where unimproved grassland has a history of manure application, do not increase the rate.
- Only use lime on unimproved grassland where it has been routinely used in the past. Do not exceed previous application rates.
- Do not apply lime or any other substance designed to reduce soil acidity on unimproved acid pastures.
- All fertilisers should be applied with care to minimise run-off.
- Follow the Code of Good Agricultural Practice.
- Consider the use of fertilisers to create nutritious grasslands for geese and other grazing wildfowl.

Changes in the composition of the plant community begin to occur at the lowest levels of application of artificial fertilisers which should therefore never be applied to unimproved grassland. Where application has been made in the past but a range of wild plants still survives (semi-improved grassland), it should not be repeated and the field should be managed to restore its interest (see page 75).

The effect of manure depends on the amount applied. The best approach is to make judgements on the basis of conditions in the field and past practice. If a field remains rich in wild plants there is no reason why past practice should not be continued, with the same amounts and frequency of manure application. If it is known that plant variety has reduced, then the level of application should be reduced or, ideally, stopped altogether for several years. Use well rotted manure, to minimise the likelihood of introducing the seeds of weed species into the grassland.

Manure from stock is now richer than it would have been in the past because

animals are fed better quality keep. This should be borne in mind if comparisons with traditional levels of application are made.

Slurry should never be applied to unimproved grasslands. The sudden release of nutrients alters sward composition. It may be toxic to invertebrates including earthworms. At high application rates, vegetation may be smothered and killed.

All fertilisers should be applied with care and the Code of Good Agricultural Practice should be followed. Do not apply fertilisers, slurry or manures close to ditches or onto land where it may be washed off the surface by heavy rain. Calculate nitrogen requirements for each field. Apply inorganics only during active growth and take into account seasonal factors such as summer drought. Avoid application to very wet soil.

In some areas of the UK concentrations of nitrates have been rising in water sources. While the effect on wildlife is not yet fully known, loss of interest can occur when levels are very high. Under the Nitrate Sensitive Areas (NSA) Scheme introduced by MAFF information is provided on practical actions that farmers can take to reduce levels of nitrate leaching.

On grasslands specially created or managed for geese or other grazing wildfowl, fertilisers or manures can be used to create a nutritious lush grass sward. Such an area can be used to provide alternative feeding areas for geese so attracting them away from cereal crops but this should never be done on land which already has wildlife interest. Set-aside land may be particularly suitable (Feature 3.4: Wintering geese on farmland).

A variety of products can be used to lime grasslands including ground limestone, chalk, sea sands, basic slag and calcified seaweed. As their application also causes change in plant composition, they should never be applied on unimproved acid grasslands and only on other unimproved grasslands where there is a history of this, in which case do not exceed previous application rates and frequency. Basic slag also contains high phosphate levels which encourage clovers, other legumes and some vigorous weeds.

3.5 Grassland restoration

- Unimproved grassland which has been abandoned, overgrazed or planted can usually be restored.
- Reinstate a traditional grazing or mowing regime.
- Chain-harrow or burn first if necessary to bring the sward into condition, taking care not to cause further loss of wildlife value. Burn only in the legal season.
- If the herbage is very poor quality, use mineral blocks and/or hardy breeds of stock.
- Semi-improved and improved grass may also be restored. Withhold all nutrient applications initially.
- Clear planted or invading trees or self-sown scrub from the grassland where they reduce the wildlife value of the area.
- Rest overgrazed grassland for at least a year, and follow with low-intensity grazing or late-season cutting.
- Enhance the sward by seeding with appropriate plants if its variety has been badly depleted.

If a grassland has been long neglected, overgrazed, planted with trees or even improved and appears to have lost its plant diversity and associated wildlife, it will still be worth restoring. Some seeds may be present in the soil and will germinate once conditions are suitable. Even scarce invertebrates may remain if conditions have maintained structural diversity – for instance, if there are seasonally-flooded areas which result in bare ground or steep banks on which growth is affected by summer drought. Small surviving unimproved grassland remnants are often in such situations.

With neglected or abandoned areas of unimproved grassland, the restoration process applies the same principles set out for grazing and mowing and the aim should be to return to the traditional regime where possible. If it is considered necessary to improve the condition of the herbage before grazing commences, mowing can be undertaken; the cut material should be removed so that the litter does not prevent good regrowth.

Chain harrowing may also be used to remove excess dead plant material but avoid destroying ant hills.

As a last resort, the grassland could be burnt, provided that it is done in small blocks over a number of years so that the likelihood of extinction of invertebrate and damage to plants is lessened. Site and weather conditions can make burning a difficult technique. Follow the Heather and Grass Burning Codes and burn only in the season legally allowed. After burning, grazing should be introduced quickly as otherwise some of the less palatable grasses may become dominant.

On shallow calcareous soils, it may take about 3.5 sheep/ha/yr or 0.7 cattle/ha/yr for 2–3 years to bring long-neglected grassland into good condition. Stocking rates will need to be higher on more fertile soils or, more wisely, the duration of the restoration period could be increased.

Restore slowly, taking regular stock of progress and adjust as appropriate, rather than attempting to hurry the restoration and causing further damage through overgrazing or poaching.

Neglected pasture may comprise much coarse growth and be dominated by vigorous or unpalatable plants. Generally speaking, the hardy breeds of animals such as hill sheep, beef cattle and moorland or New Forest ponies are better able to tackle these conditions. However, mineral blocks can enable a wide range of breeds to digest rough herbage. Because they may 'scorch' vegetation and cause localised poaching, they should ideally be placed on a part of the land that has least wildlife value – often this will be near a gateway. Once the rank herbage has been removed the mineral blocks should also be removed if the stock do not require them.

Semi-improved grassland may still hold a reasonable variety of plants and it is worth considering reverting it, especially if it adjoins an unimproved area from which other plants and invertebrates may colonise. If the site has been fertilised with artificials, cease all nutrient applications, including the use of manure, to allow levels of soil nutrients to fall. This can be a very prolonged process but will be quickest in areas of high rainfall and on fields where a hay crop can be taken as this removes nutrients faster than grazing alone. Apply the guidelines for grazing or mowing unimproved grasslands.

Where unimproved or semi-improved grassland has been planted with trees or invaded by self-sown scrub, remove them, especially if the canopy is still open and there are areas of grassland remaining. Unimproved grassland is of much higher conservation value than new tree plantings. Where the grazings are large enough a small amount of scrub and trees can be acceptable.

Grassland which has been wholly improved may be managed to restore some plant richness and value for other wildlife.

For restoration following overgrazing, it may be necessary to remove stock entirely at first. On the least fertile pastures it may be several years before grazing can be reinstated without further damage. Initially, stocking rates should be very low, increasing them slowly once the vegetation has recovered. During the resting phase, obvious changes may take place in the sward as the more responsive plants recover first. Their dominance will be re-adjusted once grazing recommences.

If, at the end of the restoration grazing phase, the field proves to have a very limited range of plants, it may be possible to increase them by seeding or planting (see page 77).

3.6 Creation of grasslands for wildlife

- Incentives and advice are available for grassland creation for wildlife.
- Do not create wildlife grasslands on areas of existing wildlife interest.
- Where the choice exists, locate new grassland next to any remaining areas of unimproved grassland.
- Analyse soil to establish nutrient status and potential restoration options.
- Deplete nutrients, if necessary, by cropping or other methods.
- The easiest course where nutrient depletion is not required is to allow natural regeneration.
- If natural regeneration produces a sward with little plant variety, it may be enhanced by seeding or planting.
- Where natural regeneration is not appropriate, seed with grass/ wildflower mix or by using hay once nutrient levels are satisfactory.
- Ensure appropriate ground preparation, aftercare and long-term management for wildlife goals.

Incentives and advice are now available to revert arable land and improved ley grassland to permanent grassland to be managed for wildlife and landscape conservation. In all cases, sustained management by grazing or cutting will be required. The intensity will depend on growth rates.

New grasslands for wildlife will normally be created on fields with a high nutrient status and little or no seedbank of the original grassland plants. These created grasslands will have a different plant composition and structure from unimproved grasslands but with regular grazing or mowing can be of value to some invertebrates, small mammals and birds. Choose reversion sites adjacent to existing unimproved grasslands where possible, so as to increase the chances of colonisation. Do not create on land with existing wildlife interest, including tillage with rare arable weeds.

The type of grassland which can be created will depend on soil type and existing nutrient status, climate, drainage and the type of management which can be carried out. It is important to give thought at the outset to the potential of the site, to wildlife objectives and to long-term management. Unless all three aspects are considered together, it is likely that much effort and money will be wasted.

For butterflies and other invertebrates, a low-fertility herb-rich sward should be the aim, with grass not too dominant. It is important to choose plants which are fed on by the larvae of grassland butterflies (see Table 3.1) or are good sources of nectar. This will be easiest to achieve on fields with soils, such as free-draining calcareous or acid land, that do not retain high nutrient levels.

For small mammals and hunting barn owls and kestrels, a species-poor grass sward is suitable. This may be the only option on heavy soils with high residual phosphate levels. Either allow natural regeneration or sow a seed mixture containing tussocky grasses such as cocksfoot and Yorkshire fog together with a mixture of slower-growing meadow grasses.

For breeding birds the vegetation structure is of greater importance than its composition and, in the case of some waders, the wetness of the site is critical (see Feature 3.1). In winter, geese and other grazing wildfowl select enriched grasslands and prefer the finer grasses with hairless leaves (see Feature 3.4).

On arable or ley grassland there are several possible courses of action to establish a sward. Before deciding, carry out soil analysis for pH and phosphate in particular (available nitrogen is quickly lost from the soil and is relatively unimportant). Determine the desirable levels of nutrients and pH by sampling the soil conditions on nearby semi-natural grasslands on similar soil types.

The easiest course is to leave the land to regenerate naturally. Initially, the result will probably be a sward dominated by common grasses and weeds, which may be used by hunting kestrels and owls plus some common invertebrates. If the soil is light and

especially if it is also in a high rainfall area, natural nutrient depletion plus grazing or mowing will enable other plants to colonise in time. If they do not, the sward may be enhanced by planting or slot seeding. For slot seeding, herbicide is sprayed in bands across the ground without destroying the whole grass sward, and selected species of wildflower and grass drilled into slots cut into the sprayed growth.

On heavy soils natural nutrient depletion will be very slow. In this case, unless the goal is to manage for birds alone, crop or apply alternative ways of depleting residual nutrients (see page 119) before attempting to bring into normal grazing or mowing management or seeding.

If a sward rich in wild plants is desired, seeding may be necessary. On low-fertility land it may be possible to sow at once but where nutrient levels are high, cropping to deplete them is advisable or many of the plants will fail to survive.

If the field has a history of weed problems, it may be necessary to treat the field with a selective herbicide prior to seeding. This can either be done using a foliar spray or spot-treated using a weed wipe.

Harrow and roll the field after harvest or in the spring. A common fault with seedbeds is that they are often too loose or uneven. The seedbed should be both firm and fine to maximise germination. This may require harrowing and rolling several times but it is essential not to disturb the soil too much. Repeated disturbance will result in soil moisture being lost leading to poor germination of some species.

There are two possible methods of seeding. One is by spreading hay taken from a nearby field before it has shed its seed. Coverage should be very thin or germination will be prevented by the mat of grass. The alternative is to sow a mix suitable for the soil type. This may be purchased, or harvested from an unimproved grassland. Examples of plants for different soil types are in Table 3.4.

The seed mixture should contain only native species, the best approach being to

Table 3.4: The suitability of plant species for different soil types

PLANT	CALCAREOUS	CLAY	ALLUVIAL	DRY ACID
Grasses				
Cocksfoot		●	●	
Yorkshire fog		○	○	●
Common bent		●	●	●
Silver hair-grass				●
Meadow foxtail		●	●	
Sweet vernal grass		●	●	●
Meadow brome		●	●	
Upright brome	○			
Crested dog's-tail	●	●	●	
Wavy hair-grass				●
Sheep's fescue	●			●
Chewings fescue	●	●	●	●
Red fescue	●	●	●	●
Fine-leaved sheep's fescue				●
Meadow barley		●	●	
Timothy	●	●	●	
Smooth meadow-grass	●	●	●	
Rough-stalked meadow-grass		●	●	
Golden oat grass	●	●	●	
Wildflowers				
Yarrow	●	●	●	
Kidney vetch	●			
Common knapweed	○	○		
Greater knapweed	○			
Wild basil	●			
Pignut			●	●
Smooth hawk's-beard				●
Wild carrot	●	●	●	
Common storksbill				●
Meadowsweet		●	●	
Heath bedstraw				●
Lady's bedstraw	●	●	●	
Dove's-foot cranesbill				●
Meadow cranesbill		○		
Mouse-ear hawkweed	●			
Horseshoe vetch	●			
Common catsear		●	●	●
Field scabious	○	○		
Rough hawkbit	●	●		
Ox-eye daisy	●	●	●	
Bird's-foot-trefoil	○	○	○	
Ragged robin		●	●	
Musk mallow		●		
Black medick	●	●		
Sainfoin	○			
Restharrow	●	●		
Spiny restharrow	●	●		
Burnet saxifrage	●			
Ribwort plantain	●	●	●	
Hoary plantain	●	●		
Tormentil				●
Cowslip	●	●	●	
Self-heal	●	●	●	
Meadow buttercup		●	●	
Bulbous buttercup	●	●		
Yellow rattle	●	●	●	

▶▶▶

Table 3.4: The suitability of plant species for different soil types (cont'd)

PLANT	CALCAREOUS	CLAY	ALLUVIAL	DRY ACID
			SOIL TYPE	
Sorrel		•	•	•
Sheep's sorrel				•
Salad burnet	•	•		
Great burnet			•	
Meadow saxifrage		•		
Pepper saxifrage		•	•	
White campion	•	•	•	
Betony		•		
Lesser stitchwort			•	
Haresfoot clover				•
Hop trefoil	•	•		
Lesser trefoil	•	•		
Tufted vetch		•	•	
Common vetch	○	○	○	
Smooth tare	•	•	•	

• Suitable
○ May be too vigorous on fertile soil

Some grasses and wildflowers have a restricted geographical distribution.

Adapted from: Wells, T C E, Cox, R and Frost, A 1989 *The Establishment and Management of Wildflower Meadows*. Focus on Nature Conservation No 21. Nature Conservancy Council.

create a mixture that incorporates the plants growing on the nearest unimproved grassland on the same soil type. Grasses should make up 80% by weight of the mixture. Incorporate at least four and up to six different species, of which none should comprise more than 30% of the total of grasses, by weight. The remaining 20% of the total weight of the mixture should be herbs. Include about 20 different species in quantities of 0.5–2% each. Seeding rates will depend upon the soil type and local conditions. Typical sowing rates for grass and wildflower mixtures on different soils are:

Chalk and limestone   1.5–3 g/m^2
                      (15-30 kg/ha)
Alluvial   2–3 g/m^2
                      (20-30 kg/ha)
Clay   3–4 g/m^2
                      (30-40 kg/ha)

If vegetation cover is required quickly, an annual nurse crop can be used. This will germinate and then die back allowing wildflowers and grasses to replace it.

Westerwold's rye grass is widely used for this purpose sown at a rate of 0.5–1 g/m^2 or 5–10 kg/ha added to the total of perennial grasses and herbs. This must be cut before it sets seed to allow grasses and wildflowers to establish. Volunteer cereals and arable weeds will also act as a nurse crop.

Management in the first year is essential both to the establishment and final composition of the grassland. The priority is to control competition from annual and perennial weeds. Newly sown sites may show a flush of annual weed seedlings which can be killed by cutting or treated with a selective broadleaved herbicide. In subsequent years the growth of grasses and wildflowers will suppress any weeds.

At least one cut to a height of 10 cm will be needed in the first summer, depending on soil fertility and local conditions. On highly fertile soils it may be necessary to cut five or more times. The aim is to prevent the most vigorous plants from taking over before other plants have germinated and become established, and to promote tillering. The need to cut means that annuals should not be included in the initial planting. They may be added later on sites which are grazed or cut only late in the summer.

In the second and subsequent years management will depend upon the type of grassland required. Grass can be managed by grazing or mowing following the guidance given in the relevant sections. For wildlife, the worst sites are those sown with vigorous grasses and mown in summer with the mowings left to rot.

To create rough tussocky grassland for barn owls, grass should be cut once a year between September and March. This will stop scrub encroachment. To create a short, dense grass sward for overwintering geese, grass should be grazed or cut to a height of 5 cm by September.

To create a succession of flowers and nectar throughout the summer for butterflies, grass should be grazed. Alternatively, half should be cut each winter, turn and turn about, to provide short and tall swards for different species, ensure that there is flower production and leave good cover for hibernation.

4. References and further reading

Butterflies Under Threat Team 1986. *The Management of Chalk Grassland for Butterflies.* Focus on Nature Conservation 17. Nature Conservancy Council.

Duffey, E, Morris, M G, Sheil, J, Ward, L E, Wells, D A and Wells, T C E 1974. *Grassland Ecology and Wildlife Management.* Chapman and Hall.

Crofts, A and Jefferson, R G 1994. *The lowland grassland management handbook.* English Nature.

Hillier, S H, Walton, D W H and Wells, D A (eds) 1990. *Calcareous Grasslands – Ecology and Management.* Bluntisham Books.

Lane, A 1992. *Practical Conservation – Grasslands, Heaths and Moors.* Hodder and Stoughton.

Oates, M 1993. *The Management of Southern Limestone Grassland.* British Wildlife 5: 2: 73–82.

Putman, R J, Fowler, A D and Trant, S 1991. *Patterns of use of Ancient Grassland by Cattle and Horses and Effects on Vegetational Composition and Structure.* Biological Conservation 56: 329–347.

Rodwell, J S (ed) 1992. *British Plant Communities* Vol 3 *Grasslands and Montane Communities.* Cambridge University Press.

Smith, I R, Wells, D A and Welsh, P 1985. Botanical Survey and Monitoring Methods for Grassland. *Focus on Nature Conservation* No. 10. Nature Conservancy Council.

Smith, R S and Jones, L 1991. The Phenology of Mesotrophic Grassland in the Pennine Dales, N. England: Historic Hay Cutting Dates, Vegetation Variation and Plant Species Phenologies. *Journal of Applied Ecology* 28: 42–59.

Wells, T C E, Cox, R and Frost, A 1989. The Establishment and Management of Wildflower Meadows. *Focus on Nature Conservation* No. 21. Nature Conservancy Council.

Feature 3.1: Breeding Waders and Grassland

FACTOR	LAPWING	REDSHANK	SNIPE
Distribution and trends	Widespread throughout the UK on suitable habitat but marked declines in England and Wales.		
Nesting	Use spring tillage, dry pastures and heaths in addition to wet grassland.	Use wet meadows, saltmarsh with smaller numbers on lowland fens and moorland.	Use wet meadows and moorlands especially on peaty soils.
	Prefer to nest in larger fields in open situations with good all-round visibility.	Nest amongst grass or sedge tussocks which provide them with protection from predators.	Nest is well concealed in tall grass and tussocks.
	Pairs often nest in close proximity to one another to protect each other from predators.	Also nest colonially for protection against predators.	Damp or wet soil or peat is important for feeding.
Breeding period	Mid March – mid June	Early April – end June	April – mid August
Sward height	Short, less than 15 cm	Medium, 12–25 cm with taller growth for nesting (30 cm)	Medium 12–25 cm with taller growth for nesting (30 cm)
Soil watertable	High watertable not essential but where possible on peats maintain within 20 cm of surface.	High watertable not essential but where possible on peats maintain within 20 cm of surface.	High watertable essential. On peats keep within 20 cm of soil surface.
Feeding	Surface pecking from bare ground or short sward of soil invertebrates such as beetles, molluscs, earthworms.	Surface pecking and probing especially from shallow pools of small insects and crustaceans.	Probe soft ground with the long bill for range of invertebrates and seeds.
Grazing and livestock	Livestock can affect breeding success of all waders through trampling of eggs and chicks. See Figure 3.1* for the effect of different stocking rates.		

* See Chapter 9 for details of watertable and other hydrological management including wader scrapes.

Snipe

Feature 3.2: Grassland Structure and Butterflies

1. Flowering plants provide an essential source of nectar for many butterflies, giving them energy for flying, mating and egg-laying. Small coppers visit a wide variety of flowers especially members of the daisy family such as fleabane.

2. Butterflies use bare ground for basking to increase their body temperature. Wall browns cannot fly until their bodies reach 25–30 °C and bask with their wings angled towards the sun.

3. Grass tussocks create their own microclimate which protects butterflies from extremes of temperature and humidity. Large skippers require tussocks of cocksfoot 8–20 cm tall for egg laying and as food for the caterpillars.

Some butterflies have very precise habitat requirements. The larval food plant of the Adonis blue is the horseshoe vetch. The caterpillars live on closely grazed plants 0.5–2.5 cm tall and usually occur on south-facing slopes where the ground is sun baked. They are attended by ants which provide protection from predators, in return receiving a sweet honey-like substance from the caterpillars' skin.

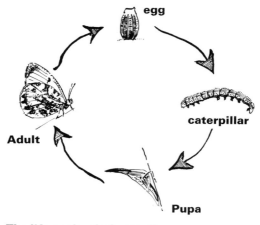

The life cycle of a butterfly.

Feature 3.3: Farming and the Barn Owl

Hunting ground
Barn owls hunt over rough pasture, hay meadows, unimproved grassland and grassy verges along field edges, woods, rivers, ditches and hedges. The barn owl's diet comprises mainly voles, shrews, mice, rats and birds, which are swallowed whole. Keep any suitable hunting grounds on the farm. Create new feeding areas by establishing rough grassland (see page 76).

Home ranges
The home range of a barn owl changes with the season and availability of food. In winter birds range up to 3-4 km from the roost site because prey is in short supply. During the breeding season ranges are

much smaller and most hunting takes place within 2 km of the nest. It is estimated that a breeding pair of barn owls requires around 1.5 ha of rough grass within a territory. This can be provided in the form of strips along streams, ditches, hedges or woods around the farm.

Risk of drowning
Barn owls are susceptible to drowning in water troughs which they use for drinking. To prevent this float a plank of wood or plastic or wire trellis in the trough. Birds that fall in will then be able to escape.

Nest and roost sites
Barn owls use traditional nesting and roosting sites on the farm. The breeding season lasts from March to September. Sites include holes in trees, farm outbuildings, straw/hay stacks and old barns. They will also use nestboxes. To provide nest sites for barn owls keep old barns and farm outbuildings. Leave old hollow trees particularly elms, oak and ash. If you construct a new farm building consider incorporating a nestbox and access hole for barn owls (see page 336).

A Code of Practice exists for the storage of animal feed in some grain stores. This may have implications for birds, including barn owls. It may be possible to allow birds to continue to use grain stores for nesting through the provision of internal attics and/or nestboxes. Seek advice from the Agriculture Department or through FWAG.

Risks from pesticides
Barn owls can die from pesticide poisoning if they eat contaminated prey. Of particular concern are the second-generation rodenticides including difenacoum, bromadiolone and broadifacoum. Where rodent infestation is a serious problem, pest control specialists should always be consulted. If rats are not resistant, farmers should use warfarin as this has a lower toxicity to barn owls.

Severe weather
Severe winters affect barn owls particularly when snow lies for many days. This makes hunting more difficult and leads to starvation.

Feature 3.4 : Wintering Geese on Farmland

Brent

Wild geese are winter visitors to the UK and some species occur in internationally important numbers. In addition feral greylag geese and Canada geese are present throughout the year.

The number of geese wintering in the UK is increasing and many now feed on winter wheat, barley, oilseed rape and rye-grass. The severity of damage will depend upon the crop type and the time of year. There are a number of measures which can be taken to reduce this conflict. Farmers may receive grant-aid payments for creating goose pasture.

ALTERNATIVE FEEDING AREAS

The most effective option for alleviating damage is to provide alternative feeding areas. Geese generally prefer a short grass sward, which may also be attractive to swans and wigeon.

Siting

These areas should be located on land without existing wildlife interest which has previously been used by geese for feeding and within 10 km of a known roost. As geese feed over a large area, liaise with neighbouring farmers or contact your local Agriculture Department office before deciding where to site fields.

Layout

Around 15 to 30 ha of alternative feeding area is required for every 1,000 geese. Use whole fields of 10 ha or more, not strips. Two or three parcels of land 10 ha each and 500 m apart are better than a single field of 30 ha as this allows geese to move between areas if disturbed.

Method

The following method is specific to brent geese but the general principles will be similar for other species.

- After harvest, prepare the ground for sowing by harrowing and rolling. Ensure the seedbed is firm. If necessary apply a herbicide such as glyphosate to control weeds (Note there are conditions on the use of herbicides under most grant schemes).

- Sow a mixture of perennial rye-grass, timothy, meadow fescue, red fescue and white (not red) clover. The mixture and sowing rate will normally be stated in the scheme regulations. A mix of rye-grass, timothy and clover in the ratio 5:1:1 sown at the rate of 30 kg/ha is ideal, with a small (5%) amount of fescue to provide a 'base' to the pasture.

- Graze or cut the sward to a height of 5 cm by the end of September. If cutting is used fields may require up to three cuts between June and September. Remove the cuttings if possible.

SCARING

Scaring geese is possible using a variety of methods including gas guns, flags, tapes, shooting and human disturbance. This will reduce the grazing pressure and can be used to scare geese to less sensitive areas. However, geese will get used to routine disturbance. Scaring therefore needs to be carefully targeted using different methods. Research in Norfolk has shown that frequent human disturbance is the best option. To be most effective scaring should be combined with alternative feeding areas.

SHOOTING

All geese are protected by law. Canada, greylag, pink-footed and white-fronted geese (England and Wales only) may be shot outside the close season. The close season is 1 February to 31 August on farmland or 21 February to 31 August below high-water mark. Shooting of these species in the close season and of other geese throughout the year requires a licence from an Agriculture Department. Licences are issued to supplement scaring and prevent serious damage to agricultural crops. They are not issued for population control. Agriculture Departments may seek information on the severity of damage and what other measures have been adopted before issuing a licence.

Case study: Grassland management (in mixed farming system with permanent pasture)

Farm details

Farm:	Manor Farm, Lincolnshire
Tenure:	Owner-occupied, plus some tenanted
Size:	105 ha plus 40 ha rented
Altitude:	5–65 m
Soil:	very variable Kimmeridge clays, Spilsby sandstones and loams
Crops:	winter wheat, winter barley, herbage seed, sugar beet, beans
Stock:	maximum 1,000 breeding ewes - prolific continental x's

The farm is set in rolling wold land with very profuse spring lines at the junction of the sandstones and clays. It was purchased in 1980 and had 13 ha of intensively grazed pasture and 24 ha of unmanaged alder carr woodland on the steepest land. The arable land had been under-drained in 1975, to the detriment of wildlife. The rented land is lowland grazing on ridge and furrow, originally wet grazing marsh but now dried out by extensive drainage including the old river bed. The owner has a very keen interest in the environment.

Farmer's aims

To integrate modern farming as a sustainable system (with reduced use of pesticides, etc where practical) with conservation and enhancement of wildlife habitats. Farm policy was to create wildlife zones which have conservation as their main aim. The rest of the land is to be farmed to its full agricultural potential (though still taking sustainability and the environment into account).

Background

Resources: Shooting interests justified expenditure on management work. Full use has been made of all forms of grant and environmental schemes, ie Landscape Improvement Grant, SSSI, Countryside Stewardship.
Constraints: Initially labour and finances were severely limited. There was no financial support in 1980 which limited the speed of progress.
Source of advice: Sought widely; including FWAG, local Trust. On a separate area of re-seeding, Institute of Terrestrial Ecology provided advice and a suitable drill.

Methods

In 1977 a professional survey found little wildlife interest on the farm. Work was then concentrated on the least productive and potentially most valuable areas, and was of two distinct types;
1) Grazed areas
a) on potentially important wildlife areas inputs such as fertiliser were stopped with spot treatment of injurious weeds only: fertilising continued on the remainder of the grazed land, and in some cases was increased to compensate for losses elsewhere.
b) the sward was carefully manipulated and stock excluded on selected areas from the end of April until mid or late July. Hay cutting in July or August was preferred but is not possible on the wet, steep, tussocky areas, which provided forage for breeding ewes at weaning time. Heavy stocking rates for a few weeks proved ideal to remove excess vegetation without damage, in particular to tussocks and anthills.
2) Hay cutting areas
This system was adopted on a selected area of old ridge and furrow with a good selection of wild grasses but low floristic interest. To reduce fertility in the first year two cuts of silage were taken, followed by hard sheep grazing to produce a very short sward. This was allowed to green up before chemically destroying strips for slot seeding with wildflowers. Drilling took place in the autumn to allow spring growth of flower seeds. During the first growing season, stock were excluded most of the time but large numbers were introduced

for short periods to reduce the competitiveness of the grass. Hay removal is normally in July with aftermath grazing during the autumn. As fertility has fallen, early spring grazing has been abandoned to allow the large numbers of cowslips to flower and seed.

Achievements

- Benefits to shooting. Integrated grazing system with reduced inputs.
- Re-creation of a rich hay meadow; all 22 species introduced now present and flowering; others have re-established. Spotted orchid, ragged robin and meadow saxifrage are the most notable successes.
- Many forms of wildlife have benefited, including plants, invertebrates, mammals and birds. Barn owls now breed and feed on or near the sites because of the increased mammal population; the wetter areas attract snipe and green woodpecker.

Future management

This will continue as before but on a much more extended basis using Countryside Stewardship to extend and buffer the most important areas. Snipe, almost lost as a breeding bird in Lincolnshire, are being encouraged by the creation of scrapes, bunding of watercourses and blocking of some drains to raise the watertable.

On some of the let land with the ridge and furrow, the rich hay meadow will be continued and possibly extended. Co-operation with the Internal Drainage Board, NRA and the Countryside Commission will allow entry into Stewardship. The old river bed and flood will be reinstated to re-create wet grazing marshes for breeding snipe with a scrape and kingfisher cliff. When attempting this type of project injurious weeds such as creeping thistle should be completely eradicated before introducing flower species. Spot treatment is now an easy annual task. A new and more advanced weedwiper has been introduced for thistles and docks, which will allow control without so much hand-work. Work will be done before weed species flower.

C H Gomersall, RSPB

E A Janes

3.1 Increased grass production has been achieved by use of fast-growing and nutritious species supported by annual inputs of artificial fertilisers. The resulting sward contains few wild plants and is unsuitable for most other wildlife. Earlier cutting dates and the speed of operation of harvesting machinery tend to lead to deaths of meadow-nesting birds.

3.2 Unimproved grasslands hold a wide range of wild grasses and herbs, in turn supporting many invertebrates, birds and mammals. Management to achieve a sustained yield with minimal inputs – the traditional skill of the livestock farmer – remains the best approach for wildlife.

David Woodfall

John Andrews

3.3 In unimproved pastures, grazing has important effects on sward structure and composition. Low-growing plants thrive. Dung itself supports a varied invertebrate fauna. Breeding birds may include lapwing and skylark. Different livestock types have different grazing habits and so tend to produce different sward structures and alter the relative abundance of different plants.

3.4 Variation in sward height and composition also result from changes of slope, the location of stock paths and the aspect of the ground. Here, bare ground will be used for basking by butterflies and egg-laying by grasshoppers. Taller growth includes a variety of food plants, and occasional tussocks offer good conditions for invertebrate hibernation.

John Andrews

R Glover

3.5 One effect of grazing is to remove flower heads. Many plants in pastures are long-lived and need to set seed only infrequently. Others spread by rhizomes or runners. However, the loss of flower production under heavy grazing affects insects by removing the vital source of pollen and nectar.

3.6 Grazing intensity affects wildlife richness. There is a fine balance between creating good variation in sward structure and overgrazing or undergrazing, both of which result in losses of wildlife. The use of horses and ponies to graze unimproved pastures requires particular care because they tend to graze preferred areas too short and to dung in 'latrine areas' which become over-enriched and rank. This can result in the loss of most of the typical herbs of pastures and the insects which depend on them.

John Andrews

Richard Revels, RSPB

3.7 On saltmarsh, like other pastures the aim for wildlife is to achieve variations in sward height and composition. Short turf serves as feeding areas for wigeon and geese whereas taller vegetation is used as nesting cover by wildfowl and waders, such as redshank, as well as habitat for specialised invertebrates including rare species.

3.8 Butterflies depend on particular plants for food in the larval stage and many species also need suitable nectar plants. Even the location of the plant can be important – sunny, sheltered sites are usually preferred. The chalkhill blue's food plant is horseshoe vetch which thrives only in pastures on chalk soils.

John Andrews

3.9 Ants play important roles in the ecology of pastures. For instance, some butterflies pupate only in ants' nests and depend on ants to guard them when they first emerge as adults. Ants' nests are a good indicator of unimproved pasture. Where grazing is abandoned and vegetation grows tall so that the nests are shaded, the ant colonies die out.

C H Gomersall, RSPB

3.10 Meadows are poor habitat for the low-growing plants which require open, unshaded conditions but favour taller species that are intolerant of intensive grazing or trampling. As plants flower freely, meadows are often very rich sources of nectar for bees and other insects though, partly because cutting makes a sudden and catastrophic change in the conditions, they tend to support fewer invertebrate species than do pastures.

David Woodfall

3.11 For a brief period, abandoned grassland flowers prolifically and appears to be very rich in plants and other wildlife. However, low-growing plants are soon shaded out, the scrub invasion follows and the area rapidly reverts to woodland with a consequent loss of its specialised wildlife.

David Woodfall

3.12 The timing of mowing affects wildlife. Traditionally, outlying fields were cut last, and often received little if any manuring. They tend to hold plant species that flower and set seed later than fields regularly cut earlier. Timing also affects nesting birds.

C H Gomersall, RSPB

3.13 **Barn owls find good hunting over unimproved meadows because they hold large populations of short-tailed voles. Where suitable feeding habitat has been lost, it may be possible to restore it as permanent grass strips at field margins or on set-aside.**

Hawk-eye Photo Library

3.14 **Natural regeneration of set-aside may produce a sward with a fair variety of grasses and herbs, providing habitat for a rich variety of wildlife. The timing of management is important – in particular avoid cutting before early July in the south or August in the north so that birds can breed and plants can set seed.**

4. Lowland Heaths

1. Factors influencing wildlife

1.1 Farming and lowland heaths

- Lowland heaths have a long history of farming management and other uses.
- Burning was employed to improve forage for stock.
- The combined effects of grazing and other activities created a complex mosaic rich in wildlife.
- Most heaths are now not grazed and this has led to much loss of wildlife. Restoration of grazing management is likely to be of great value.
- Lowland heaths are also now much reduced and fragmented but even small heaths can still hold very rare species.
- Heathland re-creation from land converted to improved grass or arable is well worthwhile.

Though heaths often look natural, all were once in farming management and in most places this has lapsed only in the last 40 or 50 years. Today, the grazing of the New Forest by cattle and ponies is a good example of the low input and low output system which was once the traditional way of using heathland. The land is infertile, with sandy, free-draining soils which do not retain nutrients, patches of bog and the occasional grassy lawn. Livestock must forage amongst a variety of wild plants some of which have only a brief season of palatability. Decisions on stocking rates have to be very carefully judged. If the land is overstocked, animals lose condition quickly and, once overgrazed, the forage can take several years to recover.

Despite this, farmers made good use of heaths. In some areas, local pony breeds grazed the mix of heathers, grasses and gorse, and browsed from trees. In others, hill livestock such as Welsh black cattle were brought in each year to fatten over the summer or from one autumn to the next. The East Anglian heaths were managed for sheep and rabbits. The Breckland grass-heaths of East Anglia were also cultivated, not on a regular basis but with very long periods of fallowing and grazing between each attempt to produce a crop.

Some heaths were first cleared of their original tree cover in the Neolithic period, about 6,000 years ago, some in the Bronze Age around 2,500 years ago, whereas others such as parts of Ashdown Forest and Cannock Chase were cleared much later, in the 15th and 16th centuries. Thus, many heaths have had a very long history of farming even if they are not currently farmed.

As well as being grazed, heaths provided bracken for livestock bedding; heathers for thatch, road foundations and drains; turfs and peat for fuel and gorse for winter fodder. In addition, there were many small sand or gravel pits. Occasionally, heaths were deliberately burned to improve grazing by encouraging new growth of grasses and heather. These combined effects resulted in a complicated mosaic of vegetation sustaining a unique mix of wildlife including rare species such as the Dartford warbler and the smooth snake, which are found in no other habitat in the UK.

Many heaths were once much larger so that even if conditions for their dependent wildlife became unsuitable in one area – as a result of burning for example – it was always likely that suitable conditions would still exist elsewhere on the heath (Figure 4.1: Major lowland heaths in south England). Thus extinction from an area was unlikely. Since the mid-18th century, the extent of heathland has been greatly reduced and, as individual sites have become smaller and been isolated from each other by afforestation, farmland or urban development, many of the less mobile or sedentary species, like the silver-studded blue butterfly, have become locally extinct (Figure 4.2: Loss of lowland heath in Surrey). Even so, small heaths may still hold very rare species.

Conservation of the wildlife of heaths is of great importance because of the scale of loss and neglect. It may be best achieved by

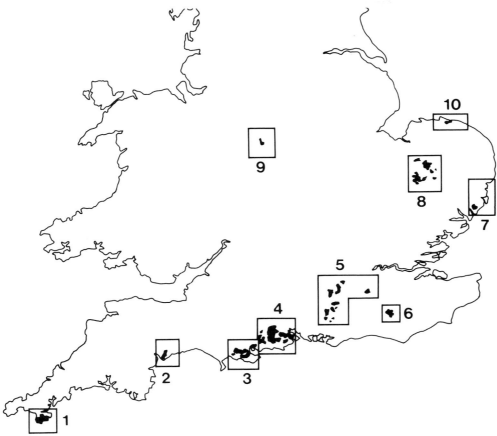

Figure 4.1
Major lowland heaths in South England

1. **Lizard Heaths.** Serpentine heaths with unusual plant communities known collectively as the Lizard rarities, eg Cornish heath.
2. **Devon Pebblebeds.** Varied heathlands; wet heath more species rich. Calcium-rich flushes.
3. **Dorset Heaths.** Important transitional areas between the oceanic heaths of the south-west and the continental heaths of eastern England.
4. **New Forest.** Still used as common grazing for cattle and ponies. Largest tract of lowland heath in UK.
5. **North Hants/Surrey Heaths.** Contains the only remaining natural inland heath population of natterjack toad, which occurs elsewhere but is introduced.
6. **Ashdown Forest.** Largest tract in South-east England — like New Forest managed by common rights.
7. **Suffolk Sandlings.** Supports population of western gorse, usually found more in the west.

8. **Breckland.** Grass heath, formerly extensively rabbit-grazed. Holds breeding stone-curlew. Least maritime heaths with low rainfall and more continental climate.
9. **Cannock Chase.** Transitional between lowland and upland heath, with corresponding plant species and communities, including bilberry and crowberry.
10. **North Norfolk Heaths.**

There are many small remnants of heath on sandy soils in other parts of England. In some counties no heath now remains but there is potential to recreate acid grassland or heathland.
The figure does not include those areas of heath vegetation with a moorland character. There are also important areas of maritime heath found along the coast in SW England and Wales.

taking them back into low-intensity grazing management. There may also be opportunities to restore heaths which have been converted to improved grass or arable and this is particularly worthwhile where it extends small sites or links two isolated areas.

Note: The following terms used regularly in this chapter are defined to avoid confusion:

Heath(s) – the habitat, sometimes called heathland.

Heather – the plant also called ling *Calluna vulgaris*.

Heathers– the group of plants that includes ling, but also for example bell heather and cross-leaved heath.

1.2 Plant composition

- Heaths are usually dominated by a small number of plants – heathers, grasses or bracken.
- They may also support a number of rare plants which require open, unshaded conditions.
- Many heathland insects depend on particular plants for food. This makes some kinds of vegetation important as feeding habitat for birds and other wildlife.
- Heaths dominated by grass and those dominated by heather have a different wildlife interest.
- Bracken suppresses other vegetation and is generally poor for most wildlife.
- Trees are valuable in small numbers but too many lead to a loss of heathland wildlife. Rhododendron and other non-native shrubs are harmful.

The vegetation on heaths is normally dominated by no more than a handful of different plant species – heathers, grasses or bracken. Several different kinds of heather grow on heaths. The commonest is ling, also confusingly called 'heather'. Bell heather and cross-leaved heath are also widespread, the former on dry ground and the latter in wetter areas. All three are important as cover and food for many heathland invertebrates plus several reptiles and birds. Cornish heath and Dorset heath have a more restricted distribution but are also important locally. Ling is sometimes subject to attack by the heather beetle which can cause large areas to die.

Grasses are present on all heaths and are dominant on some and can form areas of acidic grassland. Bracken is a common heathland plant which is little eaten by stock and can also come to dominate large areas. Differences in the relative abundance of these plants on any one heath may be the result of past management but sometimes reflects the level of nutrients present in the soil or local climatic conditions.

Some of these plants also occur on moorland in the uplands but there are rare,

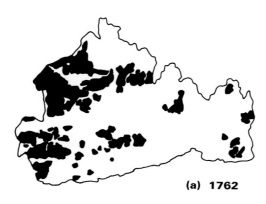

(a) 1762

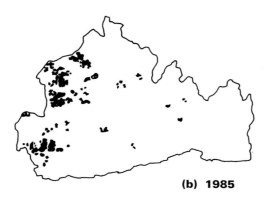

(b) 1985

Figure 4.2
Loss of lowland heath in Surrey.

(Source: Nature Conservancy Council and Surrey County Council 1988 *A strategy for Surrey Heathland*.)

specialised plants which grow only in the lowland habitat. Most importantly, lowland and upland heaths support largely different groups of animals. In particular, lowland heaths tend to hold species which require summer warmth and low rainfall such as the kinds of solitary bees and wasps that excavate nest tunnels in the sandy soils, and two rare reptiles, smooth snake and sand lizard (Feature 4.1: Invertebrates of lowland heath; Feature 4.4: Reptiles of lowland heath). Where drainage is impeded, areas of peatland can develop and these too support rare plants, such as marsh gentian.

Many of the animals that live on heaths require particular kinds of vegetation. Over 50 kinds of insects live on gorse and 35 on broom – some sucking the sap, others mining in twigs, eating foliage or taking pollen or nectar from its flowers. In turn these insects support many specialist parasitic insects and predators including spiders. Dartford warblers and other insectivorous birds find gorse a valuable feeding habitat (Feature 4.2: The wildlife of gorse). Gorse is also nutritious for stock and is browsed by ponies.

Several other native shrubs including bilberry, dwarf and western gorse and bog myrtle grow on heaths and have considerable wildlife value but are unlikely to need management.

Where bracken is dominant, it shades and out-competes other vegetation and produces a dense litter layer. Invertebrates dependent on bare ground are lost. Its dense structure does support some insects and spiders but these are common species. However, whinchats, which require tall herbage in their breeding territories, often select areas containing some open bracken growth.

Heaths are gradually invaded by trees if they are not grazed and trampled by livestock or regularly cut or burned. The main colonists are birch and pine, both of which have airborne seeds which can come from far afield. Dense stands shade out heathland vegetation and reduce the temperature at ground level, so making it unsuitable for basking and hunting by

invertebrates and reptiles. Though the trees support their own wildlife, for most part the species concerned are common so that restoration of heathland is always the higher priority. However, small numbers of trees can be an asset on heathlands. Some heathland species make use of them. For instance, nightjars are most numerous along the edge of heathland where it grades into woodland and young birch can be an important foraging habitat for them (Feature 4.3: Nightjars on heaths).

Rhododendron is now present on many heaths. It is non-native, invasive, suppresses other vegetation and supports very few invertebrates. It should be completely removed from heaths. Shallon is a low-growing, non-native shrub, originally planted as pheasant cover, which has now invaded some heaths. It too should be eradicated if possible.

1.3 Heathland structure

- Vegetation structure is important. Different species of wildlife including birds and reptiles require different structures.
- The wildlife value of heather changes with its age and structure. Mature and old heather is important for reptiles and some birds.
- Bare, sandy soil is important for invertebrates and rare reptiles.
- There can be several different types of wetlands on heaths, each with different wildlife and often including nationally rare species.

The structure of heathland vegetation is of great importance. Different species have different requirements and some may need a combination of conditions. For instance, Dartford warblers require continuous cover of dense heather and gorse for feeding and nesting whereas woodlarks feed on very short, tightly grazed or newly burnt areas adjacent to taller cover of grass or heather in which they nest. Sand lizards hunt in mature and old heather but need sunlit soft sand for egg-laying (Feature 4.4). By contrast, natterjack toads need short vegetation and shallow, sunlit ponds for breeding.

The survival of a number of uncommon plants also depends on the correct vegetation structure. For example, in East Anglia, lichens and several rare plants such as spiked speedwell thrive on dry heaths where heathers and grasses are kept short and the ground is disturbed by rabbits or by the trampling of livestock.

As they are long-lived, the structure of heather plants themselves is an important factor for wildlife. Heather undergoes changes in the pattern of its growth with increasing age (Figure 5.1: Heather growth phases and effects of grazing). As climate and soil affect the growth forms, the lengths of the phases given here are approximate. In the pioneer phase (3–6 years, max 10 years), there may be extensive areas of bare ground where invertebrates such as tiger beetles which require open conditions can hunt. As the building phase proceeds, these open areas are lost and a continuous cover develops. After 20–25 years, the heather is mature and provides cover and foraging habitat for wrens, warblers and other birds as well as reptiles. Up to this point, the life of heather can be increased by appropriate management including grazing. From about 25 years, heather begins to degenerate and the bushes open up, enabling lichens to colonise and other plants to germinate. The plants are then easily destroyed by heavy grazing, trampling or fire but with care can stay alive to 40-50 years. The open ground may then be colonised by new heather growth from seedlings. Alternatively, the heather may be replaced by grasses, bracken or trees; this has profound effects on the wildlife and may result in the loss of characteristic heathland species. For a diverse wildlife, it is important to have all stages of heather growth present on a heath at all times if possible.

Bare ground is required by many insects that are able to survive only where they can bask in the very high air temperatures existing within an inch of the surface of sun-warmed soil. Sandy soils become warm, drain freely and are ideal for many kinds of solitary bees and wasps, which burrow easily into the ground surface. Bare ground on clays and loams is much less suitable for these species.

Low-lying areas of heath where drainage is impeded support plants and animals which do not occur on the free-draining dry heath. Whereas most wetlands in lowland Britain receive quite high inputs of nutrients from the surrounding land, those on heaths usually have a low nutrient status and are relatively acid. Some plants such as marsh clubmoss and animals including several rare dragonflies can survive only in these conditions.

Increasing soil wetness leads to heather and grasses such as bristle bent or sheep's fescue being replaced by cross-leaved heath and purple moor-grass. Where grazing and trampling prevent these from becoming too dominant, scarce plants such as marsh gentian occur, particularly around the margins of pools.

Mires develop in shallow water through the accumulation of Sphagnum mosses and other plants as peat. Where peat was cut by hand for use as domestic fuel, this maintained patches of open water and regularly exposed bare, unvegetated peat for colonisation by the specialised plants that require these conditions, including the insectivorous sundews and butterwort, which make up the nitrogen deficiency by capturing insects on their sticky leaves.

Heathland pools, runnels and watercourses are extremely important for dragonflies, some of which have very precise habitat requirements. For instance, the nationally rare small red damselfly breeds in tiny, shallow and unshaded runnels, whereas the black darter and the keeled skimmer require pools with Sphagnum mosses, and the keeled skimmer will often use heaths where very little open water remains.

Livestock often concentrate where a heath is crossed by a stream or river because better forage may be available, especially if the watertable is near the surface or the area is regularly flooded in winter. The result will be a short sward containing a wide variety of plants. Some, such as small fleabane, are only found where livestock poach damp ground and are now very rare because of the efficiency of modern pasture drainage and management. If these areas hold short-lived pools in hollows after flooding or heavy rain this is an added benefit for wildlife. Such pools attract wildfowl and waders and may support the extremely rare fairy shrimp, which depends on temporary shallows.

1.4 Grazing

- Grazing is a traditional use of heaths and the best for wildlife as it can create a mosaic of vegetation structures and bare ground.
- Different types of livestock have different effects on the plant composition and structure.
- Sheep are more selective and concentrate mainly on grasses and, in winter, heather.
- Cattle eat a wider range of plants, including more coarse grasses.
- Ponies take most gorse, foliage and twigs, and less heather.
- Changes in stock type or grazing intensity can bring about major changes in the dominant plants and their dependent wildlife.
- Trampling can create important open ground conditions but can also damage old heather stands.
- Rabbits were once an important factor in creating and maintaining heaths, especially in East Anglia.

Heaths were traditionally used for grazing, which has profound effects on the composition and the structure of the vegetation and thus on all the heathland wildlife. Different livestock have varying effects on the heath, because of differences in food preferences, grazing methods, trampling pressures and dunging habits. Food preferences also vary with livestock breed and are influenced by the animals' experience and by what is available (Table 4.1: Grazing preferences and effects of livestock).

In general all stock graze grasses through the growing season where they are available. On the damper areas where purple moor-grass grows, it will be taken early in season before it becomes coarse and unpalatable. This prevents it becoming dominant and so allows many other plants to flourish. Heather is a much less important source of food and is mainly taken in winter

when grass is not growing. Ponies make less use of it than other stock – perhaps less than 10% of their diet as against 20% for cattle – but both may destroy old and woody heather plants by trampling. Sheep may make most use of heather in winter and only they will eat cross-leaved heath; bell heather is avoided by all three.

Ponies and cattle feed on a much wider range of plants than sheep, taking coarser grasses, older heather and rushes and sedges as well as more palatable grasses and younger heathers. Ponies will make considerable use of tree and shrub foliage and in winter also take gorse and poor-quality food such as twigs and mosses. Cattle and sheep also browse broadleaved scrub and, for example, eat regrowth from the stumps of newly cut birch trees. However, the degree to which they do so will depend on the size and abundance of trees and scrub, the availability of alternative food, and stocking levels.

Ponies and cattle tend to establish home ranges in which they feed. By regularly concentrating on the most productive areas, such as damper ground, they themselves enrich the soil with their dung and may create lawns of fine grasses in which many low-growing plants can flourish. Often these areas are also used for feeding by birds such as pipits, wagtails and woodlarks. Away from the lawns, grazing and trampling create a mosaic of taller and shorter cover plus small patches of bare ground, a combination that is ideal for many invertebrates.

Because they have different preferences and feeding strategies, any changes in the type of stock, the numbers present or the length of the grazing season can bring about changes in the vegetation.

Rabbits have been an important influence on heaths especially in the Breckland area of East Anglia. In some areas, numbers are again so high as to make grazing by other livestock unnecessary or even impracticable. Rabbit grazing can be beneficial, diversifying vegetation structure and modifying its composition, creating areas of bare ground suitable for lichens, annual plants and many invertebrates. At high densities they can maintain large areas

Table 4.1: Grazing preferences and effects of livestock			
PREFERENCES/EFFECTS	CATTLE	SHEEP	HORSES/PONIES
Forage a wider range of plants, including coarse vegetation (including purple moor-grass, older heather, rushes)	√	×	√
Feeders on finer leaved grasses and young heather	√	√	√
Graze heather, mainly in winter	√	√	√
Graze cross-leaved heath	×	√	×
Graze bell heather	×	×	×
Browse gorse, esp in winter	×	×	√
Browse broadleaved scrub/regrowth	√	√	√
Suitability for grazing wet heaths	√	×	√
Can do most trampling damage to old heather	√	×	√

Information is particularly relevant to hardy breeds. Increased stocking levels can 'force' livestock to forage vegetation not normally taken or preferred. For more information on effects of stocking densities and seasonal differences see text.

of short growth ideal for stone-curlew, wheatear and some scarce plants such as spiked speedwell. However, they also consume young heather and gorse seedlings, encourage invasion by weeds and the growth of grasses at the expense of heather. They can become a pest on adjoining farmland.

1.5 Fire

- Fire was used when necessary to maintain or restore the condition of forage.
- Fire kills sedentary species such as reptiles and if undertaken on a large scale can destroy a varied vegetation structure.
- Regular burning can eliminate certain plants particularly mosses and lichens and damage wet heaths and bogs.

In the past, burning was used as a means of maintaining good-quality forage for livestock, to remove coarse material and encourage new growth by grasses or regeneration of mature heather. However,

all heath fires can cause great damage. Most of the rarest heathland animals, including reptiles, spiders and many insects, are slow-moving or sedentary and fire will kill them. Although they may survive on adjoining unburnt areas, recolonisation of the burnt heath may take years. On a small, isolated heath, it is possible that a fire will entirely wipe out colonies of some sedentary species, which will never recover.

If undertaken on a large scale, burning creates stands of even-aged vegetation rather than the structural variation important to many heathland birds, reptiles and invertebrates. It can also bring about dramatic changes in the character of the vegetation, particularly if the fire temperature is too high, with bracken or wavy hair-grass replacing heathers. Regular burning can also destroy mosses, liverworts and lichens, and cause permanent damage to wet heaths and peats. The newly-exposed ground provides a perfect seed bed for invasion by nearby birch or pine, as well as heather. Finally, unless great care is taken with firebreaks and other safety measures, even controlled burning for management purposes can get out of hand and cause extensive loss of vegetation and wildlife.

This is most likely if large areas of old heather or gorse cover the heath.

2. Options and assessment: planning management

2.1 Wildlife assessment of lowland heaths

- Take stock of the condition of the heath whether currently managed or not.
- Assess wildlife value and potential for grazing or other management on the basis of amounts and condition of heather and grass.
- Map areas of invasive vegetation which may need control, such as trees and bracken.
- Map important features such as wetland areas and, where information on scarce species is available, include it in the assessment.

Because of the scarcity of the habitat and much of its wildlife, it is worth taking stock of the condition of any heath, whether it is still in traditional grazing management or has been unmanaged for some time. The basic purposes of the assessment are to allow decisions to be made on three main points. First, any need to tackle invasive vegetation such as tree cover or bracken which result in the loss of heathland wildlife. Second, the livestock numbers or other management required to bring the heath into good condition both as rough grazing and as a wildlife habitat. Third, any areas which need special treatment because they contain rare species.

A key part of the assessment is to map information on the abundance and condition of heather and grasses and on trees, scrub and bracken. This can be done at any time of year. As section 1 explains, many heathland invertebrates, reptiles and birds require a mix of conditions, such as old heather close to areas of bare ground. The mapping of vegetation and features will make it easier to identify such areas.

It is not always necessary to survey specifically for rare species but, as even small heaths may support rarities, information on their presence should be sought from the conservation organisations. Chapter 1 gives guidance on the types of information which may be available and explains the background to assessment. Table 4.2: Wildlife assessment of lowland heaths, gives more specific guidance.

Ideally, this assessment should form part of a farm wildlife plan. The method of preparing a plan is given on page 10.

If grant aid is being sought, approach the funding organisation to discuss the degree of information required to support an application before undertaking the survey.

Where consideration is being given to the re-creation of heathland on arable or improved grass, thought should be given to soil type, residual nutrient status, context, existing wildlife interest and other factors. These are discussed on page 119.

2.2 Management needs and opportunities

- Reinstatement of a grazing regime is ideal and incentives to do so may be available.
- Where grazing is impracticable, cutting and controlled burning are alternatives.
- Measures to prevent uncontrolled fires are very important.
- Management should aim to prevent losses of heathland through invasion by trees, scrub and bracken and to restore areas wherever possible.
- Funding may be available for the management and restoration of existing heaths and for re-creation of heathland on arable land.

Table 4.2: Wildlife assessment of lowland heathlands

INFORMATION REQUIRED	METHOD	REASON FOR INFORMATION
1. Conservation status and interest	Contact FWAG initially.	It may be able to provide some of the information required to assess the wildlife interest. Most lowland heaths are Sites of Special Scientific Interest (SSSI) and certain conditions may need to be satisfied before any changes of management can take place.
2. Past management	Check farm records. Contact previous owners. Examine past and present aerial photographs and maps.	To identify management practices now lapsed. To identify trends in changes to heath, eg increase in tree cover. To guide future plans, eg reinstatement of grazing regime.
3. Current management	Note current grazing practice including stock/breed type, stocking levels, grazing seasons and use of supplementary feeding, mineral blocks. Also note vegetation response. Note signs of heavy grazing by rabbits.	Evaluation of grazing regime and impact on wildlife. May suggest modifications required.
	Map mown areas, and note site and shape of area, type of cutting equipment used, time of year cut, frequency of cut, whether mowings removed. Also note vegetation response.	Evaluation of mowing practice and impact on wildlife. May suggest modifications required.
	Map all burnt areas (planned or otherwise) and note size/shape of burn, location of firebreaks and frequency of burns. Also note vegetation response.	Evaluation of burning practice and impact and control of unplanned fires. May suggest modification required.
4. Heath and grass structure	Map relative abundance of heather and grass in following categories: >75% heather <25% grass c50% heather c50% grass <25% heather >75% grass	Primarily to assess availability of forage for stock. Management decisions to change relative abundances will need to take into account reasons for current composition, eg past and current management, nutrient enrichment, effects immediately following a burn.
	Note general heather condition and map extensive areas in the following categories (see page 141 for fuller details): Pioneer Building Mature Degenerate Dead Also note 'rankness' of grass.	To assess availability of forage for stock. If grass is rank will suggest management may be needed. To assess variety and juxtaposition of heather structures and consequent management needs. To identify areas of old heather, which may require particular care in management.

▶▶▶

Table 4.2: Wildlife assessment of lowland heathlands (cont'd)

INFORMATION REQUIRED	METHOD	REASON FOR INFORMATION
5. Trees, scrub and bracken	Map areas of trees and scrub (by species) and bracken, in the following categories: Sparse and scattered <10% cover Abundant (but with plenty of heather below). Solid, closed canopy >75% cover (with little or no heather below).	To identify need for control and removal of these vegetation types. To identify priority areas for removal.
	Also note whether trees and scrub are old and mature, or are young/saplings.	To identify individuals or stands to retain, eg areas of gorse, individual trees.
6. Wetlands on heath	Record distribution and type – Wet heath Pools Streams Mires	To identify these very important features of heathlands which should be maintained and not degraded by pollution, water abstraction. Good-quality wet heath is richer in plant species than dry heath. If dominated by rank purple moor-grass, increased grazing may be needed.
	Record: Source of water Vegetation condition Degree of poaching by stock	Stock use and possible damage to these areas needs to be monitored.
	Whether pools are overgrown or overshaded.	To identify potential for enhancement, eg clearing some overshading trees.
7. Boundaries and access onto heath	Note: Location and condition of fences, hedges.	To identify necessary work to make stockproof if to be grazed.
	Land use surrounding the heath	To look at impact of surrounding land such as effect of plantations seeding onto heaths, effect of fertilisers and sprays and potential to extend heath by arable reversion.
	Routes of rights of way	Effect of public access on wildlife and management, eg increased fire risk and public reaction to tree cover.
	Access onto heath for vehicles	Provision of vehicular access for management and fire control.
8. Other ground features	Record location use and condition of other significant areas, eg bare ground, old quarries, earthbanks.	To identify features which bring diversity to heathlands, which should be maintained and enhanced. Bare ground can be caused through over-grazing and fire. Small areas are acceptable and valuable for wildlife.
9. Rare or sensitive species	Where known record exact location of rare species present. Note heathland structure in immediate vicinity. Seek specialist guidance.	Heathlands can support a number of rare and sensitive species, such as smooth snake, sand lizard, woodlark and the silver-studded blue butterfly. They are often found in discrete areas of the heath and can easily be lost, eg through fire, and may require special management.

While there are still a few large heaths, most areas are small and isolated. Very few are actively used as part of a farm or common grazing. Where traditional management has been sustained, the best course will be to continue it, modifying any details which will improve the wildlife value of the heath. However, in most cases there has been little or no management for the last 50 years. As a result, there are now four main threats to wildlife – invasion by trees and shrubs, spread of bracken, uncontrolled fire and lack of structure.

As heaths are no longer part of the farm enterprise, it may be difficult to reinstate management without either changes in the farm system or additional incentives. In many cases livestock will not be available, though it may be possible to let the grazing as there is a demand in some areas. Grazing on heaths presents problems. Although some breeds are very efficient at using the mix of vegetation, they do not put on weight as quickly as on improved pastures and those that are unfamiliar with the conditions will 'go back' initially. The introduction of grazing will need attention to fences and can conflict with established, unofficial use by the public. However, grazing is the optimum management for wildlife, and the sooner it starts, the better. Where grazing proves to be impracticable, heaths may be managed by cutting and controlled, small-scale burning.

When positive management is to be recommended, several things need to be taken into account and work on them may be handled in sequence or at the same time, depending on the available resources and the condition of the site.

If the heath still holds heather, take stock of its condition and age. If any is now past the period of vigorous growth, rejuvenate it gradually over a number of years through mowing or burning. This will ensure its continued growth, minimise the risk of attack by heather beetle, which may kill it, and improve its ability to support livestock. Gradually increase livestock numbers as the heather regrows, or maintain a regular cutting regime. Remember that old heather is a valuable

habitat for birds such as nightjar and Dartford warbler and some reptiles. It is desirable to retain enough for these species where they are present. Aim to have at least 10% of the heath with old heather, ideally in several stands.

If heather is sparse or no longer present, special measures may be needed to encourage its recovery. However, there is no 'right' plant composition for a heath. Some are grass-dominated, others predominantly heather. Where a mix of vegetation develops there will be a good range of food resources for both wildlife and livestock. A few stands of gorse and a scattering of mature trees can add to a heath's value.

One aim must be to prevent losses of heathland vegetation through encroachment by trees, rhododendron or bracken (Figure 4.3: Priorities for heathland restoration). This will require clearance by cutting, chemical treatment or intensive grazing, singly or in combination. The method will depend on the condition of the site and the presence of scarce wildlife. It is particularly urgent to halt invasion on small, isolated sites.

Uncontrolled or accidental fire can be catastrophic on small heaths. Creation of firebreaks by forage harvesting or rotovating is a high priority especially if the site adjoins public roads or footpaths.

Because of the national rarity of the habitat and the remarkable variety of rare species which may occur on any heath, big or small, management should be planned with exceptional care (Figure 4.4: Lowland Heath Management Calendar). There may be apparent conflicts between the needs of different species but on a well-managed site it should be possible to provide suitable conditions for a wide range of heathland wildlife.

It is particularly valuable to restore heathland vegetation on areas of arable or improved grassland that separate existing heathlands. By restoring the link between them, the likelihood of local extinctions of sedentary species is reduced. By enlarging a heath, its management is often made easier

Figure 4.3
Priorities for heathland restoration

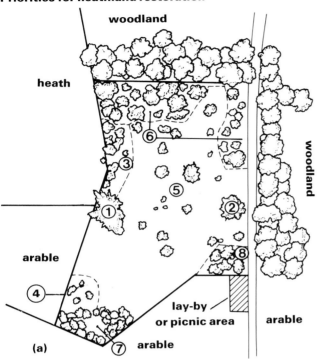

(a)

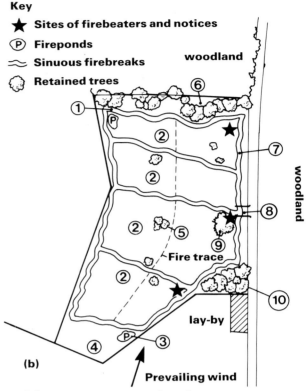

Key

★ **Sites of firebeaters and notices**
ⓟ **Fireponds**
≈ **Sinuous firebreaks**
🌳 **Retained trees**

(b)

(a) Before management

1. Rapidly spreading bracken, invading good-quality heath and creating a barrier between adjoining areas of heathland. Easy/low cost to treat.
2. Old gorse, losing wildlife value and a high fire risk near to road.
3. Established trees which separate heath from adjoining heath.
4. Small rhododendron bushes on humid heath. Unless removed now, will spread and become increasingly costly to clear, destroying valuable habitat, creating a barrier between areas of heath.
5. Sparse tree invasion on good quality heath. Present effect only slight but once more trees appear and the canopy closes, impact will be serious.
6. Long-established tree invasion. Little heathland vegetation present. Clear by stages as resources permit.
7. Established rhododendron on humid heath. Important to clear as potentially a valuable habitat but work will be very labout-intensive and costly. Create a fire pond where all heathland interest has been lost.
8. Retain trees as screen, and fire protection.

(b) Long-term restoration plan

1. Firebreak here not essential if adjoining broadleaved woodland (which does not burn) but essential if adjoining conifers.
2. Heather/grass grazed or heather managed on rotation.
3. Pond on area with no existing wildlife interest (former rhododendron thicket).
4. Wet heath. Firebreak at interface with dry heath.
5. Sparse tree and scrub cover retained on open heath.
6. Retained scalloped woodland edge for nightjars.
7. Firebreak set back 50–100 m from road.
8. Gated access for fire service.
9. Gorse here regularly coppiced to minimise fire risk.
10. Retained broadleaved scrub as screen and barrier to access.

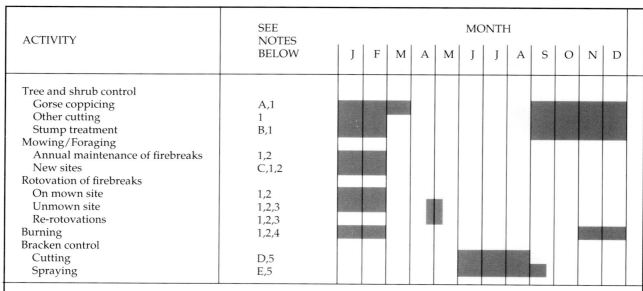

ACTIVITY	SEE NOTES BELOW	MONTH											
		J	F	M	A	M	J	J	A	S	O	N	D
Tree and shrub control													
Gorse coppicing	A,1	▓	▓	▓						▓	▓	▓	▓
Other cutting	1	▓	▓	▓						▓	▓	▓	▓
Stump treatment	B,1	▓	▓							▓	▓	▓	▓
Mowing/Foraging													
Annual maintenance of firebreaks	1,2	▓	▓										
New sites	C,1,2	▓	▓										
Rotovation of firebreaks													
On mown site	1,2	▓	▓										
Unmown site	1,2,3	▓	▓		▓								
Re-rotovations	1,2,3				▓								
Burning	1,2,4	▓	▓									▓	▓
Bracken control													
Cutting	D,5						▓	▓	▓				
Spraying	E,5						▓	▓	▓				

▓ Acceptable months for management (but see notes below)

This figure has been adapted from the Heathland Management Calendar produced by the Dorset Heathland Forum.

Figure 4.4   Lowland Heath Management Calendar

Notes:

Effective management

A   Successful regrowth most likely in March.

B   Most effective results September–November. Treatment likely to be ineffective in spring–summer as sap is rising.

C   Optimum period for harvesting mature heather seed is November–December.

D   Three cuts per year (June-August) required for maximum effectiveness. If restricted to one cut, choose July.

E   Spraying most effective in period between unfurling of fronds and first frosts (normally June–August).

Sensitive times of year for wildlife

1.   Bird nesting season (March–August).

2.   Active reptiles above ground (March–October), sluggish early spring and autumn.

3.   On heaths with rare reptiles, the safest period is late April mid-May but disturbance to breeding birds, eg stone-curlew, woodlark is a risk. Reptile eggs incubating May–September. Hibernating reptiles below ground September–April.

4.   Special care required on all heaths with important reptile populations.

5.   Breeding birds, especially nightjars breed in bracken.

and more economic. Where large areas of heathland have been entirely taken over by trees, scrub or bracken, major reclamation may be required. This will not only involve removing the existing cover and litter but may also necessitate re-seeding with heathland plants. Amongst the many national rarities which occur on heathland are several bird species, including stone-curlew, nightjar, woodlark and Dartford warbler. They are potential colonists of re-

created heaths even where the site is now isolated.

Funding may now be available from several possible sources to assist farmers in heathland management, restoration and re-creation. Most heaths are officially designated in some way, for instance as Sites of Special Scientific Interest, and there may be money available through entering into management agreements.

3. Management of lowland heath

3.1 Grazing

- Maintain or reinstate a low-intensity grazing regime that integrates wildlife needs.
- Take special care with small sites as uncommon species may be lost.
- Protect old heather especially where known to be important for scarce species.
- Restore neglected sites by cutting, burning or grazing.
- For most wildlife needs, spring and summer grazing is best.
- Hill cattle and sheep, moorland and New Forest ponies are most suitable.
- Graze over the summer (March–September) at the following rates: Sheep 2–2.5/ha; Cattle 0.25–0.5/ha; Ponies 0.1–0.2/ha; Mixed 0.25 cattle and 1 ewe/ha.
- All-year grazing, at lower intensity, is best suited to larger heaths.
- Adjust stocking levels in light of results.
- Avoid overgrazing as this leads to loss of heather and replacement by grasses.
- Avoid undergrazing as this leads to an increase in coarse grass, old, leggy heather and invasion by trees and bracken.

As with unimproved grasslands, the wildlife value of heaths was the incidental result of management designed to achieve the best growth rates for stock over the long term without inputs and based entirely on natural vegetation. The approach is still a

very good one, potentially able to produce conditions suitable for a wide range of wildlife. This is partly because of the habits and preferences of the stock themselves and partly because there will be variations in the growth rates of plants across the heath due to differences in fertility, aspect and drainage. The upshot of these two factors will be a mix of plant heights, structure and bare ground, especially where there is a variety of types of vegetation including heather and grasses.

On all heaths, animals will graze selectively, concentrating their attentions where growth is best, as it may be on damper ground, and grazing dry, unproductive areas relatively lightly. This can lead to the development of a very varied vegetation structure with 'lawns' of tight-grazed fine grasses and herbs in some areas, moderately grazed areas with varied structure over most of the heath and stands of taller grass and old heather on the more remote or inaccessible parts of the site. Aim for this ideal.

On small heaths, care is needed to avoid inadvertent damage in sensitive areas as it may cause loss of species which, on isolated heaths, may never be able to recolonise. Stock control may necessitate temporary or permanent fencing or some form of shepherding.

Compared with improved pastures, heathland grazing is of very poor quality so that stocking rates must be much lower. On the other hand, where heather, gorse and other shrubs are present, hardy stock may be able to outwinter. Generally speaking, it is hill and upland breeds of sheep such as Scottish blackface, Swaledale, Exmoor horn and Welsh mountain sheep, and cattle such as Galloway, Highland and Welsh black that are more suited to the conditions as are moorland or New Forest ponies. These hardy breeds can be particularly useful as they generally require less intensive husbandry, although it can be difficult to fence in some of the sheep breeds such as Hebrideans, which jump well.

While lowland breeds of livestock can graze heathland, they are used to high-quality herbage and are not familiar with the range of plants that the soils support so they may not flourish, at least initially, unless grazing of a higher quality is also provided. Other animals with lower nutritional needs such as cull cows can also produce the conditions needed by wildlife. It goes without saying that the welfare of stock must be considered and at least modest growth rates must also be achieved.

Where the heath has not been managed for some time, it may be necessary to clear scrub or bracken and cut or burn to bring the grass and heather into a suitable condition for grazing. Methods are described later in this chapter. Grazing itself may be used to restore heaths providing tree invasion is not in an advanced state. Cattle and ponies will tackle birch scrub, regrowth from cut stumps of trees or coarse vegetation more readily than sheep. Progress will be quicker with hardy breeds. Mineral blocks will encourage stock to tackle rank, neglected areas but they should be removed as soon as the vegetation has been brought into the desired condition. Blocks should not be put into areas of old heather as they are likely to lead to its destruction by trampling and heavy grazing by stock.

Both when carrying out restoration grazing and in continuing management, the timing of grazing can be used to bring about changes in the relative proportions of different plants. Spring and summer grazing will mainly concentrate on grasses and sedges, thus favouring heathers. Winter grazing concentrates on heather and woody vegetation, which will tend to favour grasses. As heather is a very important plant for wildlife, it is wise to restrict grazing to spring and summer where it is wished to retain or create stands of older growth.

The key factor in setting stock levels is the relative amount and condition of grass and heather. Assuming grazing from March to September, the following are approximate guidelines to levels: Sheep, 2–2.5/ha; Cattle, 0.25–0.5/ha; Ponies, 0.1–0.2/ha; Mixed, 0.25 cattle and 1 sheep/ha. Levels are likely to be at the higher end of the range on sites with abundant grasses and at the lower end where heather predominates. Graze wet heath with cattle preferably at the higher end of the stocking rates above.

If possible, use a mix of animals as this will make best use of the available forage and prevent any one type of vegetation becoming too dominant. The animals' behavioural differences will create good vegetation structure for a range of wildlife. All-year grazing at a lower intensity can also maintain heaths in a condition suitable for wildlife, because, as the animals change from one kind of food to another at different times of year, so they create variety in vegetation type and structure. However, heavy grazing in the autumn immediately after heather has flowered and put on extra growth can cause it to lose vigour. Overgrazing is not as common as on the upland heaths but the symptoms are identical with a decrease in heather cover and increase in grass species cover. This is caused by grazing which takes more than around 40% of the annual green shoot production of heather.

Cattle and ponies can cause considerable damage to old, leggy heather, which they break down while moving through it.

Undergrazing must be avoided as many of the scarcer heathland plants depend on grazing to keep in check the ranker, more aggressive species. For instance, it is important to graze wet heath in order to prevent purple moor-grass from displacing scarcer plants. These areas are usually more productive than dry heaths but stocking rates will depend on the condition of the vegetation and the amount and quality of grazing on adjoining dry heath. Cattle and ponies are most suitable.

On some heaths it may be necessary for conservation purposes to keep animals off the heath at sensitive seasons. For instance, it is believed that stone-curlews do not select nesting areas on grass heaths where sheep are grazing, so in potential nesting areas grazing should probably not start before late summer. This may mean fairly heavy grazing in the autumn in order to bring the sward back to the very short conditions the stone-curlews will seek in the following spring.

The welfare of stock is critically important and judgements on the need for mineral blocks and supplementary feeding will be required from time to time. This is more likely if the stock are less hardy and not suited to the heathland environment or if forage is at a premium. Access to alternative feeding areas may be needed in winter. At any season, the use of supplementary feeding may mean that the coarser and less palatable plants will be left by the stock. Avoid supplementary feeding if possible, but if it is needed it should take place off the heath on areas of low wildlife importance as it is very damaging. It imports nutrients, not only to the area where feed itself is made available but also in the enriched dung of animals as they move over the heath. This encourages grass growth and enables non-heathland plants to invade. Further, it causes animals to concentrate around the feeding site and may lead to localised overgrazing, damage by trampling, and weed invasion.

Where rabbits are numerous, they will compete with stock and may cause weed invasion. Control may be required. However, they do eat pine seedlings, which livestock ignore. Where a heath is not grazed by livestock, rabbits can maintain areas of short swards. If rabbits are to be encouraged it will be necessary to protect nearby crops by rabbit fencing or control to satisfy the legal obligation (see Appendix II: Legal considerations).

3.2 Heather and grass cutting

- Where grazing is not possible, cut in preference to burning.
- Forage harvesting is the best method as it removes cut material and depletes nutrients.
- On uneven ground, flail or swipe.
- Cut individual heather plots no more than 1 ha in size on around a 15–20 year rotation, mowing adjacent plots in successive years.
- Make use of cut material as a seed source of heathland plants for restoring heath or reversion of arable to heath.
- Monitor growth especially from old heather and control birch or pine colonisation.
- Mow ungrazed grass heaths on a 1–5 year rotation to benefit other plants and invertebrates.
- If rabbits inhibit recovery, undertake control or fence.
- Replace cutting by grazing if possible.

If heaths are not grazed, cutting is another method of creating the variations in structure and age required by wildlife. It may be the only option on small fragmented heaths or on farmland with no access to stock. Cutting is a more reliable and safer method than burning, and it is much easier to create small patches of different ages than with burning.

A cut height of not less than 5 cm and not more than 10 cm is ideal. If heather is cut too low, the lowest dormant buds will be lost and regrowth will not occur. Cutting should be carried out between mid-October and mid-February, when the heathers are not growing, ground-nesting birds are not present and vulnerable invertebrates or reptiles are hibernating, many of them underground or concealed in the basal parts of plants.

Forage harvesting is the best method because it removes the cut vegetation and so continues the process of nutrient depletion important to maintain heathland conditions. If the cut material and nutrients are not removed, grasses may replace heathers. Both double-chop and single-chop forage harvesters can be used. The former produces a more finely-chopped material, while a single-chop can be useful in the re-creation of heath on former arable or other sites; as well as seed it produces brash, which provides a mulch to retain moisture once spread on ground. Forage-harvested heather may also be saleable as compost.

Depending on the distance which cut material must be carted, one man should be able to forage harvest about 1 ha in 12 hours. With one man carting and the other cutting, it may be possible to cut 1 ha in 4 hours.

On very uneven or stony ground, or where there are tree stumps, forage-harvesting is impracticable. A tractor-mounted flail is preferable, as swipes tend to tear heather rather than giving it a clean cut. The cut material will have to be removed if nutrients are not to accumulate. Removal can be costly, as it may necessitate raking or sweeping by hand but there may be markets for cut or baled heather.

It is important to cut heather while it is still in its building phase. This is usually up to 15 years old (see page 141), but growth rates differ within the UK and growth in dry summers may be negligible. Older heather may fail to regrow well if cut and this presents a problem if all the heather on the heath is mature or old. Depending on the present wildlife interest, it may be wise to cut or burn about 25% of the mature heather in the first year in small, scattered plots so as to rejuvenate it but allow the rest to grow on and cut it in rotation over the next 15–20 years as described below. Burning may be better if there is a deep litter layer to clear (see page 113). There is a risk that some may die and not be replaced by new seedlings but this must be balanced against the wildife value of old heather plants, for instance for reptiles.

As a general rule for most sites, to produce variations in heather structure and age over the heath, divide it into small plots and mow them on around a 15–20 year rotation (Figure 4.5: Rotations for heather management). Ideally, have plots not more than 1 ha in size. On large sites, create several management blocks each

sub-divided into plots (eg on 30 ha of heather, two blocks each of 15 1-ha plots with one in each block cut each year). Retain some blocks of old heather.

This layout means that, at any one time, the full range of conditions are replicated several times across the whole heath. Then, if there is a catastrophic fire, there is less chance of one heather age-class being wiped out entirely, taking with it all dependent wildlife. In addition, as ground conditions are never identical across the whole site, greater habitat variation will be introduced.

Cut adjacent plots in successive years so that sedentary species can easily move from one to the next as conditions become suitable. Many species need both young and old vegetation, perhaps feeding in one and sheltering in the other, make the edges of plots as sinuous and as long as practicable.

Even with vigorous heather, regrowth after cutting is somewhat unpredictable. For instance, a very dry spring may delay recovery. Monitor the situation, particularly to deal with birch or pine colonisation which may take advantage of the lack of competition and open conditions. However, it is quite normal for regrowth to take several years and patience is sometimes needed. Other heathland plants can also take advantage of the conditions, which may also create suitable conditions for heather seedling establishment.

With grass management as with heather, forage harvesting is preferable to other cutting techniques and burning. Depending on growth rates, mow on a 1–5 year rotation aiming to prevent grass becoming rank and tussocky across the site, though a few such areas should be retained. Prepare a plot layout following the same principles outlined for heather management.

Heavy grazing pressure from rabbits will prevent recovery, especially of gorse and heather. If the effect extends over a large area, rabbit control or fencing may be required.

Once regrowth of heather or grass is sufficient to produce forage for livestock, consider the reintroduction of a grazing regime.

**10% of the heath is not cut; the site is
divided into 30 1-ha plots and two are cut
each year (ie 15-year rotation) except
near the road where a shorter rotation is
followed to reduce fire risk.**
**Many layouts are possible. Aim to create
structural variation across the heath.
Also suitable for burning rotations.**
**On a very long rotation, eg 30–40 years,
older heather should be taken back into
the rotation and other mature areas
retained to grow old.**

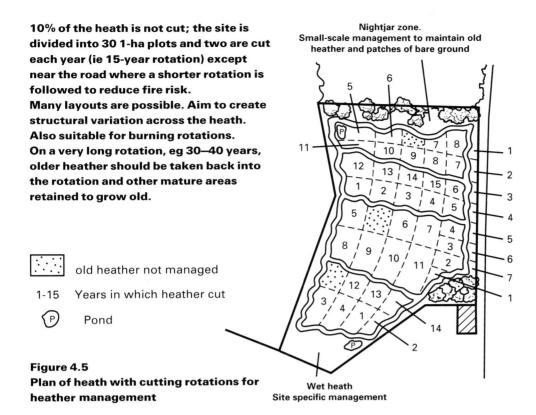

old heather not managed

1-15   Years in which heather cut

P   Pond

Figure 4.5
**Plan of heath with cutting rotations for
heather management**

3.3 Fire and heathlands

- Uncontrolled fire is very destructive to wildlife and grazing.
- On all heaths, produce a fire plan for the heath in consultation with the fire service.
- Create firebreaks 10 m wide to prevent spread of uncontrolled fires.
- Provide firebeaters.
- Fire, like cutting, can be used to regenerate heather and grass to a condition more palatable to livestock.
- Burning can be undertaken in areas unsuitable for cutting machinery and to clear accumulated plant litter and encourage seedling germination.
- Produce a burning plan before undertaking a burn and create firebreaks 5 m wide around a controlled burn site.
- Follow the Heather and Grass Burning Code and legal conditions.
- Burn between November and mid-February for least harm to wildlife.
- Do not burn more than 1 ha at a time and make the burn edge as sinuous as possible.

- Back-burn if possible as it allows more control (but is hotter).
- Monitor regrowth from the burn and control any invasion by trees.
- Rotovate and/or re-seed if no heather regrowth has occurred after 3–4 years.

All heaths should be protected from uncontrolled fires. Design the fire protection system in consultation with the local fire service, not least to ensure that they have mapped safe routes across the heath – such as main firebreaks (Table 4.3: Heathland fire plans; Figure 4.5: Plan of rotations). They will not bring equipment onto a heath where there is a risk of it being unable to evade a sudden change in the fire's direction or rate of advance.

Create permanent firebreaks. They are unlikely to stop a major fire especially in windy conditions, but provide a baseline from which back-burning (upwind) or even small downwind fires lit near the upwind edge of the break can remove vegetation before the wildfire reaches it. This denies it fuel and makes it easier to extinguish.
Site the breaks to provide protection at the

Table 4.3: Heathland fire plans

1. Survey the heath and map:
    Areas which are top priority for protection on conservation grounds. Any stands of old heather will go into this category.
    Areas of commercial value such as buildings and conifer plantations.
    Roads, public footpaths and bridleways. These are where fire is most likely to start and will provide a part of the layout of firebreaks.
    Stands of gorse, which can prove a fire risk.
    The direction of the prevailing wind as this will show the most likely direction in which any fire will progress.
    Water supplies such as streams and ponds.
    Access points for firetenders; these will have to join to firm tracks across the heath.

2. If the heath adjoins other heathland or any other area with a high fire risk, notably conifer woodland, in other ownership, produce a joint plan and help each other in the event of fire.

3. Decide on the location of firebreaks. They should be set broadly at right angles to the likely direction of advance of fire. Give particular thought to the protection of the most important areas and to isolating the zones where the likelihood of fire outbreak is greatest. As well as protecting the most important areas, it is wise to try to ensure that no more than a quarter of the whole heath can be burned by a single fire. Divide it into at least four separate protection zones and have no one zone bigger than 20 ha. As far as possible, incorporate existing paths and bridleways in the lines of firebreaks and traces (see below). This minimises the need to destroy heathland habitat and helps to isolate them as potential sources of fire.

4. Select sites for firebeaters and signs warning of the risk of fire. These should be at public access points and beside the most vulnerable areas. Signs should ask anyone finding a fire to go to the nearest callbox (give its location), phone 999 and notify the landowner.

5. Discuss the draft plan with the county fire service on site. Explain which areas are priority for protection. Ensure adequate access routes and that any keys to gates will be available. Provide a copy of the plan.

6. Implement the plan on the ground. Firebreaks should be at least 10 m wide and rotovated or mown. Fire is more likely to cross mown breaks especially in high winds or if there is substantial vegetation growth (fuel) on the upwind side. On balance, mown areas are of more value as habitat than rotovated areas, though the margins of the latter are used by sand lizards for egg-laying. A good compromise is to mow the upwind half of the strip and rotovate the downwind half. This will first deprive any small or slow-moving fire of fuel and then stop it. Firebreaks do not stop big fires but provide the basis for fighting them. They can be used as the point from which to light counter-fires to burn upwind so widening the break and depriving the fire of fuel.

7. Fire traces are strips about 2 m wide mown or rotovated parallel to the likely direction of advance of a fire. They will not stop an advancing front but will help to prevent it spreading sideways, thus reducing damage and making it easier to fight.

8. Firebreaks and traces are best for wildlife if they are sinuous, so increasing the length of the interface with adjoining vegetation.

9. If there is no water source consider creating a permanent pond beside access tracks which can be used by firetenders, on an area with no special wildlife value, for instance adjoining but not in any existing wet heath. Take advice from the fire service about capacity. Design it also for use by wildlife (see Chapter 9).

10. Consider involving local people as volunteer fire wardens at times of greatest risk such as summer weekends, bank holidays and school holidays.

11. In the event of fire, meet the brigade at the entrance and direct them to the right location. Point out the areas most important to protect. Work under their guidance. Never take risks. Heath fires can travel fast.

12. Assess the plan each year and make revisions if necessary – for instance if new areas became a priority for protection. Inform the fire service of changes.

outer perimeter and also sub-divide the heath. The greatest risk of fire is beside public roads or paths where accidental and intentional fires can occur and with areas of old heather or gorse which burn readily. If burning is a necessary part of the site's management, relate the permanent firebreaks to the areas which will be subject to it.

Maintain firebreaks by regular mowing or forage harvesting about every three years, or by ploughing or rotovation. Ploughed or rotovated land will be unsuitable for use by fire appliances but the soft bare ground, where it adjoins deep heather, is believed to provide ideal conditions for sand lizards to lay their eggs. (If sand lizards are present, rotovate in late April or May to avoid their hibernation and egg-laying periods (see Feature 4.4:).) Make the edges of firebreaks sinuous to lengthen them.

Firebeaters should be kept on the heath where they are not likely to be vandalised. If the farm has its own fire-fighting equipment this is an invaluable asset but even firebeaters may enable a small fire to be extinguished before it gains hold.

Burning is one way of bringing neglected sites back into condition to recommence grazing. Cutting will achieve this goal with fewer risks and greater precision (see page 110). Animals may also be persuaded to tackle coarse herbage by judicious siting of mineral blocks (see page 110). However, where old heather is dying and there is no regeneration because of a deep litter layer, burning the litter may be the only practicable way to expose the mineral soil and so encourage an existing heather seedbank to germinate.

If burning is to be used to manage the heath, a burning plan should be prepared indicating areas to be burnt, location of firebreaks, access onto the heath in case of emergencies and location of any water or firebeaters. It should also set out the planned rotation, typically on about a 15–20-year cycle.

Burning can be undertaken with the wind or against it. Back-burning is normally favoured, especially when the heath is relatively small, where rare species are present or where forestry is adjacent, as this method of burning makes it easier to control the fire and it moves across the heath much more slowly. However, as a consequence, the fire is hotter and there is a risk of killing heather plants. On heaths where a thick litter layer has accumulated and must be removed to allow seeds to germinate, it may be possible to clear some of the litter by forage-harvesting and then burning off the residue. Otherwise, an upwind fire will be very hot and difficult to control but a downwind fire will fail to remove enough of the litter.

On ungrazed wet heaths fire may be the only way to prevent scarce plants being lost due to the spread of rank growth but particular care is needed as a hot, slow fire may do great damage to the peat surface, and mosses will be destroyed. A downwind fire may be the lesser evil.

To reduce the risk to scarce animals on the site and to maintain vegetation diversity, do not burn more than 1 ha at a time. Before starting, create a firebreak 5 m wide around the proposed burn site. Irregularly shaped burns are better as they lengthen the interface between old and new growth, and some heathland animals require both.

For wildlife, the ideal period to burn is from November to mid-February, as breeding birds will be absent and reptiles will be hibernating. The effect on invertebrates will also be least. The burning code of practice (Appendix II: Legal considerations) should be followed and adjacent landowners and the fire service should be given due notice. Heather and grass burning is only permitted on lowland heaths in England and Wales between 1 November and 31 March. In Scotland the legal period runs from 1 October – 15 April.

Choose a day with a wind speed of force 2 to 3 but not more or there is a risk of fire jumping the break and getting out of control. If there are stands of young pine or old gorse or heather on the site, these will burn fiercely and any firebreak should be set well away from them to minimise the risk of flame crossing it.

Even when the burn is carried out under ideal conditions, the degree of vegetation recovery is unpredictable. If heathers fail to regrow after a burn, wait for seed germination. It may take 3–4 years for new plants to appear, provided the heath does not become invaded by other growth meanwhile. Should this occur, grazing or other control may be necessary. In the last analysis, it may be necessary to re-seed with heathland plants (see page 119). Failure to recover after fire is most likely if the heathers are old.

Old, leggy gorse may also be killed by fire. There is usually a prolific seedbank which can be encouraged to germinate by raking off any unburned gorse litter.

3.4 Tree, shrub and bracken management

- Maintain and manage gorse and broom by rotational cutting before they become leggy. Restrict cover to around 5% of the heath.
- Scattered trees and scrub can be of wildlife value on heaths.
- Restrict tree cover to a marginal fringe or scatter across the heath.
- Eradicate rhododendron and other non-native shrubs.
- Clear pine, birch and rhododendron by cutting.
- Treat birch and rhododendron stumps with a herbicide.
- Reduce dense bracken to less than 5% of total vegetation cover and less on heaths smaller than 5 ha.
- Clear bracken by cutting, rolling and/or spraying with Asulam.
- Remove litter by raking, forage harvesting or burning.
- Control any re-invasion. Ideally, graze very lightly as soon as heathers and grasses begin to establish.
- If the desired vegetation does not appear, re-seed with heathland plants.

Gorse and broom are most valuable wildife habitats and, as a guide, heaths could beneficially hold up to 5% gorse or broom cover as patches or scattered shrubs (see Feature 4.2: The Wildlife of Gorse). They are best kept away from public access

areas and roads as they are highly inflammable.

Ungrazed gorse becomes leggy within 10-20 years. By this stage there is a build-up of litter beneath the stand and gorse is then very susceptible to fire. Where ponies browse gorse, this produces tight, dense bushes, which in the end also become leggy. Usually the bushes tend to collapse and they may then either resprout from the base or die. The best conditions for wildlife are provided while the bushes are still dense and bushy.

Cut gorse at age 12-15 years (or when it becomes leggy) in winter, ideally in March for best response. It will then resprout from the base, like coppice. Where livestock or rabbits are present, fencing may be necessary to protect the new growth from browsing or trampling.

Where gorse is absent, it can be introduced by transplanting seedlings into areas with little or no existing wildlife value. Ensure that the roots do not dry out and water them at weekly intervals for at least six weeks. Gorse can spread into old heather and into areas that have been poached by stock, or otherwise disturbed, and may need to be controlled.

If trees are retained on the heath, it will be subject to a continual rain of seeds. However, as many heaths are adjacent to plantations and woods, total clearance is unlikely to solve the problem. A belt of trees around the boundary of a heath can have several values. It can discourage trespass or prevent agricultural spray-drift. It will provide shelter from wind and increase the temperature in its lee. For nightjars, a fringe of trees will increase feeding opportunities (Feature 4.3: Nightjars on heaths).

It is inadvisable to retain seeding trees out on the heath unless the site is grazed or cut sufficiently intensively to prevent regeneration. If it is not, these trees will create a recurring management problem.

It is worth undertaking clearance of trees, shrubs and bracken even if establishment of subsequent grazing is unlikely. It will give wildlife a breathing space and assistance may be available in the future to reinstate grazing or mowing. Before starting work, produce a clearance plan including the identification of those areas or individual trees that will be retained. Most tree felling requires a felling licence from the Forest Authority (see Appendix II: Legal considerations).

Greatest benefit can be achieved with the least effort in clearing areas with sparse tree, shrub or bracken growth. A delay will mean the scale of the task will increase each year, with a risk of extinction of scarce wildlife from the invaded areas. Another priority is to tackle colonisation that is fragmenting the heath. Substantial blocks of woodland can be cleared by contractors, whose costs may be offset against timber sales.

No cut woody material should be left on the heath nor should burning of fellings take place on the heath as both lead to localised nutrient enrichment and invasion by other non-heathland plants. After clearance, it may be necessary to undertake additional work such as litter removal to allow recolonisation by heathers or grass.

Pine is easiest to clear. Small saplings can be hand-pulled. Larger trees can be cut and carted, chipped or burned. Pine does not regrow from the cut stumps. Birch should be treated similarly but will regrow from cut stumps so it is essential to treat the stumps with a herbicide. Triclopyr (Garlon 4) and ammonium sulphamate (Amcide) have both been used to a high degree of success. Best results come from treatment in September to November. Any regrowth should be sprayed with glyphosate (Roundup) when regrowth is rapid in late spring/early summer. Stock can be used to control scrub regrowth but only if the stocking levels are sufficiently high and can be maintained without damage to other heathland vegetation.

If the site is not to be grazed but managed by forage harvester or other cutting machinery, tree stumps should be cut off at ground level to reduce the risk of damage to equipment.

Rhododendron causes problems on wet heaths. It often grows at high density, with interlacing and rooting branches, which make access and clearance difficult, and will regrow from stumps or root fragments. Bushes can be pulled out with a tractor-mounted winch but can cause large-scale disruption of the ground surface. Larger roots left in the ground regrow and follow-up work may be necessary. Where scarce plants grow in the vicinity, cutting is a safer course but remaining stumps must be killed. As with birch the most successful methods have been with triclopyr and ammonium sulphamate. Even with this treatment, there is likely to be some regrowth, which can be weed-wiped with glyphosate or triclopyr. Usually, more seedlings appear next spring: they must be hand pulled.

Wildlife benefits will come from reducing bracken cover to not more than 5% of a large heath. If it occurs in fairly small stands which are not expanding, these are the ones to retain. On sites less than 5 ha, clear the majority of the bracken.

Bracken grows from an underground rhizome system in which it stores nutrients. Carry out control at the time of year when most of these nutrients have been deployed above ground in the growing frond. Even so, mechanical methods of control will take several years, while chemical control treatment may require two or more applications. A mix of mechanical and chemical methods can be used, but total eradication is rarely achievable, except with repeated treatment over several years.

Sparse bracken can be kept under control by trampling of stock and or spot-spraying with Asulam.

Dense bracken stands should be cut or rolled two or three times a summer for two years in June, July and mid-August. This will weaken the stand and allow the remaining heathland vegetation to recover somewhat before the bracken is sprayed out in the third year. Heath plants will not respond if a thick litter of bracken remains. Ground-nesting birds such as whinchat and nightjar are affected by these operations, so check to see if they are present before starting work.

Spray with Asulam when bracken fronds are fully open, in wind speeds of force 1–3 and with rain not expected in the next 36 hours. Spraying in hot, still air conditions may lead to evaporation of the chemical and should be avoided. Spraying after the first frosts is ineffective so the best period is normally from mid- June to late August. There will be no visible effect in the season of spraying.

Typical work rates are:
(a) spraying with a tractor and 6 m boom – 1.5 hours per ha;
(b) swiping with tractor – 3.5 hours per ha;
(c) manual spraying dense growth with an ultra low volume applicator (ULVA) – 9 hours per ha;
(d) manual spraying open or sparse growth with a knapsack sprayer – 18 hours per ha.

Aerial spraying can also be successful but is more weather-dependent and it is more difficult to spray accurately. It is particularly useful in dealing with large dense areas of bracken. Expect to have to carry out some follow-up spot-spraying in the year after chemical treatment, and thereafter if regrowth occurs. Follow up is not effective in the second year.

Asulam can kill other ferns, heather seedlings, and western and dwarf gorse, and check common gorse. Fescues may die back but recover.

Heather seed can survive in the soil for well over 50 years but germination will not be possible unless the litter of pine needles, rhododendron leaves or bracken is removed. The underlying mineral soil must be exposed. If the layer is deep, forage harvesters can be used but this will not be possible where tree stumps remain. Burning with or without prior forage-harvesting is an option on large areas. On very small plots, raking, mechanical brushes or industrial suction cleaners can also be used successfully to remove litter. Trampling by livestock can be successful in small areas if there is sufficient forage to sustain them on the site.

If few heath plants remain in the seedbank then the heath will be colonised by trees, shrubs and invasive grasses unless deliberate steps are taken to re-seed with heathland vegetation (see page 119).

3.5 Management of wetlands on heaths

> - Do not undertake drainage works on or adjoining wet heaths without considering wildlife implications.
> - Restore wetland areas on heaths that have been damaged in the past through drainage works.
> - Prevent water with a high nutrient status draining onto the heath.
> - Maintain open water on heaths, particularly for dragonflies. Do not let pools become overshaded. Create new pools or ponds where there is no other interest.
> - Ensure that wet heath vegetation is correctly grazed or burned.

Like all wetlands, those on heaths depend for their continuing existence and interest on the maintenance of their water supply and can be affected by changes in drainage on the heath, on farmland or other land surrounding the heath and by water abstraction.

If attempts have been made to drain heathland areas, restore wet conditions as fully as possible.

Where a watercourse crosses a heath and channel management is necessary, care must be taken not to damage dependent wetlands on the heath. This may necessitate protective or amelioratory measures such as the construction of water control structures. The free-draining nature of heathland soils may make this a particularly difficult problem to address and specialist assistance should be sought.

Drainage from roads and villages or towns as well as fertilised farmland can bring in nutrients which will greatly affect the wildlife interest of wet heathland. No new drainage onto a site should be permitted without confirmation that the water quality will be acceptable. Levels of pH and nutrients should be no higher than those already occurring in healthy wetlands on the heath. Testing can be undertaken by the National Rivers Authority.

For all species of dragonfly it is important to retain open water on heaths and to prevent overshading by encroaching willow or other scrub. If necessary, cut down and treat stumps to kill them (see page 116). The ideal dragonfly pool is exposed to full sunlight. Keep small pools completely open. Do not stock heathland pools with fish, as they can seriously deplete dragonfly populations through eating the larvae.

Dragonfly ponds can be created on areas of heathland where the watertable is close to the ground surface and there is no existing interest. An ideal site would be where tree or shrub cover has been cleared and heathland vegetation has not recolonised naturally and where ponds may be used for fire control or for watering stock.

Correct grazing or burning of wet heath is also very important and is discussed in the preceding sections.

3.6 Heathland re-creation

- Re-create heathland on former sites, especially where this will link two isolated heaths or extend small heaths.
- Compare nutrient levels with that of a nearby heath to give a baseline for depletion requirements.
- Deplete nutrients, if necessary, through cropping or alternative methods.
- If heathland plants do not appear, re-seed with forage-harvested material from a similar heathland.
- Graze and/or cut when the vegetation has become established.
- Manage the vegetation for appropriate uncommon wildlife.
- Consider further introductions of plant or animal as some may never colonise naturally.

Because heathlands are now such rare habitats, re-creation is a very valuable wildlife conservation measure. It is particularly valuable where the land concerned will provide a link between two existing heathlands or extends a small heath which has some wildlife value. With larger heaths there is greater flexibility in management and grazing is likely to be more viable. Small sites are also more

vulnerable to catastrophe, especially fire. It is also worth considering the re-creation of heath vegetation on farmland that is now isolated from existing heaths. Though it will take some time before associated heathland plants and animals will colonise, and some may never do so, the more mobile species like birds may colonise rapidly.

There is no 'right' plant composition for a heath and because of the uncertainties of plant colonisation, it is unwise to set too rigid objectives at the outset. Some heaths are grass-dominated, others predominantly heather. Where a mix of vegetation develops there will be a good range of food resources for both wildlife and livestock. A few stands of gorse and a scattering of mature trees can add further to a heath's value. The best course is to allow colonisation to proceed naturally and, only if this fails, intervene to seed with material taken from a nearby heath. Once a cover is well established, consider how it might best be managed for wildlife. For instance, if it is mainly grass, can it be grazed or cut to attract stone-curlews? In other words, play to the strengths of the site rather than setting unattainable goals at the beginning.

If the land is next to woodland, bear in mind that this seed source may cause long-term management problems unless the heath is to be grazed or cut regularly.

Farmland will have a high nutrient status which must be depleted before heathland vegetation can be restored. If soil fertility is too high, vegetation cover will be dominated by weedy and productive species or develop bracken or scrub. The main objective is to reduce the amount of phosphate and, if the site has been limed, calcium. This has been done by cereal cropping with limited inputs of mineral nitrogen to increase growth and therefore the uptake of phosphate and to lower the pH. It is thought that an ammonia-based fertiliser is likely to have a more acidifying effect on the soil than urea.

The effects of different crops are not fully known yet and will vary with sites. There have been good results in reducing phosphate levels by cropping with spring and winter barley. Seek specialist advice before starting work.

Determine the desirable levels for soil nutrients and acidity by sampling the condition of nearby heaths as a guide. Then monitor depletion towards those base levels after each harvest. Once soil conditions are suitable, with probably a pH of less than 5 and extractable phosphorous less than 5 mg/g soil, then heather and other heathland plants may begin to appear from seed.

As an alternative to cropping, deep ploughing may bring up nutrient-poor soils to the surface. However, soil cores will need to be taken and analysed as nutrient-enriched material could be brought to the surface. This process may expose, or bury, any seedbank present so sampling is also needed before deciding on the course of action. On very small, nutrient-enriched areas surrounded by existing heathland, the simplest method may be to strip the topsoil off the whole site with a bulldozer blade and allow colonisation from the adjoining zone. Stripped material must be disposed of off-site.

Even if the land is close to existing heath, there will only be limited colonisation by plants, initially at the margin adjoining the heath. It is important to graze the area once a vegetation cover is established so as to keep the sward open for other potential colonists to gain a foothold. In the early stages, such a site may mostly support common weeds but the composition of the plant assemblage will change gradually. If heather is appearing, care is needed as it may be killed by heavy grazing; in this case, it may be as well not to graze for the first two or three years unless there is also plenty of grass on the heath; in any case restrict grazing to summer.

If there is no seedbank of heathland plants and no nearby source for plant colonisation, it will be necessary to seed the site. One option for establishment of heathers is to spread forage-harvested material cut in October to December when seed is ripening but has not yet been dispersed. If some woody material is also cut and included it can act as protective mulch. Ideally, the material should be transferred and spread at once. If storage is necessary, low heaps (no more than 1 m high at most) should be

created to minimise the risk of composting which will kill the seeds.

Do not spread the material so densely as to totally omit light, but dense enough to cover around 30% of the ground. The shoots of the heather mulch and bulk the seed and help to suppress germination by other plants and create a suitable micro-climate for seedling development. Normally, the amount of cut material is sufficient to treat an area around three times the size from which it was harvested. However, the area able to be seeded will vary depending on the size of heather plants that are cut and thus the number of seeds and amount of mulch available. A considerable percentage of seed may not germinate until the following autumn or second spring.

Alternatively, the site may be seeded with heathland grasses. They are unlikely to be available from seedsmen so that forage harvesting on an existing heath at seeding time is likely to be the only practicable method of obtaining seed.

High levels of heather seedling mortality occur in dry springs. If regeneration from the seedbank fails for this reason, it is worth rotovating in the following winter in order to bring more seeds to the surface. (The depth required will be identified through seedbank analysis by a specialist). Repeated failure may necessitate re-seeding with forage-harvested material.

Even if areas for heath re-creation form part of a larger existing heath, it is likely to be wise to maintain fences around them so that the grazing pressure can be carefully controlled. It may also be necessary to fence out rabbits especially in the first stages of heather re-establishment. If present in low numbers they may help to diversify the vegetation but when abundant they can kill young heather and gorse plants.

Once the plant cover has established, it may be appropriate to consider introduction of sedentary species such as the scarce reptiles or butterflies. This should only be done on isolated sites as those linked to other heaths are likely to be colonised naturally. Further information is given on page 8.

4. References and further reading

Andrews, J 1990. Management of lowland heathlands for wildlife. *British Wildlife*, Vol 1 No 6: 336-346.

Auld, M H, Pickess, B and Burgess, ND (eds) 1991. *Proceedings of heathlands conference II. History and management of southern lowland heaths*. RSPB.

Auld, M H, Davies, S and Pickess, B 1992. Restoration of lowland heaths in Dorset. *RSPB Conservation Review* 6: 68-73.

English Nature 1993. Lowland Heathlands. *ENACT* Vol 1 No 2.

Evans, C, Marrs, R & Welch G 1993. The Restoration of Heathland on Arable Farmland at Minsmere RSPB Nature Reserve. *RSPB Conservation Review* 7: 80-84

Farrell, L (ed) 1983. *Heathland Management*. Focus on Nature Conservation No 2. Nature Conservancy Council.

Gimingham, C H 1972. *The Ecology of Heathlands*. Chapman and Hall.

Gimingham, C H 1992. *The Lowland Heathland Management Handbook*. English Nature.

Kirby, P 1992. *Habitat Management for Invertebrates*. Lowland Heaths pp 73-92. RSPB.

Macdonald, A and Armstrong, H 1989. *Methods for Monitoring Heather Cover*. Research and Survey in Nature Conservation No 28. Nature Conservancy Council.

MAFF/WOAD 1992. *The Heather and Grass Burning Code*. HMSO

Michael, N 1993. *The Lowland Heathland Management Booklet*. English Nature.

Putwain, P D and Rae, P A S 1988. *Heathland restoration: a handbook of techniques*. British Gas.

Rodwell, J S (ed) 1991. *British Plant Communities Volume 2: Mires and Heaths*. Cambridge University Press.

Tubbs, C R 1991. Grazing the Lowland Heaths. *British Wildlife* Vol 2 No 5:276-289

Webb, N 1986. *Heathlands*. New Naturalist No 72. Collins.

Feature 4.1: Invertebrates of Lowland Heath

Bare sandy ground

Bare sandy ground, particularly on southern facing banksides, is the hottest and driest part of a heath. Good sites for invertebrates are stable and sparsely vegetated but they can be easily damaged by erosion, shading or plant growth. Many of the invertebrates are predators; many dig burrows in the sand.

- Tiger beetles. Active surface predators. The larvae live in burrows, eating insects that fall in or walk over the top.
- Mining bees. Solitary bees. Females build a series of burrows for egg-laying. Forage over the heath to gather pollen for the grub.
- Sand wasps. Solitary wasps. Also build burrows for egg-laying, stocked with a live but paralysed insect or spider.
- Wolf spider *Arctosa perita*. Waits for prey at the mouth of a burrow.

Sparsely vegetated areas

Hot but sheltered habitat with young plant growth, which provides food for some herbivorous insects.

- Grayling butterfly caterpillars. Eat grasses in hot dry areas.
- Silver-studded blue caterpillars. Eat young heathers and are always found with a species of black ant, which probably protect them from other insect predators and receive 'payment' in the form of a sugary secretion from the caterpillars' bodies.

Mature heather

This supports the most diverse wildlife, including some that need a lot of heather or a more complex vegetation structure.

- Conspicuous species. Heather weevil, beautiful yellow underwing moth, fox moth and Emperor moth, Britain's only silkmoth.
- Spiders. Wolf spiders hunt in the low canopy. Web-building spiders use the mature and old heather, gorse, bracken and scrub.

Wet heath and mire

- Large marsh grasshopper. Found in areas of wet heath and mire, associated with 'floating' sphagnum mosses.
- Bog bush cricket. Eats bog myrtle and purple moor-grass.

Open water

Lowland heaths are very rich in dragonflies including some rare species.

- Dragonflies. Species include white-faced darter, keeled skimmer, small red damselfly and southern damselfly.
- Raft spiders. The adults wait at the margins to catch insects at the water surface. The young are found in scrub.

Feature 4.2: The Wildlife of Gorse

Common gorse is often found in places on heath margins and boundary banks where soils have been disturbed. It can flower almost all year round. Western gorse and dwarf gorse are low-growing plants found among heather in open heath. Gorse was formerly of economic importance. Its uses included fuel for fires and food for livestock.

1. Over 50 kinds of insects live on gorse. Invertebrate density is much higher than on heather. Male green hairstreak butterflies use plants in full sunshine as perches from which to watch for females or potential rivals.

2. Gorse is used by many spiders. The stiff branches provide good support for webs.

3. Dartford warblers nest in gorse which, because of its abundant insects and spiders, is their main feeding habitat. Their territories average 2.13 ha, and studies have shown that their reproductive success is highest when about 0.6 ha of this is gorse. Dartford warblers and other birds, such as stonechat, also use it for winter shelter. For this reason coppicing is best done in early March after the most severe winter weather but before the start of the birds' breeding season.

4. Reptiles emerging from hibernation, especially adders, use bushy plants to protect them from cold spring winds.

5. The relatively large seeds of gorse are discharged explosively, and may be dispersed by ants, which collect them to eat. The seeds appear to survive burning well, and will last for years in the seedbank.

6. Young gorse is dense, providing excellent cover for wildlife, but after 15–20 years the bushes become leggy, leaving a relatively unshaded and open centre. Management by coppicing or burning aims to maintain it at the dense, bushy stage for maximum wildlife benefit and to minimise the fire risk from dead gorse.

Feature 4.3 Nightjars on Heaths

Nightjars are heathland birds, typically found where there is woodland edge or scattered trees on or next to the heath.

Nest and roost sites

During the day nightjars roost on the ground or on branches. They become active at dusk. The males 'churr' to advertise ownership of a territory and attract mates. Churring posts are usually exposed branches, dead trees or, occasionally, smaller shrubs or trees at the top of a steep bank. The eggs are laid in a scrape on open ground; this may be a patch about 1 m across amongst taller heather or bracken, or on leaf and twig litter between saplings but never under dense tree or scrub cover. Nightjars feed on moths, beetles and other large insects, usually taken in flight but also picked up from the ground in open areas such as firebreaks and tracks. They will fly several kilometres to good feeding areas such as other heaths, marshes and permanent pasture.

Management for nightjars

It is unlikely that nightjars will colonise small patches of heath surrounded by farmland or urban development but on larger sites adjoining woodland, it is possible to create suitable conditions by management of the interface between heath and wood. Where trees are invading a heath, total clearance is inadvisable. Aim to leave a 'scalloped' edge between trees at the margin of the site and open heath, or leave isolated blocks of trees or individual trees and patches of bracken.

Feature 4.4: Reptiles of Lowland Heath

The UK has six native species of reptiles; adder, grass snake, smooth snake, slow worm, common lizard and sand lizard. All occur on lowland heath, which is crucial for the survival of the two most threatened species, smooth snake and sand lizard.

Important areas on heaths for reptiles include sunny slopes, banks, tumuli, hillocks and heather overhangs to path-sides. They tend to be very small, and consequently extremely vulnerable to being destroyed, for example by fire. Heather takes time to develop into mature stands and colonisation by reptiles happens slowly if at all. The overall aim is to maintain an uneven-aged heathland mosaic with old heather and bare sand.

Reptile needs

All heath management should take into account the needs of reptiles, and the most important features should be managed with particular care. The following information is for smooth snake and sand lizard.

Heather
- Mature stands with thick litter, and often with mosses and lichens, are most important as their natural structure provides suitable cover, feeding, temperature and humidity. A mosaic of heather ages should be encouraged and stands of old heather should be maintained within the matrix.
- Grazing can damage old heather stands through trampling, so these may need to be fenced.
- Any cutting or burning should be undertaken mid-October to mid-February to reduce chances of reptile losses, and should be carried out on a small scale.
- Known important features may need small-scale management (see below), and may need to be excluded from the grazing, mowing or burning regimes.

Bare sand
- Bare sand is needed by sand lizards for nesting. Eggs are laid at about 8 cm deep, developing most successfully at least 40 cm from plant roots.
- Patches *c* 2 m² can be created by removing turves but may need attention every few years to keep them open.
- Sandy strips and edges to existing tracks or rotovated firebreaks adjacent to mature dry heath areas are better options. Locate firebreaks carefully to ensure that all the important features cannot be wiped out by a single fire; rotovate in late April or May if sand lizards are present, to avoid hibernation and nesting periods.
- Sandy tracks can be created with an angle bladed bulldozer. The lateral bank of spoil revegetates with heather to become ideal for reptiles.

Trees, scrub and bracken
- The bases of mature birch (but not pine) serve as territorial areas for reptiles and the root passages are used for hibernation, especially by snakes.
- Smooth snake and sand lizard prefer open heaths with scattered trees. Invasion by trees, scrub and bracken needs control.

Egg-laying substrates for grass snakes
- Grass snakes are declining, and one reason is the loss of suitable egg-laying sites. Where dung heaps occur near semi-natural vegetation, including heaths, these will be used.

Case study: Re-creation of Lowland Heath.

Matthew Rampton

Much of the land chosen for reversion to lowland heath is free draining and has received very little fertiliser in the past.

Farm details

Farm:	Easton Estates, Easton, Norwich, Norfolk
Tenure:	Owner-occupier
Size:	894 ha. Comprises 5 farms, one of which is tenanted
Altitude:	6–30 m
Soil:	mostly sandy – patches of heavy clay
Crops:	cereals 151 ha, linseed 56 ha, sugar-beet 80 ha, potatoes 12 ha, beans 49 ha, evening primrose 3.5 ha,
Stock:	sows and in-pig gilts x 420 (outdoor unit approx 49 ha)
Other wildlife features:	3 mixed woodlands, approx 260 ha, 80% broadleaf, 20% conifer. Note: approx 20% ancient semi-natural/ancient replanted woods. 75 ha permanent grassland and 31 ha set-aside. Extensive hedges, now in sympathetic management. Watercourses: River Wensum and River Tud. 1.6 ha lake and 15 ponds. Extensive dykes on grassland. A number of sluices have been installed and waterlevels can now be controlled over two areas.

The estate has been owned by the family since 1962. It is situated in a very wooded area to the west and on the outskirts of Norwich, in a rolling landscape spread over two river valleys (Wensum and Tud), and comprises what used to be three very large estates: Honingham, Taverham Hall and Costessey. It is a mixed farm; the pig outdoor unit does well, but on the whole the soil is poor. Conservation has always been a priority (because of the shoot) but in the last few years has taken on increasing significance. The estate now use Countryside Stewardship, ESA, County Council, Farm and Conservation Grant Schemes, Woodland Management Grant Scheme, Hedgerow Incentive Scheme.

Farmer's aims
Primary aim
- Own interest in wildlife potential, made possible by availability of grant aid. Objective is also to have a good mix of habitats - woodland, wetlands, heathland etc.

Secondary aims
- Sporting interest

Background
Resources: Grant: Countryside Stewardship (may cover £250/ha/year, £225/ha from year 2 onwards) lowland heath Tier 2 (reversion).

Constraints: Farm labour increasingly limited as number of men working on estate is reduced. Possibility of using volunteers?

Advice: Initial input from Norfolk FWAG; also Countryside Commission. Norfolk Naturalists' Trust management plan will start late 1993.

Methods
No work yet undertaken; it will be done by a mixture of volunteers, own labour and contractors, and fitted into farm calendar. The plan is to create lowland heathland site of approx 24/26 ha, ie of reasonable size, through Countryside Stewardship. Much of the land chosen for reversion to lowland heath is very free-draining and had been used for growing malting quality barley, receiving little fertiliser input. It is likely that there will be no need to nutrient-strip. Other land was chosen with future set-aside in mind. Some seedbank studies have been done, which show some potential for natural regeneration of heathland species.There is no local seed source if natural regeneration fails: the nearest heath from which forage-harvested heather could be obtained is over 30 km away but there are physical problems in transporting large quantities of material. Natural regeneration will eventually be managed by grazing. Gorse may also be introduced.

Achievements
Primary aim
- Stewardship scheme accepted, management plan drawn up.

Future management
This is essentially an experimental project, ie starting from scratch. It will be several years before a regular management regime can be followed. Financial records of establishment and management costs will be kept to highlight the actual costs of heathland re-creation. Norfolk Naturalists' Trust are preparing a hedgerow management plan with a combination of laying, coppicing and gapping up, plus planting up to 2,000 m of new hedge for the next five years under the Farm and Conservation Grant Scheme. Heath will be extended by a further 12 ha under non-rotational set-aside, heath option, though this is not yet confirmed (this land may have to be managed by mowing if stock grazing is not allowed). Further sluices were to be installed on land within the ESA scheme in the 1993/94 winter. After discussion with a forestry consultant, coppicing is to be re-introduced on a large scale as part of the Woodland Grant Scheme.

John Andrews

4.1 All lowland heaths were once used for grazing and in many areas were common land. Extensive grazing with cattle and ponies now continues only in the New Forest where it maintains a varied vegetation cover which also supports a range of plants and animals found in no other habitats.

C H Gomersall, RSPB

4.2 Unlike pastures and meadows, most heaths hold a small variety of plants. Often heathers are dominant. Dwarf gorse in the eastern counties or western gorse may also be present. All are fairly long-lived and, in the absence of grazing or burning, can develop a dense cover.

David Woodfall

4.3 The rare sand lizard is associated with stands of old heather. Heaths are an excellent habitat for reptiles and also hold adders, common lizards and smooth snakes as well as grass snakes in the wetter areas.

4.4 Especially as heather ages, patches of bare ground appear between the bushes and these may be invaded by trees, notably birch and pine, or by bracken. This also happens after fires. Unless management is undertaken, the heath is soon replaced by woodland or dense bracken and most of its wildlife is lost.

John Andrews

C H Gomersall, RSPB

C H Gomersall, RSPB

4.5 In the absence of grazing, heather may need mowing to maintain its vigour. Use of a forage-harvester is ideal as it removes the cut material and aids regeneration from the seedbank. On rougher ground, swiping or flailing may be the only practicable method.

4.6 Where tree invasion is serious, clearance is essential. Cut material should not be left on the heath. Chipping creates a saleable product from anything that cannot be sold as timber.

Michael Rebane

B Pickess

E A Janes

4.7 Pine dies after cutting but birch re-sprouts and must be treated with an arboricide unless stock are present; they will eat regrowth and ultimately kill the stump. Bracken can be killed by chemical treatment or by repeated rolling or cutting through several summers in succession. However, only chemical treatment is suitable where it is invading heather as mechanical methods are likely to suppress the heather also.

4.8 & 4.9 Gorse is invaluable wildlife habitat but ultimately becomes leggy and loses vigour. Up to the age of about 15 it can be coppiced and will regrow from the stumps. There is always a good seedbank under old stands and this will regenerate if the litter is raked away to expose bare ground.

John Andreas

4.10 Where heather plants have died out, there is often seed still in the soil. Rotovation can create good conditions for germination. The soft ground is also used by sand lizards for egg-laying.

John Andreas

4.11 Fire can be a valuable management tool to rejuvenate heather but can kill reptiles and many invertebrates. Correct timing and control are of the highest importance. Uncontrolled fires cause very serious harm to vegetation and the associated wildlife. Often they encourage invasion by bracken or trees. Every heath needs a fire-plan and a system of rotovated or close-mown firebreaks.

David Woodfall

4.12 Different livestock have different effects on heathland vegetation. Sheep may encourage grass at the expense of heather. In general, hill and upland breeds are more likely to thrive and tackle coarse vegetation. Electric fencing can be used to force animals to graze neglected areas sufficiently heavily, or to protect vulnerable stands of old heather from damage by grazing or trampling.

John Andreas

4.13 In small numbers, rabbits are an asset on heathlands as they maintain areas of short swards and patches of bare ground used by mining bees.

However, they can prevent regrowth of heather after management and may need to be fenced out or controlled.

Hawk-eye Photo Library

4.14 Grass heaths may hold a greater variety of plants than heather-dominated heaths, and these may include rare species such as spiked speedwell.

John Andreas

4.15 Where drainage is impeded, poor fen conditions may develop. These are rich in plants and specialised invertebrates. Low-intensity grazing maintains good conditions, and trampling creates patches of bare mud required by sundews and some other plants. Without grazing, the area may become overgrown by purple moor-grass and ultimately by scrub, with a consequent loss of wildlife.

5. Hill and Rough Grazings

1. Factors influencing wildlife

1.1 The context of farming

> - Because of climate and poor soils, farming in the uplands is difficult and most land is poor-quality grazing.
> - Overstocking is widespread due to economic factors.
> - In some parts of the UK, large areas of hill land have been converted to improved grass.
> - An increasing range of financial incentives is available to assist management which is beneficial to wildlife.

In most of the north and west of the United Kingdom, from Shetland to Fermanagh, through Wales and the Pennines to Bodmin and Dartmoor, much of the land is unsuitable for arable agriculture because of high rainfall, low temperatures, exposure to wind, a short growing season and poor soils. These conditions are not confined to the uplands but in some regions include most of the lower ground and extend to sea-level. As a result, farming is difficult and largely dependent on extensive grazing by livestock exploiting natural vegetation, mainly grasses and heathers. For these reasons, much of Wales, northern England, Scotland and Northern Ireland have long been designated as Less Favoured Areas with special support for agriculture.

Once, cattle and sheep were the main products of this land. From about 1750 to 1830, sheep farming became increasingly dominant, with grouse shooting or deer stalking interests assuming importance from the mid-19th century. Conifer afforestation has replaced much sheep walk during the last 50 years.

A number of economic factors, such as headage payments for sheep, have led to most upland grazings being stocked increasingly heavily during the last 50 years. This has led to a decline in sward quality and to the necessity for measures such as frequent and extensive burning to promote spring growth from otherwise unpalatable grasses. In some regions, such as Wales, much agriculturally unproductive rough grazing has been converted to improved grass re-seeds.

The overall trend has been a large-scale decline in wildlife richness. This is now being countered to some degree by ESA payments and other measures to enable farmers to reduce livestock densities and undertake active management to restore heather and other vegetation important for wildlife (Feature 5.3: Management for Choughs).

Typically, livestock enterprises in these regions make use of both 'unenclosed' grazings and inbye, the better land which provides relatively good-quality pasture and is used for silage or hay production. The management of inbye is covered in Chapter 3 on pastures and meadows. This chapter concentrates on the management of unenclosed grazing land.

1.2 Plant composition

> - Around 200 different flowering plants and ferns as well as many mosses and lichens occur only on upland grazing land.
> - Many of the plants associated with acid soils and peats are different from those of basic soils. Usually the latter hold a greater variety.
> - Many upland plants require wet ground conditions. Flushes are often rich in plant variety and so are good for insects and, in consequence, for birds.
> - Insects such as butterflies and moths depend on different plant species. The greater the variety of plants, the more insect species will be present.
> - Mountain hares, red grouse and other species also depend on particular plants for food.
> - Bracken has limited wildlife value but can add habitat structure on land which is otherwise overgrazed.
> - Scattered trees and stands of shrubs including gorse and juniper are valuable for some wildlife.

Unimproved grazing land, especially in the uplands, is usually thought to hold few kinds of plants but this is due to management which has tended to result in the most palatable species being grazed out and others lost as a result of burning. There are about 60 flowering plants, such as tormentil, which are largely dependent on acidic soils in the north and west of the UK and the much smaller total area with basic soils in these regions supports over 130 kinds of flowering plants including rockrose and blue moor-grass. These totals exclude mosses, liverworts and lichens which, together with ferns, flourish in many sites in the uplands especially in the high rainfall areas of the west.

Many plants, such as crowberry, mountain pansy and alpine lady's mantle, are confined to the uplands. Soil type and altitude are important influences on the vegetation. On the deeper well-drained soils where bracken grows well, it is possible to find plants, such as wood anemone, which are remnants of the flora of the woodlands that once covered much of the lower ground. On the better-drained acid soils under light grazing, heather (ling) and grasses are usually predominant. Nearly 150 of the plants, such as butterwort and marsh lousewort, require wet ground conditions. Flushes often hold a richer variety of plants than the surrounding land and in turn support more insects, so making them good feeding areas for birds such as lapwing, curlew and snipe.

As well as rainfall, terrain is an important factor influencing drainage. The flatter ground is often ill-drained and blanketed in peat. Fescues, bents and wavy hair-grass, which grow on better-drained acid soils, tend to be replaced by mat grass and heath rush on wetter land and, on the wettest areas, by purple moor-grass (Table 5.1: Ecological profiles of characteristic upland plants). Sphagnum mosses and cotton-grasses (or draw moss) are characteristic of peat bogs.

Temperature and the duration of snow-lie in the upland zone is another influence on the variety of plants. On exposed high ground heather may be replaced by crowberry and other dwarf shrubs. The area covered in mosses and lichens increases with altitude and where snow persists longest.

Three types of heather may occur. Ling is the commonest, especially on land where the natural surface drainage is reasonable: in this text it is referred to simply as 'heather'. Bell heather often occurs with it. Cross-leaved heath is more abundant on wet ground. In addition, there may be bilberry, bearberry, crowberry and other dwarf shrubs. All are important as food or cover for invertebrates, mammals and birds. Especially after burning, bell heather and bilberry may be more abundant than heather.

Many insects have specific requirements for particular plants on which they feed. For example, over 50 kinds of moths live on hill and upland grazings and more than half of them are dependent on the three heathers, bilberry or other dwarf shrubs for food. Certain widespread plants are eaten by the caterpillars of three characteristic butterflies – purple moor-grass by the Scotch argus, mat-grass by the mountain ringlet and cotton-grass by the large heath.

Particular plant species are important to both red and black grouse. Red grouse feed largely on the nutritious growing tips of heather for most of the year. In spring, the new shoots of cotton-grass are an important source of protein for egg-laying hens. Black grouse have a more varied diet – cotton-grass flowers in spring, bilberry fruit in summer, sedge and rush seeds in autumn, with heather and bilberry shoots forming a major part of the diet throughout the year. Mountain hares take a similar range of plants. Thus a range of different plants is required to provide them with adequate, suitable food all year round (Feature 5.2: Habitat and feeding requirements of black grouse).

Very few invertebrates feed on bracken but, on land which is heavily grazed or frequently burned, bracken may provide the only areas with adequate structure for orb-web spiders and good wind shelter and cover for flying insects as well as for reptiles and mammals. Patchy or open stands, particularly where mixed with tall herbs,

Table 5.1: Ecological profiles of characteristic upland plants

SPECIES	CHARACTERS	HABITAT	REGENERATION
Heather	Evergreen shrub with very varied growth forms Height <800 mm (occasionally to 1.25 m) Shallow rooting Short lived: *c*30 yrs +	Large ecological range usually well-drained soils. Soil pH <5.0	Seeds Adventitious roots Persistent seedbank
Bell heather	Evergreen Height <600 mm Shallow rooted (but up to 250 mm) Short lived: *c*20 yrs	Lower altitude than heather and more shade tolerant. Drier freely drained soils pH <5.0	Seeds Persistent seedbank Vegetative spread not important
Cross-leaved heath	Evergreen Height <600 mm Rhizomatous through adventitious roots Short lived: *c*20 yrs	Wet/waterlogged soils pH <5.0	Adventitious roots Persistent seedbank
Crowberry	Evergreen Low growing <300 mm Shallow rooting and adventitious Long lived: *c*140 yrs	Moist but not waterlogged pH <4.5	Mainly vegetative Seed establishment infrequent
Bilberry/blaeberry	Deciduous Height <600 mm Strongly rhizomatous roots: 150–200 mm Long lived	Poor tolerance of water-logging Shade tolerant (therefore found in woods) pH <4.5	Mainly by rhizomes By seed infrequent Persistence of seedbank unknown
Cowberry	Evergreen with rough leaves Low growing <300 mm Rhizomatous Long lived	Susceptible to waterlogging Shade tolerant pH 4.5	By rhizomes By seed infrequent
Purple moor-grass	Tufted deciduous grass but swollen stem bases green throughout winter Tussocks. Extensive swards Height 400–1,200 mm Deep roots	Well-oxygenated wet, acidic habitats Soil pH usually <4.0 but also in soil pH 7.0 Cannot tolerate waterlogging	Produces much seed Lateral vegetative spread
Mat-grass	Densely tufted grass with hair-like leaves Forms long-lived spreading tussocks Height to 400 mm Very short rhizomes	Frequent in grazed moorland with soil pH <4.0	Mainly through rhizomes Seeds also important
Wavy hair-grass	Slow growing, evergreen Clump or carpet-forming grass Height 200–400 mm Tufted or rhizomatous	Abundant in upland pastures/moors Shade tolerant Restricted to pH <5.0	Regeneration effective by vegetative means and by seed No persistent seedbank

Table 5.1: Ecological profiles of characteristic upland plants (cont'd)

SPECIES	CHARACTERS	HABITAT	REGENERATION
Common cotton-grass/draw moss	Flowers May-June Leaves die back autumn Height 600 mm Rhizomatous but shallow roots	Exclusively wetland Mainly acidic soils of pH <5.0	Mainly vegetative by means of rhizome extension forming large patches Seed establishment infrequent
Hare's tail cotton-grass	Forms large tussocks Height 500 mm Roots often deep and replaced annually. Long lived >100 yrs	Extensive stands on wet, acidic ground Prominent in sites water-logged in spring but drier in summer Soil pH <6.0	Primarily by seed
Bracken	Fern with deep extensive under-grown rhizome Fronds arise April–May, persist to autumn Young fronds sensitive to frost and trampling Height 1,800 mm + Life 50 yrs +	Intolerant of waterlogged soils Shade tolerant Wide soil tolerance - particularly well on deep acidic (pH 4.5) soils pH range 3.0–7.6	By rhizomes Spores – 30 millon/frond important in colonising new sites Spores viable 10 yrs +

grasses and scrub, provide habitat for breeding birds especially whinchats, tree pipits and yellowhammers. However, extensive bracken stands are much less good for wildlife than a mix of different plants and dwarf shrubs.

Trees and scrub increase the wildlife richness of rough grazings by providing food and shelter for a wide variety of wildlife. For example, rowan and hawthorn berries are taken by black grouse in autumn and they also feed intensively on birch catkins in winter and the buds of larch in spring. Gorse and juniper are eaten by insects, which provide an important food resource for songbirds. All trees and shrubs provide shelter from wind and rain and concealment from predators.

1.3 Vegetation structure

- Low temperatures, rain and winds mean that shelter is exceptionally important to wildlife.
- Many upland birds prefer varied vegetation heights to conceal their nest and provide good feeding conditions.

Most of the uplands and coastal regions of the north and west are exposed to high winds and frequent rainfall. Even in the summer months, wind shelter and cover are important. For most insects and reptiles the ideal habitat is on a small scale with open spaces, perhaps a few inches to a foot or so across, protected from wind by surrounding tall growth but open to sunlight. Stony and rocky ground is also important for many species which can adjust their body temperatures and activity levels, by basking on sun-warmed surfaces in the lee of the wind or moving into crevices for shelter from rain.

Although larger animals find it easier to maintain body heat, they too tend to seek shelter and the warmest of sunshine if possible. Mountain hares carefully select their resting sites to obtain both maximum shelter from wind and cover as protection from predators which include foxes and eagles. As well as concealing themselves in tall heather, which is also a main food plant for them, hares lie up in peat hags, amongst boulders, and excavate short burrows.

Like other wildlife, birds have particular requirements for vegetation structure. For example, curlew usually nest amongst grasses or rushes round 0.3 m tall and sometimes taller, but they need shorter swards for feeding so that moderately grazed conditions with variations in vegetation height suit them well. Golden plovers nest on areas of very short vegetation (2.5 cm up to a maximum of 15 cm) which can result from grazing or burning (Feature 5.1: Waders of hill and rough grazing).

As well as breeding waders and grouse, extensive areas of rough grazing are very important for birds of prey including red kite, golden eagle, peregrine, hen harrier and merlin, and also short-eared owl. They depend on abundant populations of other birds and small mammals. Hen harriers, merlins and short-eared owls, which nest on the ground, prefer taller moorland vegetation, often heather over 30 cm in height (Feature 5.4: Habitat and feeding requirements of birds of prey).

1.4 Grazing

- Livestock modify upland vegetation structure. They also provide food resources in the form of dung and carrion.
- Sheep, cattle and ponies have different effects.
- Overgrazing leads to a gradual replacement of heathers and other plants with a narrow range of unpalatable grasses. This leads to a loss of wildlife interest.
- Mainly because of heavy grazing pressure, most areas of rough grazing now hold a much reduced variety of plants.

Livestock are an essential element in management for wildlife. Farm animals can create or destroy the vegetation required by invertebrates, birds and mammals; their dung is a food resource for beetles, flies and other insects, which in turn are eaten by birds. When animals die, their carrion is also an important source of food.

This section deals briefly with the effects of grazing on unenclosed pasture. More information on the general effects of grazing is at page 59 in Chapter 3 on grasslands and the effects on heather are also described at page 101 in Chapter 4 on lowland heaths.

Today, most unenclosed land is stocked with sheep, which graze the finer grasses, such as bents and fescues, short and tend to cause the spread of less palatable herbage which they will not eat. In autumn and the winter

Figure 5.1   Heather growth phases and effects of grazing

	Value to stock	Value to wildlife
Pioneer	Can only tolerate light grazing.	Limited except for species needing open conditions such as nesting golden plovers.
Building	Productive and able to withstand highest level of grazing.	Moderate cover and shelter. Some insects need young heather. Good feeding for grouse.
Mature	Less productive. Can be damaged by stock relatively easily.	Highest overall value as feeding, cover and shelter.
Degenerate	Unprotective. Quickly destroyed by grazing/trampling.	Important for some invertebrates, lichens and other plants.

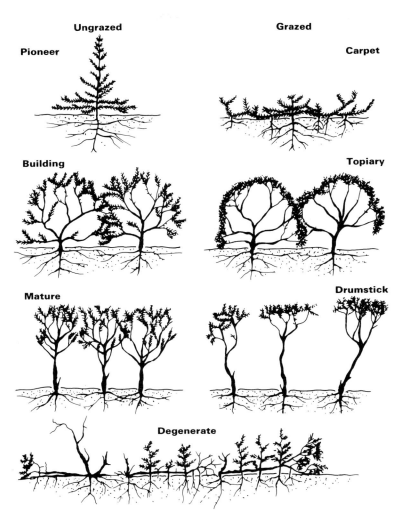

Figure 5.1   Heather growth phases and effects of grazing

Pioneer   Age 3–6 years, max 10 years. Early development with pyramidal shape. Usually only achieves about 10% ground cover which allows much light and moisture to ground level and has minimal influence on the rest of the vegetation.

Carpet   Pioneer heather under moderate grazing.

Building   Maximum of 15 years. Gradually changes to hemispherical shape. About 90% ground cover with closed, dense canopy. Exerts its greatest effects of light and moisture at ground level and excludes most other plants.

Topiary   Building heather under light grazing.

Mature   Age up to 20–25 years. Vigour reducing; oldest branches tend to spread apart. More frost sensitive. Reaches maximum height but not necessarily maximum diameter. About 75% ground cover and still strongly influencing light and moisture at ground level but conditions become more favourable for other species which begin to establish beneath it.

Drumstick   Mature heather under moderate to heavy grazing.

Degenerate   Age 25–30+ years. Central branches die leaving a gap which gradually widens as more branches die back. Outer branches remain alive for a number of years, often lying flat on the ground like spokes on a wheel and may root. Now only 40% ground cover with ground conditions more like pioneer phase. Decreasing dominance allows new heather, trees and bracken to develop.

(Diagrams modified from MacDonald, A 1990 *Heather damage: a guide to types of damage and their causes.* Research and Survey in Nature Conservation no 28, Nature Conservancy Council.)

months they make much use of heather. This means that grazing can be timed to favour one or the other and create the ideal mosaic. Bilberry is also a favoured food, particularly in late winter and early spring.

Cattle take more coarse grasses, sedges, rushes and fibrous material, and so can make good use of poor-quality grazing. Ponies are very selective where the conditions allow, grazing areas of finer grasses very short, but they also make much use of coarse material, such as browse from scrub or gorse, especially in winter. Both cattle and ponies can quickly damage stands of old heather by trampling. However, they open up dense swards and allow other plants to colonise, so increasing the variety, and it has been suggested that the spread of bracken is partly due to the absence of cattle which in the past were much more abundant and broke down the fronds by trampling.

However, as stocking densities increase, animals are obliged to be less selective and the sheer pressure of the grazing becomes the main influence on the type of plant cover and the structure of the vegetation, so that it has a very substantial effect on wildlife.

Under light grazing regimes, most rough grazings in western and northern regions support a varied plant community of grasses, herbs, mosses and ferns, heather and other dwarf shrubs such as bilberry. The structure of the vegetation is usually quite varied, with a mix of close-cropped ground interspersed by taller shrub cover. As grazing pressures increase, the plant richness is often progressively lost. Heathers and other dwarf shrubs are replaced by a restricted range of grasses.

Heather in particular provides valuable food for hill sheep throughout the year, particularly in winter. Young heather up to about seven years old is the most nutritious and is selectively grazed but it continues to be important throughout its vigorous growth stage up to about 15–20 years old. At moderate stock density there will be a balance of both grasses and heather to provide year-round food.

Heather is vulnerable to grazing pressure. If the offtake is greater than the new growth,

the bush will progressively become smaller and may die. In autumn, when the new growth is most palatable, it is particularly vulnerable. Its ability to tolerate grazing changes with age. Heather older than about 20 years grows progressively less vigorously, is more easily damaged or killed by heavy grazing or trampling and does not respond so well to burning. On better-drained soils, heather plants have a life seldom more than 40–50 years. It has therefore become the practice to burn heather once it reaches about 15 years of age in order to promote new growth. On some farms, it may be burned more often. The growth phases of heather and the effects of grazing on the plant are illustrated in Figure 5.1.

On damper acid soils, heather burning may be unnecessary as the plants can regenerate by layering. However, increasing grazing pressure can convert the habitat to one dominated by mat-grass often with heath rush. Particularly where the grassland is frequently burnt to improve palatability and early growth, purple moor-grass can become dominant. The wildlife value of these grasslands is extremely low, with a very restricted range of invertebrates and few birds either breeding or foraging.

Blanket peat and bogs can have important communities of wildlife under light grazing. Characteristic plants are Sphagnum bog mosses, cross-leaved heath, soft rush, deer sedge, purple moor-grass and the cotton-grasses, plus a range of other plants such as bog asphodel and bog myrtle. There is an enormous hatch of craneflies in early summer and this can be a vital food resource for the newly hatched young of such birds as golden plover. As well as supporting curlew, golden plover and snipe, peat bogs in northern Britain are also the habitat of breeding greenshank and dunlin. One of the first effects of intensive grazing by sheep on these areas is to lose most of the production of cotton-grass flowers because the sheep eat the shoots as they appear in spring. Thus red and black grouse are deprived of an important food source, which helps the hens to come into breeding condition.

In general, peatland habitats are particularly susceptible to damage through overstocking or burning. There is a risk of losing the vegetation cover and initiating a process of erosion which is difficult to repair.

Often it is only in areas inaccessible to grazing animals, such as ledges in stream gullies or on crags, that it is still possible to find tiny relics of the original plant cover, which it is important to protect.

As well as the effects on the variety of plants, grazing also alters the structure, which provides wildlife with shelter from the weather, concealment, breeding sites and food resources. Heavy grazing tends to remove structure almost completely, especially where dwarf shrubs are lost. The eggs and chicks of ground-nesting birds are at risk of trampling.

Supplementary feeding or fothering is a widespread practice. It encourages stock to concentrate around the feeding point for much of the day and in consequence the area becomes heavily trampled and grazed so that heather and other dwarf shrubs may be completely eradicated or so badly suppressed that they take 15 years or more to recover once the feeding point is moved.

The diet of red deer includes a higher proportion of heather than that of sheep, but deer rarely cause a conversion from heather moor to grassland. Deer are browsers and at densities of more than one per 25 ha can prevent trees and shrubs from regenerating in upland woods.

1.5 Burning

- Burning of rough grazings alters the abundance of different plants and can kill wildlife.
- Regular burning can eliminate certain plants particularly mosses and lichens.
- Large-scale burning simplifies vegetation structure and is bad for wildlife.
- Burning of heather, which creates a mosaic structure, is beneficial for many invertebrates and birds.

Burning at about 15-year intervals can maintain vigorous growth of heather and this is of value to out-wintering stock and to wildlife.

On grouse moors, heather is burned in a mosaic pattern, often on about a 10-year rotation, so as to provide an intimate mix of older stands (in which grouse nest and shelter) and nutritious young growth (on which they feed). The habitat is used by many other birds including breeding waders and birds of prey. In some situations, there is a rapid initial recovery by bilberry, bell heather or other shrubs and grasses or, on wet sites, by cotton-grass. These plants are replaced by heather in time and their presence increases the richness of the wildlife habitat.

In many regions, upland grazings are burned frequently – in some areas almost annually – in an attempt to increase the palatability and extent of grass available to stock in spring. These burns are usually large-scale and create extensive areas with little variation in vegetation age or structure. Fire-sensitive plants such as some mosses and lichens may be destroyed though a few flourish on the bare ground surface. On peats, burning can induce serious erosion which is very difficult to control. On better soils, such burning can lead to the spread of bracken and in the wetter regions it encourages purple moor-grass. Both of these plants have value for wildlife but where they dominate large areas the overall wildlife value is much reduced.

1.6 Use of fertilisers and lime

- Use of artificial fertilisers and lime is generally harmful to wildlife.

The application of nitrogen (as ammonium nitrate) and phosphate improve the growth and palatability of heather. This may increase numbers and breeding success of red grouse for a year or two but both nitrogenous fertilisers and lime lead to intensive grazing by sheep and the progressive replacement of heather by such grasses as bents and fescues. Where grasses or white clover are already present in quantity, fertiliser application will benefit them more than herbs or dwarf shrubs and thus lead to a loss of plant variety. A fuller discussion of the effects of using artificial fertilisers, farmyard manure and lime is in Chapter 3 page 62.

2. Options and assessment: planning management

2.1 Wildlife assessment of hill and rough grazings

- Because of the economics of 'hill farming', it may be difficult to integrate wildlife management so assessment of unenclosed grazings must be made with particular care.
- Advice and information should be sought from the conservation bodies.
- If grant aid is to be sought, approach the funding organisation before carrying out any survey.
- Key information is the condition of the grazings, including the amounts of grass, heathers and other dwarf shrubs.
- Small-scale features such as flushes or bogs should be mapped.
- Aerial photographs can be an aid, especially on large farms.

The aim of assessment will be to identify those parts of the unenclosed grazings which are most likely to have value for wildlife and any which could be improved, especially for some of the less-common species, without affecting the viability of the farm. Often the choices will be harder than in the lowlands because, potentially, large areas could be involved and the areas best for wildlife – such as cotton-grass bogs, may also be important for livestock. This makes it very important that the assessment is done thoroughly, a task made the harder by the likely size of the areas to be covered.

If grant aid is to be sought, approach the funding organisation to discuss the degree of information required before starting the assessment.

The background to assessment is set out in Chapter 1 which also indicates possible sources of information. Unfortunately, while most of lowland UK has been surveyed for habitats and rare species, much of the uplands has been far less intensively studied so the amount of information is likely to be small. This makes

it even more important to carry out the assessment as carefully as possible. The information to be collected is set out at Table 5.2, which also explains the reasons for its importance and how to obtain it.

The basis of assessment is to map the main different types of vegetation and their structure because, as section 1 makes clear, these have fundamental influences on the rest of the wildlife. On many hill farms these will vary little over great distances. However, especially in such an area, the value of small-scale features can take on increased importance. These include, for example, flushes, small bogs and isolated stands of heather or other dwarf shrubs in extensive grass-dominated moorland. Most farmers and crofters will know where these features are and this will enable assessment effort to concentrate on them. In addition, aerial photographs come into their own as an aid and can be used to save a great deal of time.

Within different areas, the level of use by livestock and the effects of burning will need to be recorded because of their effect on the vegetation. Again, the farmer himself is likely to have this information at his fingertips.

It is rarely practicable to survey for scarce species over large areas but the conservation organisations should be approached and, even if they have no information, may be able to say whether the 'good' areas identified by the assessment may be suitable for important species such as nesting waders. However, with some upland birds, locating nesting sites or areas may only be the first step. Waders and grouse may nest in one habitat and feed in another whereas birds of prey feed over considerable areas, sometimes covering many different farm or estate ownerships. Advice will be available on management for them.

Table 5.2: Wildlife assessment of hill and rough grazing

INFORMATION REQUIRED	METHOD	REASONS FOR INFORMATION
1. Conservation status and interest	Contact FWAG initially.	As many hill and rough grazings still contain semi-natural vegetation, information on its wildlife interest may already have been collected. Some hill and upland grazings may also have a special designation (such as SSSI or ASSI). If so, certain conditions may need to be satisfied before changes of management can take place.
2. Past management	Check farm/estate records. Check historical information. Examine past and present aerial photographs.	This will identify changes in plant composition and structure, even if only on a broad scale, eg increase in bracken and grass cover, decrease in heather area. It will help in guiding future management for wildlife.
3. Current management	Note current grazing practice including stock type, stocking levels, seasonal use and use of supplementary feeding/mineral blocks. Also note vegetation response.	Evaluation of grazing regime and its impact on wildlife. May suggest modification required.
	Map all burnt areas and note size and shape of burn, and frequency of burns. Also note vegetation response.	Evaluation of burning practice and regime and its impact on wildlife. May suggest modifications required.
4. Moorland and grass composition and structure	On acid soils and bogs map relative abundance of heather and grass in the following categories. >75% heather <25% grass *c*50% heather *c*50% grass <25% heather >75% grass	To assess availability of forage for stock and to determine degree of overgrazing, if any. To assess potential wildlife value.
	Note general heather condition and map extensive areas in the following categories (see page 141 for further details): Pioneer Building Mature Degenerate Dead	To assess availability of forage for stock. To assess variety and juxtaposition of heather structures and consequent management needs. To identify areas of old heather which may need special management. This will identify areas of overgrazed hill ground and general plant species diversity. Knowledge of the distribution of different heather ages is important. If all the same age, the wildlife interest is likely to be less and appropriate management will need to be taken. Areas of old tall heather can be of conservation importance. The location of other plants can affect decisions on future management, eg unburnt areas may have a rich lichen flora.
	On basic soils record outcrops of limestone-rich grassland (see table 3.2 page 65 for further details)	If a wide variety of herbs and grasses are present then grassland likely to have wildlife interest.

Table 5.2: Wildlife assessment of hill and rough grazing (cont'd)

INFORMATION REQUIRED	METHOD	REASONS FOR INFORMATION
5. Bracken	Map area of bracken according to following categories: Sparse and scattered <10% cover Abundant (but with plenty of heather below) Solid, closed canopy >75% cover (with little or no heather below).	Generally of low wildlife interest. If spreading then may need to undertake control. May identify potential areas for heather restoration. Retain areas that support breeding whinchat.
6. Other hill and upland features	Record tree and scrub distribution (by species). See also Chapter 7: Farm Woods.	Scattered trees and scrub can be important. May be remnants of old woodland with woodland flowers. Also add to diversity especially for invertebrates. If woodland grades into moor may be important for some birds. Will identify priorities for retention and possible enhancement through stock protection.
	Map bogs. Record location of flushes.	May contain rare plants. Also contains cotton-grass important food for grouse. Also important for invertebrates (and consequently grouse chicks and waders).
	Map location of other wetland features such as streams, burns and lochans.	Potentially of high conservation interest.
	Record major rock outcrops and screes.	Potentially of high conservation interest.
7. Rare and sensitive species	Record exact location of rare species. Note vegetation structure in vicinity. Seek specialist guidance on information.	A number of rare birds, invertebrates and plants, may occur. The locations of these are important to know and build into the management regime.
8. Boundaries	Location of dykes, dry-stone walls, fences and hedges.	To assess the potential for changes in stock management, eg for stock reduction in heather restoration.
	Location of main vehicle access routes.	To assess use of vehicles onto the hill for future livestock management.

2.2 Management needs and opportunities

- As a priority for wildlife, reduce stocking levels on overgrazed areas with little plant variety and structure.
- Where it is impracticable to reduce stocking levels, fence important areas such as stands of old heather or flushes so that grazing can be controlled.
- Control bracken where invasion is serious.
- Undertake burning only on a small scale in appropriate areas.
- Restore areas of degraded rough grazings by taking advantage of incentives and grant aid.

The character and wildlife of the hills and other areas of rough grazing have developed as a result of livestock farming. Where assessment shows that the farm holds a good range of vegetation and a varied structure suitable for wildlife, the clear course of action is to continue existing management.

However, agricultural improvement and high stocking levels may be found to have caused a decline in the extent and wildlife interest of unimproved grass, heather or other good wildlife habitats. Where grouse management is a priority, the emphasis is often on maintaining extensive cover of heather rather than a mosaic of different plant types.

In general, areas with a rich variety of plants are now rare. As a result, on all grazings, for wildlife the priority is to maintain or restore a varied plant community with a good structure to provide cover and shelter. On many farms this will only be possible through a reduction in livestock numbers and so depends on financial aid. Incentives are now available to restore areas that have been adversely affected by past management.

Where reduction of livestock levels is impracticable, it can be very valuable to fence limited areas, particularly old heather, streamsides, flushes, cotton-grass bogs or,

on limestone, flower-rich grassland, so that grazing within them can be controlled. If the right land is selected, an enclosure will produce much greater wildlife benefits than its small size would suggest. The land need not be wholly lost to the farm as low-intensity grazing at the correct time of year may be required to maintain its importance. In some instances, fencing may be a temporary measure to allow the vegetation to recover from overgrazing (Figure 5.2: Some hill farm conservation opportunities).

Livestock can also be excluded from woodland, scrub or, in Wales, ffridd in order to encourage natural regeneration by shrubs and trees. Depending on the age and condition of the existing cover, this can be a long-term process which involves only small parts of the site at any one time. Control of deer may also be needed. Grazing in woodland is considered in Chapter 7 page 208.

Although bracken has some limited wildlife value, its dramatic spread in the uplands has reduced both hill grazings and wildlife interest. Appropriate control measures should be introduced and followed by a management regime that encourages the restoration of a varied mix of plants including heather and other dwarf shrubs.

Burning as well as grazing is regarded as an important technique in the management of dry moorlands to rejuvenate heather for grazing and, on grouse moors, to produce both young heather as food and older stands as nesting cover. However, burning can be harmful because it can destroy small-scale variation in vegetation structure and, in some regions, damage the underlying peat soils and induce erosion. Where burning is too frequent, heather may be replaced by grasses and mosses and lichens will be destroyed. Such changes reduce the richness of the habitat and its capacity for supporting a wide variety of other wildlife. Good management of burning is invaluable for wildlife and the long-term productivity of the land.

In addition to stock reduction and stock exclusion measures, the re-establishment of heather and other moorland vegetation

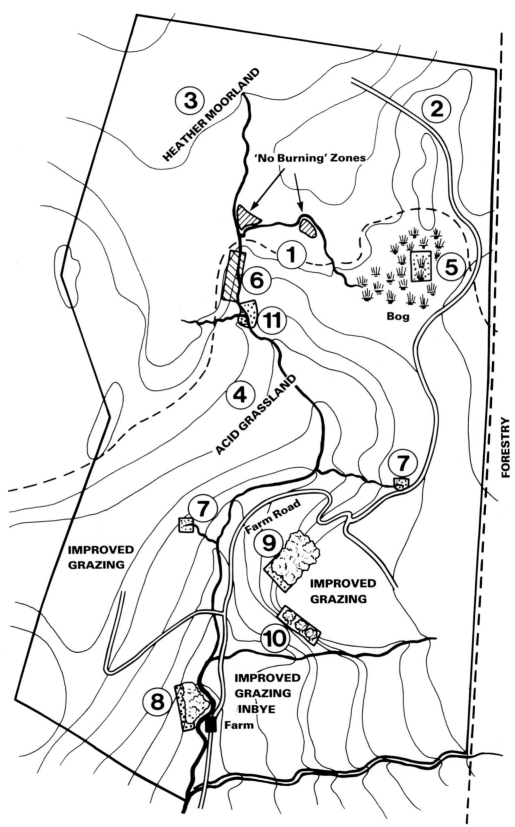

Figure 5.2
Some hill farm conservation opportunities

On many farms in the uplands or those with extensive rough grazing, by far the best way of restoring wildlife interest is likely to be to reduce stocking levels. However, unless realistic financial incentives are available, this will be impracticable. The following measures are suggested as ways of getting greatest wildlife benefit for least effect on the farm and existing livestock levels.

Refer to main text for full details of wildlife value and management methods.

1. *Heather condition.* If heather is being replaced by grass, reduce stocking rates or reduce winter grazing or fence stock out of selected areas to enable them to recover.
   Benefits breeding waders, birds of prey and game.

2. *Winter feeding points.* Ideally, keep on poor-quality grassland, if available. On young heather, move at least 250 m every 2–3 weeks or locate permanently on one sacrificial site. Do not site on old heather.
   Benefits all wildlife dependent on heather, notably breeding birds.

3. *Heather burning.* Avoid large-scale burns. If essential for regeneration, burn small patches and strips each year. Keep some areas of old heather. On wet sites where heather will regenerate without burning, protect stands from fire.
   Benefits all wildlife dependent on heather, notably breeding birds.

4. *Acid grassland.* If necessary to retain or create a varied structure, fence areas to regulate grazing pressure.
   Benefits grassland wildflowers and insects.

5. *Bogs.* Fence off to permit cotton-grass to flower and graze in autumn/winter.
   Benefits scarce upland plants, nesting waders and grouse.

6. *Crags, scree, stream gorges.* Fence against stock to protect any surviving scarce plants.
   Benefits upland plants including those of the original woodlands and birds such as ring ouzel.

7. *Springs and flushes.* If heavily grazed, so that plants cannot flower, fence to limit grazing to late summer and autumn.
   Benefits flowers, insects, wader and gamebird chicks.

8. *Plantations.* Thin to let in light. Exclude stock from part or all of site. Enhance unshaded edges by planting shrubs.
   Benefits woodland songbirds and black grouse.

9. *Native woods.* Exclude stock from at least one-third of the site.
   Benefits woodland flowers, insects and ground-nesting and shrub-nesting birds.

10. *Remnant tree cover.* Exclude stock and plant native trees and shrubs.
    Benefits all woodland wildlife. Ensures survival of wood.

11. *New woodland.* Create small plantings of well-spaced trees and shrubs.
    Benefits butterflies and other upland insects, foraging gamebirds and birds of prey.

When selecting sites for management or protection, first, protect the best wildlife areas, or those with most potential. Second, where there is a choice, it is beneficial to have several well-managed wildlife areas close together rather than scattered across the farm. This helps species that need a variety of habitats or features.

on areas which have been drained, re-seeded, heavily grazed or too frequently burned may now be encouraged through financial payments. This has good wildlife benefits.

All the techniques of management of stock and vegetation that are referred to in the following sections will be very familiar to farmers and crofters. The aim of the text is to bring out aspects related to wildlife which may not be so familiar. Farmers should modify the recommendations in the light of conditions on their land and their own experience.

3. Management

3.1 Grazing

- Maintain existing grazing regime where a good plant variety and structure still exist.
- Reduce stocking levels where signs of overgrazing appear.
- If large-scale change is impracticable, fence areas with wildlife value or potential, such as flushes and stands of old heather so that grazing can be controlled.
- Site supplementary feeding points on ground with little wildlife value, preferably on grass, well away from stands of mature heather.
- If this is not possible, reduce stock concentration by having several small feeding areas spread across the hill or by moving the feeding points frequently.
- Do not apply fertilisers or lime on unimproved grazings.

In theory, stocking rates are determined by what the vegetation can support without damage, so that stock numbers and condition can be maintained in the long-term. In practice, because of economic factors, there are now few areas of unenclosed grazing which are not overstocked and deteriorating in their ability to maintain animals in good condition and to support a good variety of plants and other wildlife. The level which different types of vegetation can support without damage varies considerably, as shown in Table 5.3. These figures are only an approximate guide, as growth rates of plants, including grasses and heathers, and the length of the growing season, can vary significantly. Stocking rates are also influenced by the types of livestock, including the size of sheep, the extent of shepherding and in what seasons the grazing takes place.

The most obvious signs of overgrazing include expanses of short-cropped grasses with prolific unpalatable species such as mat-grass, few flowering plants, few or no flowers on cotton-grass, heather and other dwarf shrubs bitten short, occurring as a sparse scattering or completely absent (Figure 5.1). The ideal for wildlife would be to reduce grazing pressure right across these areas. This would involve lower levels than those in Table 5.3. Many moorland breeding birds need extensive areas of

---

Table 5.3: Maximum year-round stocking levels for medium-sized hill sheep such as Swaledales and blackfaces on upland vegetation.

VEGETATION TYPE	(EWES/HA)
Good grass (bent & fescues)	4.7
Poor grass (mat-grass, heath rush)	1.3
Young heather (pioneer & early building phase)	1.6
Intermediate heather (late building)	0.4
Old heather (mature & degenerate)	0.1
Blanket bog	0.5

Source: Sibbald, A R, Grant, S A, Milne, J A and Maxwell, T J 1987. *In: Agriculture and Conservation in the Hills and Uplands.* (eds. M Bell and R G M Bunce). ITE Symposium No 23, Institute of Terrestrial Ecology.

Notes

1. These are maximum stocking levels and may not be appropriate on areas of high wildlife interest or where vegetation cover is being restored.
2. These are year-round stocking levels. For most areas of wildlife interest seasonal grazing is advocated.
3. There will be considerable variation across the UK in relation to latitude, altitude, exposure and rainfall, in addition to vegetation composition, height and structure.

suitable habitat supporting abundant potential food supplies. This is particularly the case with birds of prey such as merlin and short-eared owl.

Where the amount and condition of heather and other dwarf shrubs is declining, reduction or cessation of winter grazing may be sufficient to bring about a recovery. On severely overgrazed heather, cease grazing entirely throughout the year until the heather has reached the height of 20 cm or more and cover extends over half the ground at least. This may take at least seven years on well-drained ground and considerably longer on bog systems. Then graze lightly to develop greater vegetation structure. The aim should be not a continuous carpet of heather but a mosaic of tall and short heather mixed with small lawns of grasses, sedges and other plants.

Where large-scale change in stocking rates is impracticable, the next best thing is to fence off selected areas so that levels and timing of livestock use can be controlled. This will benefit plants, invertebrates, reptiles and some birds. Aim to improve overall vegetation structure to benefit invertebrates and breeding birds in particular. Concentrate care on areas most likely to bring good results quickly. These include surviving patches of dwarf shrubs, such as heather, bilberry or western gorse, bogs with cotton-grass, flushes and patches of shrubs such as juniper and gorse.

On bogs or flushes with cotton-grass, exclude sheep in spring to allow the new shoots and flower buds to be taken by grouse and hares. In autumn, sheep can be given access to graze provided that the pressure is not so great that the cotton-grass is reduced in abundance. Blanket peat bog will only sustain about 0.5 ewes/ha year round without damage to the vegetation.

Flushes are an important part of the upland habitat for plants, invertebrates and birds. Because they tend to be more productive than surrounding land, they are usually grazed heavily. For a short period in early summer, flushes support an abundance of craneflies and other insects which provide food for the chicks of grouse and waders (Features 5.1 & 5.2). Cessation of grazing is

harmful to flushes because vegetation becomes rank, many less vigorous plants are suppressed and chicks cannot move freely. The ideal is to exclude stock from the beginning of March to the end of June, so that chicks are protected from the risk of being trampled and killed, and plants can flower and set seed. Grazing from late summer through the winter should ensure good sward conditions for the following spring .

Where streamsides are heavily grazed, small exclosures will allow vegetation to grow up and provide potential nesting cover for wildfowl such as teal, mallard, wigeon and red-breasted mergansers and for common sandpipers. Grazing should not be allowed at all in these areas because some ducks settle to nest before the new growth is well advanced and, without tall cover from last year, they are easily found by predators. In these areas, taller vegetation can provide habitat for the adult stages of many freshwater invertebrates such as alder-flies and cover for otters.

Gullies to which livestock can only obtain access with difficulty may still contain plants which have survived from the original woodland cover. These are important features and here too it is desirable to ensure that stock are excluded entirely, by fencing if necessary.

Some areas may contain plants which survive but cannot flower because of grazing pressure. Where there are signs of plant variety in the sward, it is worth excluding stock on one or two small plots to see what happens. If new plants appear, consider excluding or reducing stock numbers over larger areas. Allow stock in during autumn or early spring and graze enough to prevent the dominant grasses from taking over and to open the sward so that any new seedlings may grow, but exclude stock in spring and summer so that the plants can set seed. Similarly, it may be possible to encourage the spread of plants from small areas where they still survive, such as streamsides and flushes or ledges which escape grazing altogether, by fencing adjoining ground to control grazing.

Even if the sward is mostly unpalatable grasses and no new plants appear, other benefits may still come from reducing grazing pressure. For instance, if it can be done over areas of at least 1 ha, birds such as curlew may be able to find nesting cover. They may also use smaller patches but run an increased risk of being found by foxes or other predators.

Bear in mind that fencing will put more pressure on the rest of the land unless overall stock numbers are reduced or greater reliance is placed on supplementary feeding.

Supplementary feeding points tend to cause stock to concentrate in one area, where trampling and grazing will cause damage to stands of heather or other dwarf shrubs. Enrichment from dung can cause changes in a sward and result in the loss of less-vigorous plants, which are replaced by grasses. The overall effect on wildlife is bad and can extend over several hectares. It is therefore important to site feeding points on ground with little existing value for wildlife such as areas of mat grass or moor-grass. Alternatively, to reduce the number of stock concentrating in one place, have several feeding points spread out over the hill. Good shepherding can prevent many of the problems of sheep concentrating and seriously overgrazing the vegetation.

If a feeding point must be placed on or near heathers or other dwarf shrubs, it should be sited on young growth rather than any old stands and moved at least every three weeks before serious harm is caused. When a feed block is replaced, the new one should be at least 100 m away. Where hay is provided, the distribution point should be moved at least 250 m.

Fertilisers should not be applied in areas managed for wildlife.

3.2 Burning

- Where heather must be burned to maintain its condition for grazing, develop a rotation, burning several patches smaller than 1 ha each year.
- Prepare a burning plan to ensure heather is burned effectively and safely.
- Cut firebreaks to minimise the risk of fires getting out of control.
- Burn only when weather conditions are suitable during the legal period allowed for burning.
- Follow the advice and legal conditions summarised in the relevant heather and grass burning codes.
- Identify important areas of old heather or other vegetation and do not burn them.
- Repeated, frequent firing of rough grassland is very damaging.

If it is necessary to burn heather in order to ensure its regeneration, greatest benefits to wildlife will come from creating a mosaic like that produced on grouse moors. Not only is the small-scale mosaic better for birds, mammals and invertebrates, but it also helps to spread sheep across the hill and ensures that they do not concentrate so heavily in one area as to prevent the regrowth of the heathers.

Burning should take place when the heather is 20–30 cm tall – on dry ground in the Highlands this may take 10–20 years but in south-west England as little as 6–10 years. On bogs, the length of the rotation may need to be double this if heather is not to be eliminated. Supposing a 15-year rotation, the ideal would be to burn 1/15th of the area each year in patches about 0.5–1 ha in extent. At this frequency, there will be only a moderate amount of woody material and litter so a downwind fire will be satisfactory. Burn when windspeed is light and ideally lay out the mosaic so as to burn towards recently burned areas rather than older stands where it may be difficult to stop the fire spreading.

It is difficult to muster sufficient manpower to be certain of being able to control fires if wind conditions change. This makes it all the more important to plan burns so that the risk of large areas being burned is lessened. Where there is access by roads or tracks and the terrain is reasonably smooth, a forage harvester or flail mounted on a four-wheel drive tractor can make firebreaks to minimise the risk of fires getting out of hand. Further information on the planning of heather burning is given in Chapter 4 page 113.

Ideally, for wildlife, it would be best to burn in the period from late autumn up to mid-February, as breeding birds will be absent and reptiles will be hibernating. The effect on invertebrates will also be least. Successful regeneration of heather is possible throughout this period. The burning codes of practice should be followed. Heather and grass burning is only permitted in England and Wales between 1 November – 31 March in lowlands and 1 October – 15 April in uplands. In Scotland it runs from 1 October – 15 April. In Northern Ireland it runs from 1 September – 14 April.

Some areas should be left unburnt. Ideally they should contain older heathers or vegetation other than grasses and be sited where there is the least likelihood of their being fired by accident. Suitable sites may be upwind of a stream or gully or on a steep slope.

Where overstocking has led to widespread mat grass or purple moor-grass, burning is often carried out frequently and without firebreaks, in order to encourage some palatable growth in spring. This is very damaging to wildlife and such areas should be a high priority for the restoration of more diverse swards, including heathers, on both conservation and agricultural grounds.

3.3 Bracken

- Control bracken where it is invading vegetation which has wildlife value.
- Avoid burning close to bracken stands as this may encourage bracken to spread.
- Where aerial spraying is carried out, avoid land that may contain other ferns or susceptible plants.

Bracken should be accepted as part of the vegetation mosaic and not wholly eradicated, but it should not be permitted to spread and become dominant on areas that contain a good variety of other plants, especially dwarf shrub cover. Such encroachment is encouraged by unwise burning close to existing bracken stands, draining and ploughing.

In situations where attempts are being made to restore heather or mixed vegetation cover, extensive stands of bracken can be reduced by spraying with Asulam. Cutting and rolling are also effective but difficult to carry out except on fairly flat ground. These methods are described more fully for the lowland heaths (see Chapter 4 page 116). The scale of the task and difficult terrain in upland areas may make aerial spraying necessary.

Asulam kills other ferns as well as bracken and care must be taken to avoid spraying rocky outcrops and the banks of streams, where they are most likely to occur. Gorse and some grasses can be checked by Asulam. Mature heathers are unaffected but young heather (less than five years after burning) may be killed. The accuracy of aerial application is therefore of great importance.

Once bracken has been killed, it is essential to remove the deep litter of old material so that other plants can colonise. On small areas, the trampling of stock, especially cattle, may achieve this but in most cases clearance by raking may be necessary unless the litter can be burned.

3.4 Tree and scrub management

- Do not encourage regeneration of trees or shrubs or plant them on areas with existing wildlife interest or close to breeding wader sites.
- Plant appropriate native species of tree and shrub.
- With small plantings, aim to maintain an open canopy, giving sunlit but sheltered conditions. Do not allow stock access.
- With larger plantings at conventional spacings, create sheltered, sunlit rides and glades.
- Allow livestock access to larger plantings only. Do so only when trees and shrubs are well grown.
- Manage gorse by coppicing.

Tree and shrub plantings will provide valuable food resources and shelter for wildlife. They should not be made on ground of existing importance. One problem with tree and scrub cover is that it is likely to provide nest sites and look-out posts for corvids and shelter for foxes. These are capable of increasing predation pressure on ground-nesting birds such as golden plover, curlew and wildfowl. It is therefore important to site such plantings at least 500 m away from known nesting areas.

Suitable sites for planting or regeneration may include streamsides, the margins of gullies, steep slopes which are susceptible to erosion, ground cleared of bracken and areas where a scattering of mature trees still exists.

The native willows (upland species include bay, grey, eared, dark-leaved and tea-leaved) are excellent early pollen producers for insects. Birch will grow on most sites, rowan in many areas, and native Scots pine is very desirable in the eastern Highlands. Aspen is another tree with many associated insects. The native alder grows well in sheltered wet situations. More information on tree and shrub choices is given on pages 187 and 201.

From the wildlife point of view it does not matter if the species chosen will grow slowly or remain stunted as they will still provide wind shelter and food resources. If the main aim is to produce shelter for stock and some timber revenue, choose species best suited to the local soils, drainage and weather; this may mean using non-natives in some areas and this will be less good for invertebrates in particular but some wildlife benefits will be obtained. Refer to Chapter 7 page 199 for more information on ways of integrating timber production or stock shelter with wildlife.

Great wildlife benefits can come from quite small plantings, even less than 1 ha. The aim is not to create closed canopy woodland but to plant at wide spacings – say, shrubs 2 m and trees 4 m – so that other vegetation can grow between the bushes and trees. The result will be a varied plant community, offering a wide variety of food to insects. There will also be much structural variety including areas which are reasonably sheltered from the wind but receive sunlight so that they are warm. Conditions are likely to be excellent for upland butterflies and moths, bumblebees and other insects. The habitat will also be ideal for whinchat and, where they are present, black grouse are likely to use the plantation for feeding and breeding. A variety of common songbirds will also move in, providing good hunting habitat for merlin and sparrowhawk.

In the early stages of the planting, it may be necessary to herbicide or otherwise control any vigorous vegetation growth within a metre radius of each tree or shrub in order to prevent competition for moisture and nutrients. Intervening vegetation that does not interfere with growth should be retained and management can cease once the plantation is well established.

Do not allow stock access under any circumstances because the aim is to retain good cover at ground level and this would be grazed out. Check fences frequently. As soon as the ground between the trees is becoming overshaded, thin the planting so that the tree canopy does not close. This will mean that by the time trees have reached 3 m height, they may need to be at about 6 m spacings. Keep an outer fringe of two or three trees width where the canopy is allowed to close in order to give good shelter from wind to the interior.

Larger plantings can be established at conventional spacings provided that they contain glades and rides which provide wind-sheltered, sunlit conditions. Follow the guidance set out on page 206. It may be appropriate to allow stock access to these plantations once the trees are well established and sufficiently tall.

Gorse is an excellent wildlife plant. Many invertebrates depend on it and it is used as feeding and nesting habitat by a number of songbirds. Where it is already present, the ideal management is to coppice it on about a 10–15 year rotation, depending on local growth rates, so as to maintain dense, bushy growth. Gorse can be established from seed or by planting seedlings on grazing exclusures on well-drained sites.

3.5 Re-establishment of natural vegetation

- Select the most appropriate technique for the restoration scheme.
- Where there is still heather on the moorland, all that may be required is reduction or removal of livestock, or a reduction in burning frequency.
- Land which has been fertilised, limed and re-seeded may need nutrient depletion measures, before restoration can be successful.
- Obtain heather seed by forage-harvesting material from vigorous plants.
- Scarify the ground and spread the seed with heather shoots as a mulch.
- Seek advice for all restoration proposals, especially as grant aid may be available.

The re-establishment of heather and other vegetation on hill ground and rough grazing which has been drained, re-seeded, heavily grazed or too frequently burnt may now be encouraged through financial payments. Restoration can be a complex and time-consuming process and this section can only provide broad guidelines. Experience of different techniques is being developed. In all cases seek advice from a specialist. For many areas the most practical option will be to reduce or remove livestock to

allow the heather and other plants to recover. Assess the amount and condition of heather as this will provide a guide to the management required. Where there is little heather or other vegetation except grasses, exclude stock completely for a period. Heather which has been seriously overgrazed may take seven years or more to recover on dry sites and considerably longer on wet ones before stock can be reintroduced. If the overgrazing has not been so severe, recovery may be achieved by excluding stock during the winter and using light summer grazing or simply reducing stocking levels year round.

On burnt areas where heather is not regenerating or is dying back, review the burning regime and if necessary reduce burning frequency. Follow advice contained in the Heather and Grass Burning Code. Reduce stocking levels or remove stock if the area is also grazed.

Where bracken has been sprayed out, it is important to remove litter to allow other plants to colonise and, if this fails to occur, as a preliminary to re-seeding.

Land that has lost its natural plant cover due to fire, overgrazing or bracken may still have a seedbank of heathers and other plants that will germinate naturally if grazing is removed for a period. Land that has been fertilised and re-seeded in the past may have a nutrient status too high for heathers and the pH may also be wrong if the land has been limed. It is essential to check nutrient and pH levels before attempting to restore a natural plant cover. If it is not suitable, it will be necessary to continue to graze the land without any inputs until levels fall. Alternatively, in some situations it may be appropriate to apply nitrogen in the form of ammonium sulphate to lower the pH.

Once soil conditions are suitable (see page 119), heather and other plants may begin to appear from seed. Otherwise, it will be necessary to collect heather seed in the autumn. This can be done by using a forage harvester on flat land. Ideally cut plants that are about 7–10 years old and remove about 7–10 cm so that as well as the seed there is a good amount of stem and leaf.

This will act as a mulch. As a rule of thumb, material from a site 1 ha in size will be enough to treat 3 ha. Heather seed requires light to germinate and should not be raked in. The timing of this operation is not critical although best results are obtained by sowing as soon as possible after foraging. For all the above situations stock should only be allowed back on to restored areas as part of a long-term management plan when heather and other plants are well established.

4. References and further reading

Bell, M and Bunce, G H (eds) 1987. *Agriculture and conservation in the hills and uplands.* Institute of Terrestrial Ecology.

Cadbury, C J C 1993. The Management of Upland Vegetation for Birds. *RSPB Conservation Review* 7: 12–21

Gimingham, C H 1972. *Ecology of heathlands.* Chapman and Hall.

Macdonald, A and Armstrong, H 1989. *Methods for monitoring heather cover.* Research and survey in nature conservation no. 10. Nature Conservancy Council.

MAFF/WOAD 1992. *The heather and grass burning code.* HMSO.

Mowforth, M A and Sydes, C 1989. *Moorland management: a literature review.* Research and survey in nature conservation no 25. Nature Conservancy Council.

Murray, R B (ed) 1985. *Vegetation Management in northern Britain.* British Crop Protection Council (Monograph no 30).

Pearsall, W H 1971 *Mountains and moorlands.* New Naturalist no 11 Collins.

Ratcliffe, D A 1991. The mountain flora of Britain and Ireland. *British Wildlife* vol 3 no 1.

Rodwell, J S (ed) 1991. *British Plant Communities Volume 2 Mires and Heaths.* Cambridge University Press.

Scottish Natural Heritage 1993. *A Muirburn Code.* SNH.

Usher, M B and Thompson, D B A (eds) 1988. *Ecological change in the uplands.* Blackwell Scientific Publications.

Feature 5.1: Waders of Hill and Rough Grazing

Unimproved grazings support several breeding waders including curlew, golden plover and dunlin. Each requires vegetation of a particular type and height for nesting and feeding. Other waders include lapwing, snipe and redshank which also occur on lower ground, moorland margins and inbye land.

Curlew

Curlews breed mainly on damp moors and unimproved rough grassland including enclosed inbye land. They may use re-seeded pasture for feeding. In comparison with other waders curlews nest in taller, more tussocky vegetation such as rushes, tufted hair-grass and purple moor-grass. After the young hatch they are led to damp areas with shorter grass and a rich supply of invertebrates. Curlews feed on earthworms, cranefly larvae and dung beetles. A wide variety of other beetles is also taken, and flies are important for the young.

Golden plover

Golden plovers breed on bogs and open, treeless moorland with good all-round visibility. For nesting they require short vegetation less than 15 cm tall , such as heather and cotton-grass. Golden plovers feed on beetles, caterpillars and craneflies, which are picked from the surface of the ground. Damp areas and wet flushes are an important source of invertebrates for the chicks.

Dunlin

Dunlins breed in a wide range of habitats, from machair at sea-level to mountain summits up to 1,000 m. On hill and upland grazings dunlins breed on poorly drained, peaty moorland with pools and a high proportion of cotton-grass. The nests are usually concealed in cotton-grass. Dunlins are territorial on their breeding grounds but often nest in loose colonies. They feed principally on adult craneflies, leatherjackets and chironomid midges.

Habitat requirements

	Curlew	Golden Plover	Dunlin
Heather – tall	N		
Heather – short	F	NF	
Cotton-grass		NF	NF
Purple moor-grass	N		
Rough pasture	N		
Acidic grassland	F	F	
Bogs and flushes	F	F	NF
Pools, lake shores			F

N = nesting   F = feeding area

Feature 5.2: Habitat and Feeding Requirements of Black Grouse

Decline
Caused largely by loss and fragmentation of habitats on farmland due to:

- Conversion of moorland to improved pasture through drainage and re-seeding
- Overgrazing of moorland
- Loss of shrub understorey in woodland because of foraging sheep.

Seasonal food use of black grouse

FOOD	MONTH			
	MAM	JJA	SON	DJF
Heather	●	–	·	●
Bilberry	●	•	●	●
Other shrubs eg cowberry bearberry	–	·	●	–
Cotton-grass flowers	●	–	–	–
Sedge and rush seeds	–	–	•	–
Larch buds	•	–	–	•
Other conifer buds	•	–	–	•
Birch buds, catkins, shoots	●	·	·	●
Insects and spiders	·	●	·	–
Clover	•	–	–	–

● = high importance
• = medium importance
· = low importance

Habitat
The black grouse is mainly a bird of moorland margins and upland woods. It requires a variety of habitats, which are related to the seasonal variation in its food supply. This normally includes an open patchwork of young or widely spaced trees with a well-developed understorey of heather and bilberry (blaeberry). In Northern England the use of hay meadows and unimproved pastures is particularly important as these provide abundant wet flushes with rushes, herbs and sedges.

Leks
Groups of male black grouse take part in complex communal displays known as leks to attract a mate. They occur at traditional sites and take place in the early morning and at dusk.

Feature 5.3: Management for Choughs

Nest sites

Choughs use traditional nest sites, mainly sea-cliffs, caves, quarries and old mine shafts. They will also nest in derelict buildings.

Habitat requirements

Choughs need a variety of different habitat features. Heath and unimproved rough grassland are favoured by choughs for feeding provided it has a short sward. Other important features include small patches of cultivation, arable stubbles, fallow land, rocky outcrops and anthills in pastures.

Food

Birds feed on invertebrates associated with soil such as leatherjackets and animal dung especially flies and beetles. They also eat worms, grain, crustaceans, molluscs and moth larvae.

Management

- Do not plough, re-seed or cultivate old pastures. Retain rough grazing land and heath.
- Maintain a short sward especially during the spring and summer to allow choughs access to a range of soil invertebrates.
- Heather can also be managed in rotation by burning or cutting. Aim to keep some heather as young growth, on around a 15-year rotation.
- Avoid stock treatment chemicals which have an insecticidal effect eg Ivermectin. Where there is no alternative, an injection is preferable to bolus treatment because levels of the drug will decline quickly leaving some cowpats unaffected.
- Put up nesting platforms in dark, undisturbed sites such as derelict buildings. Grant aid may be available.

Choughs and crows

Choughs can sometimes be confused with other crows. When seen at close quarters the chough has a fine, down-curved red bill and red legs. Choughs are smaller than crows, being about the same size as a jackdaw.

Distribution

Choughs used to be widespread around the coasts of the UK. However, there was a marked decline in the 18th and 19th centuries and they are now restricted to Wales, the Isle of Man, western Scotland and some coastal areas of Ireland. The decline is primarily due to habitat loss.

Feature 5.4: Habitat and Feeding Requirements of Birds of Prey

A variety of birds of prey use improved grazing for hunting and some nest on the ground where cover is adequate. The populations of golden eagle, peregrine, short-eared owl, kestrel and buzzard are all stable or increasing. However, red kite, merlin and hen harrier remain scarce and have small populations which are widely dispersed. Each species has its own nesting and feeding requirements although birds of prey can share the same habitat on their breeding grounds.

Red kite

Red kite

Conservation status: Small breeding population in Wales increasing after a long period of decline. Present population around 100 pairs. Recently reintroduced to England and Scotland.

Nesting requirements: In Wales mature, open oakwoods in steep valleys. Wooded sites in England and Scotland.

Food: Carrion, small mammals, birds (especially young of gulls, woodpigeons and crows).

Feeding habitat: Most hunting is over ffridd and unenclosed sheep walks, which extend over rough grassland and moorland.

Hen harrier

Conservation status: Increase and extension of range 1940s–1970s, subsequent decline in southern part of its range. Present population about 650 breeding females (males can be polygynous).

Nesting requirements: Mostly tall heather (>30 cm) and young conifer plantations.

Food: A wide variety of birds, rodents, young rabbits and hares.

Feeding requirements: Most hunting takes place on heather moorland and bogs but will also use lightly grazed acidic grassland and young conifer plantations.

Hen harrier

Buzzard

Conservation status: Increasing slowly but with a westerly bias in its range; rare in the south-east and eastern England. Present population 12,000–17,000 pairs*.

Nesting requirements: Trees, cliffs, crags.

Food: Rabbits, small mammals, carrion, birds and earthworms.

Feeding requirements: Hunts across a wide range of habitats including farmland, heather moorland and rough grassland.

Buzzard

Golden eagle

Golden eagle

Conservation status: Numbers stable. Present population around 420 pairs.

Nesting requirements: Ledges on cliffs and crags, occasionally trees.

Food: Hares, rabbits, grouse, carrion.

Feeding habitat: A large home range but only a small proportion may be used intensively. Hunts particularly over heather moor, bogs and other rough grazings. Deer forests in Scotland are a stronghold.

Kestrel

Conservation status: Widespread throughout the UK and the commonest bird of prey on rough and hill grazing. Estimated population around 50,000–60,000 pairs*.

Nesting requirements: Very variable. Hole or fork in tree commonest in most areas, but hole or ledge on cliff also frequent.

Food: Chiefly small mammals, especially voles. Adaptable and opportunistic.

Feeding habitats: Characteristic active hovering flight, scanning ground for prey, mainly small mammals over a wide range of open ground.

Kestrel

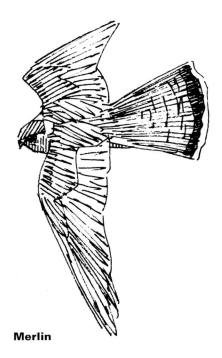

Merlin

Merlin

Conservation status: After a widespread decline appears to be increasing slowly in some parts of its range. Present population over 700 pairs.

Nesting requirements: Usually tall heather (>30 cm) or old crow nests in trees.

Food: Mainly small birds.

Feeding requirements: During the early breeding season hunts over inbye farmland and the edge of moors. Later in the season hunts over heather moorland and bogs.

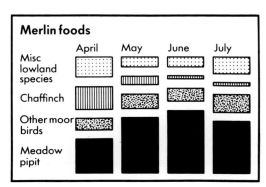

Typically, birds of prey take whatever prey is most abundant and easiest to catch in each season. This figure shows how the prey of merlins changes through the summer.
Source: Bibby, C J and Nattrass, M 1986 Breeding status of the Merlin in Britain. ***British Birds* 79: 170–185.**

Peregrine

Conservation status: Major decline in 1950s/60s due to pesticide poisoning; now increasing and has recolonised much of its former range. Present population about 1250 pairs.

Nesting requirements: Mostly on cliffs and crags including quarries.

Food: Birds, especially pigeons, waders and similar-sized species.

Feeding requirements: Open country.

Peregrine

Short-eared owl

Conservation status: Population fluctuates widely in relation to cycles of prey abundance. Present population up to 3,500 pairs*.

Nesting requirements: Tall heather and grass, young conifer plantations.

Food: Small mammals especially voles, birds.

Feeding requirements: Open country where the vegetation provides good conditions for voles (ie not heavily grazed) including moors, heaths, rough grazing, marshes, bogs, newly afforested hillsides. In winter moves to lower ground particularly farmland and estuaries.

Short-eared owl

Breeding habitat requirements of birds of prey							
	RK	GE	M	HH	B	P[1]	SEO	K
Crags, ledges		N			N	N		N
Scattered trees		N	N		N			N
Open, mature woods	N				N			N
Young conifers*			N	NF			NF	
Short heather		F	F		F	F	F	F
Tall heather		F	NF	NF	F	F	NF	
Rough grassland	F	F		F	F	F	NF	F
Bogs	F	F	F	F	F	F	F	F

*Before thicket stage (Merlin also nests in some plantations)
[1]Takes prey in flight, mostly over open habitats
N = nesting, F = feeding

Key
B = Buzzard
GE = Golden Eagle
HH = Hen Harrier
K = Kestrel
M = Merlin
P = Peregrine
RK = Red Kite
SEO = Short-eared Owl

*Source: British Trust for Ornithology

Case study: Sympathetic Grazing and Management of an Upland Farm

Christine Hall

Herb-rich grassland is grazed by sheep from mid-April to May which are then excluded for most of the summer. It is only lightly grazed in winter.

Farm details

Farm:	Milton of Ardtalnaig, Lochtayside, Aberfeldy, Perthshire.
Tenure:	Mr Mervyn Browne, owner-occupier
Size:	331 ha
Altitude:	116–677 m
Soil:	mainly schist on hill. Shallow, stony fluvio-glacial deposits by loch.
Crops:	2 ha turnips; 4 ha rape (forage); 14 ha hay.
Stock:	300 pure-bred blackface ewes; 100 blackface Cheviot or Blue Leicester cross ewes; 21 cows and followers; 1 bull
Other wildlife features:	on southern side of Loch Tay, stretching from shoreline to over 600 m, rising sharply with heather moorland dominating higher ground. Remnants of native woodland on loch side and in steep-sided gullies. Flight pond.

Mr Browne first came to Milton of Ardtalnaig as farm manager in 1950, and purchased the farm in 1954, when it had 200 ewes, 5 cows and 2 pigs. To increase the carrying capacity of the farm and retain the viability of the unit he has re-seeded 16 ha of rough grazing and grows turnips for winter feed. When Mr Browne took over the farm he was conscious of the need for sensitive management to prevent the degradation or loss of the heather, and to retain the diverse plant communities within the upland grazing. (In 1984 the Nature Conservancy Council recorded over 180 plant species on the farm). Most farms in the area are extensive stock farms, mainly sheep, with a small area of arable ground down by the loch.

Farmer's aims

- To improve the 202 ha of heather moorland for red grouse and therefore enhance the small shoot on the farm.
- To retain and enhance the flora and fauna on the farm for his own enjoyment.
- To improve the farm for stock.

▶▶▶

Background

Five years in Breadalbane ESA. Heather moorland: there is a good burning rotation and little fear of the fire getting out of control. Native woodland: regenerating woodland was fenced in 1975 to exclude stock. Since then it has not required any labour input. A contractor planted and fenced an area in 1993. Herb-rich grassland: no specific labour is required as it benefits from the grazing policy adopted for the whole 50-ha hill park.

Constraints: Availability of suitable weather, red deer grazing.
Source of advice: Joseph Nickerson Joint Reconciliation Project, NCC, FWAG.

Methods

Heather moorland: a rotational burning programme was implemented to create a mosaic of different aged stands and improve the condition of the heather. Small patches are burnt each year on an 8–20 year rotation, depending on the growth rate of the heather. Some heather is left unburnt as cover for red grouse and other species which prefer mature/over-mature heather. Burning is undertaken usually in March, when 7–10 days burning are carried out, depending on the weather. This means that burning is completed before lambing commences at the beginning of April. Grazing is controlled to prevent overgrazing and care is taken to feed the stock off the heather in winter to prevent heather damage.

Native woodland: an 8.1-ha block of grazed sessile oak, ash, birch, hazel, rowan, blackthorn and hawthorn was fenced in 1975 to exclude stock, and has regenerated without management input. Another area was stock-fenced in 1993, but could not naturally regenerate due to the dense bracken. Indigenous species were planted in guards.

Herb-rich grassland: this incorporates some interesting wet flushes and is managed to encourage botanical diversity. It is lightly grazed throughout the winter and the stock taken off in early March. From mid-April until mid to late May the sheep graze it quite heavily. Stock are then excluded for most of the summer. This regime was initially implemented for stock management purposes, but since becoming aware of the botanical interest resulting from this system of grazing, overgrazing has been carefully prevented and stock removed during the critical flowering period. Rank vegetation is thus prevented from taking over. No fertiliser or lime is applied to this area.

Achievements

- The heather moorland is now ideal for red grouse but, due to the cyclical nature of the population, at present only supports 120 grouse. When the population recovers there should be a much higher density.
- About 20 blackcock are found along the moorland edges, benefiting from the retention of the moorland, and the regeneration of the native woodland. A pair of short-eared owls appeared in the 1980s, probably due to the regeneration of the native woodland and the planting of small areas of conifers. The botanical diversity of the farm is being maintained. The herb-rich grassland supports many species of invertebrates, and five species of orchid, plus rockrose, wild thyme, quaking grass and other species thrive.
- The woodland regeneration and scattered planting provides shelter for the stock, as well as enhancing the local landscape and creating good wildlife habitat.

Future management

Mr Browne is reaching retirement, and therefore the ownership of the farm is likely to change in the near future. Mr Browne hopes that whoever takes on the farm will continue with the good grazing practice and sympathetic management of the heather, woodlands and herb-rich grassland. The new owner will be encouraged to continue the past management with payments under the ESA scheme.

Mr Browne would like to see more woodland regeneration and planting on the farm, plus additional bracken control. Another concern of Mr Browne's is the increasing numbers of red deer, which threaten the heather and woodland regeneration programme. The explosion in red deer numbers will have a serious impact on the regeneration of heather, due to the grazing pressure and may force a re-evaluation of the present heather management programme.

C H Gomersall, RSPB

John Andrews

5.2 Heather moorland can hold breeding birds of prey such as merlin and waders including golden plover. However, the intensity and timing of grazing alter the structure of the vegetation and this affects its suitability for different species. For instance, the merlin prefers to nest in deep, old heather while the golden plover require shorter cover and more open conditions.

5.1 Typical hill farms contain inbye land and unenclosed grazings which, in some parts of the UK, carry extensive stands of semi-natural vegetation including heather or cotton-grass. Because of differences in management and, consequently in their plant cover and its structure, inbye and unenclosed moor hold different types of wildlife. These include many species that are not found in the lowlands.

C H Gomersall, RSPB

5.3 Blanket bog clothes much of the uplands. Where grazing pressure is low, extensive stands of cotton-grass flower each year and provide an important springtime food for black grouse, red grouse and the mountain hare. The breeding success of these species may be reduced under higher stocking density, when the nutritious flower heads are eaten off. These areas also support high densities of invertebrates, especially cranefly, which in turn are an important food source for birds.

Mark Hamblin, RSPB

5.4 Mountain hares change their diet with the seasons. As well as cotton-grass flowers, they also eat heather shoots and grass flowers. They therefore thrive on moorland with a good mix of vegetation types. Plant structure is also important. To shelter from wind and rain, and conceal themselves from predators, hares lie up in deeper heather or rank grasses.

5.7 & 5.8 Grazing can convert heather to grass and this has occurred extensively in the uplands as sheep numbers have increased. In general it leads to a loss of wildlife interest and, as unpalatable grass species such as mat-grass or, in the wetter areas, purple

5.5 In some upland regions, the underlying rocks are limestones and their basic soils can support a much wider range of grasses and herbs than is found on the more widespread acid soils and peats. As a consequence, the invertebrate fauna is richer and numbers of breeding birds may be higher.

moor-grass spread, the land eventually supports a very restricted range of common plants, and only a few, scattered pairs of larks and pipits. In this situation, stock reduction and control through fencing may be needed to maintain heather cover and its associated wildlife.

5.6 Mountain pansy is one of a number of plants which are only found in the uplands, mainly on base-rich soils. It benefits from low-intensity grazing which maintains the open conditions that it requires.

5.9 Where fodder is provided for outwintering stock, the animals tend to remain close to the feeding point so that grazing and trampling pressure is intensified. Foddering points should be located on areas of vegetation that lack wildlife value or should be moved frequently so as to spread and thereby reduce the effects.

169

John Andrews, RSPB

David Woodfall

John Andrews

5.10 Much upland grazing has been re-seeded. Such areas hold almost none of the original upland wildlife.

5.11 (inset)   Red grouse management aims to maintain heather in a mosaic of tall stands where the birds can nest, and shorter young growth, which is the preferred feeding habitat. Patches of heather are burned to create the mix of conditions. The result can also be good for many other upland birds.

5.12 Where overgrazing has created extensive cover of unpalatable grasses, burning can help to produce fresh new growth that stock will eat. However, if burning is too frequent, it can cause the loss of most plant cover and lead to exposure and consequent erosion of the underlying peat. Such land has negligible value for wildlife or livestock.

Mike Jackson, Environmental Picture Library

David Woodfall

5.13 Bracken continues to spread in the uplands. It has limited value for wildlife and eradication of extensive stands is usually desirable. The only practicable method is to spray and, in some sites, aerial application may be the best option. Care must be taken to avoid spray-drift onto areas where other ferns are growing, such as scree slopes, ledges and woodland.

5.14 On hill land which is heavily grazed or re-seeded, the greatest variety of plants may be found to survive on inaccessible ledges. Fencing off small adjoining areas may allow these plants to spread and support other wildlife.

6. Machair

1. Factors influencing wildlife

1.1 The farming context

- Machair is one of the rarest wildlife habitats in Europe.
- Mixed farming, largely cattle production, cereals and hay, has created rich conditions for a varied wildlife.

Machair is one of the rarest wildlife habitats in Europe, being almost wholly restricted to soils formed on calcareous shell sand on the Atlantic fringes of western Scotland and Ireland. In the UK, aside from a few small pockets on mainland Scotland, most is found in the Western Isles, notably the Uists, Benbecula, Barra, Vatersay and Tiree. In these areas, high rainfall, frequent gales, lack of shelter, soils of limited potential and a short growing season mainly restrict farming to livestock production – originally cattle but now, increasingly, sheep. Hay, cereals and potatoes are grown. The small-scale, low-input system of crofting agriculture has created a range of conditions for a remarkably rich mixture of plants and birds.

Along with other marginal land in Europe, agriculture on the machair has experienced the effects of both intensification and abandonment. Both can lead to the loss of plant richness and the value of land to birds. For example, the increase in sheep numbers and a move to silage rather than hay production, with earlier mowing dates as one consequence, have contributed in some areas to loss of wildlife interest. The corncrake is one species which has declined as a result; this bird is of exceptional importance because it is now almost completely extinct elsewhere in the UK and western Europe due to changes in the management of meadows. Over the past decade or two there has also been a considerable reduction in the area of crops, which has in turn led to a marked decline in a number of plants and in the corn bunting, a bird which has suffered a great decrease in numbers throughout the UK due to changes in arable farming.

Now incentives for wildlife management on farms are becoming more widely available, and may make it possible for crofters to continue to maintain the traditional farming system.

1.2 Habitat diversity, livestock and arable

- Machair holds four habitat types – pasture, hay meadows, rotational arable and wetlands.
- The wildlife interest of the machair results from variations in soil type, low-intensity agriculture and a mixed farming economy.
- Cattle production is fundamental to the crofting system and to the wildlife richness of the machair.
- Unimproved pastures support a range of wildlife. Improved pastures are used by geese.
- Rotational arable with fallows produces ideal conditions for a wide variety of plants and some birds.
- Hay meadows support a rich mixture of plants and are important breeding and feeding areas for corncrakes.
- Improved hay and silage meadows are poor for plants. They provide cover for corncrakes but earlier cutting dates result in breeding failure and mortality.
- Conversion of meadows to sheep pasture destroys much of their wildlife value.
- Iris beds and other ungrazed vegetation provide cover for corncrakes, waders and other wildlife.

Machair holds four main habitat types. Its outer limit, facing the Atlantic, is usually defined by sand dunes, in the hollows or 'slacks' of which the ground may be moist and hold different plants from the free-draining dunes themselves. All this area may be used as rough grazing. Behind the dunes lies the dry machair, where the soil is shell sand, enriched and given a humus content by seaweed carted by generations of crofters from the beaches beyond the dunes. The machair is the main area of cultivation and also has pastures.

At its eastern, inland end, the shell sand becomes a progressively thinner layer over peats and the soil becomes increasingly moist. This is the 'blackland' zone and supports inbye grazing and hayfields. It contains pools which sometimes have an unusual mix of acid peaty and calcareous sandy conditions and may hold small reedbeds. The land is drained by a network of ditches but even so there are wet patches in many fields, with stands of yellow irises. These wetlands form the fourth habitat in the complex.

Further inland, the rising ground is clad with blanket bog and used as rough grazing. This is not part of the machair and, with a few exceptions, the wildlife of the machair does not use the moorland.

It is the mosaic of habitats in close proximity which makes the machair so rich in wildlife. Differences in soil pH and drainage produce different plant communities. Bulbous buttercup, daisy, lady's bedstraw, bird's-foot-trefoil and white clover are abundant on the dry machair pastures. Annuals like storksbill, rue-leaved saxifrage and wild pansy occur in the cultivated machair. In the hay meadows such plants as sorrel, yellow rattle and tufted vetch occur amongst the grasses. The damper parts of the blacklands hold marsh orchids and marsh marigolds while the shallow pools are often colonised by bogbean.

Whereas different types of plants are confined to one or another part of the machair and blacklands, the abundance of nesting waders reflects their need for a complex of conditions in close proximity, in order to breed sucessfully. Thus, ringed plovers and oystercatchers nest in the open on the cultivated machair but fly across the dunes to feed along the beaches. Lapwings nest on the cultivated land and on well-grazed pasture. Dunlins seek cover in damp grassland and feed in the peaty pools as well as on the shoreline. Redshanks and snipe require the taller concealment provided by hayfields. Snipe probe for invertebrates in the damp blackland fields but redshanks feed mainly around the

margins of pools and along the edges of the bigger ditches. Because the machair holds this diversity of conditions, it is one of the most important breeding grounds for waders in north-west Europe.

Agriculture on the machair has generally concentrated on livestock production, until recently on cattle but now mainly sheep. Sheep and cattle have slightly different effects on vegetation due to their feeding methods and preferences. These are described more fully in Chapter 3 page 59. Depending on the stocking density, grazing can provide a sward suitable in structure and height for some of the breeding waders and for a variety of flowering plants. Dung is itself an invertebrate habitat and the insects that feed on it, or hunt other insects attracted to it, in turn provide food for waders and other birds.

In winter, the short machair turf is grazed by flocks of barnacle geese, particularly on the remoter islands where there is little disturbance. Re-seeded grassland attracts both greylag geese and barnacle geese. The rare Greenland white-fronted goose favours the wetter machair on Coll and Tiree.

Hayfields hold some plants that do not occur in pastures because they cannot tolerate grazing. The wildlife varies from meadow to meadow depending on the intensity and history of management. Those meadows that have not been, or are irregularly, re-seeded contain a great variety of plants with stands of hogweed, meadowsweet, yellow rattle, ragged robin, and marsh and spotted orchids. These species are largely lost if the field is used as permanent pasture or improved by herbiciding, the use of artificial fertilisers or re-seeding, although grass leys may revert to semi-natural meadows in due course if they are not fertilised with artificials.

Although hay production is still widespread on machair, silage making is increasing, mainly because it is less dependent on spells of fine weather for harvesting. Both hay and silage crops provide cover for ground-nesting birds, most importantly the corncrake, but the timing and rate of cutting under the two regimes have significantly different effects on breeding success.

When corncrakes first return to their breeding grounds in April and May, they make use of the numerous small patches of damp ground, which, with their iris beds, provide cover. The birds are also attracted by the cover afforded by early-growing leys. However, silage can be harvested earlier than hay, when the corncrakes are still nesting or have young. Many nests are destroyed and young and adult birds are killed. Breeding success is better in the hayfields.

Oats and rye or other cereals are grown on the sandy lands of the machair under a rotational system. The practice of resting a cropped area after three or four years and leaving it fallow while another area is cultivated allows annual and other short-lived plants to germinate and grow. First- and second-year fallows provide suitable

conditions for such plants as corn marigold, storksbill and wild pansy. Plant variety is increased because there is a range of conditions, from recently ploughed land to old fallow.

Key factors in the abundance of wild plants in arable land are the time of sowing, the use of herbicides and the availability of nutrients. In general, high nutrient levels are bad for wild plant variety and the use of natural materials such as seaweed is beneficial. Where herbicides are used on a cereal crop, plant variety is lost.

Because the machair and blacklands cover a complex of habitats, it will be helpful to refer also to the chapters on pastures and meadows, arable, wetlands and possibly also rough grazing in order to get a full picture of the ways in which management, including grazing, mowing, tillage, herbicide, manure and artificial fertiliser use, affect the wildlife in these different habitats.

2. Options and assessment: planning management

2.1 Wildlife assessment of machair

- Record past and current management and the condition of the different habitats.
- Note the presence of rare species.
- Advice and help with assessment will be available.
- Ideally, make a full wildlife plan for the whole township.

Most crofters will have a very good knowledge of which birds nest on their land and of the changes in the plant composition which result from different management systems. Even so, a systematic assessment of areas is worthwhile to ensure that nothing of importance is overlooked.

The general principles of wildlife assessment are discussed in Chapter 1 and it will be helpful to read this before starting to compile any information. It is necessary

to record past and current management of the land and note the overall condition of swards and wetlands. By relating this information to the habitat descriptions in section 1 of this chapter, the assessment will give a good indication of the likely importance for wildlife of different parts of the croft or township.

It will also be important to record the presence of breeding birds and wintering flocks where this is known. Many of the species which are common on the machair are rare elsewhere in the UK, and advice will be available from Scottish Natural Heritage and the RSPB.

The full list of information which should be recorded, and the reasons for its inclusion, are set out in Table 6.1. Where it is intended to apply for grant aid to help with any wildlife management, it is wise to check whether additional information will be required by the aiding body before starting any assessment.

Table 6.1: Wildlife assessment of machair

INFORMATION REQUIRED	METHOD	REASON FOR INFORMATION
1. Conservation status and interest	Contact Scottish Natural Heritage, local authority, or FWAG.	Information on the wildlife interest of the machair may already be held by these organisations. Some machair may be scheduled as an SSSI and permissions may be required for changes in management.
2. Past management	Check any farm/croft records. Check past/current aerial photographs. Note any changes of management or use of land within last 15 years.	The longer grassland has been unimproved the more likely it will be of wildlife interest. May identify land that may be brought back in cultivation to the benefit of wildlife.
3. Current management	Map and note areas under cultivation, with details of crops, rotations. Map and note areas under grazing with details of stock type, stocking density, seasonal use, and use of supplementary feed. Map those areas under hay, and those under silage production. Note cutting dates and methods of cutting/mowing pattern. Note ditch and other wetland management regimes. Note use and type of fertilisers used. Note use, type and methods of application of pesticides.	Bare ground can be important both for plants and breeding birds. Linked to vegetation height and composition will identify effect on wildlife interest. If heavily grazed by sheep may reduce wildlife interest. Some grazing, especially by cattle, can create suitable conditions for a range of breeding birds. Important for hay meadow plants and corncrake. May suggest need to alter management to take account of above. Important for wetland plants and feeding/breeding areas for waders. Use can reduce wildlife interest. Use can reduce wildlife interest.
4. Plant composition and structure of wildlife habitats	For arable land/rotational cultivation refer to page 22. For grassland (both meadows and pastures) refer to page 64. For wetlands refer to page 281. For croft buildings and walls refer to page 328.	Can provide important information that determines likely wildlife interest. See relevant chapters for full details.
5. Location of rare or sensitive species	Identify location of those rare or sensitive species where known. Seek specialist guidance and information.	The presence and needs of these species should be built into the township wildlife plan.

The assessment should cover at least the whole croft and ideally the entire township lands because so much of the wildlife uses several different areas in the course of a year. Even the plants 'move' from field to field depending on whether it is being cropped or fallow. All the information could be compiled as a single wildlife plan which takes account of the range of constraints and opportunities presented by the practical and economic needs of crofting. The format of a wildlife plan is set out in Chapter 1 page 10. Help with compiling such a plan will be available from one of the conservation bodies.

2.2 Management needs and opportunities

> ● The overriding need is to maintain the traditional system in all its elements.

The exceptional importance of the machair for wildlife is due to the mixture of habitats and to the type of crofting. Virtually all the changes in management which have been introduced in order to increase output have

been damaging to the wildlife, and the overriding need is to maintain the traditional systems as far as possible. It is difficult to overstate the importance of the four key elements – rotational cultivation and fallowing, low-intensity grazing of pastures, haymaking on damp pastures, and minimal or no applications of agrochemicals.

Financial payments may be available to assist in the retention or re-adoption of crofting methods beneficial to wildlife.

3. Management of machair

3.1 Rotational cultivation

> ● Continue the rotational pattern of cultivation and fallowing on dry machair.
> ● Re-establish the system on machair cultivated in the last 15 years or on 'improved' pasture.
> ● Do not plough unimproved machair grassland that has been uncultivated for over 15 years without first taking advice.
> ● Roll or harrow only within 10 days after ploughing, to avoid destruction of wader nests.
> ● Apply at least one dressing of seaweed (at 40 tons/ha) or dung (at 25 tons/ha) to cropped areas of machair.

The mosaic of uncultivated and cultivated ground of crofting land is valuable to annual plants, dependent insects and to ground-nesting birds (Feature 6.1: Breeding waders on machair). Many of them do not occur on the land when it is being cropped but only in the fallow years, and they are mostly lost altogether from land converted to pasture. Maintenance of the traditional system is of great importance.

Where land has been taken out of cultivation, consider the possibility of ploughing and cropping. However, if it has been uncropped for more than about 15 years, it may now support a different but equally important mix of wildlife, and advice on the best course of action should be sought.

Where birds breed on cultivated land there is a danger that their eggs or newly-hatched chicks may be destroyed. As far as possible, complete ploughing in April and rolling and harrowing within 10 days after ploughing; even then some nests will be destroyed.

Application of organic fertilisers such as seaweed and dung adds humus and nutrients to the cropped land on the dry machair so maintaining its fertility and condition, including its ability to retain moisture. This also benefits the birds by maintaining good conditions for the soil invertebrates on which they feed. Apply at least one dressing of seaweed (at 40 tons/ha) or dung (at 25 tons/ha) to cropped areas of machair in spring prior to ploughing.

3.2 Hay and silage production

> ● Continue to grow grass as hay (or late cut silage) for winter feed. Do not convert hay or silage fields to permanent pasture, or 'improve' hay or silage fields that are rich in plants.
> ● Delay cutting of hay or silage until after 1 August.
> ● Cut the hay or silage in a way which will minimise the likelihood of birds being killed.

Because hay meadows hold a different mix of plants from pastures and are the main nesting habitat for corncrakes, it is important not to convert them to pasture. They should not be fertilised with artificials because this leads to grass dominance and loss of wildflowers. Similarly, herbiciding and re-seeding remove the wild plants. However, because of the high rainfall and poor soils, fields that have been improved revert relatively quickly provided that there are still unimproved fields nearby to provide a source of seeds.

To allow plants to set seed and enable corncrakes and waders to breed sucessfully, it is important to leave cutting for hay or silage as late as possible – ideally after 1 August. If earlier cutting must be done, there are a number of different mowing methods, which minimise the risk to birds by allowing them to escape the field. These are described in Feature 6.2: Corncrakes and hay.

For guidance on grazing of meadows see the next section.

3.3 Grazing

> - Do not apply artificial fertilisers, herbicide or re-seed existing unimproved pastures.
> - Graze unimproved areas of dry machair from October to end April at a stocking rate not exceeding 0.5 cattle/ha.
> - Graze wet machair, marshes and loch shores at an average stocking rate of 0.5–1.0 cattle/ha from July to April.
> - Maintain some early cover in field corners and ditch sides, if necessary by fencing.

As with meadows, pastures should not be improved but those that are may revert

relatively quickly provided that there are unimproved, plant-rich fields nearby.

To maintain good conditions for plants and cover and feeding habitat for birds, it is important to maintain a suitable stocking rate. This will vary depending on, for example, soil type, hydrology and plant species present. Overgrazing, especially on machair or sand dunes can seriously damage the vegetation, cause erosion and lead to losses of plants and a decline in the breeding bird population. As a rough guide these areas should be grazed, preferably with cattle, from October to the end of April at a stocking rate not exceeding 0.5 cattle/ha. Grazing from early May onwards will lead to nest losses from trampling.

Wet pasture, marshes and loch shores are the main breeding areas for waders such as dunlin, snipe and redshank. These areas need to be grazed regularly to prevent the build-up of rank vegetation which leads to lower plant diversity and unsuitable conditions for birds. Poaching in damp ground can also benefit waders by exposing bare ground where they can feed. Graze the wet machair, marshes and loch shores at an average stocking rate of 0.5-1.0 cattle/ha from the middle of July until the end of April or whenever the fields are shut up for the hay to grow, if this is earlier.

To provide early spring cover for corncrakes, fence off field corners or margins, especially damp areas with iris, to exclude stock from grazing them. If possible, exclude up to 5% of the total area of the field.

4. References and further reading

Boyd, J M and Boyd, I L 1990. *The Hebrides*. New Naturalist. Collins.

Boyd, J M (ed) 1979. *Natural Environment of the Outer Hebrides*. Proceedings of the Royal Society of Edinburgh 77B: 419-30.

Williams, G, Stowe, T and Newton, A 1991. Action for Corncrakes. *RSPB Conservation Review* 5: 47-53.

Feature 6.1: Breeding Waders on Machair

Machair and 'blacklands' support very high numbers of six species of breeding wader: oystercatcher, lapwing, ringed plover, redshank, dunlin and snipe. In addition occasional pairs of red-necked phalaropes are found on machair lochs. The density and variety of breeding waders makes machair and blacklands an exceptionally important habitat for breeding birds.

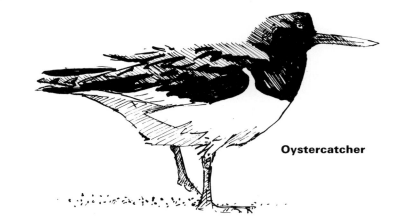

Oystercatcher

Important habitat features for waders

- Fallow, dry grazed machair, sparsely vegetated cover, cultivated ground. Used for nesting and feeding by oystercatcher, ringed plover and lapwing.
- Damp grazed marshes especially along loch shores. Used by breeding dunlin, redshank and snipe. Lapwings also lead their young to feed in wet machair.
- Sparse reedbeds, swamps and marshes. Used by breeding and wintering snipe.
- Lochs and emergent vegetation. Used for nesting and feeding by red-necked phalarope.
- Rough grazing land with rocky outcrops. Used for nesting and feeding by lapwing, redshank and snipe.

Ringed plover

Conservation

- Retain damp and wet areas on crofts. Do not cultivate, drain or re-seed permanent machair grassland. This will provide the mosaic of habitats required by breeding waders.
- On grazing land do not exceed the stocking rate of 0.5 cattle per hectare. This will provide a good vegetation structure suitable for breeding waders. Grazing during the nesting season will cause losses, especially if stocking rates are high (Figure 3.1, page 70).
- Restrict the use of herbicides or pesticides. Many plants associated with these habitats are rich in invertebrates which provide a food source for birds.
- Retain a rotational pattern of cultivation growing a variety of traditional crops. Rest a cropped area after two years and leave fallow. This will provide nesting areas and cover for waders.

Dune

Shell sand

Sea

Dunlin

Loch/Fen

Moorland

Croft

Blackland

Redshank

Wet machair

machair

Lapwing

Snipe

Feature 6.2: Corncrakes and Hay

Corncrakes are secretive and difficult to see, their mottled buff-brown plumage making them well camouflaged, and it is only in flight that the large, bright chestnut patches on the wings catch the eye.

Reasons for decline

Corncrakes were once widespread and common in the UK but are now largely extinct. Their decline began many years ago with the mechanisation of grass mowing, leading to greater losses of eggs, chicks and adult birds because of faster mowing and larger areas cut per day. Corncrakes survived in the north-west of the UK because of later cutting and slower mechanisation but more recently replacement of hay by silage (cut early) and increasing use of fertiliser are encouraging earlier cutting even in these areas. Some meadows have also been converted to grazing pasture or 'abandoned'. A survey in 1993 indicated that there are fewer than 500 calling males left, most of them in the Outer Hebrides and Tiree. This pattern is repeated through much of the rest of the corncrake's range, making it a globally threatened species.

Corncrakes need tall, dense vegetation, (over 20 cm tall) such as beds of iris or nettles to provide cover for early nests. Leys are very attractive to them because they provide good cover early in the summer, but the grass tends to be cut earlier than under traditional systems. The corncrakes will still be breeding and nests, young and adults are destroyed by the blades of the cutters.

Breeding and feeding requirements

- Tall vegetation, such as iris or nettle beds during April, May and June to provide cover for early nests.
- Hay and silage meadows and machair grassland during June and July for later nests and feeding areas.
- The chance to incubate and hatch young before the field is cut for silage or hay.
- Mowing of hay and silage in ways which reduce the risk of destroying nests and killing birds.

Conservation action

- Leave areas of iris and rough vegetation around buildings, beside ditches, in overgrown gardens and in field corners, where corncrakes nest early in the season. Try not to disturb these areas during April, May and June. If necessary, fence off field corners or strips (up to 5% of the field) to exclude stock and so provide tall vegetation.
- Consider delaying the cutting of hay or silage until after 1 August if you hear corncrakes in the area.
- Look out when mowing and if you find corncrakes in your hay or silage, stop and leave the area for several hours, if possible, to give them time to escape. If people or dogs remain in the area, the birds will sit tight.
- Avoid mowing entire fields in a spiral from the outer edge inwards – this drives the chicks towards a central 'island' where they may be killed by the mower during the final few cuts.
- Mowing by one of the methods described here gives corncrakes a chance to escape into nearby fields and ditches. Slow down, if possible, to give them time to escape. Farmers have found that once they become accustomed to these mowing techniques they are unlikely to take more time or fuel than mowing from the outside in.

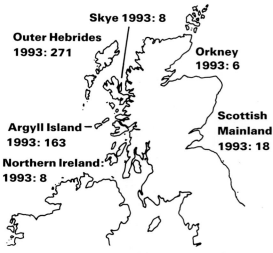

Skye 1993: 8

Outer Hebrides 1993: 271

Orkney 1993: 6

Argyll Island – 1993: 163

Scottish Mainland 1993: 18

Northern Ireland: 1993: 8

Numbers of corncrake – calling males

- If these methods are not adopted then mow out-in in smaller parcels but *do not* mow around the whole of the outside of the field first.
- If breeding is successful, avoid excavating deep drainage ditches with steep sides – these may trap and drown chicks.
- Cats will kill corncrakes. A bell attached to a collar may alert corncrakes and give them a chance to escape.
- Don't convert to sheep pasture but continue to grow hay in future years, and, if eligible, join an Environmentally Sensitive Area scheme.

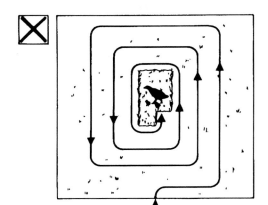

Mowing methods

Mowing from the outside in traps the birds in a central 'island'.
To allow the birds to escape, adopt one of the methods below.

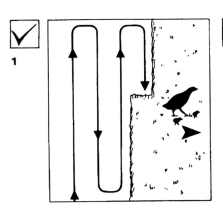
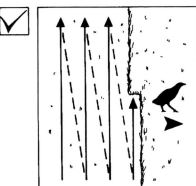

1. Cut the fields in strips from side to side (– – – – indicates reverse gear).

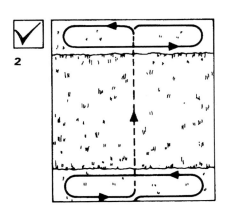
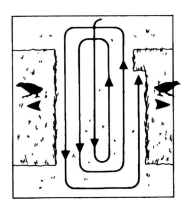

2. Cut the field from the middle outwards (suitable for drum/ rotary mowers). It may be necessary to cut a strip at top and bottom sections first.

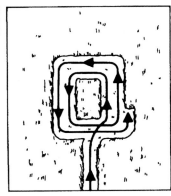
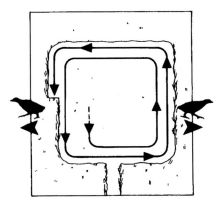

3. Cut from the gate to the middle of the field. Then cut the field from the middle outwards. The centre of the field can be cut when there is sufficient turning space. Finish the nest cutting outwards to the fences.

Case study: Traditional Croft

Farm details
Croft: Hougharry, Bayhead, Isle of North Uist, Western Isles
Tenure: Angus John MacDonald, tenant
Size: 44 ha
Altitude: around sea-level
Soil: shell sand
Crops: 12 ha of croftland and machair (oats, rye and fallow), 32 ha hill grazing and re-seed
Stock: sheep and cattle
Other wildlife
features: excellent wetland areas

Since the land was given back to the people in the 1800s the croft has been handed down from father to son. The croft is an SSSI. The area is mostly traditional rotational farming, and the machair is very rich in plants. It is also excellent for birds but especially for breeding waders such as lapwing, oystercatcher, redshank, snipe, dunlin and ringed plover. There are also large numbers of corn buntings. Traditional practices in North Uist have continued as they allow the most to be produced from this difficult environment. Whilst Mr MacDonald's aims are to get the best from his croft, he is also interested in the wildlife. There are four calling male corncrakes on his land.

Farmer's aims
- To optimise the productivity of the croft.
- To prevent death of corncrakes by changing the cutting regimes.

Background
Resources: Grants are available for all work connected with crofting. ESA grants, Corncrake Initiative, grass haylage payments (specific to Balranald – £90 /ha). Income is generated from the sale of calves and lambs in the autumn, plus subsidies on sheep and cattle.

Advice: RSPB, SNH

Methods
Croftland
Rough grazing with cattle and sheep throughout the year, with 2 ha put aside as a mixed grass silage. These 2 ha are also entered into a corncrake scheme whereby crofters receive a payment for delayed cutting and cutting in a manner less likely to kill corncrakes.

Machair
Traditional strip farming of oats and rye, five-year rotation, three years of crops then two years fallow. Crops are used as winter feed for the stock, herbicides are not used intensively so fields have abundant wildflowers within them. The machair is grazed but the stock (sheep and cattle) are taken off from May to September.

Hill grazing and re-seed
This lies farther inland on the hill ground. It is rough grazing for cattle and sheep, mainly in summer and autumn.

Achievements
- Productivity is maintained by the traditional rotational system.
- Conditions are improved for corncrakes.

Future management
Mr MacDonald intends to cut down sheep numbers and increase his cattle herd. With the reduction of sheep subsidies and poor prices for lambs, cattle are more profitable, and haylage, which he receives payments for growing, is only suitable for cattle. Cattle will also fit better into the farming calendar, as sheep shearing and lambing coincide with harvesting and this has caused problems. Cattle are better than sheep from a conservation point of view.

6.1 Until recently, the machair supported a farming system mainly for cattle production, with grass for pasture and hay, plus oats and other crops for livestock feed. Because of the low fertility of the soils, arable was followed by fallow and then by grass. This system of crop rotation supported a remarkable variety of wildlife.

John Andrews

6.2 The present trend is to sheep, and arable and meadow land has been converted to permanent pasture, causing great changes in the wildlife. Birds dependent on cereal fields, such as corn bunting, have declined greatly. With sheep fenced out of the many small wetlands, so that trampling no longer creates poached, muddy areas, they become less suitable for many plants and for feeding by waders.

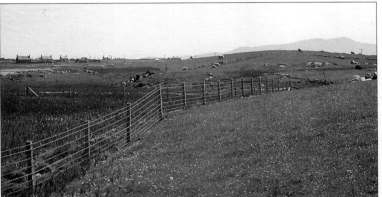

John Andrews

6.3 The outer margin of the machair, closest to the sea, are shell-sand stabilised by unimproved permanent pasture rich in wildflowers and supporting breeding waders including ringed plover, oystercatcher and lapwing. The machair holds exceptionally high densities of these species.

John Andrews

6.4 On the main expanse of the machair, small-scale cultivation and crop rotation creates a mosaic of habitats. Arable fallow in the foreground holds a variety of plants which thrive in competition-free conditions. The patch adjoins a potato bed with an area of hay beyond and permanent pasture on the higher ground.

Michael Rebane

John Andrews

C H Gomersall, RSPB

6.5 & 6.6 Many small and some larger lochs dot the machair and the 'black-lands', which lie towards the inland side of the machair. They provide feeding habitat for another group of waders, including redshank, snipe and dunlin (shown here).

C H Gomersall, RSPB

C H Gomersall, RSPB

6.7 & 6.8 There are many small patches of impeded drainage which are colonised by beds of iris and other wetland plants. When corncrakes arrive in spring the iris beds provide good cover and feeding habitat. Later, as the meadow grass becomes sufficiently tall, the corncrakes move into it to breed.

7. Farm Woodlands

1. Factors influencing wildlife

1.1 Woodland age

> - A farm woodland which has existed for generations will have more wildlife value than a recent plantation. It may hold rare plants and invertebrates.
> - Lists of ancient woods are kept by the Forestry Authority.
> - Recent plantations on farmland are usually much less important for wildlife but can hold uncommon birds and a wide range of other species.
> - Plantations are sometimes the best wildlife habitat on a farm and assume special importance for this reason.

Forest once covered most of the UK but extensive clearance for agriculture began in prehistoric times. In some regions, woodland cover was probably reduced to isolated blocks over 1,000 years ago. Many existing farm woods have direct continuity with those stands and, through them, to the original forest cover. In other areas, clearance was virtually total and existing farm woods are mostly of fairly recent origin. There was little woodland planting before the 18th century and most plantations date from the last century or more recently. Woods with continuity to the original forest cover are known as primary woods and those which stand on ground which had been cleared and farmed at some time in the past are known as secondary woods.

The origin of a farm wood is important because it affects the wildlife that lives in it. Many woodland plants and invertebrates do not readily colonise new sites. Some are sedentary and even in suitable conditions seem able to spread only a few feet each year. Others cannot survive outside the sheltered conditions within the wood so they are unable to cross open ground. This means that a primary wood having links with the ancient forests will probably contain many species that do not occur in secondary woods. However, some colonisation does occur in time and very old secondary woods may have considerable interest, including rare species.

Because most planting of woodland began in the 19th century, it is assumed that most woods that appear on the first edition one inch to one mile Ordnance Survey maps (mid-19th century) for England and Wales or the General Roy Military Survey maps (mid-18th century) for Scotland, are likely to have continuity with the original forest cover or to be very old secondary woods. Such woods are referred to as 'ancient woods'.

There are two kinds of ancient woods on farms. Those which contain native species of trees are very likely to hold rare species of plants and invertebrates. Those where the site has never been cleared for farming but the original tree cover has been replaced by non-native species, such as sycamore or conifers, may still retain some important wildlife and it is likely to be very beneficial to restore the native trees and shrubs when the timber crop is harvested.

As they are of more recent origin, plantations established on farmland are generally not as rich in wildlife. Many woodland plants and invertebrates have not colonised newer woods. However, some plantations may support uncommon birds and with appropriate management they can also support a wide variety of commoner plants, invertebrates and mammals. Recent plantations adjoining old woodland have the best chance of being colonised by the more sedentary species, but even this may take considerable time.

On some farms, plantations are the best areas for wildlife so their management and potential should not be ignored.

1.2 Tree and shrub composition

- Trees and shrubs provide food for much woodland wildlife. Different species support different wildlife.
- They also influence the condition of the soil and the growth of plants which in turn affects food availability.
- Their physical character, such as rugged bark or evergreen foliage, affects their value as shelter and foraging habitat.
- Some trees and shrubs are uncommon and are of conservation value in their own right.
- Farm woods that contain trees and shrubs native to the locality are usually of greatest value for wildlife.

Trees and shrubs provide food for birds, mammals and invertebrates which feed on pollen, nectar, foliage, buds, fruit, seeds and, in the case of some insects, decaying wood itself. Many insects are totally dependent on one particular kind of tree or shrub for food in their larval stage even if, as adults, they feed at a variety of pollen and nectar-bearing flowers. Some trees support a great variety of insects while others have very few, though these may include rare species (Table 7.1: Numbers of insect and mite species feeding on trees and shrubs). Some only have common insects associated with them but, if these insects are very abundant, they may be important as food for other woodland wildlife, especially birds. For instance, in summer, oak often supports great numbers of the caterpillars of one or two kinds of moth and these are gathered by many species of birds to feed their young.

Most non-native trees directly support fewer kinds of invertebrates and are of less conservation value for that reason. However, if it is on an ancient woodland site, a wood of non-native trees may contain a good variety of native shrubs and other plants, in turn supporting woodland butterflies and other wildlife.

As different trees and shrubs flower and fruit at different times of the year, so a varied wood offers continuity of food

Table 7.1: Numbers of insects and mite species feeding on trees and shrubs

TREE SPECIES	INSECT AND MITE SPECIES
Willow (5 species)	450
Oak (2 species)	423
Birch (2 species)	334
Hawthorn	209
Poplar (4 species)	189
Scots pine	172
Blackthorn	153
Alder	141
Elm (2 species)	124
Crab apple	118
Wild rose*	107
Bramble*	107
Hazel	106
Beech	98
Norway spruce	70
Ash	68
Rowan	58
Lime (2 species)	57
Field maple	51
Hornbeam	51
Honeysuckle*	48
Sycamore	43
European larch	38
Juniper	32
Elder*	19
Spindle*	19
Sweet chestnut	11
Holly	10
Horse chestnut	9
Yew	6

Adapted from : Kennedy, C E J and Southwood, T R E 1984 The number of insects associated with British trees: a re-analysis. J. *Anim. Ecol.* **53** 455–478. Items marked * are from Ratcliffe, D 1977. *A Nature Conservation Review* Vol 1. Cambridge University Press. Wild rose and bramble represent totals for a number of species (not specified).

supply (Table 7.2: Ripening dates of berry-bearing shrubs). Some foods, such as pollen and nectar, are prolific in summer but scarce at other seasons. Most invertebrates are inactive in winter and many early-emerging species are highly dependent on early-flowering trees and shrubs such as blackthorn and willows. For instance, in March willow pollen is an important food for queen bumblebees ending hibernation.

Different tree species have different effects on the understorey so that some tend to have an abundant and varied range of

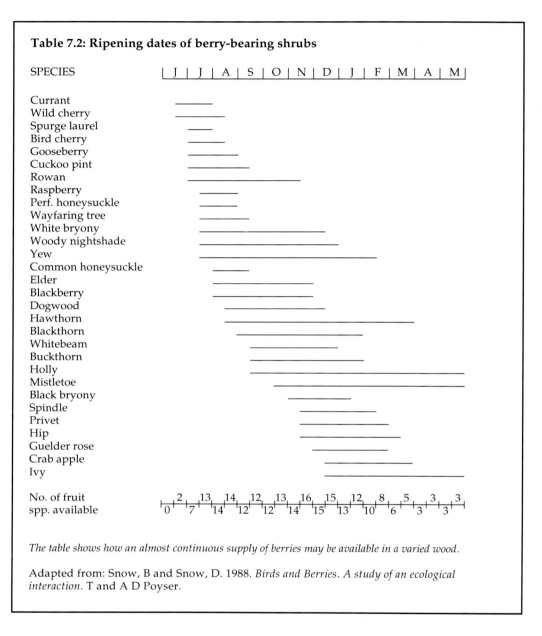

Table 7.2: Ripening dates of berry-bearing shrubs

SPECIES — | J | J | A | S | O | N | D | J | F | M | A | M |

Currant
Wild cherry
Spurge laurel
Bird cherry
Gooseberry
Cuckoo pint
Rowan
Raspberry
Perf. honeysuckle
Wayfaring tree
White bryony
Woody nightshade
Yew
Common honeysuckle
Elder
Blackberry
Dogwood
Hawthorn
Blackthorn
Whitebeam
Buckthorn
Holly
Mistletoe
Black bryony
Spindle
Privet
Hip
Guelder rose
Crab apple
Ivy

No. of fruit spp. available:
2, 13, 14, 12, 13, 16, 15, 12, 8, 5, 3, 3
0, 7, 14, 12, 12, 14, 15, 13, 10, 6, 3, 3

The table shows how an almost continuous supply of berries may be available in a varied wood.

Adapted from: Snow, B and Snow, D. 1988. *Birds and Berries. A study of an ecological interaction.* T and A D Poyser.

shrubs and plants growing beneath them while others have few. For instance, beech casts deep shade where few other plants can survive whereas ash, which comes into leaf late and has a more open canopy, can have a relatively luxuriant understorey. In addition, some conifers, sweet chestnut and beech produce leaves that decompose slowly and lie long on the soil surface, inhibiting plant germination and growth. Where plant growth is limited, so is the food resource for other wildlife.

Different tree and shrub species have different bark chemistry and so support different communities of lichens and mosses (Table 7.3: Numbers of lichens found on trees). Oak, ash and beech are notably good. There are also differences in the fungi which grow in association with different trees.

Bark structure too is important. Trees with furrowed bark give better cover to insects and spiders than those with smooth bark; this in turn makes them better foraging habitat than smooth-barked trees for birds such as treecreepers.

Evergreens have value as winter roost sites for birds, giving them additional shelter from wind. Native species include holly,

Table 7.3: Numbers of lichens found on trees	
TREE/SHRUB	NUMBER OF LICHEN SPECIES
Oak (common and sessile)	326
Ash	265
Beech	213
Elm species (not specified)	200
Sycamore	194
Hazel	162
Willow species (not specified)	160
Birch (silver and downy)	134
Scots pine	133
Rowan	125
Alder	116
Field maple	101
Holly	96
Lime species (not specified)	83
Hornbeam	44

Source: Harding, P T & Rose, F 1986. *Pasture Woodland in Lowland Britain*. Institute of Terrestrial Ecology.

ivy and yew or, more locally, Scots pine and box (Feature 7.1: Ivy and its importance for wildlife). However, if the farm wood is to be used by stock, remember that box and yew are poisonous, although they are generally avoided by animals. If the only evergreens in a wood are non-native conifers, it is worth retaining a few for their shelter value, though they may be replaced by native species in the long term.

All kinds of native trees and shrubs are themselves part of the wildlife of the wood. Some, such as wild service tree, are scarce and need conservation. Some trees, such as aspen, though common, are rarely seen as big, old individuals.

Like other wildlife, trees have natural distributions in the UK. Thus beech is native only in south England and part of south Wales: Scots pine only in the Highlands (Table 7.4: Distribution of native trees and shrubs). Locally, distribution is also influenced by soil type, altitude and drainage. So, in the English Midlands, ash, maple and oak thrive on the calcareous clays, birch is common on sandy soils, and willows and alder are present on wet ground (Table 7.5: Soil preferences of trees). Past management will also have an

influence so even adjacent woods on the same soil type may not be identical in composition. It is likely that oaks are more abundant now than they were in the original forest cover, having been deliberately encouraged because their timber, acorns and bark were useful for many purposes. Similarly, native trees have been planted outside their natural ranges – Scots pine in southern England and beech in Scotland, for example.

Farm woods most highly valued for conservation are those which contain trees and shrubs native to the locality, supporting the typical range of wildlife that depends on them.

1.3 Woodland structure

- The physical structure of the wood determines how much sunlight and wind can penetrate the site and so influences plant growth and wildlife survival. Differing woodland structures support different wildlife.
- Sunlit rides and glades and sheltered woodland edges are very important for wildlife.
- The variety of tree and shrub species present within the wood, the type of management system followed and the degree of grazing within the woodland all affect its structure.

It is convenient to think of woodland vegetation as being arranged in four layers, the ground layer of mosses and lichens, the herb layer of woodland plants, the shrub layer including young trees, and the canopy of tree foliage. Because they compete for light, each can potentially shade the one below it and inhibit its growth so it is rare for all of them to be abundant in any one part of a wood. Some trees and other plants cast very heavy shade but others let enough light through for lower-growing vegetation to survive.

Woodland structure also influences air and soil temperature because the physical obstruction created by branches, twigs and foliage deflects wind over the wood and absorbs wind energy. Thus relatively calm air conditions are created within

Map showing location of
numbered zones used in Table 7.4 opposite

*The map shows eleven
zones in which different
species are considered
native. The boundaries
are not precise for each
species, but reflect the
broad pattern of their
natural distributions.*

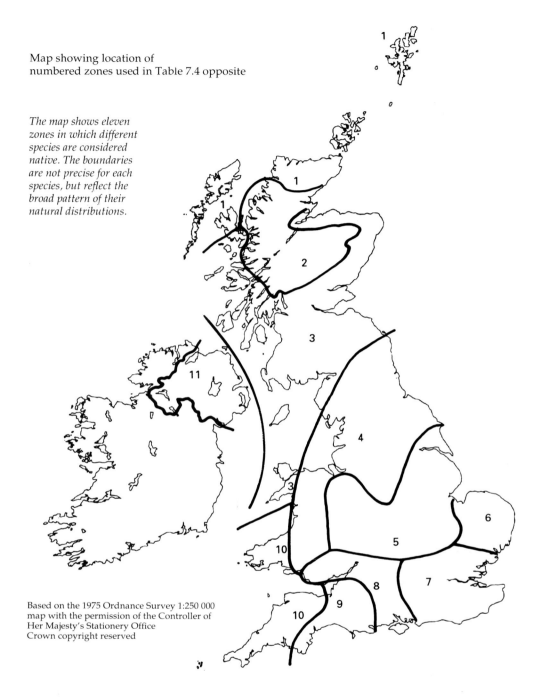

Based on the 1975 Ordnance Survey 1:250 000
map with the permission of the Controller of
Her Majesty's Stationery Office
Crown copyright reserved

woodlands. A variety of tree heights will
also help to create sheltered air pockets at
tree-top level.

Poorly draining ground protected from
wind and shaded from sunlight may
remain wet all summer, while open ground
dries out. The combination of moist ground
and warm air creates greater humidity than
there is outside the wood (Figure 7.1:
Effects of woodland structure on plants and
invertebrates). Sheltered but sunlit open
areas such as glades and rides become
extremely warm.

If the herb layer is sparse or absent, because
of deep shade or grazing by livestock, for
instance, there will be little cover for small
mammals, such as woodmice, and little food
except in autumn and winter when tree seeds
fall. Without small mammals, predators,
including weasel and tawny owl, may be
absent from the wood. However, some birds,
such as wood warbler and pied flycatcher,
favour woods with little understorey.

Many woodland invertebrates are very
sensitive to microclimate and calm warm
air is essential to them. Some need full

Table 7.4: Distribution of native trees and shrubs

Native species to be encouraged within the numbered zones of map opposite

LARGE AND MEDIUM SIZED TREES	1	2	3	4	5	6	7	8	9	10	11
Alder	•	•	•	•	•	•	•	•	•	•	L
Apple, crab		•	•	•	•	•	•	•	•	•	L
Ash	•	•	•	•	•	•	•	•	•	•	L
Aspen	•	•	•	•	•	•	•	•	•	•	L
Beech							•	•	•		
Birch, downy	•	•	•	•	•	•	•	•	•	•	L
Birch, silver	•	•	•	•	•	•	•	•	•	•	L
Cherry, bird	•	•	•		L						L
Elm, wych	•	•	•	•	•	•	•	•	•	•	L
Gean (wild cherry)	•	•	•	•	•	•	•	•	•	•	L
Hawthorn, midland				L	L	L	L				
Hornbeam							•	•			
Lime, small-leaved				L	L	L	L	L	L		
Lime, large-leaved				L	L		L				
Maple, field				L	•	•	•	•	•		
Oak, common	•	•	•	•	•	•	•	•	•	•	L
Oak, sessile	•	•	•	L	L	L	L	L		•	L
Pine, Scots	L										
Poplar, black				L	L	L	L	L			
Rowan	•	•	•	•	•	•	•	•	•	•	L
Service tree				L	L	L	L	L	L	L	
Whitebeam	L		L			L	L				
Whitebeam, Irish											L
Willow, crack	•	•	•	•	•	•	•	•	•		
Willow, goat	•	•	•	•	•	•	•	•	•	•	L
Willow, white		•	•	•	•	•	•	•	•	•	L
Yew			L			L	L				

SMALL TREES AND SHRUBS	1	2	3	4	5	6	7	8	9	10	11
Blackthorn	•	•	•	•	•	•	•	•	•	•	L
Box								L	L		
Broom	•	•	•	•	•	•	•	•	•	•	L
Buckthorn, alder				•	•	•	•	•	•	•	
Buckthorn, purging				•	•	•	•	•			
Butchers-broom						•	•	•	•	•	
Dogwood			L	•	•	•	•	•	•		
Elder	•	•	•	•	•	•	•	•	•	•	L
Gorse	•	•	•	•	•	•	•	•	•	•	L
Guelder-rose	•	•	•	•	•	•	•	•	•	•	L
Hawthorn	•	•	•	•	•	•	•	•	•	•	L
Hazel	•	•	•	•	•	•	•	•	•	•	L
Holly	•	•	•	•	•	•	•	•	•	•	L
Juniper	L	L	L	L			L	L			
Privet, wild				•	•	•	•	•	•		
Rose, dog	•	•	•	•	•	•	•	•	•	•	L
Rose, field				•	•	•	•	•	•	•	
Spindle				•	•	•	•	•	•	•	L
Spurge-laurel				•	•	•	•	•	•		
Wayfaring tree				•			•	•	•		
Willow, almond				•	•	•	•	•			
Willow, bay	•	•									L
Willow, eared	•	•	•	•	•	•	•	•	•	•	L
Willow, grey	•	•	•	•	•	•	•	•	•	•	L
Willow, osier	•	•	•	•	•	•	•	•	•	•	
Willow, purple			•	•	•	•	•	•	•	•	L

L – stock derived from local sources is preferred where possible for nature conservation reasons. The table shows which species are native to which zones. It is important to obtain advice on species suitable for the site you wish to plant, as many species have preferences for particular locations or soil types within their native zones.

Source: Nature Conservancy Council 1989 *Native trees and shrubs for wildlife in the United Kingdom.* Leaflet. NCC.

sunlight, others need high humidity and there are also some that require shade (Table 7.6: Woodland invertebrates favouring sun or shade). They cannot survive for long outside woodland or on sites exposed to wind by clearfelling.

Microclimate also affects other woodland wildlife. For example, many woodland plants favour ground that remains moist through the summer but also require sunlight to flower and set seed. Reptiles, being cold-blooded, need to bask in sunshine. Mammals and birds are relatively well insulated but depend for food on abundant plant and invertebrate life which

are in turn influenced by sunlight and temperature. In winter, shelter from wind can be vital to the overnight survival of roosting birds.

In general, the areas that hold the greatest variety and abundance of flowering plants and insects, including woodland butterflies, are sunlit glades and rides sheltered from wind by the surrounding trees. However, overall, the greatest variety of wildlife is found in woods with a variety of structure.

The type of management system affects the woodland structure. Mature woodlands with little understorey, and coppice with

Table 7.5: Soil preferences of trees

SPECIES	WET SITES	LIGHT DRY SOILS	HEAVY SOILS	ACID	NEUTRAL OR ALKALINE	EXPOSED SITES
Alder	●				●	
Apple, crab		●	●		●	
Ash	●	●	●		●	●
Aspen (zones 1–3)		●		●	●	●
Aspen (zones 4–10)			●		●	
Beech		●		●	●	●
Birch, downy	●	●	●	●	●	●
Birch, silver		●	●	●	●	●
Blackthorn	●	●	●		●	●
Box		●			●	
Broom		●		●		●
Buckthorn, alder	●			●	●	
Buckthorn, purging			●		●	
Butchers-broom				●	●	
Cherry, bird	●				●	
Cherry, gean			●		●	
Dogwood		●	●		●	
Elder		●	●		●	
Elm, wych			●		●	●
Gorse		●		●	●	●
Guelder-rose	●		●		●	
Hawthorn, common		●	●	●	●	●
Hawthorn, midland			●		●	
Hazel		●	●		●	●
Holly		●		●	●	
Hornbeam			●	●	●	
Juniper		●		●		●
Lime, small-leaved (zone 4)		●				
Lime, small-leaved (zones 5–9)		●	●	●	●	
Lime, large-leaved			●		●	
Maple, field		●	●		●	
Oak, common	●		●	●	●	●
Oak, sessile		●		●	●	●
Pine, Scots		●		●		●
Poplar, black	●		●		●	
Poplar, grey	●				●	
Privet		●	●		●	●
Rose, dog		●	●		●	●
Rose, field			●		●	
Rowan		●		●	●	
Service tree			●	●	●	
Spindle			●		●	
Spurge-laurel		●	●		●	
Wayfaring-tree		●	●		●	
Whitebeam (zones 4 & 8)		●			●	●
Whitebeam (zone 7)		●		●	●	●
Willow, almond	●				●	
Willow, bay	●				●	
Willow, crack	●				●	●
Willow, goat	●		●		●	●
Willow, grey	●			●	●	●
Willow, osier	●				●	
Willow, purple	●				●	●
Willow, white	●				●	●
Yew		●			●	

Source: Watkins, C 1991 *Nature Conservation and the New Lowland Forests*. Nature Conservancy Council. For map of zones see Table 7.4.

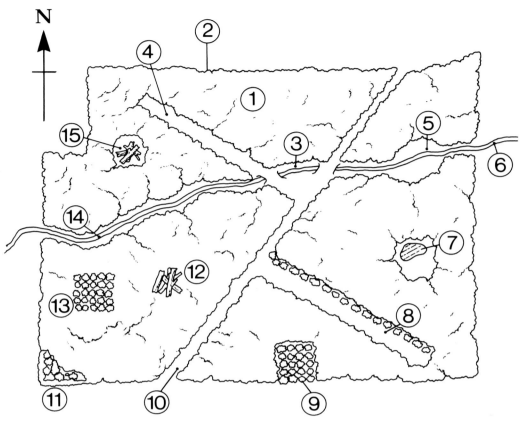

Figure 7.1
Effects of woodland structure on plants and invertebrates

1. Closed canopy: sheltered but cool. Restricted range of plants and invertebrates below canopy.
2. Wood edge: wind-sheltered but shaded. Damp ground. Poor for plants and most invertebrates.
3. Ideal glade site: sunny, sheltered ground and stream. Excellent for most wildlife. Minimal interference with productive woodland management.
4. Shaded ride with wind shelter. Damp and cool. Poor for invertebrates.
5. Stream: wind sheltered and sunlit. Good aquatic plant growth. Good for aquatic invertebrates and flying insects. Maintain some shaded sections as some scarce species need shaded streams.
6. Stream: exposed to sun and wind. Good for aquatic plants and invertebrates but less good for flying insects.
7. Pond in glade: sunlit and sheltered. Excellent for amphibians and aquatic invertebrates. Humid.
8. Wide ride with sunlit edge. Good for shrub growth, plants, invertebrates. Dry and hot.
9. New coppice panel: sunny but open to wind chill.
10. Ride open to prevailing wind, which lowers temperatures. Dry and cool. Less good for invertebrates. Could be improved by curving ride, scalloping edge or creating shrubby edges.
11. Edge enhancement with shrubs behind hedge. Reasonable shelter and good sunlight. Fair for invertebrates.
12. Dead wood shaded by canopy. Ideal for dependent insects and fungi.
13. New coppice panel. Sunny and sheltered. Excellent for plants and insects.
14. Stream: shaded and wind sheltered. Little aquatic plant growth or invertebrate activity, although some species need shaded streams.
15. 'Habitat pile' or dead wood in sunlit glade. Dried out and poor for dependent invertebrates.

Table 7.6: Woodland invertebrates favouring sun or shade

SUNSHINE-LOVING GROUPS	SHADE-LOVING GROUPS
Bees	Craneflies
Wasps	Fungus gnats
Longhorn beetles	Centipedes
Butterflies	Millipedes
Most bugs and hoppers	Snails and slugs
Hoverflies	Woodlice
Scorpion flies	
Some spiders	Many spiders
Some ground beetles	Some ground beetles
Some moths	Some moths
Many dead wood species as adults	Many dead wood species as larvae

Source: Key, R 1992. (in litt.) English Nature

---

standards have widely differing structures and support different wildlife, see section 3.3.

In small farm woods, it may be impracticable to create great structural variety. Select elements that give the best benefits for an acceptable management demand. In conifer plantations, rides and glades and woodland edges are often the areas with greatest potential for wildlife.

1.4 Streamsides, ponds, ditches and wet ground in woods

- Wetlands in woods that enjoy wind shelter and sunlight are excellent for aquatic plants and many invertebrates.
- Shaded wetlands are also essential for some species.
- Temporary pools in ruts along rides are valuable for some wildlife.

Watercourses, pools and other wetlands in woods benefit from wind shelter and often support different wildlife from their counterparts in the open. Both sunlit and shaded conditions are desirable as each supports a different wildlife assemblage.

Woods are often strongholds for plants of wet ground that have disappeared from farmland due to land drainage. Many woodland plants favour wet conditions, and wetland plants such as meadowsweet

and purple loosestrife often occur in wet woodland glades.

Wet rides on clay soils with ruts created by vehicles or trampling by livestock, for example, can hold standing water in winter and spring and are important for those invertebrates which require temporary pools where predators such as fish cannot survive. Frogs also breed in these sites for the same reason (see Chapter 9).

1.5 Wildlife value of old trees and dead wood

- Old trees and dead wood have exceptional value for many lichens, fungi, invertebrates and hole-nesting birds.
- Most trees do not reach their full wildlife value until well after commercial maturity.
- Features of wildlife value are areas of rot, seepages, dead limbs, holes and cavities and dead trees.
- Different kinds of standing and fallen dead wood are important for different wildlife and develop most value in damp, semi-shaded conditions.

The older trees become, the more wildlife they support, partly because they develop areas of rot or dead wood, which are of special value for invertebrates and hole-nesting birds. In commercially managed woods, trees are felled at economic maturity, long before they reach their greatest value for wildlife. For example, oak reaches its commercial maturity between 80–120 years but does not reach its optimum conservation value until it is over 250 years old.

In many trees, lower limbs die naturally as the upper canopy shades them out. As they decay, wood-eating invertebrates colonise them and in turn provide food for woodpeckers and other birds (Feature 7.2: Woodpeckers). This decay often creates holes and cavities. Around a third of woodland birds nest in holes because they give protection from the weather and predators.

Seepages of sap from the trunk associated with damage or decay are the breeding sites of some specialised invertebrates and fungi. Many fungi live on trees in association with rotting wood. Some of these are very rare and in turn support specialised invertebrates, which eat them or breed in them.

Most fungi and insects associated with decay are not harmful to healthy trees. The species involved are different from the pathogenic pest species responsible for the loss of plantation trees. However, there are a small number, such as honey fungus, that may cause damage in woods managed for timber production.

Mature oaks and some other trees develop heart rot and become hollow and, as they age further, the crown is lightened by loss of branches, so reducing the weight to be supported by the root system and the likelihood of windthrow. Heart rot also releases locked-up nutrients to recycle in new growth. A number of very rare invertebrates depend on the heart rot areas of ancient trees.

Depending on species, invertebrates require different types of dead wood, from rot holes, fungus-infected or heart-rotten trunks, dead wood on live trees, to fallen dead wood or trees. Dead wood in contact with moist soils in partial shade is excellent for invertebrates because it does not become sunbaked and hard, nor too cool. Very few farm woods now contain enough of these important habitats, which were abundant in the original forest cover.

1.6 Effects of grazing in woodland

- Livestock and deer alter the plant community and structure of woodlands.
- Wetland areas are particularly sensitive to heavy grazing and dunging.
- Low-intensity grazing and browsing can create conditions ideal for some birds and plants but in woods where stock regularly shelter and graze, regeneration of trees is inhibited and overall wildlife interest is reduced.
- Distribution of fodder for livestock in woods can damage ground vegetation and introduce invasive weeds.
- Where deer are numerous they prevent regeneration or regrowth of coppice.

Most farm woods are too small to contain grazing animals for long without changes to the structure. At low density, deer, cattle, sheep, horses, hares and rabbits feed selectively on the plants they prefer and may greatly reduce them. At high density, grazing mammals may destroy almost all the herbs, shrubs and young trees but the wood may still superficially appear rich in plants because a few less palatable species flourish. In addition, grey squirrels can cause serious damage to some tree species.

In larger woods, low-intensity grazing diversifies vegetation structure and is beneficial. It can be important in maintaining existing glades and open areas along rides. In the broadleaved woods of west and north Britain, sheep and cattle create ideal conditions for a characteristic bird community, including wood warblers and redstarts, which dislike a well-developed understorey (Feature 7.3: Breeding birds of western oakwoods). However, in the long term, livestock can jeopardise the survival of a woodland by preventing regeneration.

Care must also be taken in wet areas within woodlands. These habitats are most sensitive and considerable poaching and enrichment can take place if stock are allowed access.

Distribution of fodder for livestock in woodland is very damaging to plants due to the concentrated effects of trampling and dunging, which destroy the vegetation.

Locally, deer numbers can be high. All of the six species of wild deer established in the UK are expanding their range, particularly red, roe and sika deer. Their grazing and browsing can prevent regeneration by trees and destroy new plantings or coppice regrowth. Damage may also be caused to agricultural crops.

2. Options and assessment: planning management

2.1 Wildlife assessment of farm woods

- Most farm woods are small but can still be very important for wildlife.
- Assessment of wildlife value is most simply done by preparing an annotated map of the wood's structure, tree composition and the presence of important features.

Most woods on farms are less than 2 ha and though it is true that bigger woods are likely to hold a greater variety of wildlife, such small woods can be very rich and may hold rare species. On an intensively managed farm they are likely to be the main wildlife strongholds.

If the woods on a farm have been neglected for some time or if a change of management is being considered, assess both their current interest and their potential for wildlife.

The amount of information collected to form the basis for the farm wood plan will vary considerably, depending on the wood's age and interest, its size, complexity and proposed uses. However, it is usually adequate simply to produce an annotated map which includes information on the wood's structure, tree species composition and management history. The range of information required is given at Table 7.7 and background guidance on site asessments is given in Chapter 1.

Much of the information, such as the location of rides, old trees and ponds, can be gathered very quickly at any time of year. However, information on plants, invertebrates or breeding birds can only be collected in spring and summer.

Once this has been done, the wood's value for wildlife can be assessed by referring to section 1 of this chapter. Then it is possible to decide what parts of the wood are most important and what may be done to improve it. The management methods are set out in section 3 of this chapter.

If grant aid is to be sought for management, regeneration or planting, then a management plan will be required to support the application and before beginning the assessment and plan, you should contact the relevant grant-awarding body to discuss the degree of information needed (see Financial incentives and schemes leaflet, page 8).

Ideally, the assessment of the wood should form part of a farm wildlife plan (see Chapter 1).

2.2 Management needs and opportunities

- Land which has long held trees often has the highest wildlife value.
- More recent plantations, although not as valuable for wildlife as ancient woods, can be enhanced in several ways.
- Advice on the conservation potential and other uses of farm woods is available.
- Grant aid may be available for both management of existing woods and establishment of new woods.
- Management for some wildlife can be integrated with all other uses.
- The degree to which the needs of wildlife can be integrated into a farm wood managed for timber will depend on the timber production system adopted.

Table 7.7: Wildlife assessment of farm woods

INFORMATION REQUIRED	METHOD	REASON FOR INFORMATION
1. Conservation status and interest	Contact FWAG initially.	Information on the wildlife interest of the farm wood may already be known May have statutory designation such as SSSI/ASSI or Tree Preservation Order so certain conditions may need to be satisfied before change of management can take place.
2. Age of wood	Contact Forestry Authority/ Department or official nature conservation agency. (Appendix I).	If it is an 'ancient' wood it is likely to be of considerable wildlife interest. Take advice on management.
3. Management	Check farm records. Contact previous owners. Examine woodland structure and features. Note obvious signs of past management, eg old coppice stools, overgrown rides. Note current timber management practices including timescale of management. Note current game management practices.	Species associated with past management may still survive. Reinstatement of the system will benefit them. A change of system may mean they are lost but there is no compensatory gain of new species. Large-scale felling is damaging for wildlife. May need to identify and retain important features such as old trees, natural regeneration of native trees and shrubs. Locate pens and feeding areas away from areas of interest.
4. Livestock grazing and deer	If used by livestock, note numbers and seasonal use. Note evidence of deer presence and any damage.	May significantly affect understorey, tree regeneration and overall wildlife value. May constrain further management options.
5. Boundary of wood	Location and condition of fences, hedges and dykes/walls. Condition of wood at boundary. Land use surrounding wood.	To identify necessary work to make stockproof. To identify opportunities for enhancing woodland edge. To look at relationship with adjoining land, eg reducing spray-drift into woods, reducing crop shading or extension of wood into set-aside.
6. Tree canopy	Map general distribution of main tree species. Map areas with canopy closed (shade) or open (dappled sunlight). Map location and age of oldest trees, standing/fallen dead trees, and dead wood.	Different tree species support different wildlife values. Will guide decision on management, eg thinning, enhancement. Affects growth of understorey and thus plants and other wildlife. Important to retain for wildlife.
7. Understorey	Map general distribution of shrubs and young trees. Map areas with good herb layer abundance. Map areas without shrub or herb layer.	Different species and structures have different values. Will guide decisions on management, eg little shrub layer or few young trees may suggest regeneration inhibited by grazing: tall shrubs with little basal cover may suggest need for reinstating coppice.
8. Location of rides, glades or open space	Map location and size. Note vegetation type, structure and height, eg short grass. Map areas sunlit at midday.	Sunlit, open space and wind shelter is very important. Keep free from planting or natural regeneration and prevent shading.

Table 7.7: Wildlife assessment of farm woods (cont'd)

INFORMATION REQUIRED	METHOD	REASON FOR INFORMATION
9. Location of wetlands/ marshes, ditches, ponds	Map location, size and type, eg pond. Note whether holds water and remains wet all year or usually dries out in summer. Source of water. Amount of emergent or submerged plant growth. How much shaded at midday. Degree of silting. Effect of stock.	Important features of woods that should be retained or restored. Do not drain or use for dumping. Potential for enhancement, eg clearing back of some shading trees. If poaching occurs, potential for fencing off from stock.
10. Location of other features	Map old quarries, rock outcrops, earthworks, boundary banks, etc. Note conditions of feature, eg whether used for dumping, overgrown, etc.	Important features of woods which bring diversity. May be of historic interest in own right, in which case seek advice. Do not plant up.
11. Location of rare or sensitive species	If known, map exact location of rare species present. Seek specialist advice.	May be lost through woodland management- consult specialist. Retain. May need specific management.

The needs of wildlife can be integrated with other uses of the farm wood, such as timber production, or game, or stock shelter. The best timber production systems for wildlife are those based on a range of crop trees with different maturation ages.

Management is on a smaller scale, a tree canopy is always present and continuity is always provided. Even-aged conifer plantations managed by clearfelling have limited wildlife value.

The first decision to be taken when considering management is to identify the long-term aim for the wood and the amount of resources required to match this. It is important to consider manpower implications and the seasonal nature of woodland work. Most management will take place in winter but ride mowing, for instance, may need some attention in summer. If the work is not contracted out there may be capital costs for equipment. Although the skills involved may be unfamiliar, much is quite straightforward, though felling and extraction may be best left to contractors.

In planning management, also consider whether the wood affects other aspects of the management of the farm, perhaps by shading crops and grass, causing excessive lodging of cereals or harbouring rabbits or deer. There may be ways in which this can be reduced, such as putting adjoining land into long-term set-aside.

It is very important to know whether the wood is on land that has always held trees, irrespective of the current species composition of the wood. If so, the benefits of conservation management are likely to be very high. Accordingly, care must be taken as these ancient sites may contain plants and invertebrates, such as woodland butterflies, which have limited ability to colonise new woodlands. There may be strong cases for replacing non-native trees with kinds that grow naturally in the area and for reinstating the traditional management at least in part of the wood.

In deciding the goals of management, take account of what is happening in other woods in the area. For instance, if other woods are neglected and heavily shaded, it may be even more beneficial than usual to open up glades and rides or commence a coppicing regime. Similarly, if all woods are used for stock shelter and consequently contain few plants and shrubs, excluding grazing may be the most beneficial course of action.

In more recent woods, and shelterbelts planted on former farmland or moorland, scarce plants and invertebrates are unlikely to be present. However, even in small conifer plantations useful measures can be taken for wildlife without excessively interfering with the crop value. Enhancement with a selected variety of additional native trees and shrubs will be of benefit to a range of wildlife.

Decisions about woodland management rarely need to be hurried. If an area is felled by mistake, it may be a generation or more before woodland cover can be re-established. In some cases a number of plants and animals may be lost forever. Several bodies can provide advice on the wildlife value, the availability of management grants and marketable products (see Appendix I: Sources of advice).

There are also increasing opportunities and incentives to plant new farm woods, and advice on siting, planting, aftercare and long-term management is also widely available.

3. Management of farm woods

3.1 Timber production and wildlife

- Minimise large-scale felling: ideally use group selection.
- Minimise the impact of management by harvesting and restocking on as long a timescale as possible. Coppice management is an exception.
- Retain some trees in perpetuity.
- Favour and encourage natural regeneration. Retain natural regeneration by native species when harvesting, especially in conifer plantations.
- If planting is essential, preferably use local provenance stock especially on ancient sites.
- If regeneration or planting is undertaken for conservation reasons, fell and restock glades no larger than about 0.3 ha.

Depending on the system of timber production adopted, conservation may integrate fully across the whole farm wood or have to be confined to restricted areas. The best systems for wildlife are those which provide structural variety by including trees at a range of ages so that the wood always has some areas with mature trees and a closed canopy, others with young trees and an abundant sunlit herb layer, and so on. Such systems include group selection based on a range of crop trees with different maturation ages or, if markets can be found, coppice with standards. Even-aged plantations have limited wildlife interest because they lack structural and species variety, and often only contain one or two tree crop species.

Large-scale felling destroys the woodland microclimate and removes the habitat of most woodland wildlife except for those birds (and some insects) which prefer open ground or a dense herb and shrub layer.

To achieve the range of tree ages and woodland structure beneficial for wildlife, extend the length of the harvesting and restocking period over as many years as possible.

Many farm woods are fairly evenly aged and contain few old trees. In managing for wildlife, a long-term aim should be to create a spread of ages from saplings to ancient trees to give structural diversity and continuity of conditions required by particular species. Also restrict felling to the period from late summer to winter when this operation will have least effect on wildlife. If the wood contains few or no trees under 60 years old, it is worth starting a gradual process of regeneration. A felling licence will be needed from the relevant forestry authority for most felling operations. If the wood is subject to a Tree

Preservation Order then permission for felling or lopping is also required from the planning authority (see Appendix II: Legal considerations).

Due to the increase in wildlife value of older trees, it is always desirable to extend the rotation beyond that which gives a maximum economic return. The decisions on when to fell a stand, how much to fell at one time and over what period the felling takes place, require careful consideration.

Ideally, some trees should be retained in perpetuity. Provided it does not create a risk of spreading disease to healthy trees, keep those which are decaying or damaged as they have greatest wildlife value and least timber value.

Whenever possible, encourage natural regeneration rather than planting trees as this maintains the genetic characteristics of the wood (and is cheaper). For instance, some trees tend to be much more heavily branched than others, or produce epicormic growths providing more feeding and nesting opportunities for wildlife. Modern forestry has favoured trees with tall, clean, unbranched boles, which offer fewer niches for wildlife.

Not all trees produce copious seed every year and there will be losses of seeds and seedlings from many causes. However, woodland management is a long-term commitment and from a conservation standpoint regeneration is rarely urgent and can often wait for a decade or so. If necessary, selective felling after a heavy mast year can provide open conditions to lead to good natural regeneration. Where there has been natural regeneration by native species amongst a planted timber crop, retain as much as possible when harvesting. Some of the regenerating trees will be damaged during harvesting, but those that are not can go on to produce the future crop. Ideally, do not underplant them, to avoid subsequent competition and possible loss of the native species. Both for timber production and wildlife requirements, it may be useful to thin in due course. For wildlife, heavy thinning is best as it produces spreading crowns and lets light reach the woodland floor. For timber, the aim is usually to

produce tall boles with little branching, so less thinning will be done.

Normally, only plant trees if there is an urgent silvicultural need to replace a crop or to enhance an area, such as a streamside within a conifer plantation, where quick wildlife benefits are needed. If planting is necessary, use native trees and shrubs grown from local seed sources, if possible. This is especially important on ancient woodland sites, which should be reverted to native woodland if they have been planted with conifers, for example. Availability of suitable nursery-grown stock can be a problem because the trees and shrubs that are stocked are not normally derived from a local seed source. Advice on suitable sources may be available from FWAG. If all else fails, consider collecting local seed and growing it on.

Whether promoting natural regeneration or carrying out planting, always work on a small scale. Create regeneration glades just large enough not to be overshaded by surrounding trees (typically 0.3 ha, but smaller in small woods). Never fell the oldest trees to create these glades.

In plantations, opportunities exist to develop or diversify a native tree and shrub component along streamsides and ride margins as well as amongst the crop, where self-sown native trees may be retained in moderation.

Grey squirrels frequently cause severe bark stripping damage to pole stage (10–40 year old) stands of beech, oak, sycamore and occasionally other species, in May through to early August. Grey squirrels are most effectively controlled by poisoning with warfarin on wheat dispensed from hoppers specially designed to reduce the risk of poisoning of other species.

It is an offence to lay poison that may be taken by certain mammals such as dormouse, red squirrel and badger. Also the use of warfarin is prohibited in Scotland and some counties of England and Wales (see Appendix II: Legal considerations). Further guidance can be obtained from the relevant forestry authority.

3.2 Tree species choice

- In woods primarily managed for wildlife, at harvesting if not before, aim to replace any trees that are not native to the area with native species appropriate to the soil type and locality.
- It should be possible to incorporate some native trees in any farm woodland even if it is managed primarily for timber.
- When adding additional trees or shrubs, take account of the existing woodland structure and features of importance. Establish single-species groups and do not plant too many varieties.

If the farm wood contains trees and shrubs that are not native to the area, they should ideally be replaced by species typical of the locality. This should be one long-term aim for all woods managed primarily for wildlife but it can be done to a limited extent whatever the main management objective. Replacement of non-native species can usually be carried out gradually, on a small scale or left until timber is harvested and new tree cover is established. However, if the non-natives are regenerating freely and increasing substantially at the expense of native trees, immediate action will be required.

This principle applies most strongly to woods that have grown on the same land for centuries (ancient woods), or recent plantations that have replaced native trees on an ancient woodland site. It is less important in secondary woods created on farmland, where a mix of native and non-native species may be quite good for birds, for example.

Where practical, improve the wildlife value of a farm plantation or shelterbelt by increasing the variety of trees and shrubs. Select those that are locally native, are suited to the soil type and will contribute most, for example because they:

- have large numbers of dependent species (such as crab apple for insects or ash for lichens);
- provide nectar or pollen at the start of the season for newly-emerged insects (willows and blackthorn);
- mature rapidly to provide decaying and dead wood (such as birches);
- can exploit special conditions in the wood (such as alder on streamsides);
- add an element that is missing (such as native evergreens for winter shelter);
- are required by a particular species (such as buckthorn for the larvae of brimstone butterflies).

A single tree or shrub may not be sufficient to attract or sustain its dependent wildlife. Plant each of the selected shrub species in a group of five or more in a sunny situation and have at least two groups. Aim to have at least three mature specimens of each tree species; it may be possible to plant only three initially provided they are set at final spacings and any losses are replaced.

Do not make enhancements without considering the woodland structure and size. For example, do not plant up existing sunlit glades. Instead, create regeneration glades by felling small areas with little existing interest. Typically, these will be in heavily shaded areas where the existing trees do not include any very old individuals or uncommon species. Enhancement may be most easily accommodated when restocking after timber harvesting or when fencing to control grazing.

3.3 Coppice management

- Most native trees and shrubs can be coppiced.
- Mixed-species coppice is good for wildlife. Sweet chestnut coppice is poor.
- Where coppicing is to be reinstated, decide the rotation length and layout taking account of the rate of growth and the needs of associated species such as fritillary butterflies, nightingales or dormice.
- Retain some standard trees in coppice panels.
- New woods can be coppiced once the trees reach about 10–20 years old.

Most broadleaved trees sprout from the base or 'stool' when cut down and, if felled periodically and allowed to re-grow, will live for many years, even centuries. This allows underwood and small timber to be produced annually from a woodland without the need to regenerate or restock. Many broadleaved woodlands were once managed by coppicing, with scattered trees allowed to grow as standards to produce large timbers. Most conifers die when cut down and cannot therefore be coppiced. Beech, wild cherry and some poplars also do not coppice well.

Coppice is excellent for woodland flowers, which flourish once an area is harvested and sunlight reaches the ground, and for woodland invertebrates especially butterflies (Feature 7.7: Habitat requirements of fritillary butterflies). A limited variety of birds live in coppice, the most important being nightingales (Feature 7.8: Nightingales and coppice woodland). The dormouse prefers managed hazel coppice, but no other mammals show a special association with the habitat (Feature 7.6: Habitat requirements of dormice).

Sweet chestnut coppice is of less value to wildlife than hazel or a mix of different species because its regrowth is extremely rapid so that any ground flora is quickly shaded out and the dense basal cover required by nightingales and some other birds exists for a short period only. In addition, sweet chestnut leaf litter rots down very slowly and often suppresses other plants.

If the wood was formerly coppiced there will be coppice stools present, which may now carry only one or a few substantial stems. Sometimes, very old stools may die but mostly they respond well to cutting.

If the coppice is long derelict and the wood has become shaded, some species, especially sun-demanding insects, may have died out. However, some woodland plants persist in the seedbank and others have airborne seeds so they will recolonise even from a distance. Invertebrates may be able to recolonise in time if they are present nearby.

There should be enough coppice stools to give good coverage of regrowth – around 400 stools per hectare. If coppice is reinstated on an old site and the existing density of stools is very low, it will be necessary to interplant with new trees and shrubs and ultimately bring them into management. Diversify the range of species present in the wood by selecting other species native to the area. If coppice is of mixed native species this adds diversity and shrubs will have different growth rates which helps create variation in structure. Always reinstate coppicing on an experimental scale initially (0.25 ha) as not all farm woods produce a good response, some merely becoming dominated by bramble or bracken.

A few standard trees should be kept – preferably the oldest specimens. They will shade the coppice and slow its rate of regrowth, which is generally good for conservation. If all the available trees are young and their crowns are small, it may be desirable to retain as many as 100/ha but they will need to be reduced in number as they age. With old trees, aim to keep about 10/ha but no more than 10% canopy cover or the coppice growth will be unduly affected by shading.

The length of the rotation depends on the speed of coppice regrowth. When the canopy has closed and the ground layer is shaded out it should be recut because it becomes unsuitable for wildflowers, for most invertebrates and for nightingales (Figure 7.2 Effects of coppice rotations on invertebrates, nightingales and dormice). This may take about 8–15 years depending on the stool density, tree and shrub species involved, soil fertility and shading by standard trees. For wildlife, aim to have all stages of regrowth present. Divide the wood into as many compartments or 'panels' as there are years in the rotation length (ie 8 for an 8-year rotation, 15 for a 15-year rotation). If at the outset it is not known what the rotation length will be, it is better to have too many panels rather than too few.

Best of all is to have two or three separate panels cut each year: for example, in a 15-ha wood there could be 30 half-hectare

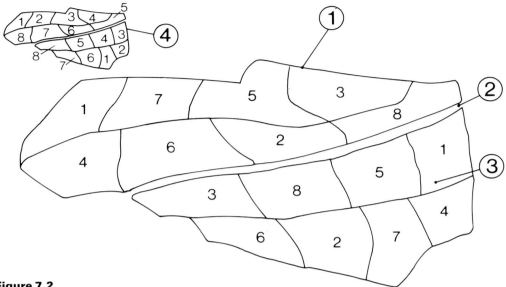

Figure 7.2
Effects of coppice rotations on invertebrates, nightingales and dormice

The size and layout of panels (also called coupes or cants) and the length of rotation will vary according to the objectives. Different wildlife groups have conflicting requirements; it is important to decide on the prime wildlife interest of a wood before deciding on appropriate management. If rare invertebrates are believed to be present in a wood, seek specialist advice before starting management.

1. 8-ha wood divided into 16 panels, and managed as two blocks of 8 0.5-ha panels each managed on an 8-year rotation.

2. Sunny sheltered rides are good for many invertebrates. Retaining overhanging branches will encourage dormice to pass across.

3. Panels laid out in 'random' pattern. Good for nightingales; good cover for nesting adjoins more open ground for feeding. Layout also satisfactory for dormice but panels are too big. These would ideally be 0·2 ha or less (but avoiding excessive shading of coppice regrowth). The rotation may be too short for hazel to begin to fruit again. This may happen after five years but in some woods it may be over 10 years (see Feature 7.6 on dormice).

4. Layout more suited to invertebrates. Cut panel next to the one cut the previous year, as many invertebrates are not mobile enough to find other suitable sites within a wood.

plots, of which three could be cut each year on a 10-year rotation. In small farm woods, it may not be practicable to cut a panel every year. For instance, in a 2-ha wood half a hectare might be cut every third year on a 12-year rotation. Panels smaller than half a hectare are unlikely to be large enough to hold the territories of coppice birds such as nightingale but may be suitable for plants, invertebrates and dormice.

For invertebrates, many of which are relatively sedentary, it is important that adjacent panels are cut in sequence, so that species can move from one to the next as conditions become suitable.

New woods may be coppiced, the trees and shrubs first being cut when they reach 10–20 years of age.

3.4 Management for old timber and dead trees

- Retain the oldest trees in the wood, plan for the long-term succession and keep at least some to the ends of their natural lives.
- Do not fell trees with decay or damage where they do not threaten the health of the remaining crop trees.
- Continue to manage pollards.
- Retain native trees that fall in gales but continue to grow.
- Retain standing dead trees and fallen timber in situ. Do not cut up fallen dead wood and pile it in heaps.
- Erect bird and bat boxes where natural cavities are in short supply.

Because of their exceptional wildlife value, identify the oldest trees and retain them. Retentions must be on wind-firm sites. Even if all the trees are relatively young, keep the oldest: a 30 year-old tree will reach its greatest value for wildlife 30 years sooner than a newly planted one. Preferably, keep specimens that have well-branched crowns or signs of damage or decay. These are likely to be better for wildlife and also have the least timber value. Thin closely grouped young trees with the aim of encouraging spreading crown development.

There may be pollards on the woodland boundary or, exceptionally, within the wood. These have high importance for wildlife and should be managed by cropping the limbs periodically (see page 258).

All old trees have value. Do not selectively remove non-native trees if they are significantly the oldest trees in the wood. Retain them at least until the native species have also reached old age.

Ideally, keep the oldest trees throughout their full natural lifespan. This will vary from species to species but some live more than 200 years. Most very old trees are wind-firm but eventually lose vigour. Do not allow them to become overshaded by adjacent trees as this may kill them prematurely. Finally, allow the dead bole to decay naturally.

When native trees fall owing to high winds, do not clear them, subject to their timber value. They rarely die and, provided some of the root system is still intact, they will sprout along the prone bole or from upstanding limbs and continue to grow. They add to the structural diversity of the wood and increase the range of variation in woodland microclimate.

Retain standing dead stems when thinning or felling. They can be under-planted and not affect the new growth. Also when thinning, consider creating standing dead trees by ring barking. On ancient woodland sites, kill non-native trees rather than native species but never kill old trees or those which already have significant damage or decay. These are of greater value alive than dead.

Retain fallen timber in situ. Small dead wood, such as brashings, is much less valuable to wildlife than large limbs, root plates and whole trunks. Dead material is better for wildlife if it is in contact with the woodland floor than if it is piled in heaps and it is better in shade or dappled sunlight rather than in full sun which dries it out (Feature 7.4: Dead wood and wildlife).

If there is a shortage of old timber with holes and cavities, nestboxes will be very valuable for hole-nesting birds. Erect the appropriate boxes for the birds' requirements. Boxes for owls and kestrels may be placed in larger trees or erected on poles in glades, clearfells and restocks (Feature 7.5: Nestboxes and bat boxes).

Bat boxes may also be beneficial. They are best sited at the edges of glades, along rides and on streamsides.

These should be seen as short-term measures. Aim to promote old timber to provide natural sites.

3.5 Management of rides, glades and woodland edge

- Keep rides and glades open to sunlight. If necessary, fell overshading trees.
- In woods where timber production is important, enhancing rides, glades and woodland edges causes little or no interference with the commercial aim.
- Where glades are absent, enlarge ride intersections, create scallops along rides, retain gaps that appear after windthrow or create glades by felling small areas.
- Manage glades and the margins of rides by cutting on a rotation to maintain a mix of short and tall grass, and herbs and some stands of dense shrubs.
- Clear scrub and trees on the south and western sides of woodland or do not plant up to fence lines. Manage shrubs and plants on rotation as for rides.
- Retain self-sown native broadleaved tree regeneration on the edges of plantations.
- Maintain a hedge or bank around woods, particularly where spray-drift may be a problem.

Farm wood rides are created for access, particularly timber extraction, and are normally too narrow to let in much sun and consequently of little value for wildlife. Always try to keep rides wide enough to let in sunlight, if necessary by felling. Open space on a ride can be increased further by cutting south-facing scallops into the wood from the ride edge 10 m wide by 50 m long (Figure 7.3: Ride with scallop and box-junction glade). To avoid creating a wind tunnel, do not open up the ends of rides, especially those aligned with the prevailing wind. If already open, plant a hedge across the end. For reasonably sunlit conditions on an east-west ride, its width should be at least as much as the height of the trees on its south side (eg if the trees are 15 m high, the ride should be 15 m wide). North to south rides get full sun briefly at midday but are very shaded through the rest of the day and need to be 2½ times as wide as the trees are

high (ie, 37 m wide for 15 m high trees). In small woods this may be impractical, in which case consider creating a glade at least 30 m x 30 m by felling trees back from the corners where rides intersect.

Some woodlands contain natural glades, which persist for many years through continued grazing by deer or other animals. These glades are often very rich in wildlife and should not be planted.

Creating glades in some woods will need to take account of the risk of windthrow. Assess whether there are areas with little exposure to wind due to topographic conditions or where trees are most likely to be wind-firm, for example, on existing ride sides or on the deeper soils. If windthrow has created a glade, and surrounding trees are now stable, retain the glade rather than restocking it.

In the smallest woods, creation of sunlit glades may leave little more than an external shell that provides inadequate internal shelter. In this case, manage the outer edges of woods instead to create open areas, particularly on the south-facing side.

When planting a new wood or restocking a clearfelled plantation, consider the value of well-designed rides, glades and edges. Ensure that their size is sufficient to remain partly sunlit when surrounding trees have reached full height; alternatively, plan to clear on the upwind face as trees begin to shade them. Clearing on the downward face may expose trees which are not wind-firm and lead to gale damage.

Where there are no special requirements for rare species, apply the following standard prescription. To allow plants to seed, mow a central strip once annually after the end of July and before the beginning of April. Maintain a margin at least 1 m wide on each side by cutting about a quarter of the total length every year at the same time as the central strip: this 4-year rotation will allow tall grasses and herbs to develop but control scrub invasion. If possible use a forage harvester or baler to remove cut grass and herbage: if left to rot in situ it will suppress the growth of flowers.

To maintain structural diversity divide the ride into a series of 'lengths' about 30–50 m in length.

1. **Central ride – approximately 2 m wide. Mown annually from late summer onwards to maintain good access and for the benefit of short-sward species.**
2. **Grass. Will need cutting about every four years.**
3. **Scrub. Will need to be cut on roughly a nine-year rotation.**
4. **Wood.**
5. **South-facing scallop – approximately 10 m wide by 50 m long.**
6. **Box junction glade where rides cross – at least 30 m x 30 m.**
7. **Scrub cut 3 years ago.**
8. **Scrub cut 6 years ago.**

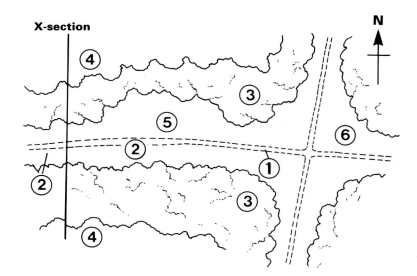

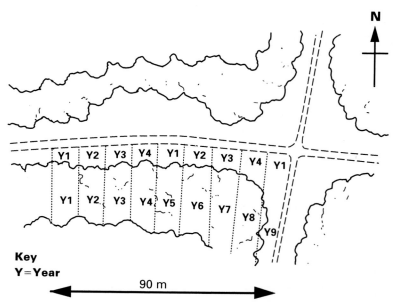

Key
Y = Year

90 m

Figure 7.3
Ride with scallop and box-junction glade

Establish shrubs at least along the sunlit sides of rides and the edges of glades, preferably by natural regeneration or by coppicing existing broadleaved trees (see page 201). Manage them to maintain the full range of conditions from newly cut areas to dense shrub growth. Supposing shrubs reach this condition in nine years, a simple management regime would be to cut down one-ninth of the total length each year or a third every three years.

Do not carry out one year's cutting of tall herbage or shrubs as a single block but divide it into several smaller patches 30–50 m long. This will mean that the sunlit areas contain great structural variety with different vegetation heights adjoining each other.

Where grazing animals, including rabbits, are present in a wood, it may be unnecessary to mow. However, if grazing pressure is heavy, reduce the level in order to develop the desired structure to the rides (see page 208).

Never burn 'lop and top' or brashings on rides as the consequent nutrient enrichment will cause weed invasion.

The sunlit south and western edges of woods can be good for shrubs and wild flowers because they are sunlit. They are less good for invertebrates than rides and glades because they are exposed to wind. Fell trees along the west and south sides and then manage them on rotation. Alternatively, fences may be moved away from the woodland edge for natural regeneration to take place or for planting with shrubs if necessary.

When restocking after felling, do not plant up to fence lines. Leave a strip 5–20 m broad where native plants and shrubs can grow. Where self-sown regeneration by native species occurs on the edges of plantations, it should be retained permanently. It is likely to be wind-firm and will shelter subsequent crops.

A well-maintained hedge makes a good outer boundary and will tend to intercept agrochemical spray-drift and fertiliser granules, preventing them from affecting plants and animals at the woodland edge.

An ideal arrangement is to maintain adjacent land as set-aside, permanent pasture or a conservation headland.

3.6 Management of wetlands in farm woods

- Retain or create areas of wet ground in woods.
- Keep open areas of marsh clear of scrub but retain existing, well-established stands of willows or alders.
- Consider land drainage implications in managing wetlands, especially streams.
- Ideally, provide a mix of conditions by planting or clearing the south sides of water bodies as appropriate.
- Ensure livestock do not damage ponds or other wetland areas.

Wetlands in woods add greatly to their overall wildlife value but need management especially to prevent excessive shading or drying out. Streams and larger ponds can benefit from some falling leaves of broadleaved trees but not from prolific conifer needle litter. Clear back conifers from the margins of watercourses and ponds. Retain or plant broadleaved trees and shrubs in patches along the southern bank to create alternate sunny and shady reaches. Trees and shrubs on the north bank can overhang the water because they will cause little shade, and falling leaves and insects are important food resources for aquatic creatures (Feature 7.9: Management of woodland streams). With small ponds, remove all overhanging trees to prevent shading.

Keep existing wet glades open and free of tree and scrub cover. However, do not open up areas of long-established alders or willows as these can be of interest in their own right. Do not drain existing wet areas in woodland.

In the past, many woods had surface drainage ditches. These ditches are now usually neglected, and existing woodland drainage should not be altered unless essential for management.

Create new or replacement wet areas by obstructing drainage channels where this will not cause a significant effect on adjoining farmland or on crop trees, for instance at the upper edges of the wood.

The use of ponds in woods by farm stock needs to be carefully monitored. A little trampling along one side can provide similar habitats to those described above, but if use is heavy, loss of plants and enrichment through dunging can occur. Fence pond margins from livestock where damage is occurring or reduce extent of use. Full guidelines on wetland management are found in Chapter 9.

In planning wetland management, particularly involving streams and ditches, consider the land-drainage implications for surrounding farmland.

3.7. Grazing and farm woods

- In farm woods where there is an urgent need for tree regeneration remove the livestock for up to 15 years or fence off sections at least 0.5 ha in rotation.
- Alternative shelter and grazing will need to be provided.
- Where fencing is planned, take the opportunity to plan for enhancements or an increase in the size of the wood.
- Where a thick mat of grass, moss or leaf litter exists within the wood, disturb the surface to provide a seedbed for woodland plants and trees.
- Keep horses, ponies and goats out of woods.
- Where deer are damaging woods, co-ordinate control with adjacent landowners and if necessary seek specialist advice.
- Use vegetation to protect areas from browsing deer.
- As a last resort, erect deer fences but note the possible hazard to some gamebirds.

Some woods on farms in the uplands, especially birch woods, are now of an age where regeneration is a matter of urgency.

A substantial proportion of these woods contain old trees which are of high wildlife value but, because of grazing, there are no or too few young trees available to take their place. Eventually, if no action is taken, the wood will be lost.

For the wood to be regenerated, stock must be fenced out completely or at least reduced in numbers. For larger woods it may be possible to fence off parts of the wood in rotation. Stock may need to be excluded for up to 15 years (longer if regrowth is slow) and alternative shelter and grazing may need to be provided. Where fencing is planned, consider fencing a larger area to increase the size of the wood.

In grazed woods a thick grass or moss mat may have developed on the woodland floor. If this is the case, the ground surface should be lightly disturbed to encourage regeneration and establishment of trees and shrubs. Chain harrowing would be appropriate but may be impossible on some sites. At worst, hand raking or 'screefing' may be needed.

Grazing can be a valuable management aid for wildlife in farm woods provided its intensity is related to clear objectives. In many upland woods it retains an open understorey important for some birds. In most lowland woods, at low grazing intensity, livestock may maintain a good vegetation structure in rides, glades and wetlands, but overgrazing and serious poaching are harmful. Fencing stock out of sensitive areas may put more pressure on other parts of the wood and it is much better to reduce the period in which stock have access; in particular avoid the spring and summer months when plants should have the chance to flower and set seed and when invertebrates are most dependent on them. Alternatively, reduce stock numbers to a level where at least a proportion of the plants can set seed and the vegetation can recover.

Horses, ponies and goats can be very destructive in woodland. They browse much tree and shrub growth and may strip bark and kill trees.

Where deer are causing serious damage to a farm wood, or where numbers are so high that they may damage new woodland planting or coppicing, culling or exclusion may have to be considered. A programme of deer management and control requires good planning and training. The aim should be to maintain a healthy population of deer, which is in balance with all aspects of the environment without doing undue damage to it.

The first course of action will be to take specialist advice. Many of the species of deer roam widely and are rarely managed successfully in isolation, therefore co-operation between estates and farms is vital. Where it is practicable, and co-operation is possible, a deer management group should be established to co-ordinate management and culling.

The number to cull each year must be based on a knowledge of the population size. Deer numbers using woodlands are usually considerably under-estimated because of the dense cover. However, it is essential to organise an initial deer count, before agreeing a cull plan. The estimation of numbers can either be undertaken through dung counts or through observation from vantage points over a long period. Culling breeding-age females is the most effective way of reducing numbers quickly, as it reduces reproductive capacity. For roe deer, for example, a cull of 15–25% in each year will normally reduce the population of deer when taking into account the annual addition from new births. Progress of culling should be carefully monitored and adjusted until damage to vegetation ceases to be a problem. Keep detailed records of all deer killed and take account of all legal requirements including close seasons (see Appendix II: Legal considerations).

If control is not undertaken or is impracticable, it is advisable to fence areas before planting new woods or undertaking management such as coppicing or restocking. Deer fencing is costly and, because it reduces the total available range for the deer, will put more pressure on other areas. Where fencing is undertaken in those upland areas where black grouse (and capercaillie in Scotland) are present, it is important to take special care in the siting

of fence lines. Black grouse and capercaillie are regularly killed by flying into deer fences. Mark the fences (eg with brightly coloured or reflective tapes) and include open ground along the fence lines to increase the fence's visibility to birds.

If little woodland management is necessary or regeneration can be spread over a very long period, it may be possible to work on a small scale, retaining as much as possible of tall herbage, bramble and scrub cover where it exists and relying on it to protect new growth from the attention of deer. Covering coppice stools with the cut material may make it harder for deer to reach the new shoots.

Even if none of the above measures are practicable, it may still be possible to regenerate the wood in the long term. Deer numbers will fluctuate from year to year and sooner or later some regeneration will probably be able to grow successfully. However, the success of tree establishment will need to be closely watched.

3.8. Game management

- Manage the wood for greatest 'edge effect' including rides and clearings in the form of permanent glades or coppice.
- Plant and maintain native shrubs and where appropriate manage coppice to provide cover.
- Site pheasant pens in parts of the wood with least wildlife value and move as rarely as possible.
- Locate and design flushing points to enhance the overall wildlife value of the wood.
- Where supplementary feeding is practised, confine it to a limited area with the least wild plant and invertebrate interest.
- Maintain permanent pasture alongside the wood to retain woodcock in winter.

In general, the aims of game management are compatible with those of wildlife conservation. Indeed, game often provides the incentive for planting, managing and retaining many farm woodlands.

Pheasant shooting and the management it encourages have many wildlife conservation benefits. Large rides and shrubby woodland edges are particularly important for many woodland butterflies while low shrubby cover is favoured by many summer bird visitors such as warblers. The provision of winter feed attracts large numbers of finches in hard winters.

Pheasants use woods as winter cover and as part of their breeding territories in the spring. During the winter pheasants require three things from woodland if they are to achieve reasonable densities:

- They prefer to live along the woodland edge and, as a consequence, small woods particularly those smaller than 5 ha, are best because they have a greater edge to area ratio than larger woods.
- They require low shrubby cover to provide warmth, concealment and ease of movement at ground level. Regenerating coppice, young conifers prior to canopy closure and scrub can all be beneficial in this respect. Shrubs are particularly important at the woodland edge, both to provide suitable cover and to make the rest of the wood windproof. Pheasants do not appear to favour particular species of trees or shrubs for cover.
- Pheasants are attracted to those woods with a good supply of food – beechmast, berries and grass seeds are particularly favoured. However, in most woods where pheasants are managed, supplementary food is provided and natural food availability is of lower importance.

The most important feature to consider for pheasants is woodland size. Numerous small plantings are best, whereas larger areas can be improved by the creation of large rides, preferably greater than 30 m in width as birds will then live along the edges of them. Low shrubby cover can be encouraged by the planting and management of shrub species and the use of tree species such as ash that cast only light shade. In existing woods, small-scale management including coppicing can provide an attractive mosaic of suitable shrubby areas throughout the wood. In

simple terms, an attractive wood for pheasants can be described as one that keeps the wind out and lets the sun in.

Pheasants breed along the woodland edge, the males setting up territories to include both woodland and open ground. Edges rich in shrubby cover are particularly preferred, as are those bordering arable land rather than grass. An attractive wood for overwintering pheasants will normally also hold high breeding densities.

A wood managed for pheasant shooting must also be carefully planned to provide high, sporting birds. This requires the creation of flushing points, open areas that encourage the birds to take flight and to fly high. New woods can be carefully laid out to make the best use of ground contours.

In most areas, hand-reared pheasants are released from pens each summer to supplement wild populations for shooting. Penned birds can damage the ground flora and, as this effect is limited to the area within the pen, they should be moved as rarely as possible. Supplementary feeding of pheasants during the winter can benefit many songbirds but also often introduces weeds such as broad-leaved dock. If the food is scattered onto straw, it should not be on areas rich in plants as the straw can smother them. Raking the straw up in spring can reduce the problem.

Open rides and small clearings are important to enable woodcock to conduct their courtship displays (roding). Tree species composition is important as the soil beneath some, including beech and conifers, supports only very low densities of earthworms, which are the main food of the woodcock. A mixture of deciduous species, including oak, ash, hazel or birch, is preferable. An established shrub layer or, in its absence, a good coverage of ground flora provides shelter from avian predators, which is especially important until the chicks are full-grown. Woodcock also use woods with shrub cover in winter for roosting, and feed in nearby fields during the night. The retention of permanent pasture or leys within 2 km of breeding woods improves the likelihood that woodcock will remain in the area in winter.

3.9. New farm woodlands and shelterbelts

- Create new woods adjoining existing woodland if possible.
- Plant areas of 5 ha or more where possible.
- Do not plant trees on open land with wildlife interest.
- Maximise the length of the woodland edge.
- Leave at least 20% of the site unplanted as rides and glades.
- Plant a mixture of native trees with a range of maturation ages, in single-species groups.
- Take care in the selection, planting, protection and aftercare of trees; it will repay itself by successful establishment.
- Plant at least some areas at wide spacings.
- Incorporate shrubs in the scheme and erect bird and bat boxes.
- Enhance new or existing shelterbelts with shrubs and nestboxes.
- Consider arable coppice as an opportunity to develop a scrub habitat.

Where possible, site new farm woods adjoining existing woodland as this may enable species present in the old wood ultimately to colonise the new one. It will also increase the size of the existing wood and make it more attractive to a greater range of species.

Aspect is important. A site on a south-facing slope receives most sunlight and protection from cold winds. North-facing woods are comparatively cold and less good for invertebrates and other warmth-demanding wildlife.

Never plant on areas with existing wildlife interest, such as unimproved, flower-rich pasture, heath or heather moorland, marshes or bogs. Least damage to wildlife comes from planting on improved farmland. However, surviving fragments of old grassland or other habitats, including ponds and streams plus old hedgerow trees, may benefit from being included in or sheltered by the wood provided they are not shaded by the new trees (Figure 7.4: Conservation features in a new farm wood).

Large woods usually contain more kinds of wildlife than small ones because it is possible to incorporate more features such as glades, ponds and streams, and vary tree and shrub composition and structure, all of which favour wildlife. Very small woods may lack a proper woodland microclimate, especially the sunlit but sheltered conditions that are important for many species of invertebrates.

Woods greater than 5 ha will support more wildlife and have a more varied structure, as it will be possible to maintain a wider range of tree ages without management becoming excessively complicated. Woods under this size are likely to be too small for some larger birds, for example breeding tawny owls in deciduous woods require about 18 ha of hunting habitat. Siting a new wood next to an existing one may increase the wood sufficiently to become large enough to sustain those birds with larger territories, including woodpeckers.

The edge is extremely important for wildlife because it benefits from light, therefore make the length of the new wood edge as long as possible. Regular shapes such as rectangles and circles have less edge than irregular shapes. If the plot is straight-edged, leave patches at the edge unplanted to create a wavy edge to the wood itself.

Aim to have 20–30% of the site unplanted. Leave wide rides and plant the edges with shrubs. Keep habitats that have been specifically incorporated, such as grassland or marsh, as glades. If you are not including existing habitats, it is still important to create sunlit glades for flowers, butterflies and other insects. The wood will give them shelter from wind and protection from spray-drift. Link them by sunlit rides or streamsides so that the dependent species can move between sites. For shelter and protection, the whole wood will benefit from a hedge around it. Either incorporate existing hedges or plant anew.

As far as is consistent with the other aims of management, plant trees that are native to the locality (Table 7.4). Table 7.8 lists trees most often planted to produce a hardwood timber crop, plus a selection of other trees suitable for improving a wood for wildlife

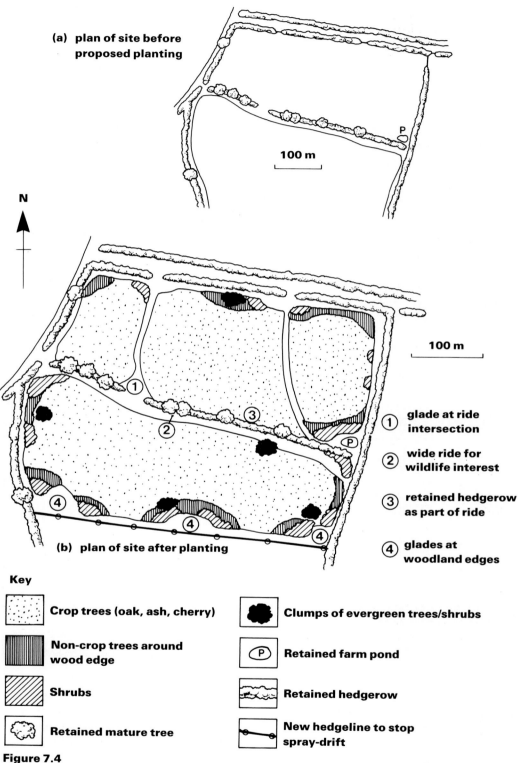

(a) plan of site before proposed planting

100 m

N

100 m

① glade at ride intersection

② wide ride for wildlife interest

③ retained hedgerow as part of ride

④ glades at woodland edges

(b) plan of site after planting

Key

Crop trees (oak, ash, cherry)

Non-crop trees around wood edge

Shrubs

Retained mature tree

Clumps of evergreen trees/shrubs

Retained farm pond

Retained hedgerow

New hedgeline to stop spray-drift

Figure 7.4
Conservation features in a new farm wood

and native shrubs, essential for creating cover near the ground and adding to food supplies for invertebrates and birds. Plant some evergreens for winter shelter.

When choosing the list of species it is often helpful to be guided by what is growing naturally in existing woodlands in the area. Most of the trees and shrubs in the list will

Table 7.8: Wildlife value of native trees and shrubs appropriate for a farm woodland planted primarily for timber production

SPECIES	IMPORTANT FOR			PROVIDES		
	DEAD WOOD INSECTS	BIRDS	INSECTS	WINTER COVER	FLOWERS	FRUIT/ SEED
Timber trees						
Ash	●					●
Beech	●					●
Pedunculate oak	●	●	●			●
Sessile oak	●	●	●			●
Scots pine	●	●	●	●		●
Wild cherry		●			●	●
Non-crop trees						
Alder	●	●	●			●
Aspen			●			
Downy birch	●	●	●			●
Silver birch	●	●	●			●
Bird cherry		●			●	●
Crab apple	●	●	●		●	●
Field maple	●	●	●		●	●
Hornbeam	●	●				●
Common lime	●		●		●	
Rowan	●	●			●	●
Yew				●		●
Shrubs						
Alder buckthorn			●			
Blackthorn			●		●	●
Bramble		●	●	●	●	●
Wild rose		●	●		●	●
Dogwood					●	●
Elder		●			●	●
Gorse		●	●	●	●	
Guelder rose		●			●	●
Hawthorn	●	●	●		●	●
Hazel			●		●	●
Holly		●		●		●
Goat willow	●		●			
Grey willow	●		●			

Note: Some of the 'non crop' trees are being increasingly planted for timber.
Source: Bayes, K 1988. *New Farmwoods and Birds*. Leaflet. RSPB.

grow in a wide range of soil conditions (see Table 7.5) but if doubt exists or if soil conditions are extreme (eg highly acid, alkaline or waterlogged), specialist advice should be taken.

Examples of the composition of possible planting schemes are given at Table 7.9.

Plant a range of species that will mature at different dates (eg cherry after 60–80 years, ash at 70–90 and oak in about 120 years). It will then be possible to spread felling and restocking over 60 years, ensuring a varied woodland structure and maximum wildlife benefit. Always try to retain a proportion of trees to reach their natural lifespan and to provide dead wood. Clearfelling is catastrophic for wildlife because it destroys structural variety.

To simplify management and the felling of the crop as it matures, plant each species in groups of 10–50 trees. Where timber production is the priority, the groups may be larger. This will not adversely affect the

Table 7.9: Possible composition/proportions of different trees and shrubs for a new woodland, showing recommended percentage of area for each tree and shrub species

SPECIES	OAK WOODLAND ON NEUTRAL CLAY SOILS %			BEECH WOODLAND ON ACIDIC SANDY SOILS %		UPLAND WOODLAND ON ACIDIC SOILS – HIGH RAINFALL %
	PRIMARY AIM			PRIMARY AIM		PRIMARY AIM
	TIMBER	CONSERVATION	40-YR OPTION	TIMBER	CONSERVATION	CONSERVATION
Pedunculate oak	60	60	90			
Sessile oak					30	60
Beech				60	30	
Hornbeam					1	
Ash	20	15	1	30	20	
Wild cherry	10	5				
Birch	2	4	1	2	4	20
Field maple	1	2	1	1	1	
Alder	1	2	1	1	2	
Aspen	1	2	1			
Goat willow				1	2	5
Rowan				1	2	10
Hawthorn	1	2	1	1	2	
Blackthorn	1	2	1	1	2	
Hazel	1	2	1	1	2	
Holly	1	2	1	1	2	
Elder	0.5	1	0.5			
Guelder rose	0.5	1	0.5			
Gorse						3
Bramble						2

Source: Bayes, K 1989 New Farm Woodland and Birds, *RSPB Conservation Review 3*: 56–58

potential for wildlife as long as a range of species is planted overall. Plant clumps of non-crop species around the edges of larger blocks to improve variety. Several small blocks of evergreens are good for winter shelter.

Vary the density at which trees are planted. Wide spacings are better for wildlife as they allow room for natural colonisation by other shrubs and wildflowers, encourage a more varied woodland and also allow some trees to develop a spreading growth form. A minimum number of trees may have to be planted per hectare to obtain grant aid but where the aims can be achieved with fewer trees, grant aid is normally paid pro rata. Vary the spacings of the trees and leave 20–30% of open ground. Shrubs should be planted at spacings of about 1.6 m. Concentrate shrub planting along rides and at the woodland edge, particularly on the south and west sides where it will not be shaded.

For planting small areas around the farm, it is possible to raise trees from seed collected locally. However, in most situations the stock of trees and shrubs will come from a nursery. Choose one that has a good reputation. Plant stock that comes from local seed sources, if at all possible. There are many leaflets on tree planting techniques and tree establishment, but again seek advice if necessary. Whips, young trees of about two years of age and 0.5–1 m in size, are the most appropriate for farm wood planting. They are cheaper and easier to establish than larger trees but they may still need protection. The degree of tree protection needed will vary from farm to farm. Livestock, deer and rabbits can all damage or kill trees. Stock fencing may be sufficient protection but if there is likely to

Type here to search

be a problem with animals other than livestock then further protection, such as rabbit netting or tree guards, may be necessary. Tree shelters are increasingly being used although they were originally developed to promote quicker growth of trees. Although they allow trees to be located for weed control, they are comparatively expensive and can be an eyesore in some situations.

Once the trees have been delivered, ensure that the roots are kept moist and protect them from wind and sun. Plant them as soon as possible, otherwise the trees will grow poorly and may die. In the early years it is necessary to control grass or weed growth within 1 m of the saplings to prevent competition for light, water and nutrients. Do not treat plant growth which is not competing with the trees, because it will support wildlife.

It may be necessary to water trees in drought conditions in spring and summer, especially in the month immediately following planting. As with all crops, check regularly to monitor growth and replace any trees as necessary.

As the wood matures, apply the management principles set out in the preceding sections. As soon as the trees are large enough, erect bird and bat boxes.

The structure of shelterbelts is of great importance to their effectiveness and depends on the correct spacing of trees, the species composition and the thickness of the belt. This means that existing belts cannot easily be modified to improve them for wildlife but they can be enhanced by planting shrubs along the outer edges, especially the sunlit side, and by the erection of nestboxes. Exclusion of stock will be beneficial.

New shelterbelts will be best for wildlife if composed of native trees or at least with a native element incorporated in them. Many of the principles of establishment have been covered earlier in this section. The choice of species will depend on the site (Table 7.5) but to be most effective as a source of stock shelter, the belt needs to be 25–30 m in width. Plant directly across the path of the

prevailing wind, and if possible plant in 'L'-shaped blocks or crosses to provide shelter from wind regardless of its direction. In the uplands it may be difficult to establish a new shelterbelt in an exposed site so it may have to be sited with care, on the lee side of a hill, for example.

Arable coppice differs from traditional coppice in that the preferred species are willow and poplar, there are no standard or mature trees and the coppice rotation is much shorter. Its value for wildlife is as yet not fully known because of the relatively recent development and promotion of this method of wood production. As the timber species are most likely to be grown on land taken out of arable production, it is unlikely that woodland plants and dependent insects will colonise, unless the site adjoins existing woodland. However it may provide a habitat for some songbirds and for pheasants. On balance, it is probably best managed for wildlife as a scrub habitat, on a rotation that provides as much a variation in age and structure as possible. Where space permits there may be opportunities for creation of other habitats, such as permanent grassland along rides, enhancement along the edges by planting with a greater range of species and allowing some trees to grow as standards or pollards.

4. References and further reading

Beckett, G and K 1979. *Planting Native Trees and Shrubs.* Jarrold.

Blyth, J, Sidwell, C, Evans, J and Mutch, W 1991. *Farm Woodland Management.* Farming Press.

Evans, J 1984. *Silviculture of Broadleaved Woodland.* Forestry Commission Bulletin No 62. HMSO.

Fuller, R J and Warren, M S 1990. *Coppiced Woodlands.* Nature Conservancy Council.

Hibberd, B G (ed) 1986. *Farm Woodland Practice.* Forestry Commission Handbook No 3 HMSO.

Insley, H (ed) 1988. *Farm Woodland Planning.* Forestry Commission Bulletin No 80 HMSO.

James, N D G 1989. *The Foresters Companion.* Blackwell.

Kerr, G and Evans, J 1993. *Growing Broadleaves for Timber.* Forestry Commission Handbook No. 9 HMSO.

Kirby, K J 1984. *Forestry Operations and Broadleaf Woodland Conservation.* Focus on Nature Conservation 8. Nature Conservancy Council.

Kirby, K J 1988. *Woodland Survey Handbook.* Nature Conservancy Council.

Kirby, P 1992. *Habitat Management for Invertebrates* – Woodlands pp. 19–45. RSPB.

Lane, A and Tait, J 1990. *Practical Conservation: Woodlands.* Hodder and Stoughton.

MAFF 1993. *Farm Woodlands: A Practical Guide.* MAFF.

Peterken, G F 1981. *Woodland Conservation and Management.* Chapman and Hall.

Rackham, O 1980. *Ancient Woodland.* Edward Arnold.

Rodwell, J S (ed) 1991. *British Plant Communities Volume 1: Woodlands.* Cambridge University Press.

Rodwell, J S and Patterson G S 1994. *Creating New Native Woodlands.* Forestry Commission Bulletin No 112. HMSO.

Smart, N and Andrews, J 1985. *Birds and Broadleaves Handbook.* RSPB.

Warren, M S and Fuller, R J 1990. *Woodland Rides and Glades.* Nature Conservancy Council.

Watkins, C 1990. *Woodland Management and Conservation.* David and Charles.

Feature 7.1: Ivy and its Importance for Wildlife

Ivy is a woody, evergreen climber, common throughout the UK, up to an altitude of about 650 m. It grows on most soils, unless very acid or waterlogged.

It is not parasitic and will not harm healthy trees. There should rarely, if ever, be any reason for removing a plant with such outstandingly high wildlife value.

1. Ivy is the food plant of the second brood of the holly blue butterfly caterpillars, which emerge in summer. The first 'brood', which emerges in spring, feeds on holly.

2. and 3. Ivy provides shelter for birds such as roosting tawny owls and for pipistrelle bats. Old ivy stems and bark are particularly rich in invertebrates.

4. Flowers appear on the climbing shoots in autumn and the nectar is used by hoverflies, butterflies and night-flying moths, at a time when little other food is available for them. Later black berries develop and are taken by many birds such as thrushes.

Feature 7.2: Woodpeckers

Lesser spotted woodpecker

- Woodpeckers have strong bills to excavate nest holes in tree trunks, and to chisel into dead wood. Their long, thin, barbed tongues extract insects from holes. Great spotted woodpeckers often feed in fallen dead wood, especially in winter, and take many caterpillars in summer. Green woodpeckers open ants' nests to eat the larvae and pupae. Lesser spotted woodpeckers feed mostly in trees, taking insects and beetles.
- On average there will be one pair of great spotted woodpeckers per 7–9 ha. The other two species live at much lower densities, varying with the suitability of the habitat.

Management
- Leave standing and fallen dead wood, especially in sheltered and shady places where it will decay, to ensure constant availability of invertebrates.
- Dead wood requirements: minimum of about 30 m^3/ha
  8 m^3 in standing dead trees
  8 m^3 fallen dead wood
  14 m^3 dead wood on live trees.

In a deciduous wood of average tree density (70–250/ha according to age) achieve this by leaving all dead limbs and fallen timber in situ, plus 2–6 whole, dead, standing trees per hectare.

Green woodpecker

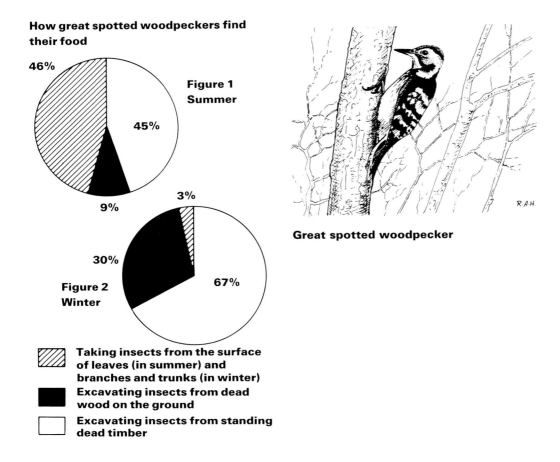

How great spotted woodpeckers find their food

46%

Figure 1 Summer

45%

9%

3%

30%

Figure 2 Winter

67%

Great spotted woodpecker

R.A.H.

Taking insects from the surface of leaves (in summer) and branches and trunks (in winter)

Excavating insects from dead wood on the ground

Excavating insects from standing dead timber

Nest sites for woodpeckers and preferred tree species, where known

NEST SIZE AND POSITION	SPECIES OF WOODPECKER		
	GREAT SPOTTED	LESSER SPOTTED	GREEN
Holes excavated in dead trunks	Birch, Elm Beech, Hornbeam Scots pine	No information on preferred species	Birch
Holes excavated in live trunks with heart-rot	Oak, Ash Hornbeam Sweet chestnut	Oak	Oak, Ash
Holes excavated in dead limbs on live trees	Beech, Hornbeam Alder	Oak, Hornbeam, Willows, Alder Poplars	Beech
Size of hole	5–6 cm	3–3.5 cm	6 cm
Usual height above ground	3–5 m	2–8 m	1–5 m
Other factors	Favour dead birch >20 cm diameter, but rarely used for more than one year	May use smaller trees	More dependent on much older trees

Feature 7.3: Breeding Birds of Western Oakwoods in Britain

The bird communities of western oakwoods are unusual. Very few species use the woods in winter as there is little understorey shelter. Few species of birds breed in the woods because there is little scrub or ground cover. However, the woods are used by three characteristic bird species; redstart, wood warbler and pied flycatcher, all of which winter in Africa.

	REDSTART	WOOD WARBLER	PIED FLYCATCHER
Breeding	Breeds at a range of tree densities; age of trees only important for a good supply of nest holes. Often selects sites beside open glades or clearings with plenty of bare ground. Also occurs in the native pinewoods in Scotland.	Needs woods with complete or nearly complete canopy (60–70%). Does not breed in areas with sparse trees. Occurs in all ages of wood with little or no vegetation beneath canopy. Also uses some conifer plantations.	Mostly in open woods where there is little understorey but will continue to nest where grazing has been excluded and a good understorey has developed.
Display	In open space under canopy, also from exposed twigs, branches, treetops and stumps.	Display flights are within 3 m of the ground, perching on branches no more than 2.5 m above ground.	In open areas under canopy.
Nest sites	Holes in trees or walls. Often uses cavities in broken limbs. Fledged young may feed and shelter in bracken.	Ground nesting. Favours woods with few shrubs and low vegetation, often with approach to nest along thin branches trailing from tree, a sapling or fallen branches.	Uses nestboxes readily, even in preference to natural holes. Can increase population. Place at 1.5–2 m above ground, maximum 8/ha.
Feeding	Structure of wood more important than tree species. Forages mainly in canopy, but regularly feeds on ground or by catching insects in flight.	Almost exclusively in canopy or on branches.	Takes insects in the air, but most feeding is on the ground or in the canopy.

Redstart

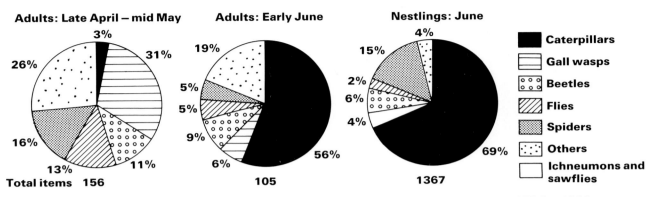

Composition of diet of adult and nestling pied flycatchers in sessile oakwoods in central Wales 1983 (expressed as the frequency of items in faecal sacs). Note the importance of caterpillars in the summer diet.

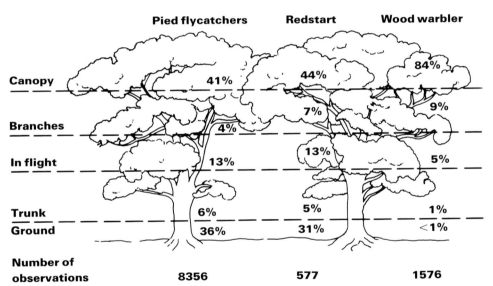

Foraging sites of three characteristic insectivorous birds of sessile oakwoods.
Pied flycatcher: spends much time in the canopy collecting caterpillars but a third of its time foraging on the ground; surprisingly little food taken in flight.
Redstart: similar to pied flycatcher.
Wood warbler: feeds largely in the canopy.

Diagrams adapted from Stowe, T J 1987. The Management of Sessile Oakwood for Pied Flycatchers. *RSPB Conservation Review* 1: 78–83.

Feature 7.4: Dead Wood and Wildlife

Dead wood may be present in a wood in many different forms, each of which may have a different assemblage of wildlife. Ideally dead wood should be left where it is and allowed to decay naturally. Timber with a large diameter is of particular importance and should not be cut up. If fallen timber must be moved, leave it as close to the original site as possible.

1. Dead outer branches on a live tree.

2. Rot-hole.

3. Fungus under bark.

4. Heart-rot in standing live trees.

5. Roots.

6. Bracket fungi.

7. Hollow trunks.

8. Fallen timber and standing timber may have different wildlife interest.

9. Dead wood including thin branches and twigs in full sun will bake and dry out and generally will support few invertebrates or fungi. Under dense shade it may support good fungal populations, but may be too cold for many invertebrates. Wood in dappled shade provides the most useful conditions for most wildlife as it is unlikely to bake but will remain reasonably warm.

Source: Kirby, P 1992. *Habitat management for invertebrates.* RSPB.

Feature 7.5: Nestboxes and Bat Boxes

The absence of natural nest holes can limit the populations of hole-nesting birds. If the plantation is young and there are no old trees present, nestboxes can be an interim means of providing nest sites.

Nestbox designs

The commonest types are open- and hole-fronted boxes. For a medium-size box, increase all dimensions shown by about a third; for a large box they should be approximately doubled.

Nestbox requirements of different bird species

BIRD	HOLE OR OPEN FRONT	SIZE/HOLE DIAMETER	
Nuthatch	H	Large/150 mm	
Pied flycatcher	H	Small/28 mm	
Redstart	H	Small or long/35 mm	
	O	Standard box with 40 mm	See sketch of longbox
Blue, coal, marsh tits	H	Small/25 mm	
Willow, crested tits	H	Small/25 mm	Fill with soft inert material, eg polystyrene or wood shavings which they will excavate. Refill for the next season.
Great tits	H	Small/28 mm	
Tree sparrow	H	Small or medium/28 mm	
Woodpeckers:			
Great spotted	H	Medium width, 400 mm deep/50 mm	All species need box sited high and filled with polystyrene (lesser spotted will accept wood chippings)
Lesser spotted	H	Medium/32 mm	
Green	H	Large/ 60 mm	
Kestrel	O	Large	Mount sideways with a perch (see sketch). Can also work well on a pole in areas with few trees.
Spotted flycatcher	O	Standard	Site with a clear view from box.
Jackdaw Stock dove	H	Large/150 mm	

Constructing, siting and maintaining nestboxes

- Wood is best as it gives good insulation, does not produce condensation and can blend in with the trees.
- Any scraps or offcuts can be used. Solid boards less than 15 mm thick may warp, but exterior grade ply of 6 mm or over should last well. Green oak is the best.
- Minimum internal sizes should not be less than those stated for individual boxes. Galvanized nails or screws last longer. The lid should be securely fastened. Wood preservatives will help prolong their life, but can be toxic and should not be used inside the boxes; they should not be used *at all* on bat boxes.
- Attach a batten to the back of the box and nail, screw or tie in place. To avoid damage to saws, use nylon, copper, aluminium or hardwood pegs or the box can be tied to the tree using plastic coated wire or binder twine. It should be strung loosely and as the tree grows can be edged up a little. Sometimes boxes can be wedged into a forked branch.
- Face boxes in a north to south-easterly direction away from prevailing winds and direct sunlight. Angle smaller boxes slightly downward to shelter the hole. The height above the ground is usually not critical, but put them where they are not easily accessible if people frequently use the wood.
- In a new wood try about 10 assorted boxes per hectare, well spaced.
- Cleaning and repairs should be done when the birds leave after the breeding season.

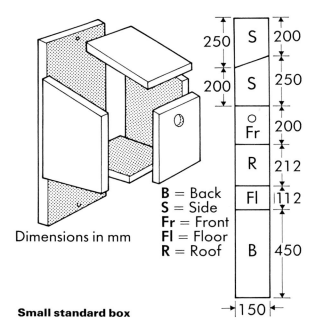

Dimensions in mm

B = Back
S = Side
Fr = Front
Fl = Floor
R = Roof

250	S 200
200	S 250
	Fr (O) 200
	R 212
	Fl 112
	B 450
	150

Small standard box

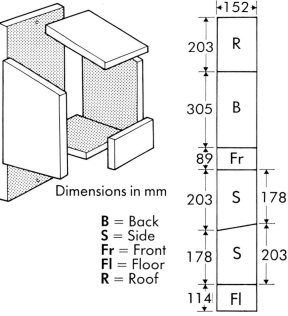

Dimensions in mm

B = Back
S = Side
Fr = Front
Fl = Floor
R = Roof

	152
203	R
305	B
89	Fr
203	S 178
178	S 203
114	Fl

Standard open-fronted box with alternative front for redstart

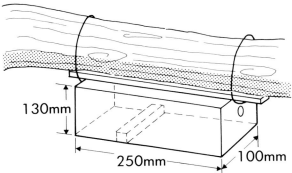

130mm

250mm   100mm

Redstart longbox

Other types of box

Dormouse hibernation box See Feature 7.6 on dormice for use of nestboxes.

Tawny owl chimney. This is designed to mimic a broken branch. Fix at an angle of 45°, as high as possible.

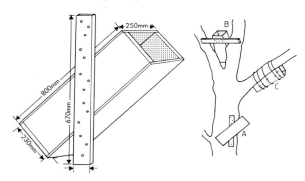

Chimney box for tawny owls
(Showing 3 different methods of attachment)

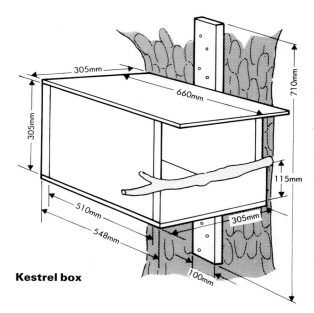

Kestrel box

Bat box Similar overall dimensions to tit box. Do not use any wood preservative inside or out. Used for summer roosting. Site 4-5 m in numbers of three and on different sides of the trunk to allow bats to choose the box with the correct temperature. If the wood is smooth cut grooves in the back board to allow bats to cling on. Most frequently used by pipistrelle and brown long-eared bats for roosting.

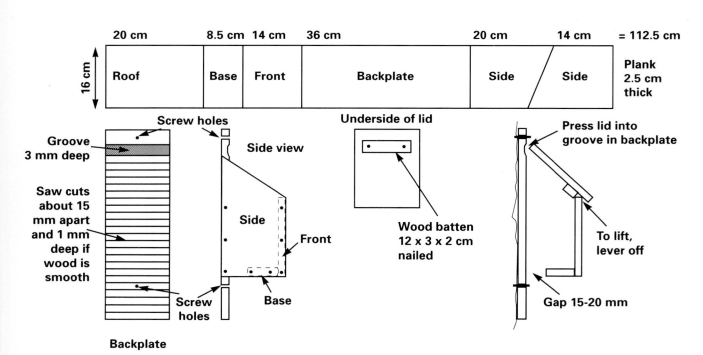

Backplate

Source: RSPB 1993. *Make a bat box*. Leaflet. RSPB

Feature 7.6: Habitat Requirements of Dormice

Dormice live at low densities (up to 10/ha), and a wood of less than 5 ha is unlikely to support a permanent population.

Feeding

They need a diverse understorey, ensuring a continuous supply of fruit, flowers, invertebrates (such as caterpillars) and nuts through the summer and autumn. Good food sources are bramble (cut part back in winter to ensure fresh growth and a good supply of fruit on two-year old growth) and honeysuckle, the bark being used to make nests.

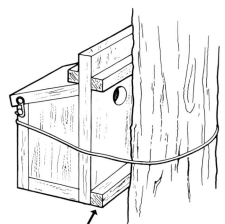

Note spacer bars

Nesting and hibernation

Dormice will nest in standard tit-boxes, ideally wooden ones, with a 3-cm entrance hole. These should be placed in groups of 10 or more, about 20 m apart, and about 1.5–2.5 m up on trunks or branches, with the hole facing towards the tree (see diagram). They hibernate in nests at ground level, where the temperature is less variable. They become torpid in summer if food supplies are poor.

Habitat management

- Coppice can be very suitable. Panels should be no bigger than 0.5 ha, dotted through the wood (see Figure 7.2); to allow access to areas of fruiting hazel for feeding. A long rotation (about 12–20 years) is needed to allow the hazel to grow sufficiently to produce a good supply of nuts.

- Hedgerows are also important, but only if grown really big, so supplying adequate food. Dormice are quite sedentary but hedges may facilitate some dispersal and possibly colonisation of new areas of wood. Cutting should be one side at a time, the other side 2–3 years later.
- Dormice prefer not to travel on the ground. Overhanging branches meeting across rides will provide a 'highway' and 'corridors' of well-grown shrubs retained to link standard trees will allow them to use standards in newly coppiced areas.
- If poison hoppers are used to control grey squirrels in a wood containing dormice, seek the advice of a pest control company to avoid accidental poisoning of dormice.

Map showing the present and former distribution of dormice in Britain.

Source: Bright, P and Morris, P 1989. *A practical guide to dormouse conservation*, Mammal Society Occasional Publication No 11.

Feature 7.7: Habitat Requirements of Fritillary Butterflies

Fritillaries have suffered serious declines this century because of the abandonment of coppice management. Most woods have become too shaded. Their larval food plants are all widespread and common, but the habitat requirements of each species are quite precise.

1. **Pearl-bordered fritillaries** have the most precise requirements, flourishing in newly cut or coppiced woodland. The larvae appear very early in spring on small, young violets growing in sparse or short vegetation.

2. **Small pearl-bordered fritillaries** need a slightly later stage in succession, using slightly larger violets surrounded by taller grass. The larvae appear later in the year when temperatures are higher. **Heath fritillaries** are the rarest, and need warm, sheltered areas cut within the last 2–3 years, with abundant common cow-wheat in short sparse vegetation. Clearings may become too overgrown for the caterpillars within 3–10 years. **Duke of Burgundy** larvae need cowslips or primroses in sheltered areas; eggs are laid on the largest leaves of flowering clumps. They avoid exposed or heavily-shaded plants.

3. No fritillaries use mature coppice or shady woodland.

4. **Silver-washed fritillaries** can tolerate shadier conditions than any of the others, but still need at least 25% direct sunlight to reach the ground vegetation. The adults feed in clearings, but do not breed in them, laying eggs on trees in adjacent woodland. The larvae feed on violets.

These conditions can all be created by coppicing or managing sheltered open areas in woods such as glades or rides or wood edges.

Silver-washed fritillary

Duke of Burgundy fritillary

Heath fritillary

Small pearl-bordered fritillary

Pearl-bordered fritillary

Feature 7.8: Nightingales and Coppice Woodland.

Territory size

Nightingales have territories of around 0.5–1 ha. They nest in dense stands of scrub from ground level up to 30 cm.

Stool density

The structure of the coppice and the individual bushes is more important than the species. Suitable stool densities may be 400–1,000 stools/ha, depending on the species. Seedling birch and climbers such as bramble, honeysuckle or clematis may produce dense cover conditions at lower stool densities.

Sweet chestnut

Sweet chestnut is less suitable for nightingales as it grows quickly, and if weeded does not provide suitable conditions for very long. It is very difficult to encourage any significant change in this situation without a loss of underwood value, but small improvements might be made by:

- increasing the number of rides – the increased light levels here could locally raise coppice density sufficiently to provide suitable habitat.
- planting different species eg hazel, hornbeam, oak and cherry along panel or woodland edges, and developing a short rotation for these.
- not weeding, allowing bramble to grow up and provide low vegetation.

Rotation lengths

Ensure a constant amount of coppice aged about 3–8 years, varying with type of coppice. By careful planning about 50% could be suitable at any one time. Commercial rotations of 12–15 years may be too long; nightingale numbers typically decline after 10 years when the structure at ground level becomes too open for nesting; however areas of 'open' floor are used for feeding. Nightingales feed on invertebrates taken almost exclusively on the ground.

Layout

Consider other wildlife interest of the site (Table 7.7). To maximise the number of pairs of nightingales, optimal nesting habitat should be scattered amongst panels of other ages, which will provide food resources.

Coppice structure and nightingales
Mixed coppice (e.g. hazel, hornbeam, bramble, etc)

1 year
Unsuitable: coppice too small

3-4 years
Suitable: impenetrable with complete foliage to ground level

6-7 years
Ideal conditions: slower growing species maintain dense areas, more rapid growing species produce 'hollow' areas suitable for feeding

Sweet chestnut, 6 years
Unsuitable: the canopy is closed, but the coppice below is open and 'hollow'

Nightingale distribution in Britain. The boundaries are approximate and a number of outlying sites have been omitted.

Source: Henderson, A and Bayes, K, 1989. *Nightingales and Coppice Woodland*, RSPB.

Feature 7.9: Management of Woodland Streams

1. Pollarding or coppicing occasional broadleaved trees can reduce shading over parts of a stream.
2. Roots reaching into watercourses can provide good cover for fish and invertebrates. Hollows in riverbank roots of ash, oak and other trees (but not willows and alder) may be used as otter holts (see Feature 9.1 on otters). Root plates of fallen trees beside the water may provide kingfisher nest sites, and overhanging branches are used as fishing perches.
3. Leave about 50% of the banks unshaded, the rest in dappled shade. Don't open them up completely, as some wildlife prefers shaded water. There will be little plant growth in shaded reaches.
4. Retain bankside and emergent vegetation. When clearing watercourses always leave a fringe of vegetation adjoining the bank (see Chapter 9).
5. Some dead wood in the water (branches or even whole trees) can be useful, provided it does not pose a flood hazard. Provides habitat for invertebrates and cover for fish. Used as nest anchorages by moorhen.
6. Keep conifers away from the water as needle litter is not beneficial.
7. Sunlit, wind-sheltered glades make excellent habitat for flying insects such as dragonflies, and if grazed, for pied and grey wagtails.

Case study: New Farm Woodland (planting for multi-purpose objectives)

Hawk-eye Photo Library

Mown ride (7–9 m) within new farm wood planted with over 5,000 trees and shrubs that are native to the area. Additional rides and glades have been incorporated into the design of the wood.

Farm details

Farm:	Milden Hall, Milden, Suffolk
Tenure:	Christopher Hawkins, owner-occupier
Size:	202 ha
Altitude:	70 m
Soil:	medium – heavy chalky boulder clay
Crops:	winter wheat 109 ha, set-aside (including bio-diesel oilseed rape) 26.3 ha, field beans 12.1 ha, sugar-beet 18.2 ha, permanent pasture 4.0 ha, tree planting areas 6.1 ha, other 6.1 ha.
Stock:	none
Other wildlife features:	good mixed hedges managed on coppice rotation, grass tracks, botanically interesting hay meadow and wet area adjacent to river, six ponds.

The farm has been farmed by the Hawkins family since the 1700s, and is run as a family company. The surrounding, rolling countryside is dissected by the occasional river valley and is predominantly intensive arable farmland, with large fields divided by ditches and ancient, mixed hedges and some large blocks of ancient woodland. Part of the farm is in the Suffolk River Valley ESA.

Farmer's aims

Primary aim

- To plant a multi-purpose 4.1 ha woodland for wildlife, landscape, timber and sport.

Secondary aims

- To utilise home-propagated trees and shrubs, grown from seeds collected in neighbour's adjacent SSSI wood following the 1987 storms.
- To provide an educational site for wife's conservation courses

Background

Resources:
- Farm capital and Forestry Commission Woodland Grant Scheme for establishment, and MAFF Farm Woodland Scheme for 25 years' annual payments. Total costs £2,262. WGS grant aid immediately after planting: £3,372.
- Farm labour (farmer plus 2 farm workers) in slack times, with additional family labour.
- *c* 50% home-propagated trees and shrubs.

Net income received immediately after planting £1,902. Profit due to some home-grown stock and using farm and family labour.

Constraints: Loss of income from arable land.

Source of advice: Suffolk FWAG

Methods

In October 1987 farmer attended Suffolk FWAG propagation course and began propagating trees and shrubs from neighbour's ancient woodland (SSSI) in small on-farm nursery. Species are suited to heavy clay, lighter and damper areas – predominantly oak (40%), ash (20%) and wild cherry (10%) with small-leaved lime, hornbeam, silver birch, aspen, alder and an understorey of mainly field maple (5%), hazel (5%), and mixed shrubs: spindle, hawthorn, crab apple, guelder rose, holly and a few wild service trees. Additional trees were purchased.

Perimeter rabbit and deer fencing was erected, being aesthetically preferable to individual protection in such a visible site. Curving 7–9 m wide rides and a 15 m diameter glade were marked out. 5,000 trees were planted in groups in mild weather in December 1989 – January 1990, mainly at 3 m spacing and allowing for easy removal of timber.

In spring 1990 the site was seeded with low maintenance native grass mix to encourage butterflies in woodland's early years, for bird nesting and overwintering cover, and to suppress injurious weeds, eg thistles. Weeding with residual chemical 1 m around the base of trees was done up to 1993 and the trees pruned as required. The grass was variously topped, creating variety in sward type.

Achievements

Primary aim
- Forestry Authority Award of Excellence for the new woodland's contribution to wildlife and landscape. Excellent tree survival and growth, plus natural regeneration of oak, hawthorn and bramble. Transplanted wildflowers have spread; good variety of grasses. Variety of birds, eg goldfinches, seen feeding on plants; pheasants nesting in good holding cover. Kestrel, snipe and sparrowhawk all sighted. Large increase in common butterflies feeding and breeding. Variety of moths, solitary bees and wasps recorded.

Secondary aims
- Education: Over 300 people have visited the new wood since it was planted, including farmers' groups, FWAG advisers, Countryside Commission staff, Forestry Authority staff. Articles on the wood have appeared in local and national press.

Future management

Chemical weed control is unlikely beyond 1993. Pruning of cherry, oak and ash will continue as necessary to achieve good timber. Thinning will probably start in 20 years or so, coppicing of hazel and ride edges in 4 years. Topping grass rows and rides will continue annually.

Local Naturalist Society, farmer and wife will continue to observe and record wildlife changes. Further tree and woodland planting courses are planned using the wood as a demonstration site.

Case study: Welsh Hill Stock Farm, Oak and Ash Woodlands

Broadleaf planting to reclaim areas lost to bracken. Old trees and standing and fallen dead wood are retained.

David Jenkins

Farm details

Farm:	Bacheiddon, Aberhosan, Machynlleth, Powys
Tenure:	Mr & Mrs E H Lewis, owner-occupiers
Size:	299 ha
Altitude:	180-440 m
Soil:	brown earths (some very shallow and eroded) over Silurian shales (rainfall 1,200 mm)
Crops:	improved grassland 180 ha, semi-natural grazing 75 ha
Stock:	1,050 hardy speckle-faced ewes and 320 ewe lambs, 55 suckler cows, mostly Welsh black
Other wildlife features:	12 ha of ancient semi-natural oak and ash woodland, 75 ha of species-rich acidic grassland of great variety, including areas of bracken and gorse. Streamside habitats on tributaries of river Dovey.

Mr and Mrs Lewis purchased Bacheiddon in 1970 and the farm is renowned for the quality of its grassland and its pedigree stock. It is in the Cambrian Mountains ESA on the edge of the Dovey valley and the views from the farm are some of the most spectacular in Wales. There is a public footpath through the woodland. Mrs Lewis runs a Bed and Breakfast business from the farmhouse and timber from the woodlands is sold to local markets. Many of the visitors to the farm come to see the wildlife (particularly the birds) and the landscape. Visitors keep a record of birds on the farm.

Farmer's aims

Aims

- To provide hardwoods for sale and for use on the farm.
- To enhance wildlife habitats.
- To improve shelter in adjacent fields.
- To enhance the landscape.
- To provide access and recreation for visitors (walking and wildlife only).

▶▶▶

Background
Resources: Grants: Forestry Authority WGS for new planting and natural regeneration; Welsh Office ESA payments for woodland management; CCW Landscape and Nature Conservation Grants. Uses existing farm labour and machinery. Income from sales of thinnings as firewood and small sawlogs (all hardwood).

Constraints: Access to the main woodland block required a new road for mobile sawmills and lorries (not eligible for grant aid).

Source of advice: Free specialist advice and supervision from Coed Cymru dealing with silviculture, conservation, timber use and marketing.

Methods
A detailed management plan includes areas of thinning (to improve a neglected oak coppice stand), selective felling for natural regeneration (oak and some ash on wet flushes), broadleaf planting in tubes (to reclaim areas of woodland lost to bracken) and minimum intervention (along wooded streamside habitats). A detailed botanical survey of the whole farm was undertaken at the start of the project in 1987. All of the woodland is fenced to exclude livestock which previously had free access at all times of year. Grazing and a very dense canopy formerly prevented all natural regeneration of oak and ash. The work is phased over five years to fit into the farm calendar and to produce a continuous supply of wood for local markets. The second cycle of thinning begins as the first ends. Old trees and standing and fallen deadwood are retained and some additional nestboxes have been provided for pied flycatchers and redstarts.

Achievements
- A greatly enhanced standing hardwood crop and a profitable thinning programme with no compromise of landscape or wildlife interest. All of the best timber has been retained to grow on. Some of the thinnings have been used in product development trials by Coed Cymru. Timber originally destined for firewood has been sold for hardwood flooring and furniture.
- The initial restoration phase is nearly complete. Successful regeneration of oak, ash and other species – the beginnings of a multi-layered woodland with many more plant species.
- Extension of broadleaf woodland into an area of low wildlife and agricultural value.
- The woodland was judged 'Best Farm Woodland' in the county by the Montgomeryshire Wildlife Trust and the farm is highly regarded in all aspects of upland farming and farm tourism.
- The establishment of a provenance trial for clonal oak jointly by Coed Cymru and Forestry Authority Research Branch.

Future management
The standing crop of oak will be thinned continuously; regenerating oak, ash and other species will be freed and thinned. The single-layer, two-species structure will change to become multi-layered with many species, including herbs and shrubs. Other woodland owners and the general public will discover from this project, Coed Cymru's promotion of sustainable woodland management for the benefit of wildlife, landscape and the rural economy of Wales.

David Woodfall

John Andrews

7.1 Most lowland farm woods are isolated by surrounding arable. Well-grown hedges can link other woods and enable wildlife to move between them. A wood with a sinuous boundary may be ancient, its shape reflecting the clearance of surrounding woods in past times. Ancient woods are usually much richer in wildlife than plantations on former farmland.

7.2 There are very few ancient woods in the uplands. Most are recent plantations with an outline reflecting straight fence lines. Conifer plantations hold a more restricted range of wildlife than broadleaved woods but may have great potential for enhancement.

David Woodfall

7.3 Tree species composition has a great influence on the wildlife. Most native species support more insects than non-natives – oaks, willows, birches and some others have outstanding value. In addition, different tree species cast different amounts of shade and this controls what can grow beneath them. For example, beech casts such dense shade that few plants can grow beneath it and in consequence the range of food and cover for invertebrates, mammals and birds is very restricted. However, its copious production of beechmast provides winter food for small mammals, finches, jays and other birds.

R Glover

7.4 Where trees cast less shade, either because they have less dense foliage or are growing at wider spacings, an understorey of herbs and shrubs can develop. This supports a wider variety of insects and food in the form of seeds and berries. Many birds nest in the good cover provided by woodland shrubs.

David Woodfall

7.5 Grazing by livestock can alter the structure of a wood. By preventing shrub growth, it removes habitat required by one group of wildlife but creates conditions suitable for others. Stock fencing may be necessary to allow the trees themselves to regenerate and ensure the long-term future of the wood.

John Andrews

7.6 Where stock are fed in woodland during the winter, they may concentrate in one area and completely destroy the natural vegetation. Wherever possible, foddering points should be outside woodland on ground without wildlife value.

Frank Blackburn

7.7 Old trees and dead wood are abundant in natural woodlands so many species of fungi, insects and some birds have evolved to exploit it. In managed woods, old trees are very rare and where they remain they should be retained. Care must be taken to prevent vigorous adjoining trees from competing with them. Fallen dead wood should be allowed to rot away on the woodland floor, not piled in heaps.

John Andrews

David Woodfall

7.8 Trees which fall in gales should be retained if possible. Often the bole sprouts new growth, like this small-leaved lime, and the resulting thicket, set in a sunny gap in the wood, adds to the variety of structure and so to the range of wildlife which the wood may support.

7.9 Watercourses and areas of wet ground are an asset in woodland. Sunlit reaches may hold a variety of aquatic plants and some shade is also valuable because this restricts plant growth and maintains the open water conditions that some invertebrates require. Ferns and other plants that require humid conditions may thrive best close to water.

John Andrews

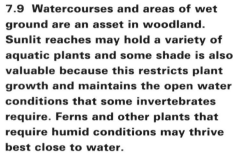

7.10 & 7.11 Woodland rides can be very rich habitats. If they are wide enough to be sunlit but not open to the wind, the combination of warmth and shelter is excellent for many butterflies, bees and other insects. Plant growth is good. Management should aim to create a mix of vegetation heights, with tall herbage and shrubs at the sides. By contrast, where the ride becomes overshaded plants are sparse and few butterflies or other species of insects occur.

Frank Blackburn, RSPB

E A Janes

7.12 Like rides, glades in the wood provide warm conditions for plants and animals. Where they do not exist, they can be created by felling back from the side of a ride or at a ride intersection. In a conifer plantation, planting the glade edges with native shrubs will much increase the wildlife value of the wood.

Juliet Bailey

7.13 Enhancement by shrub planting is also valuable at the edge of the wood and may be the only option in a small wood with no rides or glades. The best area for wildlife will be the sunny south-facing edges. In addition, any edge which adjoins arable can be protected from spray-drift by a good hedge or dense scrub cover.

C H Gomersall, RSPB

7.14 Coppicing used to be a widespread management system, mainly producing fuel wood. After cutting, the open area may be clothed in wildflowers responding to the light. Butterflies such as fritillaries breed. As the stools resprout and a close cover develops, herbs cease to flower but the conditions are favoured by dormice, nightingales and pheasants. As different parts of the wood are cut each year on rotation, it always contains habitat for each group of species, which simply moves round the wood following the management rotation.

7.15 Where standard trees are retained in coppice, they provide habitat for another group of wildlife such as hole-nesting birds and those which feed mainly in the canopy.

John Andrews, RSPB

John Andrews, RSPB

7.17 As far as possible, restock woods with species which are native to the locality as, in general, they will have the best wildlife value. For example, on suitable soils in the native pinewoods area of Scotland, woods should be restocked with Scots pine. In other parts of the UK other locally native species will be appropriate.

7.16 Woodlands managed for timber production can have high wildlife value, especially if they are not managed by clear-felling. The ideal is group selection so that the wood always contains trees of all ages up to maturity. If several tree species are grown, this will add to the structural diversity of the wood and, if they have different maturation ages, will help to extend the timescale of felling and restocking. Poor-quality trees may be retained to provide the old timber and dead wood element. Rides, glades and edges may be enhanced with shrubs.

John Andrews

8. Hedgerows, Farm Trees and Scrub

1. Factors influencing wildlife

1.1 Hedgerow age

- In some parts of the UK, farm hedges have existed for more than 1,000 years.
- Older hedges normally contain a greater number of different shrubs and trees than more recent plantings.
- Old hedges may hold rare species and should be a high priority for sympathetic management.
- Hedges of any age may be important to wildlife on the farm if other habitats are scarce.

In some parts of the UK hedges have existed for over 1,000 years, since Anglo-Saxon times at least. A small number of surviving hedges, and these are likely to be amongst the oldest, may be remnants of the original woodland cover retained to mark a boundary when the surrounding woods were first cleared. Such hedges are unlikely to be straight and they will probably contain a variety of shrubs and trees.

As well as defining boundaries and enclosing livestock, hedges were an important source of wood and in some areas were regularly coppiced, while hedgerow trees were pollarded. Planted hedges which are 300 years old or more are also likely to hold several different shrubs. Hawthorn, so common in more recent hedges, may be scarce or even absent. This is probably because these hedges were created by transplanting whatever was available locally and also reflects the fact that there has been time for other species to colonise or to be planted into any gaps.

An old hedge composed of a mixture of trees and shrubs may support plants and invertebrates which are rare because they have poor ability to colonise new sites and have not become established in more recently planted hedges. Some may have persisted in the site ever since it was part of the original wildwood. Only detailed study is likely to reveal their presence and it is wise to work on the assumption that these hedges are of great conservation value and treat them accordingly.

The most recent hedges, created within roughly the last 250 years, are usually straight except where they follow roads and tracks. In the English Midlands, most of these hedges were planted with hawthorn but there are distinctive regional variations reflecting soil types, for instance the beech hedges in parts of the Scottish Borders and the Brendon Hills in Somerset. Though they may lack the rarer species, these hedges can hold good numbers of songbirds and provide valuable sites for overwintering by beetles and spiders, which prey on crop pests (see Chapter 2 page 40). They can be central to farm conservation where other habitats are scarce.

In the last 40 years several factors have led to the removal or neglect of hedges. The decline of mixed farming means that on many farms hedges have no function in stock management. Where livestock form part or all of the enterprise, the use of wire has to a great extent replaced the need to manage hedges as stockproof structures, though they still serve a useful function in providing shelter. Hedges have been removed to increase field size, partly due to the use of larger machinery and partly to the increase in size of holdings and thus of herds. Even though the overall picture is one of continuing loss, many farmers continue to care for their hedges and there is some trend to reinstate them.

1.2 Composition

- The greater the variety of shrubs and trees, the greater variety of invertebrates the hedge is likely to support.
- Variety of composition provides continuity of food supply for birds and small mammals.

The more kinds of trees and shrubs in a hedge, the more wildlife it can support. This is particularly so with invertebrates, many of which depend on specific foodplants. A list of the numbers of species using particular trees and shrubs is in Chapter 7 page 187. It shows that

Table 8.1: Habitats and foods of common hedgerow mammals

There are 28 species of mammals which are found on lowland farmland most of which will make some use of hedges, for cover or as a corridor. Half commonly breed in hedges, and of these, almost all are associated with woodland. Some, in their turn, are preyed on by birds such as owls.

A hedge with a good variety of shrubs and plants will provide a continuous supply of fruit, nuts and berries, and plenty of invertebrates for shrews and hedgehogs. Some mammals, such as hedgehogs, will also hibernate in the hedge.

SPECIES	BREEDING SITE	OMNIVORE	CARNIVORE	INSECTIVORE	HERBIVORE	DIET
Fox	burrows (earth)		●			rabbits, rodents, birds, large insects, carrion, berries, fruit
Badger	burrows (setts)	●				earthworms, rabbits, rodents, much vegetable material (e.g. plant roots, acorns)
Rabbit	burrows (warrens)				●	plants, particularly young shoots
Stoat	vegetation		●			rodents, rabbits, birds
Weasel	vegetation		●			rodents, young rabbits, birds
Hedgehog	vegetation			●		insects, earthworms, slugs, birds' eggs
Mole	burrows			●		earthworms, insect larvae and other arthropods
Common rat	burrow	●				very wide range of foods incl. invertebrates, carrion, fruit and grain
Field vole	vegetation and tunnels				●	grasses and sedges
Bank vole	vegetation and tunnels				●	variety of soft vegetation, berries, seeds
Woodmouse	vegetation	●				seeds, plant material and invertebrates
Harvest mouse	vegetation	●				seeds, plant material and invertebrates
Common shrew	vegetation			●		insects, spiders, woodlice, snails, some plant material (eg seeds)
Pygmy shrew	vegetation			●		insects, spiders, woodlice, snails, some plant material (eg seeds)

Adapted from Dowdeswell, W H 1987. *Hedgerows and Verges*. Allen and Unwin.

hawthorn is known to support 209 species, blackthorn 153, hazel 106, beech 98 and field maple 51, for example. In practice, the total will be less than the theoretical maximum because most invertebrates have restricted distributions and may need shrubs of a particular age or condition but, even so, a hedge holding four or five different shrubs will be able to support many more kinds of invertebrates than can a hedge composed of a single species such as beech.

Invertebrates are the key food resource for many birds so invertebrate abundance is important to them. Even seed-eating species such as yellowhammer rear their young on a high-protein diet of caterpillars and other insects. Small mammals also eat many invertebrates, mainly in winter when they search out the pupae of butterflies and moths as well as hibernating beetles and other nutritious prey (Table 8.1: Habitats and foods of some common hedgerow mammals).

The shrubs themselves also provide food for birds and small mammals, especially fieldmice and bank voles, in the form of seeds, fruits and berries. As these ripen at different times, a varied hedge will offer continuity of supply through the winter (Feature 8.2: Birds and hedges). Different shrubs blossom at different times and so also give continuity of pollen and nectar supplies to bees, butterflies and other insects (Feature 8.1: Butterflies and hedges).

1.3 Hedge size and structure

- Large hedges of native species support more wildlife than small hedges.
- A hedge with a complex internal structure provides hibernation and breeding sites for wildlife.
- Dead stems and stumps will increase the range of wildlife found in the hedge.
- Regular annual trimming prevents flowering and berry production, so reducing food resources for wildlife.
- Tall, bushy hedges give good wind shelter to species requiring warmth and humidity.

The bulkier a hedge is, the more foliage, twigs and stems it will contain, thus increasing the amount of food and concealment for dependent wildlife. Most songbirds that nest in the body of the hedge prefer to site their nests at least 1.2 m from the ground to minimise the risk from ground predators. The birds also seek good lateral and overhead cover to minimise the risk of detection by magpies and other corvids. This means that a hedge needs to be about 1.4 m tall and 1.2 m wide to support successful breeding. The greatest variety and abundance of birds is found in dense hedges 2 m tall. Though birds do nest in smaller hedges, they are generally less successful than those using big dense hedges (Figure 8.1: Hedge types).

The structure of the hedge is important. The complexity of a laid hedge offers more nest sites for birds and concealed hibernating places for invertebrates than a line of simple bushes managed by cutting or coppicing (Figure 8.1). A hedge that has become leggy, perhaps with the lower growth browsed away by stock, is unsuitable for scrub-nesting species such as dunnocks.

An old hedge or one that has been laid will contain dead wood. This is of value to the large number of insects, such as beetle and moth larvae, which feed on it. Other insects, including solitary bees, nest in the abandoned borings. Many fungi also require decaying wood.

The external form of the hedge is very important to wildlife. If neat trimming takes place every year, flower and fruit production will be very restricted or non-existent. On many farms, hedges are the only substantial source of pollen early in the season and this makes them very important for the continued survival of insects such as bumblebees, which require abundant pollen supplies in March and April in order to produce eggs and feed the first generation of workers.

Some insects have precise requirements for egg-laying sites in the hedge. For instance, the brown hairstreak butterfly places its eggs singly near the junction between one- and two-year-old growth of blackthorn twigs. Laid in August, they do not hatch

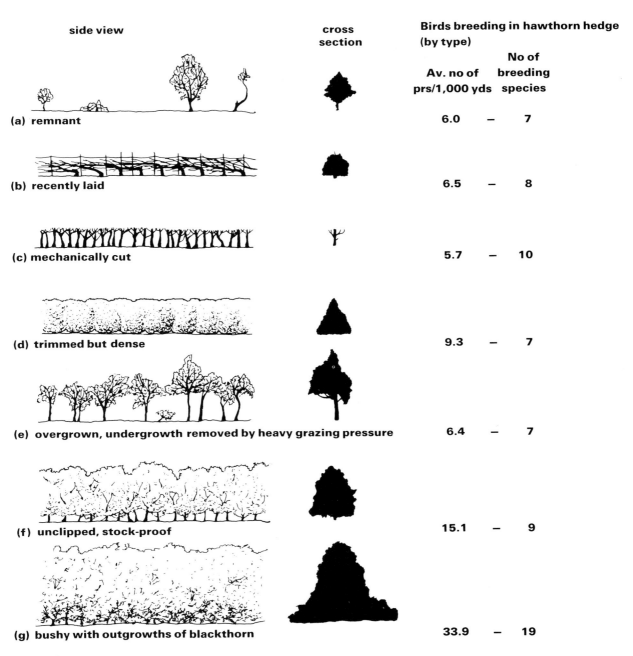

side view	cross section	Birds breeding in hawthorn hedge (by type)	
		Av. no of prs/1,000 yds	No of breeding species
(a) remnant		6.0 —	7
(b) recently laid		6.5 —	8
(c) mechanically cut		5.7 —	10
(d) trimmed but dense		9.3 —	7
(e) overgrown, undergrowth removed by heavy grazing pressure		6.4 —	7
(f) unclipped, stock-proof		15.1 —	9
(g) bushy with outgrowths of blackthorn		33.9 —	19

Figure 8.1
Hedge types and their use by breeding birds.

Adapted from Pollard, E, Hooper, M D and Moore, N W 1974. *Hedges*. New Naturalist 58. Collins.

until the next spring. If the hedge is trimmed meanwhile, most of the egg production is lost.

Restricted flowering leads to restricted fruiting. Autumn trimming will also remove berries. Blackbirds and the two winter thrushes, fieldfare and redwing, are very dependent on prolific supplies of haws and other berries to see them through the winter.

Hedges and hedgerow trees absorb wind energy through the flexing of their branches, twigs and foliage. The reduction of wind-speed means that daytime temperatures and humidity in the lee of the hedge will be higher than in the open field.

These effects are very important for invertebrates and for reptiles because their activity is greatly regulated by temperature. The best shelter is provided by hedges with a slightly open and flexible structure and a rather uneven and bushy top. Wind-speed is regained gradually on the lee side and the effects of the shelter are felt 20–30 times the height of the hedge downwind. There is also an effect extending for a short distance upwind as a result of the air 'backing up' in response to the resistance. Hedges which are tight-clipped tend not to absorb the wind. Instead, it is forced up over the top, causing an acceleration in speed and, possibly, turbulence on the downwind side.

Hedge laying and coppicing are drastic operations which temporarily change the structure of the hedge considerably. However, they may be essential to restore the dense structure of an old or a neglected hedge.

1.4 Hedgebanks and margins

- Hedgebanks provide nesting sites for birds and basking sites for reptiles.
- Many flowers, ferns and lichens survive on hedgebanks.
- Field margins adjacent to hedgerows can provide valuable habitats for butterflies and wild flowers.
- Ditches enhance the value of a hedge-line for wildlife.

Many hedges grow on banks which can be anything from a low earth baulk only a few centimetres high to a structure of stone and soil about 1 m high and 1.5 m broad at the base. Like the hedge, the bank itself is a habitat and modifies the local climate.

Banks can provide safe hibernating sites for reptiles inside the well-drained structure and warm basking places on the slopes. Especially in early spring and late autumn when the sun's angle is low, the surface of a bank gets more direct warming than the ground and these higher temperatures are critically important, enabling snakes and lizards to increase their body temperatures and so to be active on days when the ambient air temperature is low.

Ground-nesting birds like partridges have a better chance of escaping the attentions of foxes and other predators where the nest is placed on a bank. This is partly because the bank is more difficult for a predator to search than a level strip at the base of the hedge and the cover is likely to be better.

Many big hedgebanks are rich in flowers, including primroses, red campion and bluebells. Those built with a substantial framework of boulders or stones often support ferns such as the spleenworts which grow in crevices and lichens growing on the exposed faces of the stones themselves.

Up to about 50 or 60 years ago, arable field margins carried a cover of perennial grasses and herbs. Where it still survives, this is an important habitat in its own right not only for plants but as nesting cover for partridges, skylarks and other birds, and as hunting ground for kestrels and barn owls. The margins of pastures are less good for ground-nesting birds because the cover is shorter and nests may be trampled but they are still useful areas for many plants and insects. Caterpillars of the orange-tip and the gatekeeper butterflies feed on plants found at the base of hedges (Feature 8.1). Umbellifers are amongst the common hedge-margin plants of great value to wildlife. Hoverflies, solitary wasps and longhorn beetles all feed at the flowers. Cow parsley comes into bloom in April, rough chervil in May, and upright hedge parsley in July. Obviously, a hedge bottom which contains all these plants will be a reliable food source right through the period in which these insects are active.

The margin is also an adjunct to the hedge habitat itself. For instance, butterflies and moths whose caterpillars feed on the hedgerow shrubs need sources of nectar and many of the flowers which grow in the field margin will provide this.

Most modern field margins have lost their wildlife value due to a combination of factors – cultivation to the hedge base, use of nitrogen fertilisers and herbicides, pasture re-seeding and intensive management. Once the perennial plant community has been destroyed, the bare ground at the base of the hedge can be colonised time and again by barren brome, black grass, cleavers and other annual weeds that are serious crop pests (see page 26).

The presence of a ditch increases the value of the hedge-line for wildlife. Some of the birds that often nest in hedges, such as song thrushes, blackbirds and robins find good feeding conditions along damp ditch sides. Similarly, some insects that pass their larval stages in the ditch will feed as adults on the hedgerow flowers. For the management of ditches see Chapter 9 page 294.

1.5 Wildlife corridors

> - Hedges can be essential corridors to enable species that require cover or special microclimate conditions to move between habitats.
> - To be most effective, the hedgerow should link good wildlife habitats and provide suitable conditions throughout its length.

Continuity of hedges is important to enable some species to move between different areas. Many species of butterflies move along hedge-lines and the edges of woods rather than crossing open fields. Others are more sedentary and exist in small colonies. Hedges act as corridors and assist in dispersing these species provided that they contain the right food plants for caterpillars and nectar plants for the adult butterflies (Feature 8.1: Butterflies and hedges).

Many songbirds move along hedges, using the hedge to feed rather than as a corridor. However, birds also readily cross open fields and can find and exploit isolated areas suitable for feeding or nesting.

The species most likely to use hedgerows as corridors are those that move between different habitats during the year, are slow-moving and vulnerable to predators or need the microclimate conditions which hedges create – warmth, shade, humidity or wind shelter. Toads may use such corridors if they link breeding ponds with dry ground where they can hibernate. Snakes similarly move between hibernation and

breeding sites in banks or woodland and summer hunting grounds in damp grassland.

Hedgerows only work as corridors if they provide the conditions which a particular species needs throughout their length, if they are continuous and if they link the relevant habitats. Small, tightly-trimmed hedges with little cover at the base are unlikely to be of use.

1.6 Trees

> - Farmland trees are important for some birds.
> - Old trees and those which show die-back may still live for many years and are invaluable for wildlife.
> - Pollards are particularly important trees as they provide nesting cavities for birds and habitat for uncommon insects.

Isolated trees, including those in hedges, are rarely as useful for wildlife as those in woodland. The canopy is more exposed to wind so temperatures inside it are likely to be lower and conditions are less suitable for many insects. The complex of habitat features required by many species is not present. Though birds like the chaffinch nest in these trees, they also commute to the nearest wood to feed unless the surrounding hedges are tall and bushy.

Some birds prefer small stands or lines of trees surrounded by farmland. Rookeries are not placed at the centre of woodland. Some birds of prey, including the kestrel, buzzard and red kite, little and barn owls often nest in isolated trees. Buzzards and kites build their own nests; kestrels will use either a crow's old nest or a cavity in a tree trunk. Owls will also nest or roost in tree-holes. For this reason, it is important to retain trees that are developing rot holes or have become hollow. Trees have natural mechanisms for coping with decay and preventing it from affecting the load-bearing capacity of the trunk. Only when they are extremely old do they slowly fall to pieces. Old trees are also likely to be important for the many beetles which either feed in decaying wood or live in burrows vacated by insects. They should be retained.

Many farmland trees are now dying back and becoming stag-headed. There are several theories as to the cause of this. In many cases two or three factors are involved. For instance, trees which developed in pasture may have lost a significant part of their root system when it was converted to tillage. The summer watertable will have fallen if field drainage has been renewed. Dry summers will have stressed the tree further and there is the possibility of acid rain damaging the foliage so that the tree's ability to photosynthesise is reduced. It is quite normal for mature trees to retrench if they are stressed and it does not mean that the tree will die. Eventually the bare top limbs rot and fall, though with oak in particular this can take many years. Meanwhile, they are colonised by beetle larvae and make good feeding sites for woodpeckers, especially in winter when the birds may range far from their woodland breeding sites.

Pollarding was a way of producing repeat crops of wood while livestock grazed the ground beneath. Though pollards often contain areas of rot at the top of the bole where the stumps of cut limbs die back, this causes them no real harm but it does provide the right conditions for some insects that depend on decaying wood. As pollards can be extremely old, they can support colonies of rare insects which have lived in the farm's trees for many hundreds of years. It is a high priority to ensure the survival of existing specimens and create a successor generation.

1.7 Scrub

> - Scrub can support a wide variety of wildlife and its value is often underrated.
> - Young, open scrub with other wild plants growing amongst it is excellent for invertebrates.
> - Old scrub supports fewer species but they may include rarities.

Scrub can consist of a scattering of small shrubs or young trees colonising a patch of unfarmed ground or an ancient, dark thicket of giant thorns. Its wildlife interest depends on its species composition, age, structure and surrounding habitat.

Typically, young scrub consists of self-sown hawthorn or suckering blackthorn in grassland, gorse on heaths, juniper on downs or moorland, sallow and other willows on wet ground. It provides nest and feeding sites for songbirds, with yellowhammers in dry scrub, linnets in gorse and reed buntings in wet scrub, for example. All these birds also depend on seeds produced by the grasses and herbs that grow among young shrubs. The shrubs flower freely, producing pollen and nectar, and there is good wind shelter so the conditions are excellent for insects. It is common to find dragonflies hawking amongst the bushes because prey is abundant. Some butterflies also flourish in these sheltered sites. However, although the habitat is quite rich, the species it supports will usually be the mobile colonists, which are therefore common and widespread.

As the scrub becomes larger and denser, it supports fewer species. Most of the grasses and herbs are shaded out, so reducing the food resource for the seed-eating songbirds. The extent of the sunlit and sheltered ground is reduced to a zone on the south-facing edge. Flower production is largely confined to the top of the canopy. However, old scrub is not without wildlife value. Some mosses and lichens grow on the bark and in turn provide cover for a variety of insects. Other insects live in dead branches. There are also sedentary species which do not readily colonise new areas so that if the whole patch of scrub is cut down they will die out and not reappear even if regrowth is rapid. The black hairstreak butterfly is one such example which depends on sheltered, sunlit stands of blackthorn and is mostly confined to sites where there have been blackthorn bushes for generations. Thus, very old stands of scrub may have high importance.

Many trees will also colonise unmanaged land. Amongst the most frequent are oak, ash, birch and suckering elm. At first they create conditions similar to that provided by young shrubs but as they grow they outstrip the shrubs and shade them out along with other plants.

2. Options and assessment: planning management

2.1 Wildlife assessment of hedgerows and scrub

- Assess the structure, composition, presence of trees and context of the hedge.
- Attempt to age the hedge using Hooper's rule where appropriate.
- Assess scrub separately from hedges.
- Consider the relative values of managing hedges or woodland on the farm.
- Ideally, produce a farm wildlife plan.

Hedges have, or had, several functions. They define ownerships, facilitate livestock management, provide stock with shelter and sometimes delineate differences in soil capability. These functions are no longer necessary on many farms and to a great extent barbed wire has replaced labour-intensive management of hedges as a means of containing stock. Nonetheless, most lowland farms still retain hedges and, together with the field margin, they form an important habitat. Where trees are present in the hedge or isolated in the field, they too may hold wildlife which occurs nowhere else on the farm.

Scrub should be considered as a separate habitat in its own right because the conditions of shelter and shade which it provides, for insects especially, are different from those in hedges.

In assessing the wildlife value of hedges and scrub, several factors need particular attention (Table 8.2: Wildlife assessment of hedgerows, trees and scrub). These are their approximate age; whether they are composed of only one or two shrub species or of several and whether they contain trees; their structure and condition; and, last but not least, their location relative to other habitats including field margins and 'conservation headlands'. Section 1 of this chapter explains more fully why these factors are important to wildlife.

Hooper's rule has been used to estimate the age of hedges and, although it is now recognised that tree and shrub species invade more rapidly than previously thought, it is still worth using as a first guide. The rule suggests that the age of the hedge in centuries is likely to be the same as the number of tree and shrub species found in a 30 m length of it (excluding obvious new tree planting). Thus, a hedge with hawthorn, blackthorn, field maple, ash and dogwood in 30 m could be about 500 years old. It is wise to take two or three separate 30 m stretches along the same hedge and be guided by the average of the number in each stretch. The rule applies better in the south of England than elsewhere, as a greater variety of trees and shrubs grow there. In the north and west, hedges with fewer species may be equally old.

In counting shrubs, include wild roses but not bramble, honeysuckle or clematis. Elder quickly colonises new hedges. Dogwood, field maple, hazel and spindle are good indicators of older hedges. Elm is very invasive. Where planted for hedgerow timber, its suckers have sometimes spread along the hedgeline and ousted other shrubs. Now, the tree may have died but its roots and suckers live on so that an almost pure elm hedge may have a much older origin than would be judged from its restricted variety today.

Some herbaceous plants are also indicators of age because they are not ready colonists of ground outside woods. Woodland flowers, including bluebells, wood anemone and wood spurge, in the hedge bottom may be another clue that the hedge was created from a strip of the original forest cover or at least was planted near to an ancient woodland though this may since have been cleared.

Much of the wildlife of hedges and scrub also lives in or at the edges of native broadleaved woodland and, if it comes to a choice, it will usually be better to manage a wood for wildlife than to manage hedges.

Table 8.2: Wildlife assessment of hedgerows and scrub

INFORMATION REQUIRED	METHOD	REASON FOR INFORMATION
1. Conservation status and interest	Contact FWAG initially.	May be able to provide information of use in assessment. Will provide details if hedge is listed as being of wildlife or historic interest.
2. Age of hedgerow and scrub.	Check farm records. Estimate age using Hooper's rule. (see page 251).	Older hedgerows are more likely to support a greater diversity of wildlife. Scrub has different values relating to age.
3. Past management	Check farm records. Examine past/current aerial photograph.	Will provide hints on reason for current structure or species composition. May guide future management such as restoration or replanting.
4. Hedge and scrub composition	Record whether there are only one or two species or several: note identity of species if known.	Different tree and shrub species have different conservation values. Not all species are suitable for all management methods.
5. Trees	Record location and species if known. Record old trees and dead trees. Record location of pollards and condition.	Pollard trees and old trees are very important. Retain and consider repollarding.
6. Hedge and scrub structure	Record height and width of hedges and any gaps present. Note whether open or dense at base. Record height of scrub. Record whether scrub is scattered/dense.	Size of stems and branches will determine suitability for management. Scrub may need to be thinned. Will guide future plans and may suggest reinstatement of certain management practices such as laying.
7. Hedge bottom	Record whether a wide variety of plants are present. Record presence of crop weeds.	Hedge bottoms with a rich variety of plants are important and should be managed to retain this. Where contains species such as barren brome and cleaver will indicate change of management needed.
8. Hedge location and context	Record presence of adjacent features and land use.	Hedges next to plant-rich field margins, 'conservation headlands' and other habitats are important. They complement each other and can act as corridors.
9. Location of rare or sensitive species	Identify exact location of rare species present if known. Seek specialist information.	May require specific management.

However, it will usually be easier to bring a hedge into good condition for its wildlife. There is no hard and fast rule as it is important to make the assessment on the individual farm, comparing habitat quality and the practicalities of management. This may necessitate prioritising work and Chapter 1 page 10 sets out the procedure for doing this by producing a wildlife management fament plan for all or part of the farm.

Background information on the principles underlying the assessment of wildlife habitats is also given in Chapter 1.

2.2 Management needs and opportunities

- Hedgerows are important for wildlife, particularly on farms with no woodland.
- Give priority to managing old hedges, those with several shrub and tree species and those linking other habitats.
- Ideally, hedgerows need to be trimmed on a three-year cycle. They may also need to be laid or coppiced to create a good structure.
- Maintain hedgerow and other farm trees. Consider pollarding.
- Grant aid may be available for restoration of neglected hedgerows or for planting new hedges.
- Manage scrub to maintain an uneven-aged mosaic.

Especially on farms where there are no woods, hedges have a very important role and value for both wildlife and landscape. Some may be very old and diverse in species and therefore are of high conservation value.

In general, give first management priority to old hedges with several shrub species, mature trees and a location adjoining other good habitats or linking them. Consider the conservation benefits of establishing new hedgerows such as linking other important habitats or providing additional cover for wildlife, gamebirds and predators of insect pests.

Many hedges are cut too often and too small, restricting their potential for use by wildlife. Where hedges are used to enclose livestock, there are wide regional differences in approach. For instance, in much of Wales, hedges are kept tight by careful annual maintenance whereas many of those in Northern Ireland are now tall and leggy – more like lines of saplings – and no longer stockproof. Restoration of these hedges would be of great value, provided that a fair proportion of the big old hawthorns and other trees were retained. Consider laying or coppicing followed by trimming every third year to produce a berry crop and maintain a good structure.

Big, old hedgerow trees have disappeared at an alarming rate and few are replaced. Where trees along hedgelines are not acceptable, it is important to identify small areas, perhaps at field corners and roadsides, where new specimens can be established. By far the best approach is to promote self-sown specimens rather than planting. Pollarding has benefits for birds and some rare invertebrates and should be continued.

Many hedges grow on banks which themselves support uncommon wildlife. Where there is no bank, it is valuable to retain (or create) a strip of perennial grasses and wildflowers 1 m or more wide on each side of the base. On arable land, this strip is often ploughed or sprayed, resulting in ideal conditions for the annual weeds that persistently and expensively reinvade crops. Additional benefits for hedgerow wildlife will come from also creating 'conservation headlands' adjacent to the hedge.

In pasture it is to be expected that the hedgebank or margin will be grazed along with the field and, especially if pressure is such that herbs cannot flower, there are benefits to be derived from fencing off selected hedge-lines.

Grant aid is likely to be available for the management, restoration and planting of hedges on the farm.

Scrub can support a wide variety of wildlife and provide both feeding and nesting sites for songbirds, including warblers. The retention of stands of old scrub is worthwhile and they should be managed to diversify the age structure. At the same time, it is very important not to allow new thickets to take over remnants of unimproved grassland, marshy ground or other habitats that may have considerable wildlife value on their own account.

3. Management of hedgerows and scrub

3.1 Protection from spray-drift

- Protect the whole hedgerow from spray-drift.
- Spray adjoining fields only in wind speeds of force 2 or less.
- Keep pesticides and artificial fertilisers out of hedge bottoms.
- Establish a permanent unsprayed margin adjacent to the hedge where weeds are controlled by establishing perennial plants or by cultivation.

Spray-drift can kill non-target plants and invertebrates in the hedge. These may include pollinators such as bees, predatory and parasitic insects that feed on crop pests such as aphids, or perennial plants that help prevent colonisation of the hedgerow by nuisance weeds such as barren brome. The whole hedge should be protected from drift by spraying when wind is negligible (force 2 or less), turning off the nozzles on the near boom when making the pass along the edge of the field immediately upwind from the hedge or, ideally, having a permanent unsprayed margin where weeds are controlled either by establishing perennial plants or by cultivation (see page 26). Grass strips between the crop and the hedge help to control pernicious annual weeds and can be managed for wildlife, providing habitat or food for insects, small mammals and birds.

Management of a sterile strip along the field margin also needs care. It may be advisable to fit a polythene skirt to the sprayer arm in order to minimise the risk of drift into the hedge. A safer solution would be to maintain the strip by rotovation. Where a 'conservation headland' exists, it will reduce the likelihood of spray-drift into the margin and the hedge.

A tall and dense hedge will minimise the risk of spray-drift being carried into other habitats that will be harmed by it, such as ponds.

3.2 Trimming, laying and coppicing

- If possible, trim only every third year to ensure food supplies for wildlife.
- Where crop shading is a problem trim the top more often than the sides.
- Size should be at least 1.4 m tall by 1.2 m wide. Precise shape is unimportant.
- Manage between November and February.
- Do not cut all hedges at once; cut equal proportions of the total length each year to ensure continuity of suitable habitats.
- Lay or coppice when necessary to create or maintain a good structure.
- Fence newly coppiced hedges from livestock.
- Retain as much dead wood as possible.

If hedges are cut in autumn, do not cut again for three years or there will be no berry production. If cut in early spring, you can cut again after two years. Do not cut between the start of April and the end of August as this is harmful to invertebrates and breeding birds. Ideally, have a rotation so that not all the hedges on one part of the farm are cut at once.

If crop shading is a likely problem, trim the top of the hedge more often than the sides. If the hedge contains shrubs or trees which will grow too big to be easily cut if left for three years, it may be necessary to cut at least some lengths more often. Do not leave hedges to become so overgrown that your equipment will be unsuitable for the job. Limbs smashed by flails do resprout but such hedges take longer to recover than those cut regularly.

There has been much discussion of the best shape for a hedge and it is clear that larger hedges hold more birds than smaller ones, but whether the hedge is cut into an A-shape, rounded, square or chamfered appears not to be important. A good hedge size is over 1.4 m tall and 1.2 m wide at the top.

If most hedges must be cut annually, mark some stretches which can be left longer – perhaps at field corners, around old ponds or on a side facing a road or track.

If a hedge has been allowed to grow without trimming, it will become leggy and cease to be stockproof and provide cover near ground level. At this stage, it should be laid or coppiced. If possible, some saplings should be allowed to grow on as trees.

For a hedge to be laid, it needs to be 2.5–5 m tall with the main stems ideally 5–10 cm in diameter at the base. Before laying a new hedge, allow it to grow for about five to 10 years. Hawthorn is the species most commonly laid but most types of hedgerow shrub, such as elm, blackthorn, ash, field maple, hazel and willow, can be treated in this way.

Styles of hedge laying vary throughout the country where methods have evolved for different stock control purposes but the general principles are the same.

The main stems of a hedge are cut almost through near the ground in such a way that they can be lowered sideways, without breaking, along the line of the hedge. Side branches are cut off and used to stake and bind the hedge. This form of management can have fairly severe effects on wildlife in the short term but vigorous young shoots from the base of the hedge soon grow up to form a dense stock-proof fence. It is important to ensure that hedges in various stages of regrowth are present on the farm to allow wildlife to recolonise recently laid hedges.

Hedges can be coppiced on farms where a stock-proof barrier is not required, or where trimming has resulted in a short hedge open at the base so that there is not enough growth for it to be laid. Coppicing involves cutting the hedge down to just above ground level and can be done with a tractor-mounted circular saw. Cuts should be angled to enable water to run off the cut stem and not cause rotting. New shoots generally spring up from the old base but a few stumps may die if the operation is not carried out carefully. Species that respond well to management by coppicing include hawthorn, hazel, ash and oak. Hedgerow elm does not always coppice well but will regrow from root suckers. As the coppice regrows, top it annually to encourage a dense, bushy structure.

Very old hedges with many different shrub species may need to be managed by a combination of laying, coppicing and trimming in order to bring them back into good condition.

In managing hedges, always try to retain dead wood. Do not remove rotting fenceposts, dead stumps of shrubs or trees.

After management it is easy to plough close to the hedge and inadvertently destroy part of the root system as well as the plant cover in the hedge margin. If necessary, put in temporary marker posts 1.5 m from the centre line of the hedge and on both sides so as to protect it. Where the adjoining fields have livestock, coppiced hedges need wire fencing to allow regrowth and ensure they remain stockproof.

3.3 Field margins and hedgebanks

- Establish a strip of perennial grasses at the field margin to increase the value of the hedge to wildlife.
- Select sites exposed to the sun, sheltered from the prevailing wind and linking other habitats.
- Ensure pesticides and artificial fertilisers are kept out of all hedge bases.
- Encourage wildflowers by annual mowing but allow taller cover to develop for ground-nesting birds.
- In pasture, protect hedge bases by fencing a strip about 1 m wide.
- Retain hedgebanks.

Around arable fields, it is worth considering the benefits of establishing a strip of perennial plant cover about 1 m wide as this will resist recolonisation by troublesome crop weeds and have considerable value for the wildlife of the hedge itself. Details of establishment methods and management are given in Chapter 2 page 26. Most importantly, pesticides and fertilisers should not be applied so special care is needed with applications to the adjacent crop.

If it is to develop a varied plant cover, the strip will require annual mowing and the cuttings must be removed or clipped small so that they do not swamp the less vigorous plants. However, for ground-nesting birds and hibernating insects, taller cover is needed in winter and spring. The ideal may be to mow the outer edge of the strip but leave at least 0.5 m at the hedge bottom uncut. If suckering elm, blackthorn or other shrubs spread into this, an occasional cut will be needed, but do only about a quarter of the whole length in any one year.

In pasture, most hedge bases are grazed out and the only way of developing plant cover other than grass will be to fence a strip about 1m wide. In the short term this may be colonised by common, vigorous plants.

Provided that the adjoining sward is well managed these will not cause problems and they support many insects. However, such fenced strips may be invaded by shrubs and will, therefore, require some management. Ideally the space between the hedge and the fence should be wide enough to allow occasional cutting with a flail mower.

Exposure to the sun, shelter from the prevailing wind and nearness to other habitats are important factors in deciding which hedge bases and margins to develop. Thus, margins near ponds can provide good hunting ground for dragonflies, cover for dispersal by young frogs and newts and nesting sites for moorhens or sedge warblers. Other good locations would be adjoining woodland or any patch of unimproved ground carrying grassland or scrub (Figure 8.2 Wildlife corridors).

Wherever possible, retain hedgebanks, especially those which adjoin or link other good habitats.

3.4 Planting new hedgerows

- The choice of site for a new hedge is important. Aim to shelter, augment or link existing habitats.
- Use at least five shrubs of species that grow locally and incorporate native trees.
- Plant on a raised bank if possible and protect from grazing animals.
- Manage the growing hedge to create a dense bushy structure.

New hedges are best sited to augment the interest of existing habitats on the farm. There are often many possibilities, including providing shelter from wind or spray-drift to ponds, improving the potential of existing ditches or streams or linking isolated copses or stands of scrub (Figure 8.2).

Use at least five native shrub species and, ideally, choose those that grow well in existing hedges and local woods (see Chapter 7 page 191 for the list of possibilities). Because they will have different growth rates, there is a risk of the more vigorous ones swamping others, so plant several of each kind together.

It should be borne in mind that some shrubs are hosts to crop pests. Barberry and buckthorn both carry rusts that also affect cereals; black bean aphids use spindle.

Where possible, trees should be included. Crab apple, field maple, hawthorn and rowan are amongst those which do not grow very large or cast heavy shade but produce good food resources for wildlife.

Ground-nesting birds will benefit if the hedge is placed on a bank of soil at least 0.3 m high and 1 m wide. Create a tilth at least 0.3 m deep and plant during October to March, taking great care to ensure that the roots do not dry out in wind or sun before they are planted as this is a common cause of failure or slow growth. A staggered double row (0.25 m between plants and 0.5 m between rows) is preferable because it will be denser and give better cover. Initial growth and drought resistance may be better if the plants are at once cut back to about 15 cm.

Figure 8.2
Wildlife corridors: opportunities on farmland

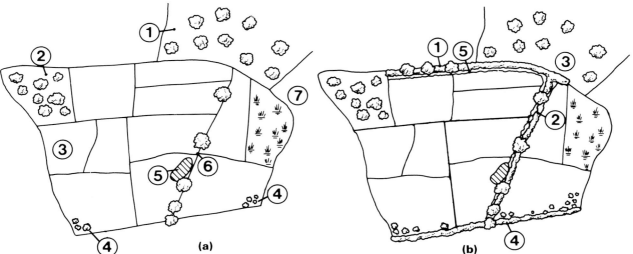

(a)   (b)

(a) Before planting
1. Area of ancient woodland on adjacent land.
2. Area of new broadleaved woodland.
3. Pasture.
4. Areas of scrub.
5. Pond.
6. Old hedge-line – now gappy and fenced, still with some trees.
7. Area of rough damp grassland.

(b) After planting hedges as 'wildlife corridors'
Note hedges are not isolated from one another, and link habitats like with like and with differing habitats.
1. Hedge-line between old and new woodland. New trees planted or selected for retention in existing hedge. Allow hedge to grow big, cut one side at a time, other side 2–3 years later. Protect ground flora carefully – scarce woodland species may spread into hedge.
2. Hedge-line gapped up and renovated, trees maintained. Allows amphibians to move to and from pond to feeding/hibernating sites eg dry grassland, scrub and woodland.
3. Linking woodland to damp grassland would allow grass snakes to move from breeding and hibernation sites in woods and on dry banks to hunting sites in damp grassland and pond.
4. Hedge linking scrub areas and scrub to other habitat types.
5. Perennial herbs and grasses allowed to develop at the base of important hedges. A good variety of nectar plants encourages butterflies, which prefer to move along hedgelines rather than across open fields.

Where stock are kept, appropriate fencing is needed to protect a new hedge from damage. Such fencing should be sited far enough away from the hedge to ensure that animals cannot browse the tops of the young plants.

Where rabbits are a serious problem, chicken netting or individual tree guards may be required. New hedges need to be protected from excessive weed growth in the early stages; grass is a most serious competitor for moisture and can check or kill plants. Careful use of selective herbicides may be the simplest option but the use of a mulch will also work and help conserve soil moisture. Natural mulches such as straw are ideal but black polythene sheeting can be used.

To encourage a bushy structure, top the hedge each autumn until it reaches the required height.

3.5 Management and planting of hedgerow trees

- Re-pollard neglected pollard trees.
- Continue to manage old pollard trees by removing new growth at about yearly intervals.
- Allow some self-sown saplings in hedgerows to grow on, but ensure they are clearly marked to protect from damage during hedge trimming.
- Always select native species of tree for planting in hedgerows.
- Where they have to be felled, replace uncommon trees with the same species.
- Retain old trees and standing dead trees if safety considerations permit.

Because of their exceptional wildlife value, old trees should be retained wherever possible. Old pollards will require management. With low spreading crowns, they are usually easy to recognise. Very old specimens are likely to be hollow and there is a danger of them splitting asunder as the boughs become ever bigger and heavier. Willows are particularly prone to this. It is therefore wise to re-pollard such specimens. However, there is a risk of killing neglected pollards if all the limbs are removed at once. The best course is to remove half the total number of limbs, cutting them about 5 cm from the bole and taking them from all round the tree so that it remains balanced. When there is good new regrowth from around the cut faces, probably after about three years, the rest of the old limbs can be removed.

New pollards are easy to make when the tree is young by cutting it off in winter at 2–3 m above the ground when the trunk has reached about 10 cm diameter at that point. It will sprout in the following spring, producing several spreading branches. These must be removed at about five-yearly intervals and, as the tree matures, it will produce progressively larger limbs.

As a general rule, success is more likely with self-sown saplings or suckers in the hedge than with planted stock. Whatever is self-sown and thriving is obviously suited to the conditions. Planted trees always have to struggle against the competition from the hedge. It is also much cheaper to work with what nature provides than to buy stock. If possible, select individuals which have not been cut at any time. Ensure that saplings in hedges are clearly marked so that they will not be destroyed during hedge trimming.

As always, it is most important to retain and promote trees where they will relate closely to other habitats. Trees contribute more to a good hedge than when growing in isolation.

If planting new hedgerow trees, always select species that are native to your part of the country (page 191) and suitable for the conditions on the farm. Oak, ash, wild cherry, field maple, hornbeam and holly all make attractive hedgerow trees and are good for wildlife. Black poplar is not a woodland tree but is typical of lowland river valleys in England and Wales. If it becomes necessary to fell an uncommon tree, it should certainly be replaced with the same species.

Elm was a very abundant hedgerow tree in many parts of the UK. Often, the root system still survives and throws up suckers. It is possible that the Dutch elm disease will run its course and that some of the suckers can be promoted to trees in the future.

If a hedgerow tree dies, retain it if safety considerations permit. Standing dead wood is a valuable habitat for woodpeckers and other wildlife.

3.6 Scrub management

- Retain stands of established scrub as these may hold rare plants and invertebrates.
- Do not allow scrub and trees to develop on rare wildlife habitats such as heath or unimproved grassland.
- Where young trees are appearing, they may be managed like scrub or allowed to develop into woodland, depending on their context.
- Where scrub is retained, manage it to maintain an open structure and a range of ages.
- Gorse, juniper and willows need special treatment.

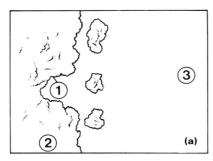
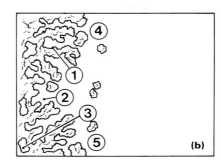

Figure 8.3
Scrub management: (a) before management – limited value to wildlife; (b) after management – diversity and value to wildlife greatly increased.

(a)
1. **Very little 'edge', few sunlit clearings**
2. **Solid blocks of dense scrub**
3. **Grass**

(b)
1. **Lots of 'edge', intimate patchwork of scrub and grass**
2. **Approximately equal amounts of scrub and grass**

3. **Lots of sheltered 'holes' – good for invertebrates**
4. **Dense blocks broken up, ideally over a few years, maintains age diversity of scrub**
5. **Keep some patches uncut – ancient scrub may support rarities**

Before decisions are taken about management, first consider whether to permit the scrub to develop or remain on the site. Old, established stands may hold rarities and should always be retained. New stands will add to the interest of other habitats but should not be allowed to occupy more than about 10% of the ground if it is unimproved grassland, heath, moor or wetland. If the patch is small, this may mean only a handful of bushes strategically sited to give shelter from wind or spray-drift. Do not allow trees to develop on rare habitats like heath or unimproved grassland. Either manage them like scrub or remove them entirely.

On grassland and at woodland edges the aim must be to keep scrub open, so that it is roughly half bushes and half small patches of sunlit clearing (Figure 8.3: Scrub management). Allow about a quarter of the shrubs to grow and age untouched and cut down one of the other quarters every third or fourth year in rotation. This will create the mix of conditions likely to support a rich diversity of species.

Juniper is a special case. Large stands of juniper and big old bushes are rare, especially on downland, and they should not be cut at all. For management of gorse see Chapter 4. To manage willow scrub in wetlands see Chapter 9.

4. References and further reading

British Trust for Conservation Volunteers 1975. *Hedging*. BTCV.

Dowdeswell, W H 1987. *Hedgerows and Verges*. Allen and Unwin.

Muir, R and Muir, N 1987. *Hedgerows: Their History and Wildlife*. Michael Joseph Ltd.

Pollard, E, Hooper, M D and Moore, N W 1974. *Hedges*. New Naturalist 58. Collins.

Lack, P 1992. *Birds on Lowland Farms* pp 12–34. HMSO.

Clements, D K and Tofts, R J 1992. Hedges make the grade. *British Wildlife* Vol 4 No 2 pp 87–95.

Feature 8.1: Butterflies and Hedges

Hedges are important habitats for butterflies on farms, providing larval food plants and nectaring plants, and as corridors around farms. The best-used hedges will provide a good selection of shrubs and herbs and wind shelter. Butterflies and caterpillars are eaten by insect-eating birds, and the pupae are eaten by beetles and small mammals.

1. In the herb layer at the bottom of the hedge are garlic mustard, hedge mustard and lady's smock, food for orange-tip caterpillars. They accumulate mustard oil from the plants in their bodies, which makes them distasteful to birds. The female spends most of her time hiding in the bushes.

2. The brown hairstreak is a scarce species, partly due to annual flailing of blackthorn hedges. Eggs are laid at the junction of one and two-year old growth, so hedges where they occur should be cut only every few years. The butterflies mate in a tall 'master' tree, often ash.

3. Drastic habitat changes cause extinction of populations of very sedentary butterflies. White-letter hairstreaks remain around a single elm tree or group of trees and have been badly affected by Dutch elm disease. Wych elm, their preferred food, is less affected and should be maintained. The adults feed on honeydew, a sweet-tasting substance exuded by plant bugs on oak or ash.

4. Sheltered fine grasses in sunny spots next to hedges are food for gatekeeper caterpillars. The adults have a short proboscis and can feed only on wide open flowers such as bramble in the hedge.

5. Nettles are important foodplants for several butterflies, such as small tortoiseshells. The adults gather in large numbers to feed on nectar, which they need before they hibernate. The adults also roost in nettles at night.

6. Commas also take nectar from brambles and other hedge flowers. Their preferred larval food plant is hops, but they will use nettles.

7. Holly blues have two broods per year, on holly flowers in spring and ivy in summer. The adults prefer honeydew to nectar.

Feature 8.2: Birds and Hedges

Hedges provide food, shelter and cover for breeding birds. Most species prefer tall hedges. The wider the hedge, the more birds will use it.

Hedges are also important to birds in winter. A dense hedge will provide cover, and if there is a good mix of shrub species in the hedge, some food will be available right through the winter. Flocks of redwings and fieldfares will take berries, as do many resident birds. Bullfinches will take seeds from any withered blackberries, and a bushy hedge bottom will contain seeds and overwintering insects.

Birds that use hedges primarily for shelter are not greatly influenced by the woody species growing within it, but to those birds feeding within the hedge, such as dunnock, blackbird, blackcap and chaffinch, they are very important. Bramble is consistently the most preferred, elder the least. The type of woody vegetation beneath the hedge is of significance to wrens, dunnock, robin, blackbird, willow warbler and greenfinch, but their preferences vary.

Key to illustration
1 **Redwing**
2 **Grey partridge**
3 **Blackbird**
4 **Dunnock**
5 **Lesser whitethroat**
6 **Kestrel**
7 **Yellowhammer**

Features of importance to breeding birds

Key: N nesting; **F** feeding; **S** songpost.

Canopy: S yellowhammer, song thrush, blackbird, robin; **S & F** Blue tit, great tit, chaffinch; **N** kestrel.

Trunk with holes: N blue tit, great tit, kestrel, little owl.

Hedge: N blackbird, song thrush, robin, greenfinch, linnet, dunnock; **N & F** Whitethroat, wren, long-tailed tit.

Hedge bottom: N & F partridges, yellowhammer, corn bunting, reed bunting; **F** chaffinch, greenfinch, linnet.

Damp ditch: F dunnock, song thrush, blackbird.

Case study: Hedgerows

Farm details

Farm:	Pasture Farm, Uppingham, Leicestershire
Tenure:	Mr J Hill, tenant farmer
Size:	247 ha
Altitude:	90–150 m
Soil:	mainly Jurassic and Cretaceous clay, some overlying ironstone, some drift covering and chalky till
Crops:	142 ha arable; oilseed rape, beans, winter wheat, barley and oats, set-aside, 105 ha grassland, (89.1 ha permanent, 16.0 ha ley)
Stock:	420 breeding ewes, 80 ewe lambs (gimmers), 200 beef cattle
Other wildlife features:	2 small spinneys being re-stocked, marsh, hedges with trees, water courses, species-rich grass meadow, meadow with scrub development.

Mr Hill has farmed here for 26 years, and employs 3 full-time workers. The farm is set in rolling countryside in an intensively farmed area and is surrounded by major commercial mixed woodlands. When Mr Hill took over the farm, the hedges were in poor condition and not stock proof. The grass banks were identified as good for gamebirds; his interest in wildlife generally has developed over past five years after initial interests in game.

Farmer's aims

- To maintain the hedges in a stock proof and manageable state.
- To rejuvenate and manage the hedges in the long term sympathetically for commercial, wildlife and landscape features.
- To make use of available resources through schemes such as Countryside Stewardship.

Background

Resources: Very little use made of grant aid as not available until recently. No contractors used for hedge or other management. Landlord/agent is sympathetic but 'good management' of the farm is essential.

Constraints: Work depends on lighter winter work loads. Commercial needs take priority and largely dictate order of management.

Source of advice: FWAG advice sought 1992.

Methods

There has been little planting of hedges as few gaps exist. Hedges are laid on a 20–25 year rotation around the farm according to stocking requirement. The aim is to lay 300–400 m/year, all around the farm. They are being cut for a second time. They are trimmed 2 years in 5 for 12–14 years after laying then allowed to grow up again, siding up occasionally. Trimming aims to encourage thickening of the hedge and allow fruiting after blossom and is done as late as possible, but cropping does often dictate late summer trimming. The rotation spreads the work load and reduces the impact on wildlife and landscape.

Hedges acting as wildlife corridors between the major woodlands tend to be wider and fuller generally. Hedgerow trees of differing ages and type (but consistent with the hedge) are encouraged. A variety of bird boxes have been put up in various locations.

'Conservation headlands' have been tried but with limited success owing to heavy silts. A partial 'conservation headland' policy has now been adopted. They are managed with care to enhance hedges and hedge bottoms. Fertilisers and pesticides are carefully chosen and applied only when 'damage' is occurring, for least environmental impact in headland zones. They are avoided here where possible and all drift is prevented.

Achievements

- Stock are contained on the farm.
- Little recording of species was done prior to 1992. Comparisons are therefore difficult, but the Common Bird Census recorded 88 species on 160 acres in 1992, some unusual sightings being included. Bird density is encouraging. Mr Hill has gained personal satisfaction and enjoyment from the work.

Future management

Locate rotational set-aside to improve field margins and to further improve the timing of hedge cutting through grass margins in the arable areas. To improve the corridors between wildlife habitats such as woodlands, herb-rich meadow and watercourses, and improve the plant diversity (to include tussocks) in unproductive grass areas. Also to make greater use of available grants and resources to forward the objectives.

John Andrews, RSPB

8.1 Where hedges are allowed to grow leggy and grazed out at the base, most of their value to wildlife is lost though they may still be used by a small variety of birds.

Hawk-eye Photo Library

8.2 The best hedges for wildlife comprise a variety of different shrub species. Such hedges may be ancient, pre-dating the enclosure hedges, which are mainly hawthorn. Each shrub species supports a different community of invertebrates, feeding on its foliage, flowers and fruits. Insects and fruits alike provide food for birds and the greater the variety, the better the continuity of supply throgh the seasons.

C H Gomersall, RSPB

8.3 Traditional hedge-management techniques vary regionally throughout the UK. In some areas, the practice is still to lay hedges, so creating a good stockproof structure. The complex internal arrangement of the regrown hedge provides good concealment for nesting birds.

John Morrison, Environmental Picture Library

8.4 Modern hedge-trimming maintains a dense exterior, but if carried out annually removes food resources for wildlife. Trimming causes least disturbance to wildlife if carried out between November-February. Birds breed most successfully in hedges which are at least 1.5 m tall and 1.2 m wide. In smaller hedges, their nests are easily seen by predators.

E A Janes

R Revels, RSPB

8.5 The winter berry crop is an important food resource for thrushes including the fieldfare and for mammals such as the bank vole. Where hedges are trimmed each year the berry crop is destroyed and there may also be little production of flowers so that pollen and nectar sources needed by bees, butterflies and other insects are also in short supply.

8.6 The brown hairstreak lays its eggs at the base of one-year old shoots of blackthorn. This butterfly has become rare through the grubbing up of hedges and is also affected through the annual cutting of the blackthorn shoots.

John Andrews

David Woodfall

8.8 By fencing stock out of the hedge bottom, a band of tall herbage will develop, greatly increasing the hedges' value for resident wildlife and as a corridor along which species including butterflies, amphibians, reptiles and some small mammals can move between breeding and wintering sites or disperse to new areas.

8.7 Much of the wildlife importance of hedges is associated with the plants that grow at its base. Apart from their intrinsic interest, they support a very wide variety of other wildlife, both by providing food and as cover where creatures can avoid predators or breed successfully.

Game Conservancy

8.9 The great decline of grey partridge on farmland has several causes including loss of good rearing habitat for chicks but another important factor is the lack of safe nesting sites where they are unlikely to be found by predators. A wide hedge base with dense and tall cover is much harder for a fox or magpie to search than one which is narrow and only holds sparse herbage.

Hawk-eye Photo Library

8.10 New hedge planting can add significantly to the wildlife value of a farm. Ideally, it should contain a mix of locally native species, plus some trees and the aim should be to develop a broad base of tall perennial herbage. This is particularly important in arable as these plants will resist invasion by weeds such as barren brome.

8.12 Scrub is now an uncommon habitat on most farms and small stands can be of considerable value especially as they are not normally trimmed, so that they continue to provide a crop of flowers and berries every year. Stands of scrub have their greatest value adjacent to ponds or watercourses or in conjunction with unimproved grassland. However, large-scale invasion of grassland is undesirable and should be cleared and controlled by grazing.

M W Richards, RSPB

8.11 Hedgerow trees are another important addition to the habitat, providing feeding and breeding sites for many species. Wherever possible, old trees, especially those with holes and cavities, should be retained and new trees should be planted in good time to provide a successor generation.

E A Janes

John Andrews

8.13 Pollarding produces regular supplies of fuel wood or small timbers on land which is grazed by stock. Often the main bole of a pollard will be of considerable age and contain cavities and patches of rotten wood which support specialised invertebrates. Such rot does not necessarily harm the tree. On the other hand, unless old pollards are repollarded regularly, the limbs can become so large that they split the bole and destroy the tree.

David Woodfall

8.14 A few native trees are rarely found in woods. One such species is the black poplar, a tree once widely planted by lowland watercourses and managed as a pollard. Now black poplars are uncommon. Old specimens should be repollarded and new trees should be planted in appropriate areas.

9. Waterbodies and other Wetlands

1. Factors influencing wildlife

1.1 The past and present farming context

- Almost all farms contain some wetland habitat.
- Land drainage and river management have greatly increased the extent of productive farmland in the UK, with consequent losses to wetland wildlife.
- Many once-functional farm wetlands, including field ponds and flood meadows, no longer serve an agricultural purpose.
- Funding is available for the restoration and creation of wetlands and for management.

There are few if any farms which do not contain at least one wetland habitat. Some, like ditches and irrigation reservoirs, have practical functions. Others such as ponds may be relics of former farming practice and now fulfil no working role. Many hill farms still contain patches of bog or marshy ground and relatively unmanaged watercourses. By contrast, in the lowlands the rivers and streams have almost all been substantially modified to aid land drainage and minimise flooding. Of the 11 million ha of agricultural land in Britain today, about half is dependent on artificial drainage and about two million ha have been won by draining marshes and enclosing saltmarsh.

Indeed, the UK has a legacy of about 2,000 years of land drainage, river regulation and flood defence, mostly carried out to help develop agriculture. By Anglo-Saxon times, large areas of wetland had been brought into farming use and, by about the year 1200, half the area of the East Anglian fens was embanked and drained, mostly to create pasture. By contrast, even as late as 1600 about two-thirds of the Somerset Levels were still natural wetlands and the other third, whilst converted to grassland, flooded every winter. In general, farms that held land in river valleys found such flooding beneficial because the annual deposition of sediment and nutrients helped maintain productivity and the land could then be used for hay production. It is only in this century that a variety of factors has led to the widespread protection of such fields from prolonged inundation and consequent declines in the specialised wildlife that depends on these conditions.

The introduction of clay pipe drains in the 19th century increased the ability to drain most farmland and allowed more widespread production of arable crops. In order to achieve adequate freeboard for discharge and to reduce flooding, most lowland rivers have been straightened and the bed lowered so as to drop the waterlevel. Shoals, islands and bankside trees have been removed. This has greatly reduced the variety and amount of habitats that rivers and their flood plains once contained.

Until the introduction of piped water supplies, livestock required access to ponds or the banks of watercourses, where their grazing and trampling maintained good conditions for a remarkable range of wildlife not found in rivers. Farm specialisation and improving standards of livestock husbandry have led to the large-scale abandonment or infilling of ponds in recent decades.

Set against these losses of wetland areas and their wildlife in the lowlands, there have been few gains. Though locally the creation of irrigation reservoirs or the excavation of wet gravel pits has resulted in new habitat, many of the species that were formerly widespread on farmland cannot live in these large, deep waters.

More wetland survives in the north and west of the UK, thanks in part to the large number of natural waterbodies, streams and rivers, but here too much marshy farmland has been drained in recent years, mainly to improve the quality and extent of inbye.

There are now financial incentives to enable farmers to rehabilitate and create wetland habitats. They cover, for example, not only the restoration of abandoned ponds but also reversion to traditional management of riverside meadows with a raised watertable. In addition, long-term set-aside offers the potential to create new wetlands.

1.2 Plant composition

> * Wetland plants are important as food, cover and breeding sites for fish, invertebrates, birds and mammals, many of which use a complex variety of plants.
> * Different types of wetlands support different plant communities.
> * Water chemistry, depth and flow, or seasonal flooding regimes, influence plant composition.

Wetland plants can be arbitrarily divided into two groups – those which grow in standing or flowing water and those which grow in moist ground and tolerate only temporary immersion. They support different groups of wildlife but a large number of species make use of both groups at different stages in their lives and so require both open water and adjacent wet ground (Table 9.1: Wetland plants, their requirements and attributes).

Submerged aquatic plants can be divided into two main groups – algae and the larger plants with leaves (macrophytes). Many algae are free-floating; others grow on larger plants or are attached to the bed. They are the food of myriad minute crustaceans and other organisms, which in turn feed larger invertebrates and fish. Some algae, the blanket-weeds, grow in long strands and mats, whereas others, the stoneworts, can carpet the bed; both of these types provide invertebrates and small fish with cover and some are important foods for birds such as the pochard. Algae are most abundant in standing and slow-flowing waters with a high nutrient status. In some situations the free-floating algae can become so prolific that they cut off light to macrophytes, which may die in consequence.

Most macrophytes are rooted and grow below the surface though they produce flowers that are held above water. A few kinds, such as water lilies, are rooted but have floating leaves while others, like the duckweeds, are free-floating. There are also some mosses which grow under water and can form extensive dense stands. Few invertebrates eat macrophytes or mosses but some species, such as snails, graze the attached algae which grow on their surfaces. These plants are very important as cover, hunting habitat and, especially in running water, as anchorages for insects, snails and other species. Many fish feed on their foliage and some, such as roach, stick their eggs to them. A number of species of wildfowl including mute swans, mallard and teal feed on the leaves, buds and seeds of these plants.

The greatest variety of submerged plants is found in standing and slow-flowing waters. Farm ditches that hold water all year contain some plants, such as the water violet and frogbit, that rarely occur in other wetland habitats. Ditches on coastal grasslands are often slightly brackish and as a result they support a somewhat different community of water plants that includes marsh mallow and tasselweed. Ditches are very good for aquatic invertebrates. The great silver waterbeetle is mainly found in them; during its larval stage it feeds on water snails, cutting their shells open with its powerful jaws. Sometimes over 50 different species of waterbeetle can be found in one ditch.

Many plants grow in lowland streams and rivers. Where the current is slower and the bed is of silt or clay, plants such as yellow water lily occur. Specialist river plants including some water crowfoots are adapted to stronger flows. The absence of plants from many upland rivers reflects the mobility of the stony bed. Few if any can grow on the mobile, rocky beds of upland watercourses or on wave-beaten shores. Some species have particular water chemistry requirements and grow only in chalk streams, for instance, but most are tolerant of a wide range of conditions provided that the water is reasonably clear. They do not thrive where water is heavily peat-stained, carries a high sediment load or suffers algal blooms.

Emergent plants such as reed and club-rush have their root systems in water but most or all of the foliage is held above the surface.

For this reason, they are largely confined to water less than 30 cm deep but a few species including reeds and bulrush can extend down to over 1 m in favourable conditions. Many emergent plants spread by a system of rhizomes or runners in the bed and can rapidly extend over the whole extent of shallows or the bed of a pond. This results in the loss of open water plants and their dependent wildlife. However, although beds of emergent vegetation may contain only one or a few different plants, their wildlife interest can still be high.

Many kinds of invertebrates lay eggs on or injected into the stems of emergent plants and their larvae live inside the stems where they have some protection from predators. Dragonfly larvae use the stems of branched bur-reed and other emergents in order to leave the water and metamorphose into winged adults (Feature 9.2: Dragonflies and damselflies). Many waterfowl shelter in the cover of emergent plants and some, such as great crested grebe, may anchor their nests among them. In southern Britain, reed warblers suspend their nests on last year's reed stems where they are safe from most dangers except cuckoos, which parasitise them. Often the warblers do much of their feeding in nearby willow trees.

Marginal and marshland plants such as purple loosestrife and greater pond sedge grow in damp ground and can tolerate occasional inundation. Unlike other wetland plants, most of which are wind-pollinated, many of them have showy flowers and are important sources of nectar. For example, brimstones and other butterflies feed at the flowers of purple loosestrife whilst water figwort attracts hoverflies. Many of these plants produce seeds that are a key food resource for dabbling ducks in winter. Sedges and rushes are particularly valuable because the seeds are large and nutritious and, on sites flooded in winter, this food is easily available to wildfowl.

Many farms contain land where the watertable is at the ground surface for part or all of the year. Sometimes these sites also flood after rain or when watercourses are running high. They vary greatly in size and character, from rushy low-spots in pasture,

through river valley meadows to peat cuttings and upland bogs containing cotton-grass, heathers and, in the wettest areas, sphagnum bog mosses. Factors including soil type, wetness, duration of inundation and management influence the plants and other wildlife they support. In both uplands and lowlands they are often particularly important feeding areas for wildfowl, waders and gamebirds.

1.3 Alkalinity and nutrient levels

- Wetlands on acid soils and peats have different wildlife from those with more alkaline conditions.
- Up to a point, plant abundance and variety increase with the nutrient status of the wetland, in turn increasing the other wildlife.
- In general, lowland sites are more productive and hold more species than upland sites.
- Both lowland and upland sites may hold uncommon species.
- Excessive nutrient levels in waterbodies cause algal blooms, which inhibit other plant growth and reduce its dependent wildlife.

Alkalinity and nutrient levels greatly influence the abundance and types of plants and hence of other wildlife in any wetland. In general, waters in the uplands come from acid soils and peats and their productivity is low compared with waters in lowland areas which flow from neutral or basic soils and often rise from aquifers in chalk and limestone. Lowland waters also tend to be enriched by run-off of artificial fertilisers and the discharge of sewage effluents.

Some insects and plants, such as water lobelia with its violet flower spikes, only occur in waters on sands and peats with very low natural nutrient levels. By contrast, water snails and crayfish are usually most abundant in alkaline waters because they require ample calcium carbonate for building the shell or carapace.

Just as changes in nutrient status bring about dramatic changes in grassland plant variety (see Chapter 3 page 62), increased

Table 9.1: Wetland plants, their requirements and attributes.

The following are species which are mostly widely distributed in still waters. Unless otherwise stated, the plants will grow in any site with a medium or rich nutrient status, medium to fine substrate, moderate to high pH. Most lowland farm ponds will fall into this category, but only introduce those which you know to occur locally.

All submerged plants and most floating and marginal species are used by a variety of invertebrates and may be assumed to be of general value. Only those which are known to be particularly favoured are indicated as such.

SPECIES	REQUIREMENTS AND WILDLIFE VALUE
Submerged plants	
Stoneworts	Good invertebrate habitat. Main food of pochard. Mostly in clear, lime-rich water.
Water crowfoots	According to species, fast-flowing rivers to ponds and ditches. Some have floating leaves. Seeds used by wildfowl.
Rigid hornwort	Unrooted. Tolerant of nutrient-rich waters. Good invertebrate habitat but can smother other aquatic plants.
Spiked water-milfoil	Favours lime-rich waters. Excellent invertebrate habitat.
Canadian/Nuttall's waterweed	Introduced but widely naturalised. Excellent invertebrate habitat.
Broad-leaved pondweed	Rivers and drains. Good seed production.
Shining pondweed	Often in lime-rich waters. Seeds eaten by wildfowl.
Perfoliate pondweed	Seeds eaten by wildfowl.
Curled pondweed	Seeds eaten by wildfowl.
Fennel pondweed	Tolerates brackish, polluted and turbid water to some degree. Seeds and tubers eaten by wildfowl.
Horned pondweed	Seeds eaten by wildfowl.
Floating leaved plants	
Water violet	Ditches.
White water lily	Rivers and lakes. Good for water scorpions, some snails and dragonflies. Good duckling foraging habitat.
Yellow water lily	Rivers and lakes. Good for water scorpions, some snails and dragonflies. Good duckling foraging habitat.
Amphibious bistort	Also on damp ground. Good invertebrate habitat. Good seed production taken by wildfowl. Good duckling foraging habitat.
Frogbit	Free-floating. Unpolluted ditches. Local. Overwintering buds eaten by wildfowl.
Duckweeds	Free-floating. Plants eaten by wildfowl.
Water starwort	Good invertebrate habitat.

Table 9.1: Wetland plants, their requirements and attributes (cont'd)

SPECIES	REQUIREMENTS AND WILDLIFE VALUE
Emergent/marginal plants	
Marsh marigold	Damp ground.
Watercress	Favours calcareous water.
Bogbean	Acid waters and peat.
Great yellow-cress	Swamps.
Fool's watercress	Favours calcareous waters.
Great water dock	Wet margins. Seeds eaten by wildfowl.
Common club-rush	Pools and rivers. Seeds eaten by wildfowl.
Water forget-me-not	Damp ground.
Brooklime	Damp ground and shallows.
Water mint	Damp ground and shallows. Good nectar plant.
Marsh woundwort	Damp ground.
Water-plantain	Shallows, margins of ponds and ditches.
Arrowhead	Rivers and drains. Brood foraging habitat.
Flowering rush	Damp ground and shallows.
Rushes	Damp ground. Seeds eaten by wildfowl.
Yellow flag	Damp ground.
Erect bur-reed	Ditches and margins of rivers. Good invertebrate habitat and seeds eaten by wildfowl.
Bulrush	Swamps and open water to 1.5 m depth. Winter cover for wildfowl but very invasive.
Common spike-rush	Damp ground. Very good seed producer. Used by duckling broods. Benefits from some cattle grazing.
Sedges, eg greater pond sedge	Damp ground and water's edge. Very good seed producers. Nesting cover for wildfowl.
Reed	To 1.5 m water depth. Ungrazed areas with high water levels. Readily grazed by cattle. Prime habitat of reed warbler. Winter cover for wildfowl.
Reed sweet-grass	Areas subject to frequent flooding. Highly invasive and limited value. Favoured grazing by cattle.
Reed canary-grass	Mostly ungrazed/partly grazed wet fields.
Purple loosestrife	Damp ground and water margins. Good butterfly plant.
Meadowsweet	Damp ground.
Great willowherb	Damp ground when ungrazed.
Water figwort	Damp ground. Good nectar and seed producer.
Mare's-tail	To 1 m depth. Good invertebrate habitat. Seeds eaten by wildfowl. Cover for duckling broods.

Information on the wildlife value of plants is largely derived from Street, M 1989. *Ponds and lakes for wildfowl*. Game Conservancy.

nutrients affect wetland plants. Some free-floating algae respond very rapidly to high phosphate levels, becoming so abundant that the water appears brown or green in colour and light penetration is reduced. This affects other submerged water plants by reducing the depth at which they can grow and restricting their growth rates and size. In most lowland waters, this effect is normal, with little growth below 2 m. In extreme cases, algae become superabundant and the resulting 'bloom' can lead to the death of all macrophytes except those with floating leaves. If this occurs, the ensuing decomposition may deplete the amount of dissolved oxygen in the water to such an extent that invertebrates and fish are killed. The same thing happens with any accidental release of large volumes of decomposing organic material, including slurry.

1.4 Water depth, fluctuation and flow

- Water less than 1 m deep is the most productive zone because light and warmth are greatest. Aquatic plants only grow where light penetration is adequate.
- Natural seasonal fluctuations in waterlevels, including floods, are valuable.
- Amphibians and some invertebrates thrive best in ponds that dry out entirely every few years as this kills their predators.
- Flowing waters contain some wildlife that does not occur in standing waters.

Water depth controls the penetration of light and heat. Light is particularly important for plant growth. In lowland waters with normal algal populations, little plant growth extends below 2 m and even in the clearest lakes few plants grow in water deeper than 6 m. Where the water's nutrient status is elevated by fertiliser run-off, for instance, and algae are abundant, macrophytes may be confined to 1 m or less.

Most plants and animals grow faster at higher temperatures. Aquatic insects complete their larval stages more rapidly in water where sunlight penetration is good.

Similarly, the tadpoles of amphibians develop faster. Other things being equal, shallow standing water is warmer than deep or running water and so it is more productive, supporting more plants and animals. This is reflected in the adaptations and feeding habits of birds. Waders like redshank are confined to depths of less than 20 cm and dabbling ducks such as mallard to the top 35 cm even when they upend. However, diving birds like the tufted duck are able to feed in depths of 5 m though they prefer rather shallower water (Table 9.2: Wildfowl feeding requirements).

Water levels fluctuate with the seasons and these changes are important for wildlife in both standing and flowing waters. The fall in level that occurs in summer exposes bare ground where plants like celery-leaved buttercup can germinate and grow without competition. When levels rise in autumn, their seeds are an important food for ducks such as teal. In farm ponds, the drop in summer levels also means lighter, warmer conditions so that aquatic plants grow better and invertebrates and amphibians also benefit.

Some ponds may dry out occasionally in dry summers. However, this is not necessarily harmful. Some water snails and dragonfly larvae can survive these conditions but fish, which prey on them, cannot, so when the site is refilled, they can complete their development and breed successfully. Frogs and newts tend to do best in ponds that dry out every few years. Although they may fail to produce young in those years, they do well in the next few seasons before predators have recolonised. A few invertebrates, such as the fairy shrimp, survive only in ponds that dry out every summer. They are now rare because such sites have either been completely drained or made into permanent ponds.

Running water contains many species that do not occur in standing water. Some aquatic insects need the high levels of dissolved oxygen found in turbulent streams, or feed by waiting for the flow to carry food to them. Several dragonflies, including the banded agrion and the white-legged damselfly breed mainly in flowing water. Some fish, including the grayling,

Table 9.2: Wildfowl feeding requirements

SPECIES	SEASON	ADULT DIET				WATER DEPTH (M)	DUCKLING DIET
		AQUATIC PLANTS	MARGINAL PLANTS	SEEDS	INVERT-EBRATES		
Mute swan	all year	+++++	+++++			1	probably invertebrates
Wigeon	winter	+++	+++++++			–	
Gadwall	summer	++++	++++	+	+	0.35	invertebrates
	winter	+++++	+++++				
Teal	summer	+	+		++++++++	0.2	invertebrates
	winter	+	+	+++++++	+		
Mallard	summer	+		++++	+++++	0.35	invertebrates
	winter	+	+++	++++	++		
Shoveler	summer			+	+++++++++	0.3	invertebrates
	winter	++		++	++++++		
Pochard	summer	++			++++++++	to 2.5 but can dive deeper	invertebrates
	winter	++++++	+		+++		
Tufted duck	summer			+++	+++++++	usually <5m rarely >7m	invertebrates
	winter			++++	++++++		

Key: + = approx 10% of diet

live only in clear, well-oxygenated rivers with strong currents. The populations of several bird species are largely dependent on rivers. They include the kingfisher, sand martin, dipper, common sandpiper and goosander.

1.5 Shoreline hydrology and structure

- The damp ground zone at the margin of open water is a distinct habitat.
- Small variations in wetness are significant to wildlife.
- The zone is an important feeding habitat for wildfowl and waders.
- Vertical earth banks are used as breeding sites by kingfishers and other wildlife.

Damp ground at the margins of standing and flowing water is a very important habitat. Where the surface is bare, due to flooding or trampling by livestock, a remarkable variety of invertebrates can occur. The larvae of several species of flies live in soft mud with a high organic content and the adults form dense swarms on the surface. Slightly higher up the margin, the mud may be drier, firmer and less organic; it will support flies of several other species, and burrowing beetles can also be present. The soil conditions are also ideal for some species of earthworms. Predatory and scavenging beetles roam over the open surface.

Because of the abundance of invertebrates, these areas are excellent feeding grounds for birds. Ducks sieve the softest muds, wagtails run over the surface to take flies, and waders such as snipe and probe for worms and larvae. The open conditions are also required by some species of chaser dragonflies, which perch on bare ground from which they can see possible prey, or potential mates, and take off instantly in pursuit.

Usually, livestock access to margins is beneficial. Cattle in particular graze some of the most invasive plants such as reed sweet-grass and reed canary-grass, preventing them becoming too dominant and allowing other plants to grow, while their poaching creates muddy margins good for feeding birds such as snipe and woodcock. However, heavy, sustained grazing pressure will destroy much cover and remove bird breeding sites.

On large waters, the character of the shoreline may be affected by wave action. Shores which are wave-beaten will be rocky or clothed in shingle or sandy beaches. Unvegetated shingle is a hot, sunlit habitat with abundant crevices where invertebrates can shelter. Higher up the shore, where the shingle is stabilised and sparsely vegetated, a different insect and spider fauna lives. Especially in the north and west of the UK where summer temperatures are low and rainfall is high, these free-draining, unshaded and rapidly-warming habitats are of particular value. The shores are also the main feeding areas for common sandpipers, and in some regions ringed plovers and oystercatchers may nest. Only the most sheltered bays can accumulate finer, more organic sediments where plants can grow. Such bays provide feeding areas for dabbling ducks. such as teal and mallard. and breeding habitat for waders.

Different species of fish and birds have developed particular adaptations to feed in the specialised conditions. For example, the shoveler's beak is designed to sieve invertebrates and plant seeds from soft sediments and the dipper takes invertebrates only from watercourses with stony or rocky beds.

Where erosion by wave action or current creates steep or vertical unvegetated banks, these too have considerable interest. Solitary bees and wasps can burrow into the face to create breeding sites. These species live by hunting or parasitising other insects, including many kinds of caterpillar. Nesting burrows are also excavated by sand martins and kingfishers, which find reasonable protection from predators such as rats and weasels where the face falls sheer to the water.

1.6 Grassland hydrology and flooding regimes

- Grassland which floods in winter and has a high watertable in spring and early summer has great value for plants and birds.
- Water depth influences the bird species able to utilise flooded grassland.
- The types of breeding birds and plants found on wet grassland are influenced by soil watertable levels and vegetation management.

Farmland that floods in winter immediately attracts birds to feed. The range and abundance of food resources are likely to be greater on flooded grassland than on arable, and richest of all on unimproved grassland because of the wider variety of plants and invertebrates which live in it.

Winter floods of less than two to three weeks' duration probably have little effect on grassland composition or on invertebrate populations. Longer floods may alter the composition of the earthworm fauna, because some species are more tolerant than others of the anaerobic conditions that develop in the soil. Floods that last into the growing season can cause the death of grasses and some other plants, leaving bare ground and the probability of a weed-control problem to come but where such floods are annual and there is a high watertable in summer the sward will consist of tolerant species such as marsh foxtail.

If flooding is shallow and short-lived, gulls may be the main beneficiaries, taking worms, beetles and other invertebrates washed out of the vegetation and the soil surface. If flooding persists, wildfowl numbers usually build up, exploiting plant seeds as well as invertebrates. Depending on water depth (Table 9.2), they may be mostly dabbling species, upending to work over the waterlogged ground surface itself, or diving duck. From the point of view of birds, late-winter floods are probably of the greatest value. By this time of year, food resources in other wetlands have been greatly depleted and females are in need of a high protein intake to prepare them for breeding.

Grassland that still has a high watertable in spring and early summer can hold breeding waders, most likely lapwing, snipe and redshank. For them to breed successfully, three factors are of great importance. First, sward heights must be suitable – lapwings need open conditions but redshanks and snipe seek cover about 25–30 cm tall for their nests. The intensity of autumn and early spring grazing will determine this. Second, exclusion of livestock in spring and early summer is required to avoid nest losses due to trampling. The traditional use of these areas for hay production with aftermath grazing is ideal. Management of this type of habitat by mowing and grazing is discussed in Chapter 3 page 71. Third, the level of the watertable and the condition of ponds and ditches will determine whether birds and their young can obtain enough food.

1.7 Wetland trees and shrubs

- Trees and shrubs support a diverse invertebrate fauna, which provides other wildlife with a valuable food resource.
- Shading by trees reduces the growth of marginal and submerged plants.
- Tree roots resist bank erosion.
- Trees can give shelter from wind which causes waves, uproots plants and erodes shores. Wind also chills water and disrupts the activities of animals and birds.
- Shrubs can provide ponds with excellent shelter from wind and spray-drift.

Trees and shrubs rapidly colonise banksides and some species will spread right across areas of wet ground including reedbeds and meadows if they are not managed. Their effects need careful evaluation as they have both benefits and disadvantages.

All native trees and shrubs support particular groups of invertebrates (see page 187). Willows support an exceptionally large invertebrate fauna. A total of around 450 different species are known to feed on them, including over 160 kinds of moths. Poplars have 189 known species of invertebrates and alder 141. Of course, on any one farm, the total will be less than this, depending on its location in the UK and on the age and condition of the trees, but they are always an important habitat.

Many insects have complex life cycles which require both water and trees. Some lay their eggs in overhanging foliage and, on hatching, the larvae drop into the water to develop. Some spend the whole larval stage on exposed tree roots below water and others use submerged limbs. A few species have larvae which leave the water to pupate in crevices in the bark of nearby trees. Sponge flies, whose larvae feed on freshwater sponges, spend their adult stages in the treetops.

Because they support so many insects, trees are a very significant source of food for other wetland wildlife. Many of the insects fall or get blown into water and are taken by fish. Birds glean through the foliage or catch insects in flight. In upland regions, it is the riverside trees that first provide good feeding conditions for migrant birds such as warblers when they arrive in spring and it may be another fortnight before conditions in the hillside woods become suitable for them.

Grey wagtails breed most successfully where the banks are tree-lined, not only because insects are abundant but also because it is easier to catch them in the sheltered air between the two lines of trees. Some aquatic insects also benefit from the shelter. They include those which fly weakly, like mayflies, and those which hunt them, especially dragonflies.

Trees can be important for otters, which find good holt sites in cavities washed out amongst the roots (Feature 9.1). Because they have very fibrous root systems, willows and alder do not produce good holt cavities but oak, ash and sycamore are often used. Root systems are also important because they resist erosion. Tree-lined watercourses are narrower and more stable than ones where the trees have been removed.

Where there is no bankside cover, due to grazing for instance, tree branches that dip into the water may be used by moorhens, coots or grebes as nest anchorages. Though they are not hidden, they are difficult for some predators to reach.

Leaf-litter from broadleaved trees provides an input of organic material, which helps feed many invertebrates that are in turn consumed by fish and other wildlife. However, in small ponds or streams, prolific leaf litter may form a layer on the bed, which decomposes only slowly and inhibits submerged plant growth. This is more likely with conifer needles and with large-leaved hybrid poplars than with leaves of trees such as ash and willows. Deoxygenation, which can harm fish, may also occur.

Where trees shade the water, they can reduce or even prevent the growth of marginal and submerged plants. On some chalk rivers where growth of submerged plants is so prolific that it impedes the flow of water and may affect land drainage, shading is beneficial as it obviates the need to cut and remove the weed. On the other hand, the suppression of marginal plants removes nest sites for grebes and several other waterfowl species. Shading of a small pond may greatly reduce its productivity and make it too cold to support amphibians and many kinds of insects and fish.

Trees can provide waterbodies with shelter from wind and this is beneficial to wildlife. Wind affects waterbodies in several ways. Most importantly, it generates waves, the size of which is a function of the downwind extent (fetch) of the waterbody and the speed of the wind. In shallow waters, waves may interact with the bed so that mobile sediments are stirred up and submerged plants may be uprooted. Waves erode soft shores, for instance in gravel pits, and may uproot emergent plants. Many upland lakes have rocky shores almost devoid of plants because of their exposure to waves.

Wind also affects temperature, cooling the water. It affects animals directly by chilling. This is most important for some wetland invertebrates. Thus, damselflies are almost completely inactive in cool conditions and their breeding success may be affected by prolonged cold wind. Even well-insulated creatures like ducks will have to expend more energy maintaining core body warmth in exposed sites. Wind also seriously disrupts the activities of flying insects, simply because it can prevent them from flying.

Where a pond or the shoreline of a larger water is screened by shrubs and trees which do not shade it, the combination of wind-shelter and sunlight creates very favourable conditions for wildlife. If the adjoining land is in arable, the shrubs will also give protection against pesticide spray-drift.

2. Options and assessment: planning management

2.1 Wildlife assessment of waterbodies and other wetlands

- All farmers have a clear picture of the drainage needs and problems of their land. This can provide the basis for identifying and assessing the wildlife value or potential of wetlands.
- Wetland assessment is mainly based on readily-observed hydrological factors.
- Information on species may be obtained from the conservation bodies.
- Because wetland management may affect farm operations, it is best considered in the context of a farm wildife plan which will take full account of the implications.

Since land drainage is such an important influence on farming operations, every farmer will have a very clear knowledge of the seasonal changes in soil watertable, of incidents of flooding and of the standards to which watercourses are managed. This provides an ideal basis on which to identify not only areas that retain wildlife value but those where re-creation of valuable habitats would be practicable.

The principles of wildlife habitat evaluation are described in Chapter 1. With wetlands, much can be deduced from the hydrology of the area, such as water depth, the wetness of ground, the frequency and duration of flooding. The importance of these factors is described in section 1 of this chapter. Other readily-assessed factors such as the degree of shading or exposure to wind and evidence of algal blooms due to artificially high nutrient levels are also straightforward to record. Detailed surveys of plants and other wildlife are not essential but, because wetlands have attracted a great deal of attention from the wildlife conservation bodies, it is worth an approach to them as they may have

information, especially on the presence of scarce species.

The complete list of information to be recorded is given at Table 9.3. If it is possible that grant-aid will be sought, ensure that the information collected also meets the needs of the relevant grant scheme.

Some aspects of wetland management may impinge directly on the management of the farm. For instance, any change in the frequency of ditch management, the grazing of a hill bog or the penning levels for a riverside meadow will have both financial and practical implications. To ensure that these are taken into account properly, it may be considered worthwhile to prepare a farm wildlife plan using the format given in Chapter 1 page 10.

2.2 Management needs and opportunities

- Almost all farms have potential to improve or create wetlands.
- Reduction of over-enrichment is a need with most waters, especially in the lowlands.
- Manage neglected ponds to let in light and protect from spray-drift.
- Most farm ditches can be enhanced for wildlife.
- Continue low-intensity grazing on marshes and bogs but regulate its timing.
- Maintain hay meadows with a high watertable in spring and early summer.
- Create new wetlands on land taken out of production.

Almost all farms still contain wetland habitats and without exception there is potential to improve or create them. Although the range of habitats is enormous, from Fenland reedbeds to Highland loch shores and Ulster bogs, with countless

Table 9.3: Wildlife assessment of waterbodies and other wetlands

INFORMATION REQUIRED	METHOD	REASONS FOR INFORMATION
1. Conservation status and interest	Contact FWAG initially.	Information on the wildlife interest of wetlands may already be available. Some farm wetlands may be of high wildlife interest and may be designated as SSSI or ASSI. In this case certain conditions may need to be satisfied before any changes in management can take place.
2. Past management	Check farm records. Examine past and present aerial photographs	Can highlight loss of open water through spread of emergent plants. Will also identify increase/decrease in bankside vegetation and changes in extent of wetlands on farms.
3. Current management	Note effects of livestock through grazing and trampling.	Beneficial and essential to many wetlands particularly wet grasslands. Excessive poaching/dunging can damage ponds.
	Note run-off or discharges of sewage effluent, animal wastes, silage liquor and fertiliser.	Can kill wildlife and damage wetlands. Take necessary action to prevent further discharges and run-off.
	Note any dredging operations, including frequency and extent and disposal of spoil.	While waterbodies may need to be dredged from time to time, large-scale operations undertaken too frequently can reduce wildlife interest. Dredgings should not be placed on land of wildlife interest.
	Note bankside management operations.	May be needed from time to time to prevent overshading from trees or shrubs. However, some cover, including tall bankside plants, is beneficial.
	Note use of pesticides in and around waterbodies and wetlands.	Inappropriate use can kill plants and invertebrates. Advice should always be sought.
	Note cutting/mowing régimes of wet grassland, reedbeds and marshes, including frequency, area cut and time of cut.	May suggest review is required and modifications needed.
4. Plant composition	For waterbodies including ponds, rivers and ditches. Note percentage cover by: floating aquatic plants emergent plants algae	The richer the plant diversity the more important the wetland. If little open water in ponds or other standing waterbodies then may suggest plant clearance needed. If algae cover is extensive may identify over-enrichment as a problem.
	For marshes Note: – variety of herbs and grasses and height of vegetation. – presence and depth of litter layer. – presence and % cover scrub and trees.	The richer the plant diversity the more important the marsh. If deep then may suggest increase in intensity of management needed. Can be beneficial unless they cover a substantial area.

▶▶▶

Table 9.3: Wildlife assessment of waterbodies and other wetlands (cont'd)

INFORMATION REQUIRED	METHOD	REASONS FOR INFORMATION
	For reedbeds Note:	
	– presence and depth of litter layer.	If litter layer is deep then may need to be removed and management régime may need to be amended.
	– presence and % cover scrub and trees.	Scrub and trees can be beneficial but if they cover a substantial part of the ground, may need to be controlled.
	For wet grassland Note:	
	– presence of herbs and grasses (other than 'agricultural' species).	The richer the plant diversity the more important the grassland.
	– presence and % cover of scrub and trees.	
	– height of vegetation, litter layer and bare ground.	Will guide decisions on stocking rates.
	(Also see Chapter 3)	
	For all wetlands and waterbodies Note:	
	– Presence of non-native invasive plants such as giant hogweed, water fern.	Will identify degree of control required.
5. Water depth and levels	Note water depth and any major variations and gradients.	Water depth is a major influence on wildlife.
	Note seasonal fluctuations in water levels, especially in relation to breeding birds.	Can be both beneficial/detrimental to wildlife depending on the wetland and dependent wildlife. If fluctuations are catastrophic consider greater water control.
	Note wetness of land in reedbeds, wet grassland and marshes.	
6. Shoreline, bankside and other features of waterbodies	Note bare mud, wet shelves, shingle.	Unvegetated shingle and mud can be valuable for invertebrates.
	Note whether bank slope is gentle or steep.	Shallow-shelving waterbodies are important.
	Note presence of vertical earth banks.	Banks can be important as nest sites for sand martins and kingfishers.
	Note presence of islands, meanders, backwaters and other features.	Can be very important for wildlife and need to retain.
7. Bankside vegetation	Note occurrence of bankside trees and shrubs and tall herbage.	Important for wildlife and need to retain. However, where causing excessive overshading around, for example, small ponds, then some clearance may be needed.
8. Adjoining ground	Note land use of ground adjoining wetland.	May suggest potential for extending wetland. May identify changes in land management to reduce impact on wetland eg spray-drift.
9. Rare or sensitive species	Map location of rare species. Seek specialist guidance on species and management.	The presence and needs of these species eg otters should be built into future management.

ponds, ditches and watercourses in between, there are some widespread management needs and opportunities. Many of these can increase the sporting potential of the farm.

In the lowlands, most farm waterbodies are over-enriched due to fertiliser run-off. Measures which will reduce this range from diversion of land drains to creation of a buffer zone, perhaps in the form of permanent set-aside, or construction of a reedbed to reduce nutrient inputs. Treatment with barley straw may help prevent algal blooms.

Many farm ponds would also benefit from attention such as the selective clearance of over-shading scrub or trees so as to let in more light. On arable farms, the risk of spray-drift causing damage to plants and insects could be reduced by allowing scrub to form a screening belt set back far enough from the water to avoid shading.

Farm ditches are sometimes the only wetland habitat that remain on a farm and they can be improved for a range of wetland wildlife without interfering with their functional purpose.

Maintenance of a low-intensity grazing regime is important for several types of wetland including the margins of watercourses and waterbodies, marshes and bogs. However, timing of grazing is a key factor where ground-nesting birds are present. Unimproved grassland that has a high watertable and is managed for hay production and aftermath grazing is of exceptional value for wildlife. Continuation or restoration of the system is most desirable.

New wetlands are simple and rewarding to create as a range of common wildlife will colonise rapidly and, with correct design and aftercare, rarer species may colonise in time. There is potential on land put into long-term set-aside and other schemes.

3. Management

3.1 Plant management

- In waterbodies, the main plant management need is to prevent emergent species from taking over all shorelines and shallows.
- Low-intensity grazing or mechanical clearance are usually preferable to herbicide use.
- Aim for a mix of conditions, with some stands of emergents retained.
- Many wetland plants are good colonists of new sites or can easily be introduced from local sources.
- Never fertilise wetland plants.
- Protect new plantings from grazing by livestock and birds.
- In marshes, bogs and wet grasslands, regulate grazing pressure; do not use herbicides or artificial fertilisers.

Submerged aquatic plants should need no management. In general, the greater their abundance, the larger the invertebrate populations and the more food resources for fish and birds. There may be changes in

their extent from year to year and the dominant species may alter over time. This reflects changes in fertility and other factors and does not require a management response.

Emergent plants can be invasive and, except where currents or wave action keep them open, usually rapidly occupy shallows needed for wildfowl feeding or for breeding by amphibians. Where livestock have access, their grazing and trampling should be regulated by fencing to maintain a mix of conditions with at least half the shoreline kept open. However, except where cattle or horses have access to small ponds, stock are unlikely to be able to keep extensive areas of shallows clear so alternative methods will be required. Depending on the reach required, a hydraulic digger or dragline may be needed. Cutting is unlikely to be effective except with reeds in summer (see page 307).

Several herbicides have been developed for the control of aquatic plants. When managing for wildlife, the only types likely to be needed are those to kill invasive emergents where simultaneous desilting is not required. Some aquatic herbicides kill a wide spectrum of plants, some may be toxic to invertebrates and most can be translocated by currents and have effects outside the area of application. In small waterbodies, such as ponds, the decay of treated vegetation may cause deoxygenation of the water or algal bloom, leading to deaths of invertebrates and fish. The risk of damage is least in large waters, with very limited spot applications or the use of formulations which adhere to plants. On balance, it is safer to use manual or mechanical methods wherever possible.

If it is essential to use herbicides, identify the target plant and choose an appropriate formulation. Bear in mind that it may take some weeks for the plants to die after treatment. In England and Wales, the National Rivers Authority should be consulted before using any herbicides in water.

Whatever control method is chosen, develop a rotation based on the rate of spread and clear small adjoining sections in successive years, rather than repeatedly working the same one or 'blitzing' the site at infrequent intervals, as it will result in a good succession of conditions from freshly exposed margin to fully revegetated, each with a different wildlife community. Never clear all the vegetation at once or you will cause the loss of all the creatures which depend on it for cover or food.

A number of non-native plants that occur beside or in waterbodies are very invasive, dominating large areas and suppressing other vegetation. They may have serious effects on the whole wildlife community. They include giant hogweed, Japanese knotweed, water hyacinth and water fern. Control may be difficult and where they are present, take advice from FWAG on the best approach. Act as soon as the plants are noted. Canadian waterweed and Nuttall's waterweed are vigorous non-natives which are also invasive but as they are now very widespread and appear to be good habitat for many invertebrates, control may not be worthwhile. However, they should not be introduced to new sites.

Many wetland plants have several means of spreading and colonising new areas. Some produce seed which is wind-dispersed, like great reedmace, or floats, like bur-reed. Some have rhizomes or rooting stems, like fringed water lily, or can grow from root or stem fragments broken off by waves and currents. As a result, new wetland areas are quickly colonised by plants. Algae are always present in water. It is not, therefore, essential to introduce plants to a new wetland or to enhance an existing site. However, it can be beneficial especially if species that have particular value are chosen, such as those most favoured by invertebrates or birds. Only introduce plants that are native to the locality (see Chapter 1 page 8).

It is usually easy to obtain common plants from river dredging operations, bodies that are managing wetlands for conservation, or simply by taking material, with the owner's consent, from a nearby site. The commoner wetland plants are most useful because they support the greatest variety of other wildlife. Plants can be purchased and this is the best course for uncommon species or very large quantities. Deal only with suppliers whose stock is of UK origin. A list of the commoner wetland plants, their growth requirements and value for wildlife is at Table 9.1.

Most wetland plants can be easily introduced. The work is best done in winter or early spring when they are not growing. Emergent or marginal plants can be cut back if necessary, lifted from the donor site with a spade or digger bucket and relocated in appropriate conditions. Emergents can simply be located at the water's edge and will rapidly spread down to their maximum growing depth (but for reeds see page 307). Initially, they may need anchorage with stakes driven through the root clump or stones to weigh them down. Once established, emergents can give reasonable protection to shores exposed to wave action and so prevent erosion but in such areas they will need initial protection by a timber boom or a reef of stone until the roots are well into the bed.

Aquatic plants can be tied into hand-sized bunches, attached to a weight and dropped into the water. Lilies need a good section of budded rhizome to get started.

Put the plants in groups of one species and do not put small, slow-growing emergents next to fast-spreading species or they will be rapidly overwhelmed. Think twice before introducing the most vigorous species because they can dominate a water and suppress slower-growing plants. On the other hand, if the water is enriched with nutrients, it may be appropriate to introduce rapidly growing plants, which will utilise the nutrients and can reduce algal blooms more quickly.

Never apply fertiliser to wetland systems. The greatest variety of plants will develop where fertility is low to moderate. For this reason, do not put topsoil on the bed of a new pond. Where fertility is high, the site will become dominated by a few very vigorous species only. In standing waters, fertilisers may induce algal blooms which result in the death of other plants, fish and invertebrates.

New plants will need protection from grazing animals - not only livestock but swans, geese and coot may eat and uproot them so that wire-netting enclosures may be necessary.

Aim to achieve a balance, with areas of open water containing submerged plants, some shallows without vegetation, fringes or beds of emergents and stands of marginal plants plus some tree cover (see page 310). It will require management to prevent the emergents occupying all the shallows and, in turn, willows and other trees replacing the marginal and emergent plants.

3.2 Water quality

- Minimise nutrient inputs to farm wetlands.
- Prevent escape of slurry, silage liquors and polluted drainage from buildings and yards.
- Take advice on nutrient reduction by using beds of emergent plants or buffer zones, including permanent set-aside.
- Reduce algal blooms by treatment with barley straw.
- Dredge out enriched sediments from waterbodies.
- In peatlands and coastal sites, carry out soil and groundwater surveys before land drainage, to avoid acidification, saline intrusion and other problems.

Look at all wetlands on the farm to assess whether they are suffering from or at risk of nutrient enrichment. Ditches, ponds or other waterbodies where the water is pea green in the summer months, full of blanket-weed or covered by a mat of floating duckweed are seriously over-enriched. Identify the likely cause and consider remedial action. If it is due to the escape of slurry or silage liquors, or polluted water drainage from buildings and yards, it will be necessary to improve containment. This must be carried out in accordance with the Control of Pollution Regulations 1991. Guidance can be sought from the NRA or equivalent body.

The most usual cause of over-enrichment is simply fertiliser run-off. MAFF guidelines in the Code of Good Agricultural Practice for the Protection of Water should be followed to reduce this and ensure maximum uptake by the crop.

In ditches and drains carrying drainage from fertilised fields it is not possible to solve the problem of nutrient enrichment. The best that can be done is to ensure that there is no direct input due to careless application on the field. Ideally, the solution would be to select stretches at the top end of the farm's drainage system and put the adjoining fields into permanent set-aside or any other scheme which funds the creation of habitats where fertilisers will not be used, such as unimproved grassland, woodland or heath. Such areas will also be ideal for the creation of ponds and other wetlands.

Ponds may sometimes be affected by lack of care in applying artificial fertilisers to adjoining land and it may be wise to put up guide posts to keep drivers away from the margin. Creation of a buffer zone at least 5 m wide where no nutrients are applied may assist in reducing nutrient inputs as a result of surface run-off. However, many ponds were designed to receive field drainage and it may be impossible to isolate them without diverting ditches or underdrainage.

If this is impracticable, consider the possible benefits of establishing a bed of emergent plants such as reed or reedmace on the inflow as this will take up some of the nutrients in the summer months while the plants are growing. However, the bed will release nutrients during the winter so the method is probably only likely to be successful where winter flows are high and will flush through the pond. The process is still experimental and the size of the bed will depend on the nutrient status of the inflow, its volume, the soil type and the vigour of reed growth. No harm will come from creating a reedbed on ground adjoining a polluted pond and passing the inflow through it, and it will benefit wildlife, but it may not much improve water quality unless it is properly designed. Take specialist advice (see Appendix I) before embarking on anything costly.

If nutrients cannot be kept out of the water, it may be possible to counter their effects. Decomposing barley straw in water may inhibit algal growth and so reduce or prevent blooms. The amount required is small – 10 g/m^3 of water volume. The better the water circulation through the straw, the better the effect, but as loose dry straw may drift ashore before it sinks, either net it loosely or soak it first. If whole bales are used, they will be easy to anchor but the application rate should be at least doubled as only the outer layer is likely to be effective. The straw does not start to take effect for about a month and needs to be replenished every six months. As it appears

to inhibit the onset of algal blooms but not to clear them once they start, the best application times are early spring and autumn. Macrophytes are unaffected. There is evidence of increased invertebrate production, benefiting fish and birds. Barley straw appears to be more effective than wheat straw or hay.

If a small waterbody has become so enriched that it has lost most or all of its submerged plants and their dependent wildlife, the only solution may be to dredge or pump out the bottom sediments during the winter months. At this season most of the phosphate will be in the mud and, though the disturbance of the sediments will cause some release of nutrients, much will be removed, and macrophytes should recover progressively over two or three years provided further enrichment is prevented.

In peats, installation of land drainage can lead to acidification of waters in ditches or the release of iron oxides. In coastal areas where fresh water overlies saline groundwater, the deepening of ditches may permit it to enter them. All these effects are catastrophic for the existing wildlife. They may be identified as potential problems by proper survey of soils and groundwater so that an informed judgement can be made.

3.3 Ponds

- Do not top up ponds that dry out in summer.
- Ideally, manage emergent and marginal plants by controlled grazing and trampling to maintain open water and some bare mud at the edge.
- Where stock do not control it, prevent take-over by emergent vegetation by clearing up to one-third of the pond each year.
- In neglected ponds, remove any substantial layer of silt or rotting vegetation to expose the bed.
- Clear overshading trees and scrub. Retain such cover on the north side.
- Provide cover, wind shelter and, if necessary, protection from agrochemicals with a buffer zone of shrubs set back from the water's edge.
- Do not introduce fish if you want frogs, newts or dragonflies.
- Pond creation is worthwhile but should not destroy sites with existing value such as marshland.
- Select a site with a good-quality water supply.
- If the substrate is permeable, use a liner.
- Create gently shelving margins and a maximum depth of 2 m or less.
- Introduce locally-native plants if desired.

Farm ponds are usually shallow and so they warm up quickly in spring. Levels fall through the summer. If they dry out, they should not be artificially topped up as some wildlife benefits from this. When in use, they are rarely shaded and stock trampling keeps the margins open. They are excellent for frogs and newts but sometimes too shallow for toads (Feature 9.3: Amphibians). They often hold thriving dragonfly populations. Though ponds are visited by feeding mallard and sometimes teal, wildfowl rarely breed successfully because there is often insufficient food for the growing duckling broods. However, many ponds have breeding moorhens. Snipe and other waders may visit the margins to feed.

Ponds which are not used by stock require periodic maintenance to ensure they do not fill up with accumulating plant debris and get taken over by emergent vegetation. Very small ponds may be cleared manually but in most cases a mechanical excavator or even a dragline will be needed and should remove accumulated silt and leaf litter. Many ponds have a puddled clay bed which may be protected with a layer of stone. Extreme care should be taken not to damage this.

Never clear the whole pond at once, no matter how overgrown and silted it may be, or you will cause the loss of some species. At most clear two-thirds and do the rest after a lapse of two or more years. Thereafter emergent vegetation should be managed by clearing no more than one-third of the pond in any one year. Do not dump spoil on areas with wildlife value.

Livestock access to pond margins can be beneficial. Trampling by cattle or horses breaks up areas of dominant plants such as reed sweet-grass, creating areas for annuals and other short-lived plants to grow. Trampled margins also provide good feeding areas for wading birds including redshank and snipe. However, heavy grazing pressure will destroy too much plant cover and, as tall cover is also beneficial, access should be restricted by fencing to one side only.

On arable farms, leave a zone at least 5 m wide between the pond and the cropped area for the development of an outer screen of scrub with tall herbage between it and the water. The zone will also help protect the pond from the effects of agrochemicals including fertiliser run-off and those insecticides that are toxic to aquatic invertebrates. It will also provide cover and hibernating habitat for amphibians, nesting cover for moorhens or other waterbirds such as sedge warbler and hunting habitat for dragonflies.

Clear overshading trees and scrub from the south side but if there are several ponds on the farm, allow one to be shaded as some invertebrates require these conditions.

Do not introduce fish to a small pond because they will eat many of the aquatic invertebrates, prevent some amphibians from breeding and compete with waterfowl for food.

Pond creation offers the opportunity to increase wildlife diversity on farms. Take account of four factors in deciding on the site. Do not place the pond on ground with existing wildlife value, especially not on marshy ground as this is likely to have more wildlife value than the pond itself. However, a site adjacent to an existing marsh or other wildlife habitat such as unimproved grassland or woodland will be ideal. If the site is adjacent to improved pasture or arable or does not adjoin an existing habitat such as moorland, plan to give the pond a belt of tall herbage and scrub at least 5 m wide as described above.

It is essential to know whether your site will hold water. If there is any doubt, dig a trial pit. If there is no naturally impermeable site, consider using a butyl or polythene liner or traditional puddled clay. Liners must be laid over a smooth bed of stone-free sand and fully covered by soil. They can be punctured by the hooves of stock or by machinery and so the manufacturer's advice should be followed where these forms of management will be applied.

If possible, use a water supply least affected by nutrients such as fertiliser run-off (see page 273). It may be possible to site the pond on land to be put into long-term set-aside so that this problem will not arise. Otherwise, consider diverting a good-quality supply or passing it through a small reedbed. If none of these options is possible, go ahead anyway because the pond will at least support marginal and emergent plants and their dependent invertebrates.

The amount of water supply does not have to maintain the pond brim full all year. Ponds that dry out in summer are valuable for some wildlife and can provide good feeding for mallard and teal in winter. Figure 9.1 illustrates many of the main features that can be included in a wildlife pond.

If the pond will be less than 10 m across, have it sloping to a depth of no more than 1.5 m as any greater depth will mean that the bed slopes so steeply that the area of

shallow water is too small. This will mean that the whole bed may be invaded by emergent plants but it will be within reach of the arm of a mechanical excavator. If the pond is over 10 m across, make the centre 2 m deep so that emergent plants cannot colonise but submerged plants can grow - provided that the water quality and hence the light penetration are good. Introduce plants if desired (see page 284). Fish may colonise naturally in time but introduction is not recommended.

3.4 Natural waterbodies, gravel pits and fishing lakes

- In general, shorelines of large natural waterbodies need little management.
- Prevent excessive grazing pressure on banks.
- In new sites, maximise the extent of shallows and create bays and spits.
- Plant trees and shrubs to provide wind shelter but do not shade the south bank or shallows.
- Construct islands or install rafts for nesting birds.
- Where there are livestock, give them controlled access to some shorelines.
- Create other habitats adjoining the water, such as marshland.
- On waters used for fishing, consider applying an extended close season to avoid disturbance to breeding or wintering birds.

Usually, larger waters, because they are more likely to offer a greater variety of habitats, support a greater variety of wildlife than small sites. They provide more feeding opportunities for birds and, as a consequence of both diversity and size, many larger waters are extremely important as wintering or breeding grounds for waterfowl. Large numbers of birds may be present, including rare species. Some sites, including gravel pits, are valuable fisheries.

The shorelines of larger natural waterbodies need little if any management. Where there are livestock, they should have controlled access to the banks. A good arrangement would be to fence off half completely so that tall cover can develop and allow access at all times to the rest. If grazing pressure is

Figure 9.1 Pond restoration and design

(i) Restoration of a neglected pond

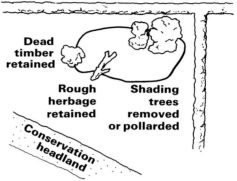

Before

After

Hedge trimmed alternate years/sides

Dead timber retained

Arable

Rough herbage retained

Shading trees removed or pollarded

Conservation headland

Arable

(ii) Pond design

(a) Depth 1–1.5 m. Emergent plants can colonise whole bed, so requires frequent management.

Keep about 1/3 emergents, 2/3 mix of open water, bare shallows, recolonised emergents, submerged plants.

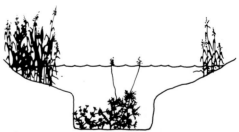

(b) 1.5–2 m deep
Depth of centre dredged to more than 1.5 m. Emergent plants cannot colonise. Management need reduced.

Continue to manage shallows to maintain about 50% open margins.

heavy and cannot be reduced, at least fence off some patches 10 x 10 m or more in size to allow cover to develop.

Do not allow dense tree cover to shade shallows or prevent the growth of stands of tall herbage close to the water, but well-spaced trees will be valuable for invertebrates and thus contribute to the food resources of the site.

If necessary, manage marginal and emergent plants to maintain diversity and keep areas of bare mud and, especially, open shallows.

If shingle is excavated from a lake shore to build tracks or make concrete, do not excavate the whole extent of any stable shingle beds but try to keep patches at all stages of stabilisation and plant colonisation.

Large new sites such as gravel pits and fishing lakes usually offer great opportunities for conservation and for carefully integrating the needs of wildlife with recreational uses. It is wise to take specialist advice at the outset, so that a suitable restoration plan can be agreed and form part of the planning application.

If possible site the new waterbody close to but not on good existing wildlife habitats. As a rule of thumb, for greatest wildlife benefit have about a third of the bed shelving gently to about 1 m deep and the rest to a maximum depth of 2 m. Often gravel pits will be worked much deeper than this so use all available overburden or inert spoil to produce the biggest possible area of shallows less than 1 m deep and let them shelve steeply into the deep water. If there is very little material with which to make shallows, a convoluted shore-line will increase the extent of margins in which emergent plants can grow.

If the site is big enough, create sheltered bays. This will be good for wildlife – for instance, it enables wildfowl to establish more territories than on an open shore. If the water is to be used as a fishery, build up the spits between bays or plant them with shrubs so that some areas can be protected from disturbance while others are in use.

Even on small sites, create sheltered water with tree shelterbelts. Shelterbelts usefully reduce wind energy for about 20 times their height downwind. They should be sited to intercept the prevailing wind and set back at least 25 m from the water's edge to avoid shading the shallows; the sunlit, sheltered conditions this creates will be ideal for a very wide range of wildlife including creating good rearing areas for ducklings. See also Chapter 7 page 211 for more information on shelterbelts.

Closer to the water, plant some blocks of low shrubs to provide more shelter and cover along the shoreline without shading out plants in the water. Aim for a mix of roughly equal proportions of shrub cover, tall herbage and shorter swards around the water. Cut one-third of the tall herbage each year to prevent scrub spreading into it and leave the rest as cover for invertebrates, amphibians and nesting wildfowl. Sow the short sward area with a wildflower mix and manage by mowing or grazing (see page 76).

On large waters where tree shelter will be inadequate to control wave action and serious erosion, install reefs of rock, or timber booms in shallow water a few yards

offshore so that organic sediments can accumulate in bays or lagoons. Reefs are better as they are a habitat in their own right; plants can grow on them and the rocks and plants both provide cover for fish and invertebrates. Booms are relatively short-lived and have no particular value as habitats. Take account of the value of wave-swept beaches with shingle and do not alter the regime where good examples exist.

Create and manage islands to provide the best conditions for breeding waterfowl. If there are no islands, artificial rafts may provide an alternative (Figure 9.5).

Spoil from the excavation can be banked up and sufficiently compacted to form a steep face suitable for nesting by sand martins and kingfishers (Figure 9.2). Other habitats such as a stand of reeds (Figure 9.7) or a marshy area may be combined with the waterbody.

Fishery management will have some detrimental effects on other wildlife. Waters that are heavily stocked are unlikely to be good for invertebrates or for breeding wildfowl. Disturbance may also be a problem but this can be reduced by good site design and by applying a close season from the end of February until mid-July. This is longer than the normal close-season for coarse fishing but takes account of the needs of birds that nest early, such as mallard, and those which nest late, such as reed warblers. For wintering wildfowl, close the fishery at least from mid-December to the end of January.

Figure 9.2 Artificial cliff and bank creation

Kingfisher nests are invariably within 50 cm of the top of a bank, and anything from 75 cm to 2 m above normal water level. The birds excavate a tunnel up to 1.5 m long. Exposed tree roots or overhanging branches nearby are important as perches when excavating, bringing food to young, or as fishing posts.

Sand martins, which are summer visitors, breed colonially in tunnels which they excavate in sandy, dry, vertical banks, suitable sites being used for years. New tunnels will be dug as the cliff collapses, or as the old holes become too big (when they may be taken over by sparrows or starlings).

(a) When creating a bank the face must be vertical and rise at least 1.5 m above normal water level. It should be as long as possible, ideally over 5 m. Wooden stakes, boulders or gabions may be used to protect the toe of the cliff, but if erosion is prevented the bank may become unsuitable. Both species normally use actively eroding banks. If the banks stabilise they may weather and form a resistant crust, after which the bank will be abandoned; or they may slump, allowing predators to get to the nest, or simply become overgrown.

(b) If the banks are less than 1.5 m above low water, or the substrate is stony or liable to slumping, then stoneless spoil may be brought in, packed behind shuttering, finished with turf or re-seeded, trees or shrubs planted and the area stock fenced if necessary. It should be left at least a year to settle, and the shuttering removed in early March before kingfishers and sand martins start prospecting for a nest site.

(c) Banks have been made for sand martins using a weak or dry concrete mix around clay or polythene pipes. If this option is chosen, the bank must be vertical with water at its foot, with pipes of at least 6 cm internal diameter set in rows 0.3 m apart with the pipes at 0.2 m spacing, and the bottom row at least 1 m above summer waterlevel. The pipes should be no more than 1 m long, sloping very slightly up into the bank, with the opening flush to the cliff face. The pipes are best filled with sand for the birds to excavate, with the entrance hole half-blocked with cement. The birds should be able to tunnel farther into loose sandy material at the other end of the pipe, and it is essential that the pipes are dry inside, not acting as drains.

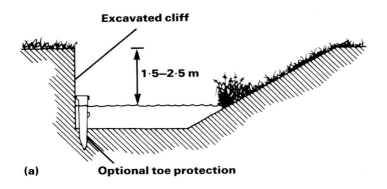

Excavated cliff

1·5—2·5 m

(a)

Optional toe protection

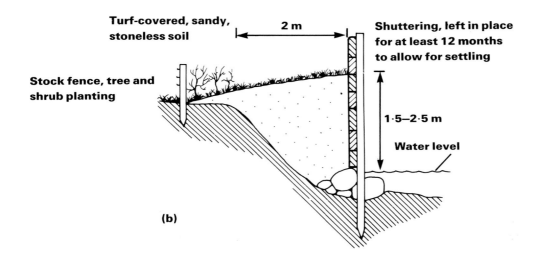

Turf-covered, sandy, stoneless soil

2 m

Shuttering, left in place for at least 12 months to allow for settling

Stock fence, tree and shrub planting

1·5—2·5 m

Water level

(b)

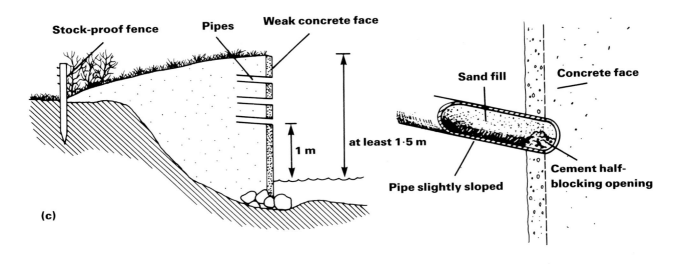

Stock-proof fence

Pipes

Weak concrete face

Sand fill

Concrete face

at least 1·5 m

1 m

Pipe slightly sloped

Cement half-blocking opening

(c)

3.5 Ditches and drains

- All farm ditches can be managed to benefit wildlife.
- Desilt and clear invasive vegetation on rotation, allowing some recolonisation.
- If necessary, widen some stretches to retain plants without impeding flows.
- Where ditches are dry for part of the year, deepen stretches to retain water.
- Prevent excessive shading and allow access to grazing livestock.
- If possible, isolate high-quality ditches from the effects of fertiliser run-off.

On all farms, ditches can be managed to give them value for wildlife (Figure 9.3). This is so even if they do not hold water in the summer. Obviously, there is greater potential with wide drains that hold water permanently.

Whether or not a ditch or drain holds water throughout the year or it simply channels water away and then dries up, it must be kept clear of excessive vegetation and of silt to fulfil its drainage function. When this was done by hand, roots and rhizomes were often left in the bed and, as successive stretches were cleared each year, the plants were able to regrow. This meant that there was a range of conditions for wildlife, with some ditches newly clear, some being recolonised by plants, some silted and well vegetated. The result was that they held a wide range of species. With machinery, ditches can be cleared of silt and plants more thoroughly and much more can be done at once. This means slow plant recolonisation, few if any well-vegetated sections and little wetland wildlife.

If possible, revert to rotational management on about a five-year cycle, depending on the rate of regrowth and siltation. Take care not to clean ditches so thoroughly that all the roots and rhizomes are removed. Best of all, on wider drains which hold water year round, do not clear the full width but leave about a third of the channel width untouched. Next time round, clear this and leave the third on the other side. If leaving plants will seriously interfere with drainage capacity, consider widening some stretches

of the ditch, for instance at ditch junctions, to create a little pool, say 1 m wide by 10 m long, and when it silts up clear half one year and the rest once plants have recovered in the first section.

Where ditches regularly dry out, as they do on most farms, they have little value for aquatic wildlife, though the bed sometimes carries wetland plants such as stands of meadowsweet and bulrush. Where possible, widen and overdeepen stretches so that they will remain as pools in the bed without interfering with field drainage. As a minimum, aim to hold at least 30 cm and ideally 1 m depth of water in stretches at least 3 m long. They will trap silt and need periodic cleaning out; do not do them all in the same year.

If none of this is practicable, when clearing, at least leave some patches of different plants. Mark them with canes in summer as they may die back and be hard to see when work starts in the winter.

With narrow, deep ditches, the bottom is often shaded by overhanging vegetation and the high banks. This inhibits aquatic plant growth but the damp shady conditions will be good for some invertebrates and many small mammals and birds will forage in the cover of the herbage. Plant growth will be most luxuriant in wide drains where the water is sunlit. Do not plant willows or other trees along the south side.

Grazing or annual mowing of the banks helps to prevent plants such as reed sweet-grass becoming too dominant and to create good conditions for a wider range of plants and for feeding by birds including waders and wildfowl.

In many ditches the water quality is poor because of the effects of fertilisers. As a result, the surface may be carpeted by duckweeds and the submerged aquatics are replaced by blanket weed or the water may be bright green with algal blooms. Most invertebrates, fish and amphibians are lost and there is little food for birds. Emergent plants may continue to grow luxuriantly and, as they help to use up the available nutrients, it is wise to retain them as far as

Figure 9.3   Retaining wildlife value of ditches

(a)

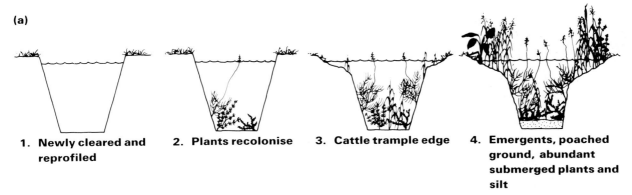

1. **Newly cleared and reprofiled**
2. **Plants recolonise**
3. **Cattle trample edge**
4. **Emergents, poached ground, abundant submerged plants and silt**

Development of ditch structure and vegetation. By the time ideal conditions for wildlife are reached (see (a) 4) drainage is becoming seriously impeded and it will be necessary to clear unless the ditch is designed to have spare capacity. When managing and clearing ditches there are many possible options to create extra capacity so as to be able to retain plants.

(b) Ditch enhanced for wildlife — widened and deepened

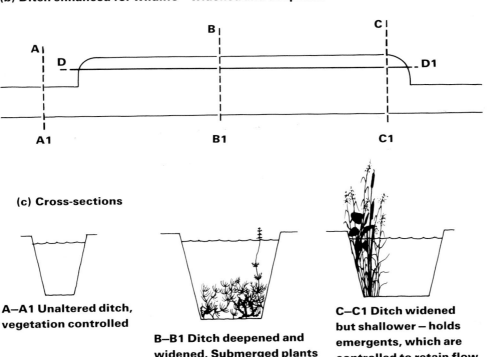

(c) Cross-sections

A–A1 Unaltered ditch, vegetation controlled

B–B1 Ditch deepened and widened. Submerged plants do not reduce flow unacceptably

C–C1 Ditch widened but shallower — holds emergents, which are controlled to retain flow in half of channel

(d) D–D1 Longitudinal section through widened and deepened stretch

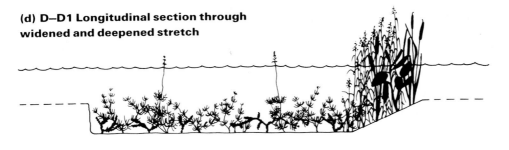

possible. Management of water quality is discussed on page 286.

Where drains are managed by an Internal Drainage Board there is a statutory regulation to further nature conservation.

3.6 Rivers and streams

> - Where works are to be carried out by the relevant statutory authority, ensure that a river corridor survey is carried out.
> - On all watercourses, ensure that dredging does not lower the bed or remove channel features including pools, riffles and bars.
> - Trees should be retained where they do not cause excessive shading.
> - Bank features including muddy margins and earth cliffs should be retained or reinstated.
> - Create 'two-stage channels' to avoid the need for works on the existing river.
> - Accept limited erosion to create vertical banks.
> - Plant trees for their intrinsic value and to combat serious bank erosion.
> - Use only bank protection measures which allow plants to grow.
> - Maintain and restore islands, meanders and oxbows.

Rivers and streams can contain a range of habitats. The more varied the river, the greater its overall wildlife importance. Features of particular value include shallow reaches and deep pools, sand bars and islands, eroding vertical banks, muddy margins with beds of emergent plants, calm backwaters and meanders. The number and type of plants found in any river depends on factors including water chemistry, river velocity and geographical location.

Normally, the farm will not have control over the management of rivers and larger streams. However, maintenance and improvement works should be discussed with the managing agency. In England and Wales, Internal Drainage Boards and the National Rivers Authority have a statutory obligation to further the conservation of wildlife when managing any drainage

channel. Specialist staff are employed by the NRA. In Northern Ireland, the Drainage Division of the Department of Agriculture aims to apply the same standards of care. In Scotland there is a requirement for River Purification Boards and local authorities, or private bodies undertaking schemes receiving public financial support, to pay due regard to the needs of wildlife.

Before any work is carried out, request that a river corridor survey is done; this will identify and assess the value of wildlife habitats likely to be affected. Ask to discuss the results. The work should be designed and carried out to incorporate conservation measures. You can seek to have river habitats restored or created as well as retained during the work.

Whether the work is on main river or on minor farm streams, the same care should be taken. In some respects, small streams are easier to damage because important features such as gravel beds used by spawning fish may be small and easily removed or buried by silt disturbed by work upstream. Walk the stretch to be worked plus a good distance downstream to identify important and vulnerable features before starting work. As watercourse management can affect neighbours both upstream and downstream, discuss it with them if necessary.

On lowland rivers, the main work is dredging to remove accumulated silt and so maintain flows. Dredging should not cut down into the bed and cause the river level to fall. If it does, nearby wetland habitats may dry out. Low bars of sand or silt exposed when flows are low should not be removed. They have little influence on overall channel capacity or rate of flow when levels are high but they are important feeding areas for birds such as wagtails and may support invertebrate populations.

A skilled operator can remove significant deposits of silt from a channel without touching the bank. Marginal fringes of emergent plants should be retained at least on one side of the river. It should be possible for the operator to work round trees. Limbs that hang into the water should be retained unless they pose a flood hazard. If trees must be cleared to permit working, they should be coppiced or pollarded, not uprooted. Where stock are present, coppice should be fenced to allow it to regrow.

If maintenance has not been carried out for many years, both banks may be tree-lined. On narrow channels, it will be beneficial to open up the sunlit side but on larger watercourses where shade from the south side does not extend to the other bank, it may be preferable to maintain cover on both banks. If so, it is sometimes possible to work the channel either by tracking along it if the flow is low enough, or to operate from a barge. This will permit retention of the tree cover. Where tree removal is essential, undertake it only on one bank, preferably the south side.

Dredgings should never be dumped in wetland areas such as patches of marsh or backwaters, nor on other valuable habitats like unimproved grassland.

A major scheme to reduce flooding may involve increasing channel capacity by widening or deepening, the removal of islands, straightening the channel to speed flows and the construction of new flood banks. The potential impact on wildlife is very severe and many species may be lost entirely. There is a legal requirement for an environmental assessment to be carried out.

Ideally, if the existing channel is good for wildlife, it should be left untouched and new flood banks should be built set back from it so that it can overtop and still be contained in the 'two-stage channel'. The flood channel can be grazed for most of the year or cropped if the risk of damage or loss is accepted.

If the channel must be modified, the bed form should be restored to provide a variety of habitats for fish and invertebrates. Most river beds naturally have alternate deep and shallow stretches. This 'pool and riffle' form should be re-created. Islands should always be retained. At the foot of the banks, the bed should be shaped to create a wet shelf close to the summer waterlevel and emergent and

marginal vegetation should be replaced. Stock drinking points are useful because they create the trampled, bare areas which many invertebrates and some birds require.

Willows, alder and other trees and shrubs should be planted, especially along the north bank, and fenced against stock.

Limited erosion is beneficial to wildlife, for example, creating bare earth banks where kingfishers and other wildlife breed. River management can have very substantial effects on the rate of erosion. An increase may result from the removal of trees whose roots protect the bank. It is also caused by river works which remove large volumes of material from the bed so that current energy formerly absorbed in transporting sediment or stones along the bed is now freed to erode material from the banks. Erosion may be slowed or halted by tree planting but, at least as an interim measure, bank protection may be required.

Although the simplest way of protecting a bank from erosion due to waves or currents is to armour it with blockstone or gabions, such treatments are not satisfactory for wildlife as they do not support plants. There are several alternatives that allow plants to grow through. They include wattle hurdles and geotextiles, interlocking concrete blocks and bio-degradable fabrics, which can be used to protect the bank while specially planted vegetation takes over. A traditional method is to drive in fencepost-sized willow stakes and interweave willow wands; the stakes root and bind the bank (Figure 9.4). However, measures that successfully halt all erosion result in the loss of a habitat.

Where they still exist, avoid the loss of backwaters, oxbows and secondary channels. Such areas may need some work if they are to continue to retain water and flows after the scheme is complete. They should not be filled in with spoil.

Opportunities should be sought for restoration and re-creation of backwaters if they have been reclaimed in the past.

Figure 9.4
Bank protection treatments

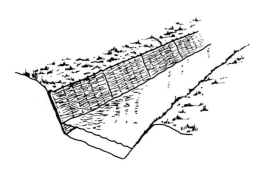 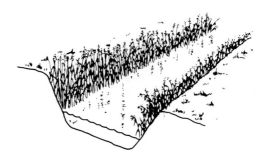

(a) *Stabilising banks using wattle ('spiling')*
Drive stakes more than 2 m long into the base of the bank in a staggered double row. Weave freshly-cut (and therefore pliable) willow or hazel branches between them to a height above the highest expected water level. Fill in behind with soil and plant to stabilise the surface. Willow stakes will sprout, which would give greater protection to a toe particularly affected by scour.

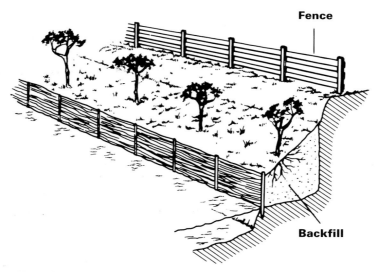

Unstable section cut back, spiled with hazel.
Fill with soil and use willow or alder to stabilise
the sector.

(b) *Stabilising banks using trees*
Trees and shrubs have extensive root systems. Alder is the best species for planting at the base of the bank in small watercourses. Willow is as effective and more easily established but is too bushy for small channels. Planting can also be done at the top of the bank. By the time the wattle rots away, the root system will have developed and continued to stabilise the bank. Do not plant trees close to drainage outfalls as the root systems may block them.

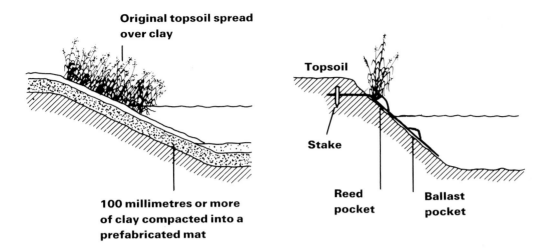

Original topsoil spread over clay

100 millimetres or more of clay compacted into a prefabricated mat

Topsoil

Stake

Reed pocket

Ballast pocket

(c) Stabilising the banks using prefabricated materials
**There are various types, including geotextiles through which plant roots can grow, others with pockets to
hold plants during establishment and interlocking cellular concrete blocks. Lay out the mat units and stake
in position. The flexible nature of the mat enables it to fit the contours of the site. The toe of the mat must be
below the base of the bank to prevent it being undermined, and the top of the mat above the top waterlevel.
Machinery for desilting has to be used very carefully so as not to catch and lift the mat.
Adapted from: Newbold, C, Honnor, J and Buckley, K 1989. *Nature Conservation and the management of
drainage channels*. Nature Conservancy Council and Association of Drainage Authorities.**

3.7 Irrigation reservoirs

- Consider installing nesting rafts on irrigation reservoirs.
- If practicable, plant the banks of irrigation reservoirs with native shrubs or allow herbage to grow tall.

Irrigation reservoirs are usually steep-sided and fairly deep. Often, they are built with raised sides so that the water surface is exposed and windswept when full in winter. The rapidity of drawdown in summer may result in conditions unsuitable for many invertebrates. Amphibians may be unable to breed successfully. The range of feeding opportunities and nest sites for birds is very restricted. Small numbers of diving ducks, coots or grebes may use the site but dabbling ducks will probably only flight in to roost. Anyone appearing on the edge of the reservoir immediately puts birds to flight because of the lack of cover.

Provided they are not too disturbed, reservoirs can be improved for birds by installing nesting rafts. One surfaced with shingle may attract terns. A raft with tall herbage may be used by a variety of waterfowl. Bear in mind that a reservoir stocked with fish is unlikely to produce much invertebrate food for ducklings and, though adults may nest, production will be low. However, such sites may appeal to herons and great crested grebes. If it can be done safely, plant the inside of the bank above the top waterline and the outside with low-growing shrubs such as bramble, guelder rose and dogwood. This will give some wind shelter, cover and screening. Otherwise, allow grass and herbage to grow tall.

New reservoirs can be designed to improve their wildlife value by the incorporation of an internal bund so that a proportion of the water is not drawn down until late in the season, if at all. On balance, the costs and additional land-take involved are such that it would probably be better to create a pond separate from the reservoir.

3.8 Islands and rafts

> - Waterfowl breeding success is often better on islands, and otters use islands as holt sites.
> - Ensure existing islands are retained during river management work.
> - Create islands in ponds and other standing waters, ideally in shallow water.
> - Surface islands with shingle or soil depending on the wildlife objective.
> - Rafts make good substitutes where island creation is impracticable.

Islands are valuable for several reasons. Many species of waterfowl prefer to nest on them because they offer reasonable protection from ground predators such as foxes. Birds breeding on islands are less subject to human disturbance and this too may help to increase nesting success. Wildfowl will also use islands as resting places when they are not feeding. Islands provide shelter from waves because, whatever the wind direction, birds can always move to the lee side. If they are surrounded by shallows, islands make excellent areas for duckling broods to feed.

Where otters are present or likely to recolonise in future, islands are favoured lying-up and breeding sites because they are relatively safe and undisturbed.

It is important to retain islands in watercourses. They are sometimes at risk from major channel improvements, in which case it may be better to cut away marginal shallows or adjoining land than lose the island. The choice must take account of the amount of these different habitat types in the reach and their likely overall value to wildlife.

Islands can be created in new waterbodies such as gravel pits, irrigation reservoirs or wildfowl flight ponds. They should be sited as far offshore as practicable because this gives the greatest protection, though birds will breed on an island close to the bank if there is no alternative. Islands may need protection from waves if they are composed of soft materials so that siting them under a lee shore may be essential on an exposed

site. Alternatively, an island can be protected by a reef or booms.

Several small islands will usually hold more birds than one large one. The minimum practical size is likely to be about 10 x 10 m. With very small sites, if predators such as mink gain access they can easily search the whole area but they may miss nests on a larger island. If erosion is a problem, larger islands are likely to be more cost-effective to protect or simply last longer.

The margins should slope at 1:4 or less to make access easy for waterfowl. Have the largest possible extent of shallows less than 1 m deep. If there is insufficient material for this, make the shoreline as convoluted as possible to increase the extent of this shallow zone (Figure 9.5).

Islands surfaced with shingle may be occupied by nesting terns or some waders, such as little ringed plover. Spread 10 cm of shingle over a layer of plastic sheet or fertiliser sacks but do not extend the layer down into the zone affected by waves or it is likely to be washed out. The plastic will prevent deep-rooted plants from colonising and other plants may die of drought in summer or can easily be cleared by raking in winter. In fact, a sparse cover of plants can be useful as chick shelter on hot days so it is not essential to clear all plants every year.

For wildfowl, the surface of the island should be irregular. If the island is built with a hydraulic digger then have the surface finished by dumping each bucket of soil beside the last one and not levelling it. The uneven surface will make it easier for birds to hide nests and more difficult for predators to search systematically.

Surfacing with soil will speed up the development of a dense cover of grass tussocks and tall plants such as hoary willowherb and brambles. This provides good overhead concealment for nesting ducks - many fewer nests are found by crows where cover is at least 0.5 m tall.

**Figure 9.5
Island design**

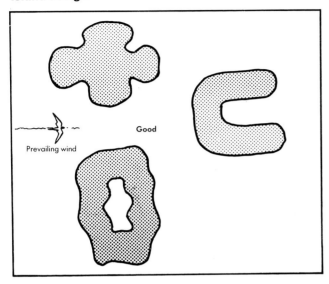

Good island forms to provide abundant
'edge' for feeding waders and dabbling
ducks.

(a) Poor island design

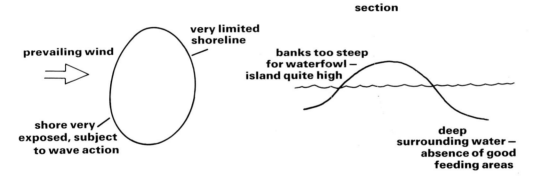

(b) Good island design

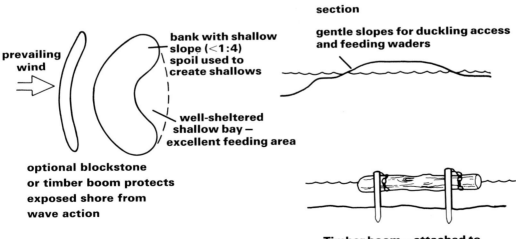

Figure 9.6 Raft designs

(a) Tern raft

Removable protective wire frame bolted at ends to surround all four sides of raft

3·0 m × 230 mm high, externally covered with 25 mm chicken wire

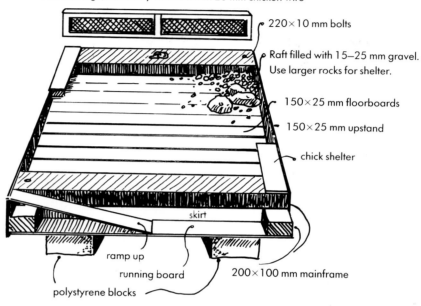

220 × 10 mm bolts

Raft filled with 15–25 mm gravel. Use larger rocks for shelter.

150 × 25 mm floorboards

150 × 25 mm upstand

chick shelter

skirt

ramp up

running board

200 × 100 mm mainframe

polystyrene blocks

This raft is a 3 m x 3 m platform which will hold up to 10 pairs of common terns. Assembly time about two man-days. If transported flat by road, the completed raft is a wide load and the police will require 48 hours' notice.

1. **Mooring ring connected to chain or polypropylene rope at opposite end to re-entry ramp. Anchor with four or more buckets, each with an eye bolt set at the centre and filled with concrete (practical to transport). Connect in pairs by shackles to 30 cm lengths of chains, crossed to provide a single point to shackle to the mooring line.**
2. **Fence to keep off ducks and geese. Four frames 3 m x 23 cm of 5 x 5 cm poles, covered with chicken wire and bolted on.**
3. **15–25 mm gravel, plus rocks for cover, added until raft floats with running board at water level.**
4. **Deck: planking 3 m x 15 cm x 25 mm attached with 75 mm galvanised nails to lower main frame timbers.**
5. **15 cm raised sides to retain shingle and chicks.**
6. **Simple shelters protect chicks from rain and hot sun – 1 m length at alternative corners.**
7. **Main frame: four 3 m x 20 cm x 10 cm timbers bolted together through overlapping corners. One upper timber inset from the ends of the two lower timbers by 15 cm to allow for re-entry ramp. Sub-frame 3 m x 7.5 cm x 5 cm battens attached flat and parallel to lower main frame ▶▶▶**

Plan

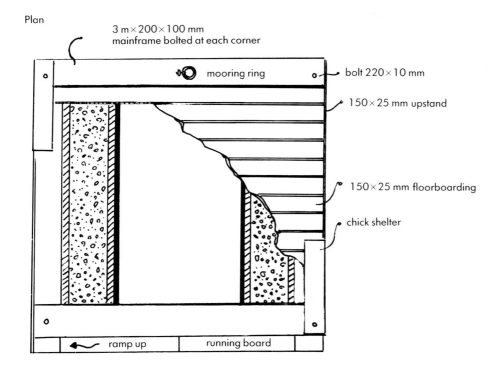

3 m × 200 × 100 mm
mainframe bolted at each corner

mooring ring

bolt 220 × 10 mm

150 × 25 mm upstand

150 × 25 mm floorboarding

chick shelter

ramp up   running board

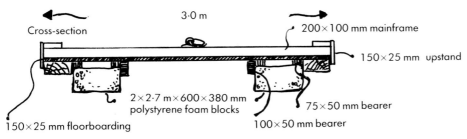

Cross-section

3·0 m

200 × 100 mm mainframe

150 × 25 mm upstand

2 × 2·7 m × 600 × 380 mm
polystyrene foam blocks

75 × 50 mm bearer

150 × 25 mm floorboarding

100 × 50 mm bearer

Figure 6 (b)

members by nailing through planks, the outer two against the inner sides of the main frame members, the inner two each at 45 cm spacing from the outer two.

8. **Running board allows chicks to clamber out of the water.**

9. **Sloping re-entry board allows chicks to get back on if necessary; block the gap behind it to stop them getting under the raft.**

10. **Flotation: 2 high-density polystyrene foam, 2.7 m x 60 cm x 38 cm, can be water sealed with Aquaseal 44 bituminous paint, which will also strengthen them. In water, the weight of the raft holds them in place but for extra security polypropylene webbing can be nailed across them to hold them in place.**

11. **'Angels' can be attached along the anchor line to damp effects of wave action.**

12. **760 mm circumference marker buoy.**

13. **Main flotation holders: two 3 m x 10 cm x 5 cm timbers attached on edge against the inner edges of the two inner battens, by nailing through the planking. Sides: four 3 m x 15 cm x 25 mm planks; two nailed to the lower frame timbers with their upper edges level with the top of the upper main frame timbers at the corners, thus forming a tray to hold shingle. Two nailed to the ends of the lower main frame timbers and battens with their upper edges level with the deck to hold in the flotation material.**

(b) Waterfowl raft

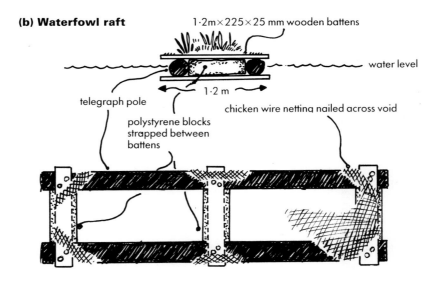

1·2m × 225 × 25 mm wooden battens

water level

telegraph pole

polystyrene blocks strapped between battens

chicken wire netting nailed across void

1·2 m

Telegraph pole

chicken wire

polystyrene blocks

The aim is to create a frame that will hold growing plants with their roots in water.

1. **Main frame is 2 telegraph poles held apart by 3 planks 1.2 m x 23 cm x 25 mm attached by 75 mm coach screws (2 at each plank end), 3 planks above and 3 below.**
2. **Flotation: 3 polystyrene blocks 75 x 30 x 23 cm slipped between the pairs of spacing planks and retained by galvanised wire.**
3. **Vegetation trays, consisting of 1.2 m width of 25 cm chicken wire, stapled to the upper surface at the sides and ends with sufficient slack to form a shallow tray.**
4. **Place clumps of vegetation with root systems placed in the galvanised wire tray. Suitable plants include iris, rushes, reedmace, reed sweetgrass and other marginals.**

Because mallards nest very early in the year, often before the new season's growth has begun, it is important that this cover is not cut in the winter. However, these islands are likely to be colonised by willows or other trees and once these get tall they will shade out the ground cover and make the site unsuitable. They must therefore be cleared while small or regularly coppiced to maintain dense growth.

Where it is not possible to create islands, rafts make an excellent substitute and have been used widely for ducks, terns and grebes. They can also be designed for rare species and have improved breeding success for black-throated divers on several Scottish lochs. There are many possible designs but the basic principles are the same. The structure must be buoyant; polystyrene blocks are better than metal drums as they do not rust. The raft bed must be able to support the required covering - a solid tray for shingle and a wire mesh base for vegetation so that the roots can reach the water. Low sides are important for access; it may be necessary to make ramps along the edges. Size should be at least 2 m x 2 m but not so big it cannot be moved once assembled. The anchoring arrangements should make it easy to detach the raft and tow it ashore for maintenance.

Rafts are best sited in calm waters but must be robust enough to ride out the occasional storm.

3.9 Wet grassland

- Do not alter the hydrological regimes of grasslands which flood in winter and have a high watertable in spring and early summer.
- Continue traditional mowing and grazing management. Do not improve the sward.
- On peat sites maintain a high watertable in spring and early summer by managing adjacent ditch waterlevels.
- Sites with clay or silt soils rely on surface flooding to maintain wet conditions suitable for breeding waders.
- Where land drainage has lowered the watertable, reinstate former conditions by 'reverse drainage' or surface re-wetting.
- Re-wetting by surface flooding is inappropriate where the sward is plant-rich.
- Where the whole field cannot be re-wetted, modify ditch sides and pools or create a wader scrape for feeding and manage the adjoining sward to provide nest cover.

Where a high watertable maintains surface dampness across ground through the spring and into July, the land will usually have been managed for hay production with aftermath grazing. If this continues to be the practice and the sward has not been re-seeded, herbicided or treated with artificial fertilisers, it is likely to be rich in plants. Conditions are also potentially suitable for breeding waders. Such fields are now rare throughout the UK. Continued maintenance of a high watertable and traditional management are of great importance. Chapter 3 describes how the sward should be managed to get the best results for wildlife. An important consideration is the timing of mowing and grazing as this will affect the composition of the plant community and birds' breeding success.

On peats, the aim should be to maintain the watertable within about 20 cm of the soil surface in spring and summer. At this time of year, evaporation and transpiration by plants result in water loss from the surface of the field and this needs to be replenished by flow from the ditches which must therefore be penned at a high level. Often, water moves sideways through the peat more slowly than it is lost from the surface and the result is that the watertable tends to drop in the middle of the field. This means that to keep the largest possible area in good condition for the birds, the ditch waterlevels should be as near the ground level as possible. However, it is very important that water does not flood over the surface as this will affect the sward and be bad for hay production and plant richness.

By dropping waterlevels in the ditches in July, the ground can be dried to permit haycutting and grazing through into the autumn. In winter, inputs of rain exceed evapo-transpiration and the watertable in the centre of the field rises, with sub-surface flow towards the ditches. The penning level can be dropped further but it is important to bring it right back up in March to restore the conditions that birds require.

On peats, it is often necessary to fence ditch sides as stock can become mired. If this is done, ensure that they are cut when the field is mown to prevent them becoming so overgrown that aquatic plants are shaded out. They will regrow in the autumn and provide nesting cover for wildfowl in the following spring.

Where peats have been dried out by underdrainage, re-wetting may be possible by raising penning levels in the adjoining ditches or by mole ploughing to allow water to flow back under the field. Precise spacing will depend on site conditions and advice should be sought. An alternative is to re-wet the land by prolonged surface flooding. This will destroy the existing sward and its invertebrate fauna. However, from a wildlife standpoint this is unimportant if the field is improved grassland or former arable. A new sward will develop once the peat is re-wetted and the waterlevel drops below the surface.

Depending on the amount of rainfall, sites on clays and silts dry out rapidly when surface flooding recedes. This makes them unsuitable for snipe because the birds cannot probe the ground to feed. Redshanks

and godwits are less affected because they feed more at the margins of ponds and ditches. Lapwings will breed on dry sites but if possible move the chicks to damp ground to feed, which suggests that food is more abundant there. It is possible to improve conditions for waders by keeping the sides of ditches open. On these soils there is less risk of miring stock, whose trampling and grazing may be sufficient to produce wet open ground in the form of a shelf along the ditch side. Usually, however, it is desirable to reprofile the margins when the ditch is being managed, and to create a shelf at least 0.5 m wide at or up to 10 cm below the normal summer waterlevel along the full length of the ditch. An alternative approach is to create a wader scrape (see page 307) and manage the adjoining sward conventionally, timing grazing to avoid destruction of nests (see page 68).

However, it may be possible to create good conditions for breeding waders across the field if there is an adequate water supply to keep the site surface-wet until the end of June or mid-July if possible. Water must flood over the surface so that it can soak into the ground and keep it soft, but the field must not flood as this will destroy nests. In some sites it may be possible to do this by setting penning levels in adjoining ditches but usually it will be essential to pump on to the field and control the rate of run-off with a penstock at the outflow point. Considerable volumes of water will be required to keep pace with evapo-transpiration and close attention must be paid to water supply to ensure neither flooding nor drying.

The effect of this regime will be to alter the sward composition and the invertebrate community, especially the earthworm population. It is not appropriate on a traditional hay meadow with a rich variety of plants as it will result in changes in the sward. It could be applied to improved grassland or to arable land. The seeds of grasses and other plants adapted to the conditions may arrive in the water which flows onto the site in summer and in winter flooding, if any, so that colonisation will probably be rapid. The resulting cover may comprise large amounts of plants such as reed sweet-grass and grazing will be essential to keep this in check or breeding waders will be lost. Therefore, at the end of the breeding season, in mid-July, the site must be drained down and grazed.

3.10 Wader scrapes

- Where a high watertable cannot be maintained or restored but conditions are otherwise suitable for nesting waders, good feeding conditions can be provided by creating a very shallow scrape.
- The site should be open and at least 100 m from any hedge or trees.
- The scrape should be 1 ha or more in size, with a maximum depth of 50 cm.
- It is essential to be able to draw down or top up levels by very small amounts.
- High productivity is required so nutrient-enriched topsoil with a good organic component should be used.
- Control the spread of emergents.

Where it is not possible to manage the watertable across a whole field, feeding conditions for some waders can be provided by the creation and management of extensive shallow pools. Pools smaller than 1 ha are unlikely to be able to support birds right through the breeding season. If possible, choose areas for flooding which are at least 100 m from hedges or trees as some waders will not use sites close to cover where predators may hide. Ground where existing winter flooding lies longest may be ideal as the amount of earth-moving will be least, but do not destroy a good existing wetland such as a marsh.

Water can be retained either by excavating or by constructing an earth bank. Commonly, both are done, with material from the bed scraped up to provide material for embanking.

Water depth is critical for waders. Chicks can only feed in the shallowest areas - typically less than 5 cm deep, and adults will go to about 10 cm, depending on species. The ideal is a site in which levels can be controlled precisely, with the ability to top up or draw down 1 cm at a time. If there is no means of controlling levels, a dry spring may mean that the whole area dries out before hatching, or a wet one may mean

that the water is too deep for them. If half the area of the scrape is 0–25 cm deep and the rest 25–50 cm deep, a gradual drop in levels throughout the spring and summer will regularly expose fresh areas to the birds. At least half the site should remain too deep for birds to feed until the chicks hatch, so that they can be given access to untouched food supplies.

The productivity of the site is most important. The best site will have a high nutrient status with plenty of organic matter in the soil. On former arable, plough in a green manure or cover crop. This is ideal to support superabundant larvae of midges and other flies on which the birds will feed. Such conditions are also particularly attractive to wildfowl, which will use the site in large numbers in winter.

The pool will be colonised by emergent vegetation. Patchy cover, occupying up to about a quarter of the area is useful as it provides cover, especially for chicks, and increases the types of food available. Once it extends beyond this point, it should be controlled by mechanical means or herbicides. Do not remove cut or dead material as its decomposition will replenish the important organic component.

3.11 Reedbeds, marshes and bogs

- Reedbeds in deep water need no management.
- Where a reedbed is drying out, prevent build-up of a litter layer by harvesting reed every second year.
- Control tree and scrub invasion.
- Small reedbeds are easily created by transplanting rhizomes.
- Large reedbeds may attract rare species and could be created on land taken out of arable production.
- Specialist advice should be taken.
- Low-intensity grazing is desirable in marshes and bogs.

Reedbeds in deep water need no management. However, in order to protect open water in shallows, it may be necessary to control reed that is colonising them. Where the waterlevel can be controlled, draw down enough in summer to cut the reed and then reflood the stubble. This will kill it. Try to time draw-down so that it has least effect on any breeding birds, which will probably be after the young have left their nests. Alternatively, herbicide can be used, but see the caveats on page 284. Established reed is not easy to remove mechanically as the rhizomes can extend at least 0.5 m into the bed.

It is important to protect reedbeds, marshes or bogs from drying out due to any change in waterlevel as this permits colonisation by scrub and trees.

In reedbeds, the annual accumulation of dead stems can result in a rapid build-up of litter, leading to drying out and colonisation by other vegetation. All stages of the process have different associated wildlife, so the ideal is to have each represented in a reedbed but it is very difficult to control the process; it is better to keep the bed wet than to allow it to dry out. Unless the waterlevel can be raised, the best solution is to start a cutting regime. About half to one-third should be cut each winter and the cut stems removed. Do not cut all the bed every year as this removes the old, dry stems which are required by reed warblers to suspend their nests and used by some invertebrates. If the site is large, seek advice on the best management as rare species may be present. In some regions it should be possible to sell large stands of reed to be cut for thatch.

It is important to prevent extensive colonisation by willow scrub. No more than 10% scrub or tree cover should be allowed to develop. When cut, the stumps will regrow rapidly, so they must be treated with an arboricide. Once larger growth has been removed, reed cutting will prevent reinvasion. A scattering of bushes should be retained as some species feed on the bare ground beneath them and the foliage of willows in or adjoining the reedbed will give good feeding habitat to warblers.

Exclude stock from drying reedbeds as their trampling will damage the reed and may aid colonisation by common weeds such as willowherb and nettles. However, it is best to continue light grazing in areas that hold

a mix of willow scrub, grasses and herbs on the drier ground and patches of reed in the wet. Such sites are still fairly common in parts of Scotland and Northern Ireland. If these are abandoned they may quickly become dominated by willow and much of their wildlife value will be lost.

Reed can be easily established by transplanting clumps of rhizome in the winter, spacing the clumps about 1 m apart. It is important to plant them just above the watertable in damp ground at the margin; if it is below water initially, the plant will die. Once established, it will spread into water about 1 m deep at a rate of up to 1.5 m a year or more in some sites. Reed can be confined to a specific area by surrounding it with a trench with a water depth of at least 1.5 m.

The creation of a large reedbed on land taken out of arable production could be of great conservation value and provide income from reed cutting for thatch. This would require a water supply sufficient to maintain summer waterlevels and simple water control structures to drain the bed in winter for cutting (Figure 9.7). Establishment could be by seeding, with rooted cuttings, or by transplanting rhizomes. Reedbeds of over 20 ha are very rare and important habitats, which may hold or attract nationally rare birds such as bitterns and marsh harriers. Take specialist advice on their creation and management.

Where marshes or bogs remain, ensure that improvements of drainage or management of ditches or other watercourses do not result in their drying out. Their interest is best maintained by low-intensity grazing, ideally from mid-summer to the end of the season only. Plant variety will be reduced or destroyed by the application of artificial fertilisers or herbicide use. However, if this has already occurred, the areas may still have some wildlife value and there is usually good potential for restoration.

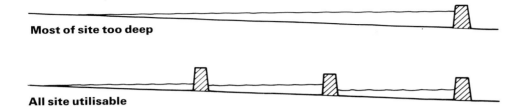

Most of site too deep

All site utilisable

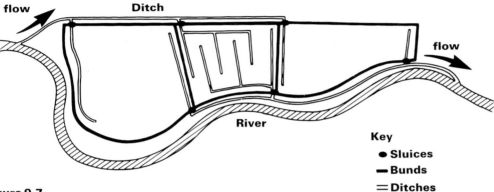

Figure 9.7
Reedbed creation

Key
● Sluices
▬ Bunds
═ Ditches

- Disused mineral workings, such as gravel pit silt lagoons are ideal sites. So is farmland in a river valley but bunding may require planning consent and there may be opposition to a scheme which reduces flood-storage capacity. Consent for water abstraction and discharge may be required.
- There must be water movement through the bed in the growing season. Supply must be sufficient to prevent drying out.
- Subdivide the site into at least two and ideally four parts, each with its own water control structures. This will enable you to draw down or flood areas for management without disrupting use of most of the site by wildlife.
- On a sloping site, cross-bunds also permit the creation of more areas of shallow water, vital for bitterns and some other birds.
- Consult the relevant authority (NRA in England and Wales, DANI in Northern Ireland, or RPB in Scotland) for advice on licence and approval of large bunds or dams.

- Water channels within the bed should be at least 1.5 m deep to stop reeds from growing across them and impeding flows.
- For illustrative purposes, the three-part bed shown has one part with additional internal channels to benefit wildlife.

Bitterns feed on fish, especially eels, in water up to 25 cm deep and mostly close to ditch sides as fish do not penetrate far into the bed. Maximise the length of ditches and aim for the greatest possible area to be flooded less than 25 cm deep. Bitterns build their nests up in these shallows where they are safest from predators.

Bearded tits feed on insects and reed seeds. They nest in accumulations of reed litter about five years old or more. Leave reeds in the shallowest areas of the bed uncut. Eventually weeds and willow scrub will invade; to control this, cut about a fifth of these patches each year and reflood them.

3.12 Trees and Shrubs

- Broadleaved trees and shrubs at the waterside have many benefits and should be retained or planted, especially on north banks.
- Open up the south sides of most small ponds and streams to let in sunlight.
- Overhanging branches should be retained unless they pose a serious risk of impeding flow and causing an unacceptable degree of flooding.
- Ideally, manage willows and alders along watercourses by coppicing or pollarding on rotation.
- Permit willows and alders to invade damp ground which has no other wildlife value.
- Retain existing stands of alder or willow carr.

On large waterbodies, maintain tree and shrub cover along most of the northern bank where the effects of shading are least. Keep half to three-quarters of the southern bank open so that light can reach marginal shallows (Figure 9.8). Take account of the need for wind shelter. On ponds and small streams, keep shading away from the whole water surface unless there are several ponds or more than 200 m of stream, in which case keep one pond or about 10% of the stream shaded.

Willows and alder can be managed by coppicing, which produces rapid, dense regrowth and gives good cover at ground level for the first 2–3 years but then tends to become open at the base and less suitable for nesting wildfowl. Decide on the best rotation length; then divide the area into as

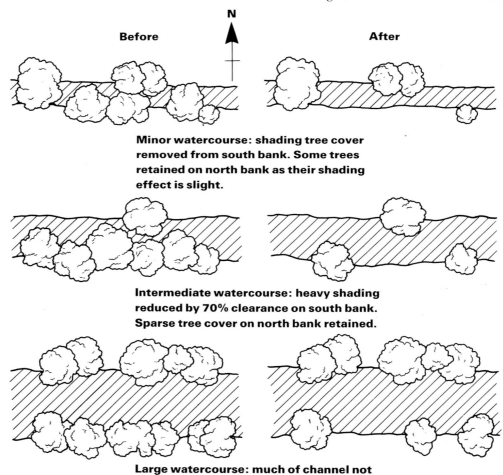

Before

N

After

Minor watercourse: shading tree cover removed from south bank. Some trees retained on north bank as their shading effect is slight.

Intermediate watercourse: heavy shading reduced by 70% clearance on south bank. Sparse tree cover on north bank retained.

Large watercourse: much of channel not seriously shaded but some clearance on south bank to open up marginal shallows to sunlight.

Figure 9.8
Tree cover and watercourses

many plots as there are years in the rotation and cut one each year.

Traditionally, willows were pollarded and this prolongs the life of the tree. Do not pollard more than one-third of the trees in any one year, so that some always have young growth available for the invertebrates that require it.

Willows can easily be established by pushing freshly-cut lengths of twig or branch into damp ground; they can be from pencil to fence-post size.

Willows in particular can rapidly invade damp ground. Alder may also do so. Where the area has no existing interest and cannot be kept open by grazing or cutting, allow the stand to grow. It may be coppiced or simply left.

Existing stands of old willows and alder are usually of considerable wildlife interest as they are likely to support invertebrates that depend on decaying wood, and many hole-nesting birds. They are often shallowly flooded in winter and may hold uncommon marshland plants such as tussock sedge. Drier sites often support thriving nettle beds, which make good feeding habitat for warblers.

Such woods should not be cleared and care should be taken to ensure that alterations to land drainage, or river management works, do not result in any change in the seasonal pattern of flooding and drying. Large willows often fall or split asunder but will go on growing despite their ruined appearance provided that stock cannot browse off all the shoots. When they fall, they create short-lived glades in which wetland plants will grow.

4. References and further reading

Andrews, J and Kinsman, D 1990. *Gravel Pit Restoration for Wildlife*. RSPB.

Andrews, J and Ward, D 1991. *The Management and Creation of Reedbeds*. British Wildlife Vol 3 No 2 pp. 81–91.

Barrett, P R F and Newman J R 1991. *Aquatic Weeds Research Unit Progress Report*. AFRC Long Ashton Research Station.

British Trust for Conservation Volunteers 1976. *Waterways and Wetlands*. BTCV.

Furniss, P and Lane, A 1992. *Water and Wetlands*. Hodder and Stoughton.

Green, R E and Cadbury, C J 1987. Breeding Waders of Lowland Wet Grasslands. *RSPB Conservation Review* 1:10–13

Kirby, P 1992. *Habitat Management for Invertebrates* pp. 93-119. RSPB.

Lewis, G and Williams, G 1984. *Rivers and Wildlife Handbook*. RSPB/RSNC.

Newbold, C, Honnor, J and Buckley, K 1989. *Nature Conservation and the Management of Drainage Channels*. Nature Conservancy Council.

Street, M 1989. *Ponds and Lakes for Wildfowl*. Game Conservancy.

Ward, D (ed) 1992. *Reedbeds for Wildlife*. RSPB/University of Bristol.

Feature 9.1: Otters

Otters are found in all types of wetland, even in coastal waters. They used to be widespread in Britain but declined drastically in the late 1950s and '60s, chiefly due to organochlorine pesticides accumulating in fish (the bulk of their diet), plus widespread habitat destruction and increasing disturbance. Numbers seem to be increasing in Wales, south-west and northern England at least, and remain relatively high in Scotland and Northern Ireland. If you think you have otters on your land, seek advice from FWAG. Otters are protected by law.

Habitat requirements

- Otters rest during the day in holes, dense vegetation, fallen timber and flood debris, and need stretches of well-vegetated banks to lie up undisturbed. They need up to 30 of these 'holts' throughout their home ranges. They are very shy and except in very secluded areas are mostly nocturnal. Favoured sites are under bankside oak, ash or sycamore trees, whose roots grow horizontally and allow water to erode hollows underneath.
- Alder and willow are usually unsuitable as holts because the roots form a dense mat behind which tunnels do not readily form. Crowns of pollarded willows may be used.
- Otters breed in very secure well-concealed holts near the water.
- Home ranges are large, varying with availability of food and cover. A dog otter's home range may stretch to 40 km and may overlap with a bitch's but not another dog's.

Key

1. Bramble and dense scrub are often used and should be retained and allowed to develop on islands.

2. Retain and plant oak and ash on the bank. Retain mature trees by pollarding or coppicing, leaving the roots intact. If necessary, using blocks of stone as current deflectors can help contain erosion. Planting is secondary to retaining existing habitat; careful trimming of new trees will help prevent future problems.

3. In quiet areas with no cover, log piles wired to the banks (above flood levels) will provide short-term cover.

4. Wetlands, such as reedbeds, provide good resting and feeding places. Exclude livestock by fencing.

5. Ponds and quiet tree-lined tributary streams are used for feeding.

6. Keep livestock away from the river bank (allowing for selected access for drinking) to give scrub a chance to grow.

7. Fence off a river meander and plant with trees and scrub.

Note: People and dogs by rivers can disturb otters and should be kept away from known habitat where possible.

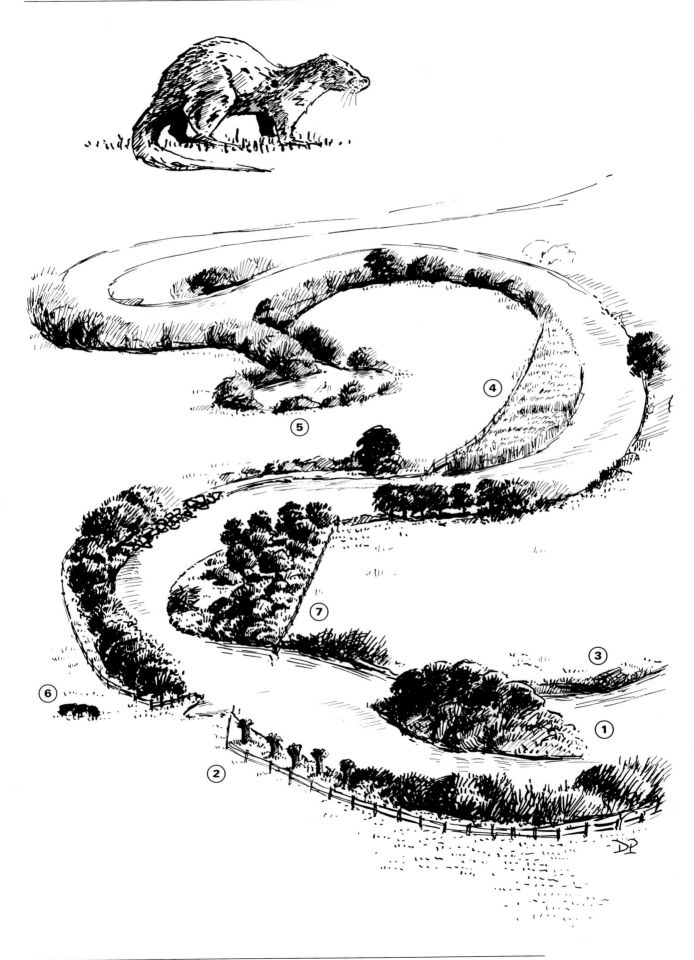

Feature 9.2: Dragonflies and damselflies

Dragonflies are bigger than damselflies and usually hold their wings at right angles to the body. Damselflies usually fold their wings back over the body. In this feature we have used the name dragonfly to cover both groups. There are about 40 breeding species in the UK.

Hunting habitat

Dragonflies often range far from water searching for places where there are abundant flying insects, such as sunlit woodland glades, stands of patchy scrub or big hedgerows. Damselflies mostly hunt near the ground, flying amongst the stems of tall plants such as rushes or reedmace, or even through hay crops.

Shelter

Dragonflies are inactive in cold weather, especially wind and rain, when they roost for hours or days at a time in tall herbage or amongst the foliage of hedges, scrub or trees. Some damselflies stay very close to the breeding sites so nearby cover and hunting habitat are essential to them.

Breeding sites

Most species need still water but a few breed in rivers. Some have very specialised needs, such as shallow runnels through sphagnum mosses, but many are capable of breeding in a typical farm pond. The best sites are sheltered from wind by nearby trees and shrubs but not shaded, so that the summer water temperature will be high and even the weak-flying damselflies can be active on quite windy days.

Key to Dragonflies and Damselflies

1. **Adults hunting in wind shelter provided by trees and scrub**
2. **Patches of bare ground used for basking**
3. **Mating pair in wheel formation**
4. **Larva hunting by sight**
5. **Larva emerging on plant stem**
6. **Adult taking prey in flight**
7. **Egglaying**

Egg laying

There are important differences in the needs of different species. Some scatter their eggs on damp marginal vegetation or mud, or across the water surface. Others lay their eggs on or in plant stems. In some species, the female actually descends beneath the water to do this. To support a range of species, a pond will have stands of emergent plants, beds of submerged aquatics and muddy margins.

Predators

Other dragonfly larvae, water beetles, fish and ducks all eat the larvae. The best dragonfly sites are without fish or large numbers of wildfowl. As dabbling ducks can only reach down about 35 cm, the best ponds will have extensive shallow areas no deeper than 1 m where aquatic plants can grow, providing habitat for the larvae out of reach of such wildfowl.

Larval habitat

Larvae feed on insects, fish fry, tadpoles and worms. Some bury themselves in mud and hunt by touch, others hunt by sight through water weeds. The best habitat offers a mix of conditions.

Emergence

When it is mature, the larva selects the stem of an emergent plant, such as bur-reed, crawls up it and the adult emerges through the split larval skin. It takes some time for the wings and body to harden properly and meanwhile the adult needs cover in which to shelter. Beds of emergents, nearby scrub and trees are important for this. Before they can fly well, many adults are taken by predators, especially birds.

Management

Some species favour ponds with an almost complete cover of emergent plants – though reedbeds are poor dragonfly habitat. To maintain a pond in good condition for a range of species do not allow emergent plants to occupy more than a third of the water area.

Drying Out

Even if the pond dries out, some dragonfly larvae can survive in damp mud. The advantage of occasional drying out is that it removes many of the predators. The disadvantage is that most dragonfly larvae will also be killed. On balance, permanent ponds are best for dragonflies but do not introduce fish.

Key to Amphibians (See Feature 9.3 on page 316)

1. **Tall vegetation provides cover**
   Shallow sloping sides
2. **Shallow water for frogs to spawn**
3. **Newts attach their eggs to submerged plants**
4. **Water beetles eat tadpoles**
5. **Logs and stones provide hibernation sites**
6. **Toads spawn in deeper water**
7. **Fish eat great numbers of tadpoles**

Feature 9.3: Amphibians

There are three newt species in the UK. The great crested or warty newt is widespread in lowland waters above pH 5.5. The palmate newt is the rarest, found mostly in rather acidic pools on heaths and in the uplands. The commonest is the smooth newt, which is the only species found in Ireland.

There is one native frog, which is widespread in the UK but very rare on intensive arable farms. Frogs are mostly found in marshes, river valleys and poorly-drained pastures.

There are two toads, neither found in Ireland. The common toad often uses drier habitat than frogs. Natterjack toads are confined to a few heaths and sand dune systems in England (eg Lincolnshire coast) and Scotland (eg Solway coast).

Feeding requirements

The adults all feed on invertebrates including slugs, beetles and worms in rough grassland, heathland or woodland margins. Field margins may be suitable if unsprayed and not grazed short. Ideally, maintain about 0.5 ha of uncultivated ground beside the pond plus 'corridors' of tall vegetation and unsprayed hedgelines linking to woods or other suitable habitat.

Hibernating sites

Frogs hibernate in marshes or at the bottom of ponds. Toads use holes in dry ground: provide linking 'corridors' to join ponds to hibernating places. Newts hibernate close to ponds, under stone piles or logs and in cracks or burrows in the soil.

Breeding sites

All species use ponds. Shallows are very important because they warm up readily. Frogs lay clumps of spawn in water 10–50cm deep, preferably with little aquatic plant cover, and will breed in tiny sites, even flooded wheel ruts on tracks or rides. Toads spawn in water up to 1.5 m, in larger ponds, and need aquatic plants or fallen branches round which to wind their egg strings. Newts usually lay single eggs on submerged plants. See illustration with Feature 9.2 on page 315.

Competition and predation

Toad tadpoles are unpalatable but all the others are eaten by sticklebacks, dragonfly larvae, water beetles and other predators. Adult newts eat frog tadpoles. Newts and frogs rarely breed in the same pond. Both do better in sites which dry out occasionally in late summer, so temporary pools should not be drained or converted to permanent water. Do not introduce fish to any amphibian sites.

Vegetation management

Retain submerged plants in deeper water and a fringe of marginal plants (protect from grazing by fencing if necessary) but keep shallows less than 0.5 m deep free of vegetation.

Edges

Shallow sloping sides allow easy access and escape. Frogs and toads may drown in steep-sided ponds.

Case study: Farming with Good Conservation Practice in Wetland Areas

Stan Terry

One of the four ponds on Seddon Fold Farm renovated to increase their wildlife value. Two additional ponds have also been created.

Farm details

Farm:	Seddon Fold Farm, Bolton, Lancs
Tenure:	Stan Terry, tenant farmer
Size:	77 ha
Altitude:	106–137 m
Soil:	poorly drained surface water gley on boulder clay
Crops:	permanent grass
Stock:	50 Limousin x Friesian suckler cows and progeny, plus ewes November–April at 1.5 ewes/ha.
Other wildlife features:	new hedgerow and laid hedges, restored ponds

The farm is on the urban outskirts of Bolton and is subject to trespass. It has been farmed for nine years in its present format. Previously the land was divided into three small dairy farms. The land is in a hollow surrounding an 8-ha lake and there is a reedbed adjacent to the water.

▶▶▶

Farmer's aims

Primary aims

- To farm traditionally on an extensive system, hence providing birdlife already attracted to the area with suitable habitat.

Secondary aims

- To improve the landscape.

Background

Resources: Work started in 1986. Labour was provided by the local conservation volunteers. The capital costs were grant-aided by the Countryside Commission.

Source of advice: An overall plan was drafted in 1986 by ADAS. In 1987 the annual planning was taken over by Lancashire FWAG.

Methods

A conservation plan was prepared. A thick well-maintained hedge was created around the farm perimeter either by laying of existing hedgerows or planting new ones. The hedge was to be stockproof, a wildlife corridor and a barrier to trespass. Four ponds were renovated and two old farm tips cleared. The soil from within the tips was to be excavated and used to cover the rubbish. In the resulting hollows a pond was formed, the banking planted out with whips and the whole area fenced off. Of the six resulting ponds, three not needed for cattle watering were planted around the margins and newts were introduced. The lake and the reedbed were fenced off from adjacent agricultural land and two small islands created in the centre of the lake as a bird refuge. To maintain the enthusiasm of the volunteers and to keep the annual capital cost after grant aid to around £1,000 the plan was implemented as follows. Each year 100 m of hedge layered, 100 m of new hedgerow planted, 1,000 whips planted and a pond renovated. The new hedgerows and whips needed a stock-proof fence.

Farm Management: The whole farm is grazed by sheep from 1 November to 1 April at a stocking rate of 0.6 ewes/ha. At the beginning of April the pasture land is lightly dressed with fertiliser, repeated approximately every six weeks throughout the summer, the land receiving in the order of 180 units of nitrogen. At the end of April or early May, depending on the weather, suckler cows with calves at foot are turned out on the pasture land. About 50 twelve-month-old beef cattle also graze this land during the summer. Stocking rate is about 0.6 cattle per ha. 40 ha are shut off for a hay crop. This land, having received farmyard manure during the winter now receives a supplement of 50 units of nitrogen. Cutting usually takes place in late June or early July depending on the weather.

Achievements

Primary aims

- a) The ponds and lake are now valuable areas for overwintering duck and attract nesting species such as moorhen, coot, mallard. b) The wet pasture fields have provided good feeding grounds for species such as plovers, snipe and redshank. c) The wildlife islands have been a disappointment as they have been taken over by Canada geese. The number of Canada geese on the farm has increased to around 280 birds and is an ever-growing nuisance. d) The perimeter hedge is now well established and has become stock-proof and has considerably reduced trespass.

Secondary aim

- Landscape improvements have been achieved via the work detailed above.

Future management

Conservation is at present confined to maintenance work, pending the landlord's development plans. Future work may involve controlling the lake waterlevel so as to expose a gravelly shoreline in spring and summer. It is also hoped to sow a wildflower meadow. Both of these projects would be of benefit to bird life whilst detracting nothing from the farming enterprise.

Case study: Enhancing the wildlife interest of riverside meadows on a mixed farm in north Buckinghamshire

Chris Smith

Work has begun to extend the periods of winter flooding in the meadows alongside Padbury Brook for wetland birds.

Farm details

Farm:	Warden's Farm, Padbury, Bucks
Tenure:	Mr G H Ward, tenant
Size:	160 ha
Altitude:	80–90 m
Soil:	Oxford clay with some sandy areas; alluvium along watercourses
Crops:	wheat, barley, oats (plus set-aside); rotational grass leys
Stock:	75 pedigree Holstein dairy herd plus followers
Other wildlife features:	broadleaved woodland, good hedges with hedgerow trees, ponds, field corner plantings of trees and shrubs, an old orchard and a wildflower-seeded field margin.

Warden's Farm is set in a very attractive landscape, fringed and traversed by the Padbury and Claydon Brooks. Dairying and arable have been the main farm enterprises. Rotational grassland is managed for strip-grazing and silage with longer leys as well as permanent pasture. Most of the arable is currently under set-aside. Other interests include a small flock of breeding sheep and a low-key pheasant shoot. A speciality of the farm has been catering for educational visits for school children and others (the Open University's Farm Interpretation Project was involved for a time). The farm provides a venue for FWAG, Agricultural Training Board and other demonstrations and events.

The Wards' approach has always been to integrate fully practical conservation with farming, rather than to see these as separate interests. The conservation work is entirely the farmer's own idea and initiative (generated by his interest in birds) which he was keen to carry out himself with existing farm machinery.

Farmer's aims

Primary aim

- To extend the periods of winter flooding in the meadows alongside the Padbury Brook to enhance their value to overwintering wetland birds.

Secondary aims

- To increase the diversity of plants and invertebrates in the grassland by reducing fertiliser inputs.
- To enhance the visual attractiveness of this part of the farm.

Background

Resources: Grant-aid, when the Countryside Stewardship Scheme Waterside Landscapes was introduced.

Source of advice: FWAG, who brought in the RSPB and Anglian Water. Agreement was obtained from the landlords regarding reduced inputs, and from the Buckingham Internal Drainage Board over the need to modify management of the flood-plain.

Methods

Work commenced in the autumn of 1991. Top-dressing with N fertiliser was discontinued. 2 long shallow scrapes 0.5 m deep and 1 m wide, with short spurs about 3 m long, were dug across one of the meadows about 30 m apart, with a Hy-Mac excavator, spreading the spoil in shallow ridges alongside to enhance the topographical effect and to provide conditions for the germination of dormant seeds from the meadow's seedbank. In the adjoining meadow, a new pond was constructed, and a programme of both willow pollarding and riverside tree planting begun.

Achievements

Primary aim

- Sightings of overwintering birds recorded for the first time have included tufted duck and pochard, both on the new pond. Detailed bird counts have yet to be resumed, but there has been a definite increase in numbers of snipe and green sandpiper. Numbers have remained about the same for golden plover, lapwing and curlew, but there have been signs that the last may be breeding in the vicinity.

Secondary aims

- Increase noted in Lady's smock – likely to attract egg-laying orange-tip butterflies, which have been noted on the wing in spring here. Also an increase in other visually attractive species such as meadow buttercup, dandelion and common daisy.

Future management

Modify scrapes, which have tended to dry out more quickly between wet spells than anticipated.

Pete Addis, Environmental Picture Library

9.1 Farm ponds are best for most wildlife if they contain open water with submerged plants over most of the area, a marginal fringe of emergent plants, and shelter from wind in the form of trees and shrubs that do not shade the water surface. Such a mix of conditions will support dragonflies, amphibians and some birds such as moorhen and sedge warbler.

9.2 ▼ Stock access to ponds is valuable because it prevents emergent plants from spreading too much and taking over the whole pond. The bare mud created by trampling is used by some plants and makes good feeding areas for waders. However, all-round access may reduce marginal cover so much that birds cannot breed for instance, so watering points are best fenced.

R Glover

9.3 ▲ Ditches that hold water throughout the year develop a rich variety of plants provided that the water quality is not over-enriched or otherwise polluted. The plant assemblage in turn supports water beetles, dragonflies and other aquatic insects. Ditches that drain dry for part of the year may be overdeepened in short stretches to retain some water and improve their wildlife value.

John Andrews

9.4 ► When a ditch becomes choked by vegetation, the variety of plants is reduced, its overall wildlife value falls and it ceases to function as a drainage channel. Ditches should be cleared on rotation so that there are stretches with plants at all stages of regrowth. Clearance must not be so effective that plants are lost entirely. Ideally, leave roots still in the bed or, if sediment must be removed, leave a fringe of plants along one edge.

John Andrews

9.5 Much farmland in river valleys used to flood in winter; this was turned to advantage, with the land being used for hay production or as water meadows to produce spring grass for sheep. The flooding attracted wildfowl and waders to feed on seeds and invertebrates. After the floods recede, if the ground remains moist into spring and the land is shut up for hay, some of these birds may also breed.

9.6 Where flood control and field drainage have removed conditions suitable for the wildlife of flood meadows, it is possible to create an artificial wetland. By progressively drawing down water-levels as the season progresses, fresh food-rich mud where birds can feed can be exposed.

9.7 Upland streams and rivers hold few plants but can be rich in insect-life and fish. In most situations the banks are grazed by stock and there is little marginal cover or feeding habitat. By fencing off small areas it may be possible to improve breeding conditions for common sandpipers and wildfowl.

John Andrews

John Andrews

Colin Carver

David Woodfall

9.8 Dippers are characteristic of tumbling upland watercourses, plunging into the water to search for insect larvae. Dippers nest in cavities among water-side rocks and also on ledges or in holes under bridges. They will use nestboxes erected above the reach of flood waters in such a site.

John Andrews

9.9 Lowland watercourses can contain luxuriant plant growth in the channel and on the banks. The best reaches have a varied bank cover with a mix of shaded and open conditions, a fringe of emergent plants and marginal shallows. Good conditions can be created by sympathetic river management and no work on rivers should be carried out without a survey of existing wildlife interest and the potential to enhance it.

John Andrews

9.10 The shores of upland lakes are often wave-beaten and rocky. Beaches of shingle are gradually colonised by plants and have good value for a variety of wildlife. Stands of emergent plants may be confined to sheltered corners where organic muds accumulate. It is best if these are protected from heavy use by stock but occasional access may help to open up the vegetation and allow new plants to colonise.

9.11 Gravel pits have great potential for restoration for wildlife. The aims should be to maximise the extent of shallow water, provide islands and a varied bank structure. On larger waters, wave action can uproot plants and cause erosion so shelterbelts should be planted to reduce wind energy and create calmer conditions. They should be set back from the water far enough to avoid shading the surface.

John Andrews

E A Janes

9.12 Stands of reed form a valuable habitat with a distinctive wildlife and may be used to strip nutrients from water and improve conditions in polluted farm ditches and ponds.

M R Richards, RSPB

9.13 Kingfishers will colonise sites where eroding banks provide a vertical face in which they can excavate a nest burrow inaccessible to predators such as rats. River management should aim to retain and create suitable sites, which may also be designed into irrigation reservoirs and gravel pits.

John Andrews

9.14 Islands are preferred nesting and loafing sites for many waterfowl because they are relatively safe from predators. If surfaced by tall herbage they will be used for nesting by wildfowl; shingle is used by common terns and three waders — oystercatcher, ringed plover and little ringed plover. Where islands cannot be provided, rafts can form a good substitute

10. Farm Buildings and Walls

1. Factors influencing wildlife

1.1 Structure, siting and context

> - Farm buildings and walls provide an important habitat for a number of specialised plants and animals, including lichens and ferns, barn owls and bats.
> - The value of buildings and walls for wildlife depends on their design, building materials, age and siting. Generally the older the building or wall the greater the value.
> - Different building materials have different physical and chemical properties, and consequently have their own individual characters and value to wildlife.
> - Warm dry walls are especially good habitats for insects and spiders, lizards and snakes.
> - Walls are more valuable to wildlife where they adjoin less intensively managed land.
> - Important features of buildings for birds and bats include eaves and access holes to roof spaces.
> - Farmyards, rough ground and farmhouse gardens can also be of value to wildlife, especially where water and spilt grain are available.

Buildings and walls are constructed and maintained for purposes other than providing a wildlife habitat. However, in addition to being central to farming activities, they have also traditionally complemented the appearance of the countryside and contributed to the survival and spread of wildlife. Some plants which are common on limestone exposures in the uplands occur in the lowlands only where walls have been built using lime mortar. For example, rusty-back fern seldom grows anywhere except among limestone and in the crevices of mortared walls. This means that old farm buildings and walls may hold wildlife found nowhere else in the locality.

The value of buildings and walls depends on their method of construction, age and siting. Generally the older the building or wall the greater the value. This is partly because it may take time for weathering to make the surface of a stone suitable for colonisation by a particular lichen or moss. Also, it may be many years before the spores or seeds of the plant get carried there by the wind or some other agency.

Different building materials have different physical and chemical properties, and consequently have their own individual character and value to wildlife. Over time, sandstones crumble, cavities form in limestone, schists split along cleavage-planes, granite weathers into a fine gravel. As a result, different types of building material have different wildlife associated with them.

The decay of lime mortar is comparable to that of limestone. Modern mortar is harder, very alkaline and more resistant to weathering which makes it a hostile environment for plants. However, plant growth can develop in crevices or the pores of most rough surfaces where both water and fine soils have built up. Establishment of vegetation on new walls by natural means is slow. Lichens normally appear unnoticed, followed by mosses.

Dry-stone walls are as important a feature of the countryside as traditional farm buildings, though the availability of suitable stone is largely restricted to the uplands. In some areas they are a very extensive habitat. For example, Northern Ireland has some 8,000 km of dry-stone walls. Although they can last for centuries, they still require maintenance from time to time. Many are now in disrepair and can be costly to restore. The gaps in dry walls make good cover for many invertebrates including spiders and larger crevices may be used by nesting birds such as wheatears.

The siting of buildings and walls is an important influence on the wildlife which uses them. Many mosses and ferns prefer cool shady positions, while south-facing warm dry walls are especially good for insects, spiders, lizards and snakes. They can adjust their temperatures by moving from sun to shade or into situations sheltered from the wind.

As with hedges (Chapter 8 page 255), the wildlife value of a wall is enhanced where it adjoins at least a small width of uncultivated or less intensively managed ground. If the base of the wall has no vegetation cover it offers less protection from extremes of weather, and if the ground is cultivated right up to the base of the wall then there will be effects of spray-drift on the plants and invertebrates that try to live on or in it (Feature 10.1: Walls).

Buildings may hold wildlife which does not find suitable conditions elsewhere on the farm. While some, like barn owls, will also use hollow trees, others such as swifts, swallows and martins nest almost entirely in buildings. Important features for birds and bats include eaves, access holes and the roof space. House martins construct nests under eaves, swallows on beams or other surfaces within buildings and owls on larger ledges or the tops of stacked hay or straw. Swifts will nest within the enclosed roof space provided that there are gaps under the eaves through which they can enter. (Feature 10.2: Wildlife and farm buildings).

The ground around farm buildings also has a contribution to make to the value of the farm for wildlife. Spilt grain provides food for finches, insects attracted to livestock are sought by bats, swallows, house martins and pied wagtails, and rodents are preyed on by barn owls. Rough ground brings diversity to the farmyard where weeds can thrive and attract insects that feed on nectar, such as butterflies and hoverflies. Water may be another attractive feature, particularly during cold winters and hot summers when it is less available in the countryside.

Over time, many old farm buildings, wooden and stone barns and dry-stone walls or dykes have fallen into decay or been demolished. This has been a considerable loss to wildlife. Wire fences and most modern farm buildings are far less attractive to wildlife as they do not possess suitable features and surfaces.

2. Options and assessment: planning management

2.1 Wildlife assessment of farm buildings and walls

- Assess the likely wildlife value by noting plant growth, features such as crevices and the presence of birds and bats.
- Seek advice if uncommon species are thought to be present, or before applying for grant aid.
- Review the impact of management practices, such as the use of rodenticides, in and around farm buildings.

Many farmers will already be aware of some of the features of buildings that wildlife such as barn owls and swallows put to good use. In addition to birds, another major value of buildings is their use for breeding or roosting by bats. If bats are known to use a roof space or other part of a building then specialists should be contacted as they are fully protected and species can be difficult to identify.

A list of the information required for a full assessment is given in Table 10.1. An important part of this is to note plant growth on surfaces, the presence of gaps or cavities which may be home to invertebrates or other small creatures and, in buildings, whether birds or other wildlife have access to nesting or roosting structures such as ledges. The value of these features is described in section 1 and the principles underlying wildlife assessment are explained in Chapter 1. Advice on the importance of features or particular species is available from FWAGs and the other conservation bodies.

Where survey is a preliminary to maintenance or restoration work which will

Table 10.1: Wildlife assessment of farm buildings and walls

INFORMATION REQUIRED	METHOD	REASON FOR INFORMATION
1. Conservation status and interest	Contact FWAG initially.	Information may already be available on wildlife interest, such as bats. The farm building, itself, may be listed as being of historic or archaeological interest. In which case, permission may be required before repairs or alternations are made.
2. Current use and condition of farm buildings	For each building identify: Whether in use or derelict. If derelict, state of repair and main areas of deterioration. If used, note use ie, grain store, for livestock, machinery, silage stores. Note presence of features likely to be of value for wildlife – traditional building materials (stone, slate) internal roof spaces, eaves, access holes, straw bales.	May identify need to restore to maintain value for wildlife in addition to main farm use. May identify potential conflicts with wildlife, eg leaks from silage stores into watercourses. May indicate use by wildlife.
3. Current use of farmyard and immediate surrounds to buildings	Map areas of rough ground with vegetation, trees, scrub. Map areas of standing water. Note areas used to place rodenticides, types used, and methods employed.	To identify other areas of wildlife interest adding to the value of the feature. To identify possible conflicts with use of buildings by barn owls. May suggest repositioning required.
4. Current extent and condition of stone walls	Map and note condition of walls, ie fully stockproof, partially stockproof, derelict. Note wildlife interest of walls on above map, especially presence of lichens, mosses, flowering plants, nesting birds, eg wheatear.	To identify any restoration work required for both wildlife and grazing control needs. Take into account in any restoration programme.
5. Current use of farmland adjacent to stone walls	Map use of land and note use of artificial fertilisers and pesticides. Map any semi-natural/rough grassland adjoining walls.	Fertiliser and pesticides can harm wildlife that use walls. Adjacent semi-natural vegetation can enhance the wildlife value of walls. May suggest opportunities for creating/managing grassland next to walls.
6. Location of rare and sensitive species	Note presence of rare or sensitive species, such as barn owls and bats where known. Seek specialist guidance.	May need specific management or conservation measures. May have special legal protection.

be supported by grant aid, check with the funding agency to ensure that its needs will be met by the assessment.

Assessment of the farm buildings can usefully be extended to consider the impact of operations such as the use of rodenticides and the prevention of pollution, for instance due to the escape of silage liquors.

2.2 Management needs and opportunities

> - Grants are sometimes available for renovation work.
> - New buildings can be designed to incorporate features of value to wildlife.

The value of buildings and walls to wildlife is very specific and the potential to improve these features can be sometimes quite limited. The most important thing is to retain them. If they are old it is possible that a certain amount of restoration will be required. This may appear to conflict with the needs of wildlife which has colonised the habitat; for instance, it may be necessary to rake out plants growing in crumbling mortar before it can be replaced. Aim to retain at least a few individuals in situ where safety permits, so that they can seed other areas.

As many old buildings can also be important in their own right, special permission may be required before work can be started. However, it is possible that money may be available to carry out building restoration, and wall repairs may also be grant-aided where they also contribute to landscape character.

There are many small-scale works that can improve the interest of both old and new buildings and walls to wildlife. Consider installing nestboxes and modifying management of the field margin alongside walls.

3. Management of farm buildings and walls

3.1 Retaining and enhancing old farm buildings

> - Retain old farm buildings and stone walls.
> - If works are required to make them sound, check with the planning authority in case they are listed buildings.
> - Undertake necessary renovation in a manner sympathetic to wildlife.
> - Avoid disturbing breeding or roosting birds or bats. Permission is required before work starts.
> - Do not use surface-coating or roof treatments that are toxic to wildlife.
> - If carrying out pest control around the farm buildings, use rodenticides with care and according to instructions. Barn owls can be killed by misuse.

While derelict and decaying buildings can be extremely important features in the countryside, they will lose their value to wildlife once they fall down or are demolished. As with many habitats, value increases with age, therefore it is essential to retain these features.

Where works are required to make them sound or functional again, check with the local planning authority to see if they are 'listed buildings' as consent may be required. Where any renovations are required, consider the needs of wildlife and restore in a sympathetic manner. Retain features that are of benefit, such as eaves and access points for birds and bats (Feature 10.2: Farm buildings and wildlife), and consider adding nestboxes and ledges. Undertake any works outside the bird breeding season to avoid disturbance, and check for presence of bats as they are fully protected and the official conservation body must be contacted before any work starts.

Any treatments to the inside or outside of the building should be carefully considered. Do not use surface coating or roof timber treatments that are toxic to wildlife.

Grants may be available for restoration work especially if the building is of historic interest, contributes to the landscape or has special wildlife interest.

Wildlife also makes much use of the ground around the farm building and the presence of rough ground, grain and water all contribute to the value of farmyards to wildlife. Obviously grain should not be distributed if there is a rodent infestation problem. If pest control is necessary, use rodenticides with care and follow instructions, as barn owls can die from poisoning if they eat contaminated prey. Avoid second generation rodenticides such as difenacoum, bromadiolone and brodifacoum, and consult a pest-control specialist.

3.2 Design of new farm buildings

- For new farm buildings choose a site that has no conservation value.
- Retain as much existing vegetation around the building as possible and do not build too close to trees.
- Incorporate features useful for wildlife such as bird and bat boxes.

The construction of new farm buildings provides many opportunities to incorporate features that will be attractive to wildlife. Stone is to be preferred as it provides a substrate for plants such as ferns, which cannot colonise metal, plastic or similar claddings. Lime mortar is better for colonisation by plants than are modern mortars.

Nestboxes for a range of species including flycatchers, tits and wagtails may be attached to the outside of a building, especially on a side which is undisturbed and adjoins good cover such as a line of shrubs or trees. Subject to regulations on crop storage, access points may be provided for swifts, swallows or owls and nest ledges or boxes provided.

For new farm buildings choose a site that has no existing wildlife value, avoiding

areas of natural vegetation. Retain as much vegetation around the building as possible. Consider effects on trees, including damage to roots and disruption of the supply of groundwater. Trees may also damage buildings so keep them separate.

Where buildings lack features of use to wildlife, it may be possible to incorporate bird and bat boxes or nesting platforms (see Feature 10.2).

3.3 Dry-stone walls

- Rebuild dry-stone walls with local stone if possible.
- Manage the strip of field adjoining the wall to allow tall cover to grow up.
- Avoid spray-drift affecting the wildlife of the wall.

For wildlife, walls should be retained and not be replaced by wire fences. Rebuilding should use local stone and be undertaken outside the bird breeding season as some birds nest in the crevices.

Most walls are situated in north and west Britain in areas of pasture. Where an intensive grazing system is followed consider erecting temporary fences at least 1 m from the wall to allow a tall grass and herb cover to establish. This will provide habitat at the base of the wall for a variety of wildlife (Feature 10.1: Walls).

Where land is cultivated, do not spray herbicides or insecticides right up to the base of the wall as these may kill some of the plants and invertebrates living in it. If possible, consider the creation of a conservation headland alongside the wall (see Chapter 2 page 30), where a crop is grown alongside the wall.

4. References and further reading

British Trust for Conservation Volunteers 1986.
  Drystone Walling. BTCV.
Carr, S and Bell, M 1991. *Practical Conservation:
  Boundary Habitats*. Hodder and Stoughton.
Darlington, A 1981. *Ecology of Walls*. Heinemann.

Feature 10.1: Walls

Aspect is important: north-facing walls are generally more suitable for plants as the temperature variations are less extreme than south-facing walls. Lichens and mosses usually colonise a fresh wall first, followed by ferns and flowering plants. Colonisation of concrete may not go beyond lichens and mosses.

Walls provide perches and vantage points for birds such as stonechat, whinchat and wheatear. Dry-stone walls are nest sites for wheatears, wrens and pied wagtails. Ivy and other creepers growing on walls give excellent cover for birds and insects.

Where walls are permanently damp a different plant community may grow, including some algae. Disused buildings generally support more wildlife than inhabited ones as heat travelling through the walls to the outside increases dryness and reduces plant growth.

Horizontal window-sills of decayed buildings develop cushions of mosses, which allow colonisation by other species. Crevices are usually colonised first. Dry-stone walls have lots of these; mortared joints make colonisation more difficult, but if rich in lime can support some plants.

Plants most often appear at the top and bottom of walls. The top is the most likely spot for seeds to be dropped by birds. The base is likely to be dampest and most likely to receive nutrient-rich soil particles.

Flowering plants in crevices attract butterflies. Caterpillars may crawl up to pupate. Crevices and cavities are used by black-bodied red tail bumblebees and mining bees for nesting, and by fertilised queens overwintering.

Short tumbledown sections may be used as nest sites by wheatear and other birds which should be borne in mind if rebuilding wall.

Lizards bask on walls heated by the sun and shelter in crevices.

Feature 10.2: Wildlife and Farm Buildings

Rodenticides
Barn owls hunt for rodents in and around buildings, especially in poor weather. To control vermin use warfarin where possible as it is less toxic to owls than second generation rodenticides. Consult a specialist if in doubt.

Wintering finches and other birds
Undressed grain, grass seed or 'tailings' can be spread regularly near buildings or hedges, especially during snow, where this will not attract rodents.

Water
Attracts birds such as finches and other seedeaters, especially during dry or very cold weather. Wet mud at the edge of puddles attracts house martins. Owls and other birds can drown in water troughs as they try to drink; float a plank or plastic mat in it to enable them to climb out; this will not prevent stock drinking.

Insects
Buildings are used by overwintering insects, which need sheltered, cool conditions. These include queen wasps, ladybirds and butterflies, such as small tortoiseshell and peacock. Pupae may also overwinter on the outside of walls.

Roosting bats
Roost in/on farm buildings, especially in summer. Some colonies very important; may attract bats from many kilometres around. Unlikely to cause problems in buildings, but harmed by toxic timber treatments. If present, seek advice before using preservatives, altering roof structure or enclosing or opening roof space.

Swallow nests

Nests may be used for years, built inside on a high ledge, beam or projection, where there is constant access. Frequently nest near livestock, especially cows, as they feed on insects.

House martins

Nest under eaves about 5–10 m above ground, especially at gable apex or near windows. Feed on insects taken in flight.

Swifts

Nest in holes under eaves and roof-tiles, but not on low buildings as swifts take flight by dropping from the eaves. Boxes may encourage them to nest if they are already in the area, and can be placed under eaves or in loft spaces.

Pied wagtails

Pied wagtails will use a small, open-fronted nestbox mounted low or at medium height, in various situations such as farm outbuildings, walls or beams.

Improving buildings for birds

Boxes may encourage barn owls to roost or nest, but to breed they must also have suitable hunting habitat. If owls are present near buildings from which birds must be excluded, provide a box with a tunnel entrance so owls do not enter the building itself. Swallows will use small platforms, undisturbed and safe from predators (eg cats). Will also need a permanent opening. Use a small shelf/plastic bag to catch droppings to prevent fouling of floor. Pied wagtails and spotted flycatchers can also nest in boxes on external walls.

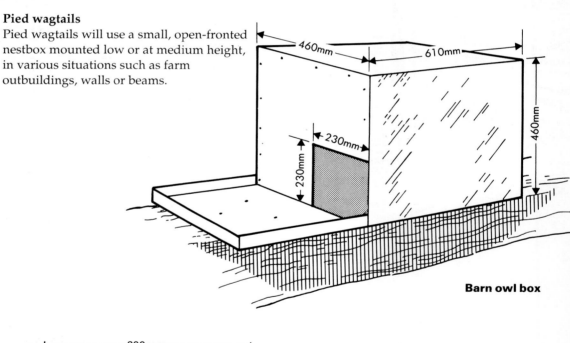

Barn owl box

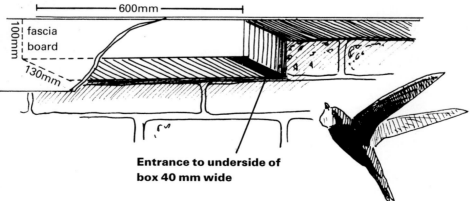

Entrance to underside of box 40 mm wide

Swift nestbox

Case study: Providing Nesting/ Roosting Sites for Bats and Birds on Farm Buildings

Sara Smith

Swift boxes and artificial house martin nests have been installed on the front of an estate house. Crevices used as bat entrance holes have been retained.

Farm details

Farm:	Chatsworth Farms, Chatsworth, Derbyshire
Tenure:	Owned and farmed by the Trustees of the Chatsworth Settlement
Size:	2,400 ha
Altitude:	60–100 m
Soil:	thin upland soil on slopes of gritstone valleys rising to peat moorland.
Crops:	predominantly permanent grassland and heather moorland, interspersed with mixed conifer and broadleaved woodland.
Stock:	250 milking cows, 100 cow suckler beef herd, 5,000 sheep and lambs
Other wildlife features:	all within the Peak District National Park

The farm includes 450 ha of traditional parkland and over 400 ha of moorland. It surrounds or adjoins about 400 ha of traditional mixed Estate woodland, varying from pure broadleaved woods in and around the Park to pure conifer woods on the highest land adjoining the moors. There are a number of lakes and ponds within the area, and the River Derwent runs through the centre of the parkland. The only hedges are in house gardens, all woods and fields being enclosed by drystone walls.

Farmer's aims

Primary aims

- To establish one or two breeding pairs of barn owls by providing suitable nesting sites/boxes.
- To provide artificial boxes/nest sites for swifts and house martins

Secondary aims

- To manage all the buildings sympathetically to provide nesting/roosting sites for a range of bats and birds.

Sara Smith

Entrance cut away for access to barn owl boxes. There is plenty of rough grass for hunting nearby.

- To raise awareness regarding the provision and management of suitable habitats for wildlife, particularly birds.

Background

Resources: work was carried out in the 'own time' of an estate worker. Financial outlay is relatively small as 'recycled' materials may be used.

Source of advice: literature of the British Trust for Ornithology, RSPB.

Methods

Numerous bird boxes have been installed over the last 4/5 years. Barns (empty and in use) were selected for barn owl boxes, on the following criteria: quiet location; sufficient suitable hunting ground in the vicinity; adequate access to the barn for the birds; no change of management planned for the barn in the short term; access not going to be blocked; suitable structure for fitting boxes; adequate shelter from the weather, eg in derelict barns. Wooden boxes were installed in sheltered locations usually attached to an existing beam and positioned lengthwise to allow the young birds easy access to the beam. Where access to the barn was restricted an opening was made in line with the box. Where roofs were in disrepair boxes were sited in the most sheltered areas. In used barns boxes were sited near an access point and operations such as the stacking of hay bales were carried out to cause the least disturbance to the birds and leaving clear access.

Swift boxes were incorporated into the woodwork of an estate house and painted to match the surrounding woodwork. The position of the entrance slit was varied to see if this had any bearing on the suitability of the box. Artificial martin nests were made from rolled up chicken wire and 'Polyfilla'. Tags were left for attachment to a wooden board under the eaves of the house and then finished with 'Polyfilla'. Both swift and martin boxes/nests were installed on the front of the house where the aspect is very open allowing a clear line of access into the boxes/nests. Cracks and crevices which are or may be used as bat entrance holes have been left unfilled.

Maintenance and monitoring is important to assess the success of the project and to provide information that may be used to improve or modify new and existing installations.

Achievements
Primary aims
- Barn owls pellets have been found in some of the selected barns but to date they have not nested in the boxes provided. One of the boxes is being used by an owl, probably a little owl. Swifts have been observed 'banging' the boxes provided at the end of the season and it is hoped that they will return to nest. The martin 'nests' have only recently been installed. Other boxes have been installed on the estate with great success, eg pied flycatcher, kestrel.

Secondary aims
- There has been some success as boxes have been used by other species of owl and positive signs have been observed. Other birds, such as swallows and wrens have used the undisturbed barns for nesting. Large numbers of bats, particularly pipistrelles, roost in various buildings where access openings have been left.
- Encouraging barn owls on the estate has raised awareness of the importance of habitats such as rough grass banks and young tree plantations for hunting barn owls and other raptors.

Future management
Existing boxes will be maintained and monitored. Damaged boxes will be replaced. Where possible new boxes will be installed; the number is largely related to available man hours. Schools may be involved in an 'Adopt a bird box' scheme.

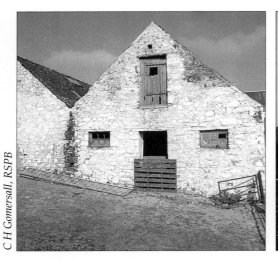

10.1 Older farm buildings often support a surprising variety of wildlife. Plants such as rustyback fern colonise mortar in the walls. Mosses grow where the roof eaves drip and lichens cling to the roof tiles. Peacock and tortoiseshell butterflies hibernate in dark lofts. Swallows and barn owls may have safe nesting places within the building, and house martins stick their mud nests under the eaves.

10.2 Modern buildings are often made of materials which do not support plant life and may be designed to prevent access by birds. They can be modified to provide nesting sites for owls without contravening regulations about grain storage.

10.3 Derelict buildings are excellent habitats for plants which may otherwise be able to grow only on rock outcrops. They also provide cavities for hole-nesting birds. In time, however, **they fall to pieces and lose their value. Where such buildings remain, it is worth trying to keep them in a reasonable state of repair and, ideally, with the roof intact.**

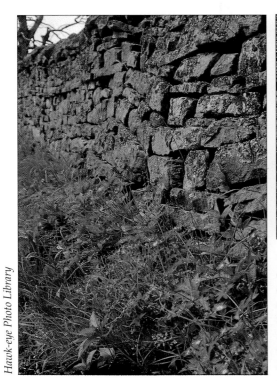

10.5 In both arable and grassland, it is valuable to attempt to retain or restore a flower-rich band of plants at the base of walls and to ensure that it is protected from the effects of spray-drift.

10.4 The wheatear nests in rock cavities, rabbit burrows and holes in dry-stone walls. Feeding on insects caught on short turf, they are now largely confined to the uplands where livestock grazing creates the conditions they require. Once wheatears were abundant on the chalk and limestone country of lowland Britain but since its conversion to arable use they have virtually disappeared from these areas.

10.6 Where walls fall into decay they go through a phase of great wildlife value, with mosses, ferns and ivy among the plants which colonise them. Small mammals, solitary bees, spiders and birds use them. Once they become too overgrown, much of their wildlife is lost so it is desirable to maintain and restore walls where possible.

Appendix I. Sources of Advice on Land Management for Wildlife

The following organisations provide advice on land management for wildlife and a number produce leaflets and management handbooks. Many of the organisations listed also have regional and local offices. The degree of specialism varies with the organisation.

Government Organisations

1. Agriculture Departments
Ministry of Agriculture, Fisheries and Food (MAFF)
Welsh Office Agriculture Department (WOAD)
Scottish Office Agriculture and Fisheries Department (SOAFD)
Department of Agriculture Northern Ireland (DANI)

In England and Wales advice is provided by ADAS through consultancy centres. In Scotland advice is provided by the Scottish Agricultural Colleges Advisory Service (SAC). In Northern Ireland advice is provided directly by DANI through agricultural advisory centres.

Ministry of Agriculture, Fisheries and Food, 3 Whitehall Place, London SW1A 2HH Tel: 0645 335577 (MAFF Helpline – all calls charged at local rate).

Welsh Office Agriculture Department, Cathays Park, Crown Buildings, Cardiff CF1 3NQ Tel: 0222 825111.

Scottish Office Agriculture and Fisheries Department, Pentland House, 47 Robbs Loan, Edinburgh EH14 1TW Tel: 031 556 8400.

Department of Agriculture Northern Ireland, Dundonald House, Upper Newtownards Rd, Belfast BT4 3SB Tel: 0232 520000.

2. Countryside Commission (CC)
The Countryside Commission is the principal government body in England with responsibility for promoting landscape conservation and informal recreation in the countryside. Provides advice on these matters.

John Dower House, Crescent Place, Cheltenham, Gloucester GL50 3RA Tel: 0242 521381.

3. Countryside Council for Wales (CCW)
The Countryside Council for Wales is the principal government body in Wales with responsibilty for nature conservation, landscape conservation and informal recreation in the countryside. Provides advice on these matters.

Plas Penrhos, Ffordd Penrhos, Bangor, Gwynedd LL57 2LQ Tel: 0248 370444.

4. Department of the Environment for Northern Ireland
Responsible for wildlife conservation, landscape and national heritage in Northern Ireland. Provides advice on nature conservation especially relating to Areas of Special Scientific Interest (ASSIs), historic buildings and monuments.

Countryside and Wildlife Branch, Calvert House, 23 Castle Place, Belfast BT1 1FY Tel: 0232 230560

5. English Heritage (EH), CADW (Welsh Historic Monuments), Historic Scotland (HS).
Responsible for the conservation of the national heritage of England, Wales and Scotland. Provide advice on scheduled monuments, other historic areas and listed buildings.

English Heritage, Fortress House, 23 Savile Row, London W1X 2HE Tel: 071 973 3000.

CADW, Brunel House, 2 Fitzallan Road, Cardiff CF2 1UY Tel: 0222 465511.

Historic Scotland, 20 Brandon Street, Edinburgh, EH3 5RA Tel: 031 244 3107.

6. English Nature (EN)
The principal government body in England with responsibility for nature conservation. Provides advice on all aspects of nature conservation through regional offices, especially relating to Sites of Special Scientific Interest (SSSIs).

Northminster House, Peterborough PE1 1UA Tel: 0733 340345.

7. Forestry Authority (FA)
The Forestry Authority is responsible with the Forest Enterprise for promoting, managing and advising government on forestry. The Forestry Authority provides advice on woodland management and issues felling licences.

231 Corstorphine Road, Edinburgh EH12 7AT Tel: 031 334 0303.

In Northern Ireland the Forest Service of DANI is the relevant body (see 1. Agriculture Departments for address).

8. Local authorities
Local authorities can provide advice on nature conservation, landscape conservation and

countryside recreation at a local level. In England and Wales advice is provided through county and district or borough councils. In Scotland advice is provided through regional and district councils. A number of local authorities provide more specialised advice on habitats, for example woodland and lowland heath.
Addresses of local authorities are found in the telephone directory.

9. National Park Authorities and the Broads Authority
Administer National Parks (England and Wales only) and the Norfolk and Suffolk Broads. Provide advice on landscape and nature conservation in these areas.

Addresses of National Park Authorities are found in the telephone directory.

10. National Rivers Authority (NRA), River Purification Boards and DANI Watercourse Management Division
The NRA is responsible for pollution control, water resources management and conservation in England and Wales. Provides advice on conservation of the water environment, water quality, fisheries and recreation. River Purification Boards perform a similar function to the NRA in Scotland and the Watercourse Management Division of DANI does so in Northern Ireland.

National Rivers Authority, 30–34 Albert Embankment, London SE1 7TL Tel: 071 820 0101.

Scottish River Purification Boards. There are seven RPBs – Clyde, Forth, Highland, North-East, Solway, Tweed and Tay – consult telephone directory for details.

DANI, Watercourse Management Division, Hydebank, 4 Hospital Road, Belfast BT8 8JL Tel: 0232 647161

11. Scottish Natural Heritage (SNH)
SNH is the principal government body in Scotland with responsibility for nature conservation, landscape conservation and informal recreation in the countryside. Provides advice on nature conservation, landscape conservation and informal recreation in Scotland.

12 Hope Terrace, Edinburgh, EH9 2AS Tel: 031 447 4784.

Voluntary Organisations

1. British Association for Shooting and Conservation (BASC)
Promotes interests in conservation, country shooting, firearms policy and training. Provides advice to members on all aspects of shooting and conservation.

Marford Mill, Rossett, Wrexham, Clwyd LL12 OHL Tel: 0244 570881.

2. Coed Cymru
Established to maintain and enhance the woodlands of Wales for the benefit of landscape, wildlife and the rural economy. Provides advice on woodland management, marketing and wildlife conservation.

Frolic Street, Newtown, Powys SY16 1AP Tel: 0686 650777

3. Farming and Wildlife Advisory Group (FWAG)
The Farming and Wildlife Advisory Group aims to reconcile the needs of modern farming with nature conservation. Provides advice on integrating farming with nature conservation and the landscape through a network of county groups and advisers.

National Agricultural Centre, Stoneleigh, Kenilworth, Warwickshire CV8 2RX Tel: 0203 696699.

4. Game Conservancy Trust (GCT)
Aims to conserve and increase game through the promotion of responsible management practices. Provides advice on the management of land for game including moorland, woodlands, arable crops and wetlands.

Fordingbridge, Hampshire SP6 1EF Tel: 0425 652 381.

5. The Heather Trust
The Heather Trust aims to restore heather moorland for the benefit of grouse and other wildlife. Provides advice on techniques for restoring degraded heather moorland.

Arngibbon House, Arnprior, Kippen, Stirlingshire FK8 3ES Tel: 0360 85420

6. Landowners' Associations
Represents the interests of members in countryside matters. Provides advice to members on a wide range of subjects.

Country Landowners Association, 16 Belgrave Square, London SW1X 8PW Tel: 071 235 0511

Scottish Landowners' Federation, 25 Maritime Street, Edinburgh EH6 5PW Tel: 031-555-1031

7. Farmers' Unions
Farmers' Union of Wales (FUW)
National Farmers' Union (NFU)
National Farmers' Union of Scotland (NFUS)
Northern Ireland Agricultural Producers' Association
Scottish Crofters Union
Ulster Farmers' Union (UFU)

Represent the farming industry in negotiations with government and promotes farming to the public. Provide advice to members on all aspects of farming.

Farmers' Union of Wales: Llys Amaeth, Queens Square, Aberystwyth, Dyfed SY23 2EA Tel: 0970 612 755.

National Farmers' Union: 22, Long Acre, London WC2E 9LY Tel: 071 235 5077.

National Farmers' Union of Scotland: Rural Centre, West Mains, Ingliston, Newbridge, Midlothian EH28 8LT Tel: 031 335 3111.

Northern Ireland Agricultural Producers' Association, 15 Molesworth Street, Cookstown BT80 8NX Tel: 06487 65700

Scottish Crofters Union, Old Mill, Broadford, Isle of Skye IV49 9AQ Tel: 0471 822529

Ulster Farmers' Union: Dunedin, 475/477 Antrim Road, Belfast BT15 3DA Tel: 0232 370222.

8. Royal Society for Nature Conservation (The Wildlife Trusts Partnership – RSNC)
Established to undertake nature conservation at a local level, wildlife trusts now cover the whole of the UK and provide advice on land of wildlife interest.

The Green, Witham Park, Waterside South, Lincoln LN5 7JR Tel: 0522 544400

9. The Royal Society for the Protection of Birds (RSPB)
The RSPB is Europe's largest voluntary wildlife conservation body and provides advice on conservation of birds particularly threatened species and habitats.

The Lodge, Sandy, Bedfordshire SG19 2DL Tel: 0767 680551.

10. Soil Association
The Soil Association sets standards for organic agriculture and the environment and monitors registered organic growers. It provides advice on conservation and organic farming.

86 Colston Street, Bristol BS1 5BB Tel: 0272 290661

11. Wildfowl and Wetlands Trust (WWT)
Formed to promote the conservation and study of wetland birds throughout the world. Provides advice on establishing and managing wildfowl reserves.

Slimbridge, Gloucester GL2 7BT Tel: 0453 890333.

Appendix II. Legal Considerations

The following section contains brief information on the legal considerations relating to wildlife, wildlife habitats and farm management. It includes reference to the most relevant conservation legislation. Much of the legislation is very detailed and can be very complex. Anyone requiring further information should consult the relevant organisations or turn to the Acts themselves.

The following publications issued by the relevant Agriculture Departments are very useful sources of information.

- *At the Farmer's Service* (England and Wales)
- *For your information* (Scotland)
- *At Your Service* (Northern Ireland)

1. Protection and conservation of special areas for wildlife on farmland

National Parks
There are 10 areas that have been designated as National Parks in England and Wales. There are none in Northern Ireland or Scotland. These have been designated to protect natural beauty and provide opportunities for recreation and enjoyment. The area of Norfolk and Suffolk Broads, whilst not a National Park, operates with similar objectives and mechanisms. While there are more extensive planning controls, farming operates under similar conditions as those that exist outside National Parks. However certain moorland or heath areas may have special protection, and farmers should check with the National Park Authority before changing their management.

Further information
Countryside Commission, Countryside Commission for Wales, Broads Authority, National Park Authorities.

National and Local Nature Reserves
These are established through nature reserve agreements with farmers and other landowners by government nature conservation agencies and local authorities. Farming operations, where essential to the maintenance of the wildlife interest, are agreed between farmers and agencies as part of a management plan. There may be restrictions on certain other operations.

Further information
National Nature Reserves: CCW, EN, DoE(NI), SNH
Local Nature Reserves: Local authorities

Sites of Special Scientific Interest (SSSI) England, Wales, Scotland

Areas of Special Scientific Interest (ASSI) Northern Ireland
Sites or Areas of Special Scientific Interest are designated by government nature conservation agencies because of their wildlife, geological or physiographical interest. Farmers and all other owners and occupiers are informed of that interest and provided with a list of operations that might harm the wildlife (or other) interest of the land. Where farmers wish to carry out any of these operations they must first notify the agency and seek consent.

Further information
CCW, EN, SNH, DoE(NI).

Special Protection Areas (SPA)

Wetlands of International Importance (Ramsar)
There are some wildlife habitats on farmland that support important species or populations of birds and are of international importance. Some of these may have been designated as Special Protection Areas or Ramsar sites. Prior notification as an SSSI is necessary and the further designations do not mean any additional constraints on farming operations.

Government proposals for the implementation of the 'Habitats Directive' are likely to lead to the designation of further areas of international importance.

Further information
CCW, EN, SNH, DoE(NI)

Environmentally Sensitive Areas
The Environmentally Sensitive Areas (ESA) Scheme was introduced in 1987 to encourage farmers in certain areas of the country to adopt agricultural practices that help protect and enhance the environment. This is a voluntary scheme and farmers within these areas may enter into management agreements with the Agriculture Department for which they receive payments.

Further information
MAFF, WOAD, SOAFD, DANI

2. Conservation of species

Birds
Wild birds, their nests and eggs are protected by law. Some species are afforded a higher degree of protection by special penalties. There are certain exceptions to this, notably in respect of wildfowl, gamebirds and various species that may cause damage. See *Wildlife and Countryside Act 1981.*

Schedule 1 – Part II

Birds and their eggs protected by special penalties during the *close season, 1 February to 31 August* (21 February to 31 August below high water mark) but which may be killed or taken at other times.

Goldeneye
Greylag Goose *(in Outer Hebrides, Caithness, Sutherland and Wester Ross only)*
Pintail

Schedule 2 – Birds Which May be Killed or Taken
Schedule 2 – Part 1

Birds which may be killed or taken outside the *close season, 1 February to 31 August* except where indicated otherwise.
NOTE: the close season for ducks and geese when below high-water mark is 21 February to 31 August.

Capercaillie – *close season 1 February to 30 September*
Coot
Tufted Duck
Gadwall
Goldeneye
Canada Goose
Greylag Goose
Pink-footed Goose
White-fronted Goose *(fully protected in Scotland)*
Mallard
Moorhen
Pintail
Golden Plover
Pochard
Shoveler
Common Snipe – *close season 1 February to 11 August*
Teal
Wigeon
Woodcock – *close season 1 February to 30 September, except in Scotland where 1 February to 31 August.*

A general licence has now replaced Schedule 2 – Part II ('pest species') contained in the 1981 Wildlife and Countryside Act.

General licences need not be applied for but copies of the actual licences can be obtained from the Government department responsible for their issue. Unless stated otherwise the licence permits authorised persons to kill or control the following birds to prevent serious damage to agriculture.

Carrion Crow
Collared Dove
Great Black-backed Gull
Lesser Black-backed Gull
Herring Gull
Jackdaw
Jay
Magpie
Feral Pigeon
Rook
House Sparrow
Starling
Woodpigeon

Further information
DoE, MAFF, Scottish Office Environment Department
EN, CCW, SNH, DoE(NI), RSPB.

Mammals
Some mammals found on farmland are specially protected by law. These include all species of bat, badger, wildcat, common dormouse, otter, pine marten, and red squirrel. Protection also extends to breeding sites and places of refuge

Red, fallow, roe and sika deer are also protected during the close season, when it is an offence to kill them.

Further information
CCW, DoE(NI), EN, SNH, RSNC
Red Deer Commission, BASC, Game Conservancy.

Other animals (including invertebrates)

Most species of amphibian and reptiles, and a small number of fish and invertebrates, are also protected in some way by legislation. These may be difficult to identify and their presence on farmland is likely to be indicated by the relevant organisation. A full list of these animals can be obtained if required from the Government's statutory nature conservation organisations.

Further information
EN, CCW, SNH, DoE(NI).

Wild plants
There are many species of wild plant including mosses, liverworts, lichens, stoneworts and fungi that have declined substantially over the last 50 years. Many of these rare species are protected through site designation but a small number are fully protected in their own right, and it is an offence to pick, uproot or destroy these protected species. Currently there are 107 species of vascular wild plant, 33 mosses and liverworts, 20 lichens and 2 algae on the British schedule. The equivalent schedule for Northern Ireland contains 56 vascular plant species. A full list can be obtained if required from the Government's statutory nature conservation organisations. It is also an offence, except for authorised persons (the land-owner or someone authorised by the landowner), intentionally to uproot any other wild flower.

Further information
EN, CCW, SNH, DoE(NI).

Introduction of species

The introduction of certain species such as trees and shrubs is accepted as part of habitat creation. In most situations the best option is to try and create the right conditions for species to find for themselves. On land with special protection such as an SSSI, permission must first be sought from the statutory nature conservation organisations. It is also an offence to release certain animals and plants that have become established in the wild such as American mink and giant hogweed. Similarly, protected species may not be taken for purposes of translocation without a licence.

Further information
EN, SNH, CCW, DoE(NI).

Weeds and Pests

A small number of animals and plants have become pests on farmland. Injurious weeds comprise spear thistle, creeping or field thistle, curled dock, broad-leaved dock and common ragwort. Occupiers of land are only required to prevent the spread of these 'injurious' weeds when there is a real threat to agricultural land or production.

Rabbits, grey squirrels and rats and mice can also become pests and advice on control can be obtained from a variety of sources. Deer can become pests in some parts of the UK but red, roe, fallow and sika deer can only be killed outside the close season. Badgers and their setts are fully protected.

- Farmers need to be aware of the potential effect on protected species when undertaking weed or pest control, for example, through use of herbicides and pesticides. In SSSIs and ASSIs pest control may be listed as a potentially damaging operation.

Further information
MAFF, WOAD, SOAFD, DANI.

3. Farm management

Building

Planning permission is generally required for the change of use of agricultural buildings. All buildings listed as being of historic or archaeological interest need planning permission for changes. Any changes should take into account the use of the buildings by certain species, for example barn owls and bats, which are protected by law. Contact the statutory nature conservation organisations for advice.

Further information
Local Planning Authorities (England, Scotland, Wales). DoE N I Divisional Offices.

MAFF 1992, *A Farmers' Guide to the Planning System*. HMSO.

Ancient monuments

Ancient monuments can sometimes also be of wildlife interest and if scheduled, are protected by law. Information on ancient monuments on farmland can normally be found in local authority planning departments. Nearly all, such as earthworks, can be damaged by insensitive management, ploughing or tree planting.

Further information
Local authorities, English Heritage, CADW. Historic Scotland, DoE (NI).

English Heritage 1987. *Ancient Monuments in the Countryside*. English Heritage.

Trees and woodland management

Local authorities may protect trees by making Tree Preservation Orders. This can apply to a single tree, a group of trees or an area of woodland. Farmers need consent from local authorities to fell, lop, top, or uproot protected trees.

A felling licence is normally required from the Forestry Authority to fell growing trees. In any calendar quarter up to 5 m^3 of timber may be felled by an occupier without a licence, provided not more than 2 m^3 are sold.

These provisions do not override any Tree Preservation orders in place.

Further information
Forestry Authority, Local Authorities, DANI (Forest Service).

Heather and grass burning

The date and conditions under which heather and grass can be burnt are defined by law. The permitted period for burning is as follows:

England and Wales	1 October – 15 April (uplands):1 November – 31 March (lowlands)
Scotland	1 October – 15 April
Northern Ireland	1 September – 14 April

Further information
MAFF, WOAD, SOAFD, DANI
MAFF 1992. *The Heather and Grass Burning Code*.
SNH 1993. *A Muirburn Code*.

Pollution

Some farming activities have the potential to harm wildlife and damage habitats through pollution of air, water or the ground. Farm wastes such as slurry and silage effluent can cause pollution if they get into a watercourse, and there are minimum standards for farm waste stores.

The use of sewage sludge on farmland can cause water pollution and guidance is given within codes of practice.

Pollution to water sources can also be caused by fertiliser and manure. Guidance is given on the level and timing of applications and the storage of manure. The areas of most concern have been identified as Nitrate Sensitive Areas (NSAs).

The burning of crop residues is now banned, and legislation through the Clean Air Acts covers other air pollution matters. A code of practice gives farmers advice on how to minimise air pollution.

Further information
Air and soil: Local Authorities
Water: Local Authorities, NRA (England and Wales) River Purification Boards (Scotland), DANI.
MAFF 1991. *Code of Good Agricultural Practice for the Protection of Water.*
MAFF 1992. *Code of Good Agricultural Practice for the Protection of Air.*
MAFF 1993. *Code of Good Agricultural Practice for the Protection of Soil.*

Pesticides
A wide range of pesticides is now available and used by farmers. It includes herbicides, insecticides, fungicides and molluscicides. The use of pesticides is strictly controlled by law, and anyone using pesticides must take measures to safeguard the environment. This applies to the storage, use and application and disposal of pesticides.

Further information
MAFF, WOAD, SOAFD, DANI.
MAFF and Health and Safety Commission 1990.
Pesticides: Code of Practice for the Safe Use of

Pesticides on Farms and Holdings. HMSO.
FWAG 1993 *Pesticides.*

4. Legislation
There are many Acts relating to farm management, wildlife and the environment. The following are some of the more important pieces of legislation, some of which will be covered by different legislation in Northern Ireland and Scotland.

National Parks and Access to the Countryside Act 1949
Wildlife and Countryside Act 1981 (and amendments)
The Nature Conservation and Amenity Lands (Northern Ireland) Order 1985 and amendments
Badgers Acts of 1992
Heather and Grass Burning Regulation 1986 and amendments
Environmental Protection Act 1990
Water Act 1989
Water Resources Act 1991
Control of Pollution Regulations 1991
Control of Pesticides Regulations 1986
Forestry Act 1967
Agriculture Act 1986
Local Government Act 1972
Clean Air Acts of 1956 and 1968
Sludge (use in Agriculture) Regulation 1989 as amended.
Pests Act 1954
Weeds Act 1959

Appendix III. English and Scientific Names of Species Referred to in the Text

1. Plants

Alder	*Alnus glutinosa*
Alder Buckthorn	*Frangula alnus*
Almond Willow	*Salix triandra*
Alpine Lady's-mantle	*Alchemilla alpina*
Amphibious Bistort	*Polygonum amphibium*
Arrowhead	*Sagittaria sagittifolia*
Ash	*Fraxinus excelsior*
Aspen	*Populus tremula*
Babington's Poppy	*Papaver lecoqii*
Barberry	*Berberis vulgaris*
Barren Brome	*Bromus sterilis*
Bay Willow	*Salix pentandra*
Bearberry	*Arctostaphylos uva-ursi*
Beech	*Fagus sylvatica*
Bell Heather	*Erica cinerea*
Betony	*Stachys officinalis*
Bilberry	*Vaccinium myrtillus*
Bird Cherry	*Prunus padus*
Bird's-foot-trefoil	*Lotus corniculatus*
Black Bryony	*Tamus communis*
Black Horehound	*Ballota nigra*
Black Medick	*Medicago lupulina*
Black Poplar	*Populus nigra*
Black-grass	*Alopecurus myosuroides*
Blackthorn	*Prunus spinosa*
Blanketweed	A variety of green algae eg *Enteromorpha*
Blue Moor-grass	*Sesleria albicans*
Blue Pimpernel	*Anagalis arvensis* subsp. *foemina*
Bluebell	*Hyacinthoides non-scripta*
Bogbean	*Menyanthes trifoliata*
Bog-myrtle	*Myrica gale*
Borage	*Borago officinalis*
Box	*Buxus sempervirens*
Bracken	*Pteridium aquilinum*
Bramble	*Rubus fruticosus*
Bristle Bent	*Agrostis curtisii*
Broad-fruited Cornsalad	*Valerianella rimosa*
Broad-leaved Cudweed	*Filago pyramidata*
Broad-leaved Dock	*Rumex obtusifolius*
Broad-leaved Pondweed	*Potamogeton natans*
Broad-leaved Spurge	*Euphorbia platyphyllos*
Brooklime	*Veronica beccabunga*
Broom	*Cytisus scoparius* subsp. *scoparius*
Buckthorn	*Rhamnus catharticus*
Bugloss	*Anchusa arvensis*
Bulbous Buttercup	*Ranunculus bulbosus*
Bulrush	*Typha latifolia*
Burnet-saxifrage	*Pimpinella saxifraga*
Bush Vetch	*Vicia sepium*
Butcher's-broom	*Ruscus aculeatus*
Buttercup	*Ranunculus* sp.
Butterwort	*Pinguicula vulgaris*
Canadian Waterweed	*Elodea canadensis*
Cat's-ear	*Hypochoeris radicata*
Cat-mint	*Nepeta cataria*
Celery-leaved Buttercup	*Ranunculus sceleratus*
Chewings Fescue	*Festuca nigrescens*
Cleavers	*Galium aparine*
Clematis	*Clematis vitalba*
Cock's-foot	*Dactylis glomerata*
Common Bent	*Agrostis capillaris*
Common Club-rush	*Schoenoplectus lacustris*
Common Cotton-grass	*Eriophorum angustifolium*
Common Dog-violet	*Viola riviniana*
Common Figwort	*Scrophularia nodosa*
Common Fleabane	*Pulicaria dysenterica*
Common Knapweed	*Centaurea nigra*
Common Mallow	*Malva sylvestris*
Common Poppy	*Papaver rhoeas*
Common Ragwort	*Senecio jacobaea*
Common Reed	*Phragmites australis*
Common Restharrow	*Ononis repens*
Common Rock-rose	*Helianthemum nummularium*
Common Sorrel	*Rumex acetosa*
Common Spike-rush	*Eleocharis palustris*
Common Spotted-orchid	*Dactylorhiza fuchsii*
Common Stork's-bill	*Erodium cicutarium* subsp. *cicutarium*
Common Vetch	*Vicia sativa* subsp. *sativa*
Common Whitebeam	*Sorbus aria*
Corn Buttercup	*Ranunculus arvensis*
Corn Gromwell	*Lithospermum arvense*
Corn Marigold	*Chrysanthemum segetum*
Corn Parsley	*Petroselinum segetum*
Corncockle	*Agrostemma githago*
Cornish Heath	*Erica vagans*
Cow Parsley	*Anthriscus sylvestris*
Cowberry	*Vaccinium vitis-idaea*
Cowslip	*Primula veris*
Crab Apple	*Malus sylvestris*
Crack Willow	*Salix fragilis* var. *fragilis*
Creeping Thistle	*Cirsium arvense*
Crested Dog's-tail	*Cynosurus cristatus*
Cross-leaved Heath	*Erica tetralix*
Crowberry	*Empetrum nigrum* subsp. *nigrum*
Cuckoo Pint	*Arum maculatum*
Curled Dock	*Rumex crispus*

Curled Pondweed	*Potamogeton crispus*
Currant	*Ribes* spp.
Cut-leaved Dead-nettle	*Lamium hybridum*
Daisy	*Bellis perennis*
Dandelion	*Taraxacum officinale*
Dark-leaved Willow	*Salix myrsinifolia*
Deergrass	*Trichophorum cespitosum*
Dense-flowered Fumitory	*Fumaria densiflora*
Devil's-bit Scabious	*Succisa pratensis*
Dog-rose	*Rosa canina*
Dogwood	*Cornus sanguinea*
Dorset Heath	*Erica ciliaris*
Dove's-foot Crane's-bill	*Geranium molle*
Downy Birch	*Betula pubescens*
Downy Oat-grass	*Avenula pubescens*
Duckweeds	*Lemna* spp.
Dwarf Gorse	*Ulex minor*
Dwarf Mallow	*Malva neglecta*
Dwarf Spurge	*Euphorbia exigua*
Eared Willow	*Salix aurita*
Elder	*Sambucus nigra*
Erect Bur-reed	*Sparganium erectum*
European Larch	*Larix decidua*
Fennel Pondweed	*Potamogeton pectinatus*
Field Maple	*Acer campestre*
Field Scabious	*Knautia arvensis*
Field Woundwort	*Stachys arvensis*
Field-rose	*Rosa arvensis*
Fig-leaved Goosefoot	*Chenopodium ficifolium*
Fine-leaved Sheep's-fescue	*Festuca tenuifolia*
Flixweed	*Descurainia sophia*
Flowering-rush	*Butomus umbellatus*
Fool's Water-cress	*Apium nodiflorum*
Foxglove	*Digitalis purpurea*
Fringed Water-lily	*Nymphoides peltata*
Fritillary	*Fritillaria meleagris*
Frogbit	*Hydrocharis morsus-ranae*
Garlic Mustard	*Alliaria petiolata*
Giant Hogweed	*Heracleum mantegazzianum*
Globeflower	*Trollius europaeus*
Goat Willow	*Salix caprea*
Golden oat-grass	*Trisetum flavescens*
Gooseberry	*Ribes uva-crispa*
Gorse	*Ulex europaeus*
Great Burnet	*Sanguisorba officinalis*
Great Water Dock	*Rumex hydrolapathum*
Great Willowherb	*Epilobium hirsutum*
Great Yellow-cress	*Rorippa amphibia*
Greater Knapweed	*Centaurea scabiosa*
Greater Pond-sedge	*Carex riparia*
Green Field-speedwell	*Veronica agrestis*
Grey Poplar	*Populus x canescens*
Grey Speedwell	*Veronica polita*
Grey Willow	*Salix cinerea* subsp. *cinerea*
Guelder-rose	*Viburnum opulus*
Hare's-foot Clover	*Trifolium arvense*
Hare's-tail Cotton-grass	*Eriophorum vaginatum*
Hawthorn	*Crataegus monogyna*
Hay Rattle	*Rhinanthus minor*
Hazel	*Corylus avellana*
Heath Bedstraw	*Galium saxatile*
Heath Rush	*Juncus squarrosus*
Heather	*Calluna vulgaris*
Hedge Mustard	*Sisymbrium officinale*
Hedge Woundwort	*Stachys sylvatica*
Henbit Dead-nettle	*Lamium amplexicaule*
Hoary Plantain	*Plantago media*
Hoary Willowherb	*Epilobium parviflorum*
Hogweed	*Heracleum spondylium*
Holly	*Ilex aquifolium*
Honeysuckle	*Lonicera periclymenum*
Hop Trefoil	*Trifolium campestre*
Hornbeam	*Carpinus betulus*
Horned Pondweed	*Zannichellia palustris*
Horse-chestnut	*Aesculus hippocastanum*
Horseshoe Vetch	*Hippocrepis comosa*
Irish Whitebeam	*Sorbus hibernica*
Ivy	*Hedera helix*
Japanese Knotweed	*Reynoutria japonica*
Juniper	*Juniperus communis*
Kidney Vetch	*Anthyllis vulneraria*
Knapweed	*Centaurea* sp.
Knotted Hedge-parsley	*Torilis nodosa*
Lady's Bedstraw	*Galium verum*
Lady's Smock	*Cardamine pratensis*
Larch	*Larix* sp.
Large-leaved Lime	*Tilia platyphyllos*
Lesser Burdock	*Arctium minus*
Lesser Hop Trefoil	*Trifolium dubium*
Lesser Knapweed	*Centaurea nigra*
Lesser Quaking-grass	*Briza minor*
Lesser Snapdragon	*Misopates orontium*
Lesser Stitchwort	*Stellaria graminea*
Long Prickly-headed Poppy	*Papaver argemone*
Long-stalked Crane's-bill	*Geranium columbinum*
Loose Silky-bent	*Apera spica-venti*
Lucerne	*Medicago sativa*
Mare's-tail	*Hippuris vulgaris*
Marsh Clubmoss	*Lycopodiella inundatum*
Marsh Foxtail	*Alopecurus geniculatus*
Marsh Gentian	*Gentiana pneumonanthe*
Marsh Lousewort	*Pedicularis palustris*
Marsh Orchid	*Dactylorhiza majalis* group
Marsh Woundwort	*Stachys palustris*
Marsh-mallow	*Althaea officinalis*
Marsh-marigold	*Caltha palustris*
Mat-grass	*Nardus stricta*
Meadow Barley	*Hordeum secalinum*
Meadow Brome	*Bromus commutatus*
Meadow Buttercup	*Ranunculus acris*
Meadow Crane's-bill	*Geranium pratense*
Meadow Fescue	*Festuca pratensis*
Meadow Foxtail	*Alopecurus pratensis*

Meadow Rue	*Thalictrum flavum*
Meadow Saxifrage	*Saxifraga granulata*
Meadow Thistle	*Cirsium dissectum*
Meadowsweet	*Filipendula ulmaria*
Midland Hawthorn	*Crataegus laevigata*
Mistletoe	*Viscum album*
Mountain Pansy	*Viola lutea*
Mouse-ear Hawkweed	*Hieracium pilosella*
Mousetail	*Myosurus minimus*
Narrow-leaved Hemp Nettle	*Galeopsis angustifolium*
Night-flowering Catchfly	*Silene noctiflora*
Norway Spruce	*Picea abies*
Nuttall's Waterweed	*Elodea nuttallii*
Osier	*Salix viminalis*
Oxeye Daisy	*Leucanthemum vulgare*
Pedunculate Oak	*Quercus robur*
Pepper-saxifrage	*Silaum silaus*
Perennial Rye-grass	*Lolium perenne* subsp. *perenne*
Perfoliate Honeysuckle	*Lonicera caprifolium*
Perfoliate Pondweed	*Potamogeton perfoliatus*
Pheasant's-eye	*Adonis annua*
Pignut	*Conopodium majus*
Plantains	*Plantago* spp.
Primrose	*Primula vulgaris*
Purple Moor-grass	*Molinia caerulea*
Purple Willow	*Salix purpurea*
Purple-loosestrife	*Lythrum salicaria*
Quaking-grass	*Briza media*
Ragged Robin	*Lychnis flos-cuculi*
Raspberry	*Rubus idaeus*
Red Campion	*Silene dioica*
Red Clover	*Trifolium pratense*
Red Fescue	*Festuca rubra*
Reed Canary-grass	*Phalaris arundinacea*
Reed Sweet-grass	*Glyceria maxima*
Rhododendron	*Rhododendron ponticum*
Ribwort Plantain	*Plantago lanceolata*
Rigid Hornwort	*Ceratophyllum demersum*
Rosebay Willowherb	*Chamerion angustifolium*
Rough Hawkbit	*Leontodon hispidus*
Rough Meadow-grass	*Poa trivialis*
Rough Poppy or Rough-headed Poppy	*Papaver hybridum*
Round-leaved Fluellen	*Kickxia spuria*
Rowan	*Sorbus aucuparia*
Rue-leaved Saxifrage	*Saxifraga tridactylites*
Rustyback Fern	*Ceterach officinarum*
Rye Brome	*Bromus secalinus*
Sainfoin	*Onobrychis viciifolia*
Salad Burnet	*Sanguisorba minor* subsp. *minor*
Sallow	*Salix cinerea*
Scots Pine	*Pinus sylvestris*
Selfheal	*Prunella vulgaris*
Sessile Oak	*Quercus petraea*
Shallon	*Gaultheria shallon*
Sharp-leaved Fluellen	*Kickxia elatine*
Sheep's Sorrel	*Rumex acetosella*
Sheep's-fescue	*Festuca ovina*
Shepherd's-needle	*Scandix pecten-veneris*
Shining Pondweed	*Potamogeton lucens*
Silver Birch	*Betula pendula*
Silver Hair-grass	*Aira caryophyllea*
Slender Tare	*Vicia tenuissima*
Small Fleabane	*Pulicaria vulgaris*
Small Toadflax	*Chaenorhinum minus*
Small-flowered Buttercup	*Ranunculus parviflorus*
Small-flowered Catchfly	*Silene gallica*
Small-flowered Crane's-bill	*Geranium pusillum*
Small-leaved Lime	*Tilia cordata*
Smooth Hawk's-beard	*Crepis capillaris*
Smooth Meadow-grass	*Poa pratensis*
Smooth Tare	*Vicia tetrasperma*
Soft-rush	*Juncus effusus*
Sorrels	*Rumex* spp.
Spear Thistle	*Cirsium vulgare*
Spiked Speedwell	*Veronica spicata*
Spiked Water-milfoil	*Myriophyllum spicatum*
Spindle	*Euonymus europaeus*
Spiny Restharrow	*Ononis spinosa*
Spotted orchid	*Dactylorhiza maculata* group
Spreading Hedge-parsley	*Torilis arvensis*
Spurge-laurel	*Daphne laureola*
Stinking Mayweed	*Arthemis cotula*
Stone Parsley	*Sison amonum*
Stoneworts	*Chara* spp.
Sundew	*Drosera* sp.
Sweet Chestnut	*Castanea sativa*
Sweet Vernal-grass	*Anthoxanthum odoratum*
Sycamore	*Acer pseudoplatanus*
Tasselweed	*Ruppia* sp.
Tea-leaved Willow	*Salix phylicifolia*
Teasel	*Dipsacus fullonum* subsp. *sylvestris*
Thale Cress	*Arabidopsis thaliana*
Thyme-leaved Sandwort	*Arenaria serpyllifolia*
Timothy	*Phleum pratense* subsp. *pratense*
Tor-grass	*Brachypodium pinnatum*
Tormentil	*Potentilla erecta*
Treacle Mustard	*Erysimum cheiranthoides*
Tufted Hair-grass	*Deschampsia cespitosa*
Tufted Vetch	*Vicia cracca*
Tussock Sedge	*Carex paniculata*
Upright Brome	*Bromus erectus*
Valliant's Fumitory	*Fumaria vaillantii*
Venus's-looking-glass	*Legousia hybrida*
Wall Rocket	*Diplotaxis muralis*
Water Crowfoots	*Ranunculus* spp.
Water Fern	*Azolla filiculoides*
Water Figwort	*Scrophularia auriculata*
Water Forget-me-not	*Myosotis scorpioides*
Water Hyacinth	*Salvinia molesta*
Water Lobelia	*Lobelia dortmanna*
Water Mint	*Mentha aquatica*
Water Starwort	*Callitriche* spp.
Water-cress	*Nasturtium officinale*
Water-plantain	*Alisma plantago-aquatica*

Water-violet	*Hottonia palustris*
Wavy Hair-grass	*Deschampsia flexuosa*
Wayfaring-tree	*Viburnum lantana*
Weasel's Snout	*Misopates orontium*
Western Fumitory	*Fumaria occidentalis*
Western Gorse	*Ulex gallii*
White Beak-sedge	*Rhynchospora alba*
White Bryony	*Bryonia dioica*
White Campion	*Silene alba*
White Clover	*Trifolium repens*
White Dead-nettle	*Lamium album*
White Water-lily	*Nymphaea alba*
White Willow	*Salix alba* var. *alba*
Wild Basil	*Clinopodium vulgare*
Wild Carrot	*Daucus carota* subsp. *carota*
Wild Cherry	*Prunus avium*
Wild Pansy	*Viola tricolor*
Wild Privet	*Ligustrum vulgare*
Wild Rose	*Rosa* sp.
Wild Service-tree	*Sorbus torminalis*
Wild Thyme	*Thymus praecox* subsp. *arcticus*
Wild-oat	*Avena fatua*
Wood Anemone	*Anemone nemorosa*
Woody Nightshade	*Solanum dulcamara*
Woundwort	*Stachys* sp.
Wych Elm	*Ulmus glabra*
Yarrow	*Achillea millefolium*
Yellow Flag or Iris	*Iris pseudacorus*
Yellow Water-lily	*Nuphar lutea*
Yellow-rattle	*Rhinanthus minor*
Yew	*Taxus baccata*
Yorkshire-fog	*Holcus lanatus*

2. Invertebrates

Beetles
Great Silver Water-beetle	*Hydrophilus piceus*
Heather Beetle	*Lochmaea suturalis*
Tiger Beetle	*Cicindela sylvatica*

Bumblebees
Black-bodied Red-tail	*Bombus lapidarius*
Browns	*Bombus pascuorum* (and rarer species)
Two-banded White-tails	*Bombus lucorum, Bombus terrestris*
Three-banded White-tails	*Bombus hortorum* (and rarer species)

Butterflies
Adonis Blue	*Lysandra bellargus*
Black Hairstreak	*Strymonidia pruni*
Brimstone	*Gonepteryx rhamni*
Brown Argus	*Aricia agestis*
Brown Hairstreak	*Thecla betulae*
Chalk-hill Blue	*Lysandra coridon*
Chequered Skipper	*Carterocephalus palaemon*
Common Blue	*Polyommatus icarus*
Dark Green Fritillary	*Argynnis aglaja*
Dingy Skipper	*Erynnis tages*
Duke of Burgundy Fritillary	*Hamearis lucina*
Essex Skipper	*Thymelicus lineola*
Gatekeeper or Hedge Brown	*Pyronia tithonus*

Grayling	*Hipparchia semele*
Green Hairstreak	*Callophrys rubi*
Heath Fritillary	*Mellicta athalia*
Holly Blue	*Celastrina argiolus*
Large Heath	*Coenonympha tullia*
Large Skipper	*Ochlodes venata*
Lulworth Skipper	*Thymelicus acteon*
Marbled White	*Melanargia galathea*
Marsh Fritillary	*Eurodryas aurinia*
Meadow Brown	*Maniola jurtina*
Mountain Ringlet	*Erebia epiphron*
Northern Brown Argus	*Aricia artaxarxes*
Orange-tip	*Anthocharis cardamines*
Peacock	*Inachis io*
Pearl-bordered Fritillary	*Boloria euphrosyne*
Ringlet	*Aphantopus hyperantus*
Scotch Argus	*Erebia aethiops*
Silver-spotted Skipper	*Hesperia comma*
Silver-studded Blue	*Plebejus argus*
Silver-washed Fritillary	*Argynnis paphia*
Small Blue	*Cupido minimus*
Small Copper	*Lycaena phlaeas*
Small Heath	*Coenonympha pamphilus*
Small Pearl-bordered Fritillary	*Boloria selene*
Small Skipper	*Thymelicus sylvestris*
Wall Brown	*Lasiommata megera*
White-letter Hairstreak	*Strymonidia w-album*

Dragonflies
Banded Agrion	*Calopteryx splendens*
Black Darter	*Sympetrum danae*
Keeled Skimmer	*Orthetrum coerulescens*
Small Red Damselfly	*Ceriagrion tenellum*
Southern Damselfly	*Coenagrion mercuriale*
White-Faced Darter	*Leucorrhinia dubia*
White-legged Damselfly	*Platycnemis pennipes*

Grasshoppers and Crickets
| Bog Bush-cricket | *Metrioptera brachyptera* |
| Large Marsh Grasshopper | *Stethophyma grossum* |

Moths
Beautiful Yellow Underwing Moth	*Anarta myrtilli*
Emperor Moth	*Pavonia pavonia*
Fox Moth	*Macrothylacia rubi*

Spiders
| Raft Spider | *Dolmedes fimbriatus* |
| Wolf Spider | *Arctosa perita* |

Weevils
| Heather Weevil | *Lochmaea suturalis* |

3. Crustaceans
| Fairy Shrimp | *Chirocephalus diapharius* |

4. Fish

Grayling — *Thymallus thymallus*

5. Amphibians

Common Toad	*Bufo bufo*
Common Frog	*Rana temporaria*
Great Crested Newt	*Triturus cristatus*
Natterjack Toad	*Bufo calamita*
Palmate Newt	*Triturus helveticus*
Smooth Newt	*Triturus vulgaris*

6. Reptiles

Adder	*Viper aberus*
Common Lizard	*Lacerta vivipara*
Grass Snake	*Natrix natrix*
Sand Lizard	*Lacerta agilis*
Slow-worm	*Anguis fragilis*
Smooth Snake	*Coronella austriaca*

7. Birds

Barn Owl	*Tyto alba*
Barnacle Goose	*Branta leucopsis*
Bearded Tit	*Panurus biarmicus*
Bittern	*Botaurus stellaris*
Black Grouse	*Tetrao tetrix*
Blackbird	*Turdus merula*
Blackcap	*Sylvia atricapilla*
Blue Tit	*Parus caeruleus*
Bullfinch	*Pyrrhula pyrrhula*
Buzzard	*Buteo buteo*
Canada Goose	*Branta canadensis*
Capercaillie	*Tetrao urogallus*
Carrion Crow	*Corvus corone*
Chaffinch	*Fringilla coelebs*
Chough	*Pyrrhocorax pyrrhocorax*
Cirl Bunting	*Emberiza cirlus*
Coal Tit	*Parus ater*
Common Sandpiper	*Actitis hypoleucos*
Coot	*Fulica atra*
Corn Bunting	*Miliaria calandra*
Corncrake	*Crex crex*
Crested Tit	*Parus cristatus*
Cuckoo	*Cuculus canorus*
Curlew	*Numenius arquata*
Dartford Warbler	*Sylvia undata*
Dipper	*Cinclus cinclus*
Dunlin	*Calidris alpina*
Dunnock	*Prunella modularis*
Fieldfare	*Turdus pilaris*
Golden Eagle	*Aquila chrysaetos*
Golden Plover	*Pluvialis apricaria*
Goosander	*Mergus merganser*
Great Crested Grebe	*Podiceps cristatus*
Great Spotted Woodpecker	*Dendrocopos major*
Great Tit	*Parus major*
Green Woodpecker	*Picus viridis*
Greenfinch	*Carduelis chloris*
Greenshank	*Tringa nebularia*
Grey Partridge	*Perdix perdix*
Grey Wagtail	*Motacilla cinerea*
Greylag Goose	*Anser anser*
Hen Harrier	*Circus cyaneus*
Hobby	*Falco subbuteo*
House Martin	*Delichon urbica*
Jackdaw	*Corvus monedula*
Kestrel	*Falco tinnunculus*
Kingfisher	*Alcedo atthis*
Lapwing	*Vanellus vanellus*
Lesser Spotted Woodpecker	*Dendrocopos minor*
Linnet	*Carduelis cannabina*
Little Owl	*Athene noctua*
Long-eared Owl	*Asio otus*
Magpie	*Pica pica*
Mallard	*Anas platyrhynchos*
Marsh Harrier	*Circus aeruginosus*
Marsh Tit	*Parus palustris*
Merlin	*Falco columbarius*
Montagu's Harrier	*Circus pygargus*
Moorhen	*Gallinula chloropus*
Mute Swan	*Cygnus olor*
Nightingale	*Luscinia megarhynchos*
Nightjar	*Caprimulgus europaeus*
Nuthatch	*Sitta europaea*
Oystercatcher	*Haematopus ostralegus*
Peregrine	*Falco peregrinus*
Pheasant	*Phasianus colchicus*
Pied Flycatcher	*Ficedula hypoleuca*
Pied Wagtail	*Motacilla alba*
Pochard	*Aythya ferina*
Quail	*Coturnix coturnix*
Red Grouse	*Lagopus lagopus*
Red Kite	*Milvus milvus*
Red-breasted Merganser	*Mergus serrator*
Red-necked Phalarope	*Phalaropus lobatus*
Redshank	*Tringa totanus*
Redstart	*Phoenicurus phoenicurus*
Redwing	*Turdus iliacus*
Reed Bunting	*Emberiza schoeniclus*
Reed Warbler	*Acrocephalus scirpaceus*
Ring Ouzel	*Turdus torquatus*
Ringed Plover	*Charadrius hiaticula*
Robin	*Erithacus rubecula*
Rook	*Corvus frugilegus*
Sand Martin	*Riparia riparia*
Sedge Warbler	*Acrocephalus schoenobaenus*
Short-eared Owl	*Asio flammeus*
Shoveler	*Anas clypeata*
Skylark	*Alauda arvensis*
Snipe	*Gallinago gallinago*
Song Thrush	*Turdus philomelos*
Sparrowhawk	*Accipiter nisus*
Spotted Flycatcher	*Muscicapa striata*
Stock Dove	*Columba oenas*
Stone-curlew	*Burhinus oedicnemus*
Stonechat	*Saxicola torquata*
Swallow	*Hirundo rustica*
Swift	*Apus apus*
Tawny Owl	*Strix aluco*
Teal	*Anas crecca*
Tree Pipit	*Anthus trivialis*
Tree Sparrow	*Passer montanus*
Treecreeper	*Certhia familiaris*

Tufted Duck	*Aythya fuligula*
Wheatear	*Oenanthe oenanthe*
Whinchat	*Saxicola rubetra*
Whitethroat	*Sylvia communis*
Wigeon	*Anas penelope*
Willow Tit	*Parus montanus*
Willow Warbler	*Phylloscopus trochilus*
Wood Warbler	*Phylloscopus sibilatrix*
Woodcock	*Scolopax rusticola*
Woodlark	*Lullula arborea*
Woodpigeon	*Columba palumbus*
Wren	*Troglodytes troglodytes*
Yellowhammer	*Emberiza citrinella*

8. Mammals

Badger	*Meles meles*
Bank Vole	*Clethrionomys glareolus*
Brown Hare	*Lepus capensis*
Brown Rat	*Rattus norvegicus*
Common Shrew	*Sorex araneus*
Dormouse	*Muscardinus avellanarius*
Field Vole	*Microtus agrestis*
Fox	*Vulpes vulpes*
Grey Squirrel	*Sciurus carolinensis*
Harvest Mouse	*Micromys minutus*
Hedgehog	*Erinaceus europaeus*
Mole	*Talpa europaea*
Mountain Hare	*Lepus timidus*
Otter	*Lutra lutra*
Pygmy Shrew	*Sorex minutus*
Rabbit	*Oryctolagus cuniculus*
Red Deer	*Cervus elaphus*
Red Squirrel	*Sciurus vulgaris*
Roe Deer	*Capreolus capreolus*
Sika Deer	*Cervus nippon*
Stoat	*Mustela erminea*
Weasel	*Mustela nivalis*
Wood Mouse	*Apodemus sylvaticus*

Index

The alphabetical arrangement is letter by letter.

Numbers in *italics* refer to photographs, with accompanying text.

Numbers in **bold** refer to features, case studies, figures and tables.